*"Information, inspiration and ideas to help you
make money doing what you love!"*

Turn Your

Passion

into

PROFIT

**A step-by-step guide for turning ANY hobby, talent,
or new product idea into a money-making venture!**

WALT F. J. GOODRIDGE
author of Lyrics for Living

REVISED US TAX LAW EDITION

Dedication
This book is Dedicated to Isolene Rebecca Golding
1907-1988

Photo Credits:
Images of Walt: Tony Cordoza (www.tonycordoza.com)
Cover image ("Forging A Fortune"): Colin Anderson

Acknowledgments:
Special thanks to:
• Sidney Harleston of the National Money League (Thanks for the title!)
• Odette Flemming (Editing and contribution to the "Passion" Chapter)
• Zelda Owens-Waters (for her invaluable contribution to the Cycle of Success)
• Andrew Morrison (the world's greatest mentor!)
• Mike Jones (for coming through in the clutch!)
• Delxino Wilson-DeBriano of TagTeamMarketing.com (for freeing my mind!)
• Ernest Capers (for always being there through thick and thin)

And to those whose love and support helped me on my journey to freedom turning my passion into profit: Thelma Goodridge, Nyembane Goodridge, Christine Karmo, Reina Joa, Courtney Munroe, Wayne Wright, Gurdeep Singh, Kenneth McRae, Courtney & April Gibson, Nicole Drew, Diamond Davis, Ernest Capers, Erroll Paden, C. Thomas Gambrell II, Tony & Judy Cordoza, Gary Ervin, Dawn Greenidge, Marilyn DeFreitas, Aaron, Stacey, Atiya and Sekou Spencer-Willoughby, Anika Moore, Kelly & Zelda Owens-Waters, Andrew Morrison, Ronson & Delores Lennox, Kim McNeil, Sharon Lewis, Siew-Li Ng, The American Communications Network family, and the one and only TagTeam Marketing!

Special thanks also to the authors of the many books mentioned in this guide whose words, opinions and examples informed, inspired and moved me to create the life of my dreams so that I might help others do the same!

When you really think about it, EVERYONE whom we meet along the way in life, plays a part in our journey. Therefore, I'd like to thank everyone I've ever met:

Thelma Rose Goodridge • Nyembane Goodridge • Nicole Ndobe Goodridge • Loris Parkinson • Ernestine Golding
Cynthia Golding • Clement Golding •Everold Golding • Aunt Emmie • Ms Mac • Viola Crooks • Michele Stoute
Valentine Parkinson • Zoy Parkinson • Margaret Broomfield • Faye Golding•Marco Golding •Tracy Golding
Deeno Golding • Claire Golding • Manager• Mas' Opie • Andrew Walters • Wayne Walters • Lisa Walters
Baron Brissett • Horace Hall • Ian Smith • Desmond Anderson • Ferdinand White • Norman Hemmings
Perez Cross Gail Germaine Scott • Dion Thompson • Daighn Jones • Mrs Sutherland • Richard Sutherland
Philip Sutherland • Mrs Downy • Gary Scott • Mrs Scott • Tanya Nash • Mrs Nash • Gillian Johnson • Paul Johnson
Peter Samuels • Paul Samuels • Lorraine Samuels • Sophia Samuels • Camille Samuels • Mrs Barton • Marcia Barton
Herbert Barton • Mrs Britain • Lora Miller • Mrs. Stewart • Mrs. Greene • Keith Goodman • Tracy Crumb
Mark Brown • Latricia Pimento • Jimmy and Tony Battle • Serge Desvarieaux • Mrs.Cumberbatch • Joseph Latto
Mrs. Fiore • Charlotte Huey • Harrison Claiborne • Carmela Abiuso • Neal Gardner • Ian Gardner • Edward White
Ray Wilson • Ingrid Lim • Charmaine Fyffe • Carol Gray • Raymond De La Vega • Billy Levine• Mitchel Primas
Glen Bustrim • Dawn Dobson • CB • Courtney Drummond • Pauline Drummond • Janine Comrie
Errol Drummond • John Bines • William Gillespie • Craig Henley • Derek Hawkins • Brian Barnett • Rhona Julien
Reina Joa • Dalma Tejada • Hector Tejada • Amanda • Christine St Hilaire • Jose Ithier • Randy Hyde
Sharon Farnum • Karen Lue Yat • Ronson Lennox Dick • Delores DeSouza • Lenore Dick • Lynette Dick
Heather Massiah • Sylvia Dick • Dean Blackman • Yves Jean • Tony Dick • Carlton T. Gambrell II
Marianne Gambrell • Trappio Horne • Terrence Woody • Delroy Millers • Chantal Jean-Baptiste • Terry Walcott
Trevor Parris • Karen Best • Corynne Carter • Mahalia Joseph • Manuel Martinez • Rod Brathwaite
Archie Cumberbatch • Greg Gonsalves • Yesilernis Pena • Warren Heusner • Cecil Chang • Edwina Molina
Glenda Bethel • Kingsley Chin • Marcia Narine • Homer Hill • Hearns Charles • Wilton Cedeno • Chris Davis
David Small • Mark Spence • Jerry McCall • China • Diane Myles • Dr. Alan Beckles • Rhona Julien • Ta M.
Kent Wythecombe • Mike Tavis • Bob Bolan • Shirley Banker • Erica O Smith • Courtney Munroe
Andrew Campbell • Camille Chin • Vincent Chin • Beverly Chin • Wayne Chin • Carol Frances • Ian Oliver
Darren Oliver • Ira Weitz • Rasta in Long Beach • George Brash • Rina Bontemps • Andell Fogie • Wayne Wright
Gurdeep Singh • Lew Chang • Clinton (Bubbles) Rowe • Luke Sewell • Horace James • Val Jarrett • Patricia Jarrett
Leroy Graham • Vinton Lindo • Sheila Broza • Chris Chin • Patricia Jarrett • Maria Barry • Janine Murray
Dennis Haliburton • Jeff Sarge Barbara Pope • Kenneth McRae • Andre Shabazz • Glen Brooks • Mike Liburd
Pascal Antoine • Michelle Pessoa • Phyllis Thomlinson • Tony Cordoza • Charlie Pizarello • Paula Benjamin
Mortimer Philbert • Lance Caine • Ken Greenblatt • Michelle Estrello • Yasuko Ito • Mariah Britton
Lewis Savage • Kurt Lampkin • Deidre Young • Yseult Beecher • Kandace Simmons • Eric Butler • Pam Lewis
Sam Bailey • Pat Johnson • Capone • Alula • Irin (Iroc Records) Sherlyne • Shalandra • Glen Ford • Manny Ayala
Sheila Cargill • Percy Bratton • Shawn Burgess • Shanette Bryant • Lillie Collins • Charles Taylor • Terry Beals
Keith Ruddock • Chuck D • Majic • Harry Allen • Geraldine Williams • BenWhite • Carlotta Piper • Garret Fortner
Josh Nathan • Andrew Munroe • Neal at Ornall Glossies •Joe Colon • Arlington Edwards • Chris Wilson
Mark Went • Havelock Nelson • Wendy Day • Pat Boothe • Simon Ajose • Dion Ashman • Roma • Norm Schreiber
Gabriel Tolliver • Wildman Steve • Dominique Taylor • Michelle Scott • Jay Eberhardt • Antoine Garnier
Sharon Thomas • Cheryl Haab • Nancy, Jamie • Cathy & Patsy at Bookcrafters • Mary Frances Carr
Sandra Arias • Paul Tsang • Yon Sim • Jia D Lee • Mario Arias • Si Brown • Sandra Melicharek • Sandra Ernst
Chyril Denbow • Andrew Wallace • Aileen Del Prado • Cesar Silva • Rich Lendor • John Potter • George Keller
Devon Mitchell • Don Ferdinand • Francois Villejoint • Michele Douyon •Alvin Tan • Reza Maleki • Tita Payomo
Oscar Villanueva • Bruce Vitelli • George Soriano • Quentin Brathwaite • Catherine James • Ron Shaw • Mike Zutell
Peiling Hui • Richard Allen • Tony Carlesi • Harry Schmerl • Richard Franklin • Millie Taylor • Pramod Khanna
King Lee • Jaime Morales • Audie Robinson • Barry Lucas • Janet McDonald • Lophney Knight • Rhonda Kearse
Kelly King • Audrey Smith • Thomas Nicklas • Catherine Young • Kelly Washington •Joe Bruzzo
Angela Baptiste •Bob Pruno • Joe • Kim Magloire • Ed&Marie Bronshvag • Bernice Robinson • Estherline
Tai Sun Chen • Courtney and April Gibson • Bruce Ford • Chantal Jean-Baptiste • Monica Carroll • David Jones
Nadine • Courtney White • Neville George • Jeff Sarge • Malika Lee Whitney • Catherine Shaw • Mahalia Joseph
Tasha Hinds • Maurice Archibald • Rula Brown • Ted at Romoba • Andel Forgie • Jacquie Hatch • Jeneane Murray
George Brash • Ernest Capers • Stacey Spencer • Salimah Abdullah King • Khadijah Abdullah • Marilyn DeFreitas
Mary Roberts • Tim Jackson • Gene Flynn • Andrew Grant • Nicole Drew • Monique Shaw • Erika Fikes
Bruce Vitelli • Wanda Faye • Dawn Greenidge • Aaron Willoughby • Diamond Davis • David Owens • Masaai Kush
Odette Flemming • Eugene Bussey • Erroll Paden • Anika Moore • Akilah Moore • Julius Moore
Shehara Smallwood • Kim Johnson • Monica Blache • David Weeks • Gigi & Willie@drumandspear.com
Glenda Coleman • Paul Facey • Dean Simmonds • Denise Laing • Derek Dingle • Dorothy Phaire • Tonya Moxey
Percy Sutton • Shailesh • Howard Walters • Alvin Hartley • Ancil Tyrrel • Sam Chekwas• Terrie Williams
Charlene Turner • Roussan Etienne • Karon Mason Etienne • Sharon Lewis • Salimah Abdullah-King
Kim McNeil • Siew-Li Ng AND to everyone who has ever purchased my books or joined my mailing list

What People Are Saying About
Walt's books, workshops,
coaching, websites and life rhymes

"Walt, next to my Bible, your book, *Turn Your Passion Into Profit* is the book I reference the most in my house! It is the only other book that is constantly visible (it's on the dining room table right now)!"

Karon Mason Etienne

"...My husband had a total revelation about his passion as a result of your book two years ago and we both really like your work. Peace and Blessings, Ruth!"

Ruth Kirby, Medford, OR

"Do you know how it is when you've run across something that is just what you've been looking for, but didn't know you were looking for it? Well, that's how I feel about having found your [Passionprofit.com] site! I am excited about what I see in your company and am looking forward to becoming more involved. Honestly Walt, I haven't seen anything on the internet that has so moved me as what I've experienced visiting your site! Thanks again and again!"

Henry Street

"I have read many "self-help" books, but yours is actually instructional and answers questions. It addresses how I feel and what I am thinking. I also e-mailed you several months ago about how I [pursue my passion] when I have a house to pay for, a child to support, etc...and you told me to start out slowly and build. Like you said in your book, it is scary. However, I am doing what you said and am starting to feel so much better. I realize I have a long way to go but, I think just realizing that I don't have to stay in one of those 9-to-5 jobs working for someone else gives me so much courage to get out there and start doing what I want! Thank you so much for the book and the inspiration. I truly appreciate it!"

Tammy van der Leest

"I want to thank you again for all the insights you shared with me yesterday. Listening to you enabled me to see my situation in a whole new light. As a result, I'm now focusing on various activities I would like to engage in rather than fretting over my life's purpose, which I'm sure will show itself to me in time."

Shelly

"Yeah, why else did I go to college for 8 years to be turning someone else's key!! Time is important. Better to start right away with my own business than to juggle a bunch of part-time stints with no long-lasting benefits to me or society. You are right... I just hope to God that I find my way through the obstacles, and plethora of get-rich-quick schemes and information out there on the net! Your book will be a fine manual for putting this business together."

a client

"I will be eternally grateful to know that there is a mentor out there who is available to offer advice on turning my passion into profit! Again thanks... I will ponder over what you've just shared with me for the remainder of the day and I am certain my God-given brain will come up with some answers and thought-provoking questions! Thanks!! PS. I was up for 5 hours last night browsing your site and taking in information! What swell work you have done!!"

T., a consulting client

Master the Art of Thoughtful Living!

"They're not poems. They're called 'life rhymes'! Sort of like LYRICS FOR LIVING!"

What is a Life Rhyme?

Life rhymes are *"...positive, situational, success-oriented, lyrical, rhyme-based poetry designed to inspire new ways of thinking."*

They are a new genre of inspirational poetry created by Walt F.J. Goodridge, an author, inspirational speaker and career coach known as the "Passion Prophet".

"What a great way to communicate positive words of wisdom!"— **L. Hawthorne**

"…I receive these every Friday, and I love them all because they inspire and uplift me so, but never has one of your poems ever read my heart and soul as this one has. It was as if you were writing to someone else for me. I'm not sure what to do just yet because I'm still afraid to "go out on a limb," but hopefully after reading it a few more times, I'll get the courage to actually taste the 'sweetest fruit.' "-**Lashunda Bailes**

"Walt, I swear GOD is trying to talk to me through you. Unbelievable, as usual. Thanks!"-**Dst22**

"…just wanted to drop you a quick note to let you know that I enjoy reading your Friday Inspirations. I'm a faithful reader and find it amazing that week after week you can continually come up with something new. Thanks for the inspiring words and keep up the good work. Sincerely." —**Todd Johnston**

"You have no idea of how much your inspirations affect people. It's like you heard me talking with my girlfriends yesterday about my relationships. This inspiration hit the nail on the head for me. It is just what I needed to start my day." -**T Bos**

"Hello Walt: especially liked your poem - "The Art of Creation." It is very much in tune with what I believe as hard as that philosophy is to accept (i.e. that we create our own experiences)." -**Pamela Beatty**

"This is so authentic. It captures so much of what you shared with us and I'm totally impressed at how well you used language to capture some of the intangibles that seem to make up the crucial pieces of our growth. Thank you." --**Reina Joa**

Andrew A. used them to save his marriage.

DST22 believes God is using them to speak to her.

Lorna P. uses them to teach values to her 7th graders.

Thomas uses them to motivate his employees....

HOW WILL THEY AFFECT YOU? Find out! Order at www.lyricsforliving.com

Books by Walt F.J. Goodridge

The Lyrics for Living Series
Some lyrics you sing. Some lyrics you live.

The Tao of Wow/Art of Wow
Discover your "wow factor." Become a "wow master." Create your dream life.

Change the Game (formerly *Rap: This Game of Exposure*)
A "How To" guide for Hip Hop Entrepreneurs who want to follow their passion for music and release their own records by starting an independent record label.

The Game of Artist Management
At the request of many buyers of *Change the Game* (see above), *The Game of Artist Management* was created to give the scoop on managing artists Hip Hop style! (Features "24 Ways to Get a Record Deal" by Chuck D.)

The Niche Market Report (Discovering, Understanding and Selling to the Niche Consumer of the 21st Century)
As the Internet grows and the world gets smaller, the information in this manual becomes essential to everyone doing business in the new millennium. Learn how to market anything to everyone from Generation X to Baby Boomers, African Americans, The Hip Hop Generation, Asian Americans and more.

Lessons In Success Volume I: The Silent Performer
Life rhymes and commentary that provide an intimate, revealing peek into a year in the life of Walt Goodridge. *"Complex thoughts expressed in the simplicity of rhyme/Walt's Lessons In Success is a classic for all time!"*

Come Into Our Whirl (The First Cyber-Anthology of Poetry From The PoetsNiche)
Edited by Monica Blache, and featuring life rhymes by Walt Goodridge, *Come Into Our Whirl* features the story behind the creation of The Poets Niche (www.poetsniche.com) as well as the poetry of 40 poet-members of this unique online community.

Turn Your Passion Into Profit: A Step-by-Step Guide for Turning ANY Hobby, Talent, Interest or Product idea into a money-making venture!
Discover the value in your passion. Create a unique product or service from your talents. Make money doing what you love!

All titles are available at www.passionprofit.com

Table of Contents

List of Illustrations, Forms and Charts

About The Author

*"I share what I know,
so that others may grow!"
--Walt F.J. Goodridge*

Walt F.J. Goodridge is known as the *Passion Prophet.*

A graduate of Columbia University, Walt is a former civil engineer who walked away from his career to follow his passion for music, writing, and helping others. He has been an artist manager, radio dj, record label owner, inventor, poet, network marketer and consultant.

He is the author of 10 books including *Turn Your Passion Into Profit (A Step-by-Step Guide for Turning ANY hobby, talent, interest or idea into a money-making venture!)*, and owns and operates several profitable websites.

He is the creator of "Walt's Friday Inspirations", a popular weekly email of "the thoughts that create success" that he sends to the thousands who subscribe.

Walt writes for Entrepreneur Magazine and Black Enterprise, and has been featured in Time Magazine, Wall Street Journal Online, the Dallas Morning News, The Kip Business Report and numerous publications and websites. Walt offers personalized coaching and conducts workshops around the country and through the Learning Annex™ to help others make money doing what they love!

Walt's workshops are ALWAYS interactive, solution-focused, fact-filled, process oriented, "How To, What To, and When To" events. If you leave without a solution to the SPECIFIC challenge you're facing in turning your passion into profit, it'll only be because you didn't ask for one!

You may contact Walt at P.O. Box 618 Church Street Station, New York NY 10008, or by faxing (323) 693-9425 or calling (800) 363-5197 or via email at Walt@passionprofit.com.

"I am proud to offer the world a philosophy and formula for turning one's passion into profit. I encourage its use by parents, teachers, coaches, as well as within institutions of higher learning. It is my hope that it will foster a greater understanding and appreciation of our inherent value as spiritual beings and the expression of that value within the physical marketplace. It is my wish that these ideas lead a revolution in thought and in deed and usher in a new era of entrepreneurial expression, financial independence, and personal freedom."

— Walt F.J. Goodridge.
The Passion Prophet

The Passion Profit Philosophy

Your PASSION is part of your life's purpose
HAPPINESS in life starts when you pursue it
EVERYONE has a passion
ALL passions have value
ANY passion can be turned into profit

The Formula: The Cycle of Success

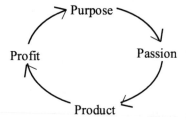

Value No One Can Steal

"If you create and market a product or service through a business that is in alignment with your personality, capitalizes on your history, incorporates your experiences, harnesses your talents, optimizes your strengths, complements your weaknesses, honors your life's purpose, and moves you towards the conquest of your own fears, there is ABSOLUTELY NO WAY that anyone in this or any other universe can offer the same value that you do!"

> *"One step beyond
> the wish, is the way."*

Chapter 1: Permission to Dream!
"The Passion Profit Life-style"

Welcome to the World!

Congratulations! You are about to enter a brave new world!

Everything that you now accept about the world, about money, about value, about making a living, about your self-worth, your value to the world, even your purpose on the planet is about to be challenged. By choosing to turn your passion into profit, you've given yourself permission to dream. If you follow through with that dream, you'll be doing something many people talk about and wish for, but few actually find the courage to do.

The reason more people don't take this journey, is that it's uncomfortable. Growth is always about stretching beyond the known. The answers you're looking for, the guidance that you need to achieve your goal won't sound like what you're used to hearing from the people around you. It's that discomfort that tends to make people fearful and give up dreaming. Most of your life you've heard that in order to be a good child, a good student, good employee, good spouse and a functioning member of society that you have to give up your dreams, and do what's practical. You've heard essentially that you have to choose between passion and profit.

Now, if you're open to seeing things differently, I want to suggest to you that unless you're pursuing your passion, then your life is only being half-lived. And that if you're not doing it for profit, that you have no clue what you're missing out on. There's a whole other world that you haven't experienced yet. There's a world of freedom, of growth, of living each day with a sense of purpose and passion. There's a world where you get up every day eager to see what happens next! A world where you make money simply by being and becoming who you are and who you were meant to be. A world that rewards you for the uniqueness you bring to the party, not for doing what someone else decides is important for their balance sheet bottom line.

You've paid a few dollars for the chance to really change your life, and I'm going to deliver on the promise of the title of this book. I'm going to share with you a philosophy and a formula for turning your passion into profit. Remember, one step beyond the wish is the way! So, again congratulations, welcome to the world, and let's take that step!

Dream a World.

Ninety-five percent of society finds itself working for someone else, and many will continue to do so until they leave this planet. Have you ever had the thought that it was unnatural and demeaning to be forced into confinement for 8 or more hours every day, told when to eat, how to dress and how to speak?

Imagine for a moment what your life could look and feel like if you were making money on your own terms. Imagine being free and in control of life, free to go to a movie in the middle of a weekday, play golf on a Tuesday, pick the kids up for lunch, or just make decisions about how to spend your days without an employer's input. Imagine breaking free from a life of servitude in order to start doing something that inspires you.

Imagine making more money in a month than you currently make all year. Or at least removing your employer's limit on the amount you can make. Imagine not having to play someone else's game in return for security and benefits.

Imagine creating your own definition of success, experiencing a bigger world of bigger people, places, and ideas while making a difference in the world.

This book is for people who have started to imagine something different. It's for people who may have spent many years building someone else's dreams and have started to wonder if that's all they were put here to do. It's for people who are feeling the need to do more, be more, experience more and leave a lasting legacy. They've started asking questions like "What am I building? What am I really doing here? Is this all there is?"

If this sounds like you, you're not alone. Others have found themselves questioning their lives, and daring to dream a different world.

> So what am I building? as I work every day
> am I constructing my future or just temping for pay?
> my efforts are bricks my foundation my dreams
> my faith are supports and my prayers are beams
>
> is it a road of regrets that I build sure to fail?
> is it a wall of defeats with no ladder to scale?
> is it a fortress of fear to bind dreams that can't fly?
> is it a prison for hopes that then wither and die?
>
> is it a fence 'round my wishes with no way out, through or in?
> is it a castle for others while without I peer in?
> to build bridges of victories over doubts I must choose
> to build tunnels of experience that help others get through
>
> to build towers up high from there vast lands survey
> to build a temple inside and show others the way
> and then built by design from a plan to be grand
> my monument to life over time will still stand!

What am I building?
Walt's Life Rhyme #48

Passion Seekers

By taking this bold step, you'll join the ranks of a unique group of people I call "Passion Seekers."

Passion Seekers are men and women of every age, ethnic group, educational background, profession and religion. They include entrepreneurs, housewives, inventors and artists. They are a diverse group of people from every corner of the globe. However, Passion Seekers do share one common trait: they've all found something they enjoy doing and have decided to keep doing it.

More significantly, not only do Passion Seekers enjoy what they do, they get paid to do it! They've found the hidden value in their talents, interests or pastimes, offer that value to the world in the form of unique products and services, and do so for profit. In other words, they've created businesses that allow them to make money doing what they love. As a result, many have walked away from frustrating jobs to live the Passion Profit life-style. They set their own schedules and control their time. They live according to their own personal value system rather than someone else's. Furthermore, Passion Seekers experience the joy, empowerment and unique satisfaction of being compensated for being who they choose to be, honoring what they believe in, and doing something they feel divinely called to do.

ANYONE Can Do This

The Passion Seekers is not an exclusive club. I contend that EVERYONE can turn their passion into profit because of a few special beliefs I have about people.

I believe that everyone is creative. We are each an individual expression of creation. Therefore, we each have within us the ability to create as well.

I also believe that success is a process that can be taught and learned. Everything that I've listed as the keys to my own success are ways of being that I learned and practiced until they became my own habits. I believe people can learn to be successful.

Yes, I believe that ANYONE can turn their passion into profit. It doesn't matter if you've never run a business before. It doesn't matter if you don't believe that you're creative. It doesn't matter what you think your present skills and talents are. I've seen people who considered themselves very ordinary, do some very extraordinary things once they were given a vision that inspired them and which was presented in a way which moved them to action.

I believe that people sometimes need more than motivation. I've found that many people who attend motivational seminars find themselves "back at square one" shortly after the seminar. They leave high on momentary motivation, but with no definite direction in which to apply it. They leave in awe as they marvel at another person's success, but often don't make the necessary connection in their own lives. I believe people can succeed if they simply know what to do next in the process.

I believe that everything you need to become successful is already yours. Every desire, motivation, talent, skill, reason and rhyme you need is already a part of you.

And finally, I know one individual who went to school for engineering, who never took a writing course, and who couldn't bring himself to strike up a conversation with a stranger who is now inspiring others as a successful entrepreneur, author and public speaker. Yes, my friend, if I can do it, you can too!

How This Book Came To Be

The story of how this book came into being is itself a good example of the power of pursuing one's passion. I was living in Silver Spring, Maryland at the time, and had just sent *Lessons In Success* off to the printer. Because of the success of my websites, I was being sought for my expertise on launching online ventures. I was invited by an organization called the National Money League (NML) to give a talk entitled "Doing Business on the Internet" as part of their Eagle's Nest workshop-- a seven week course which focuses on mastering different elements of prosperity.

As I always like to do when I give public talks, I involved the attendees from the very beginning and tailored my presentation towards their immediate needs and interests. I discovered that people were more interested in discovering what their passions were, and how they could make money doing it, than finding some turn-key online business they couldn't really get excited about. As a result, the discussion evolved into a brainstorming session in which we all contributed suggestions to help individual attendees discover what it is they loved to do and to come up with business ideas with which to capitalize on their unique interests. It was an exciting and enlightening night!

According to NML founder, Sidney Harleston, what happened that night really got people excited. She invited me to return as one of several presenters in a single-day workshop which would allow more people to experience the magic of that evening.

Over the course of the next week, she shared with me the enthusiastic response she was receiving to my topic. So much so, in fact, that Sidney said she could sell all the available seats just on that section alone. She then added, "It's great that your book [*Lessons In Success*] will be out by then, too!" I replied, "Sure, but *Lessons In Success* isn't really a how to book on creating a business around your passion." I added jokingly, "I'd probably have to write a separate book for that!" At that instant, that old familiar light bulb went on and shone brightly on an idea that I now realize had been in production for most of my life. It reached completion at that very moment.

The idea that was conceived at that moment was the perfect embodiment of what my life had been about for the previous 8 years. Ever since I walked away from my corporate job, friends, family and strangers seemed inspired by my commitment to my passion, and have asked me to share my experiences, insights, tips and advice to help them do the same. A book on that very topic was actually long overdue. I decided to call the book *How To Make Money Doing What You Love*.

Sidney called a few days later to announce the name she had come up with for my section of the all-day workshop. She would call it "Turn Your Passion Into Profit."

"Hmmm," I thought to myself. "That's a catchier title. Perhaps I'll use that."

The next day, I sat down to write the book you are now reading. My task, over the next several weeks was simply to add the words to the idea; to put the knowledge that already existed in my mind, into a form that others could access. This book, therefore, is filled with information that I have been living and sharing with thousands of people in many different ways. It is nothing less than every single word of advice and guidance I've given to the questions people have asked over the years.

What This Book Can Do

This book will offer **information** through practical steps to get you from where you are now to where you want to be.

This book will provide **inspiration** in the form of success thoughts, step-by-step instructions, as well as real-life examples of people who are turning passion into profit.

This book will offer **ideas** for businesses that you may never have considered.

If you have never been in business for yourself, but feel that following your passion is the next important step in your life, this book can help you think differently about the task ahead in a way that will increase your chances of success.

If you are already in business for yourself, but still haven't found something you're passionate about, this book can help you to reclaim some of the things that used to get you excited, and perhaps help you find some forgotten dreams to commit to.

This book will help move you in the direction of your desire. It will offer a process to lay the foundation for a successful business as well as a fulfilling life.

This book will answer the most frequently expressed concerns about turning your passion into profit.

Frequently Asked Questions About Turning Passion Into Profit:

1. How do I find my passion?
2. How do I overcome the fear I have of pursuing it?
3. Are all passions profitable?
4. Should I take a business class?
5. How much money will I need to start my passion business?
6. Where do I begin?
7. How long does it take to start making money?
8. How do I know if what I've chosen is my real passion?
9. What should I do if I don't like selling?
10. Can I make enough money to pay my rent?
11. How can the Internet help me turn my passion into profit?
12. How much should I charge for what I do?
13. When should I quit my job?
14. Should I distribute my product myself or work with a distributor?
15. How do I know if and when it's time to throw in the towel?

By the time you've finished reading this book, you'll have the answers to all these questions and many more!

What This Book WILL NOT do for You:

At the same time, this book will not make you happy, but happiness may seem a more attainable goal by reading it.

This book will not think for you, but the way you think may be changed forever by reading it.

This book will not dream for you, but your dreams may cause you more excitement by reading it.

This book will not act for you, but the actions you choose may be more effective by reading it.

This book will not exempt you from the challenges you will face or the life tests you will be given, but it will help you to interpret the lessons they offer.

This book will not be the definitive source on every topic that's covered. It's designed to highlight the areas that are connected to your success, and offer guidance if you wish to pursue more knowledge in those areas.

This book will not guarantee a specific profit from your venture, nor will it guarantee that the first passion you choose will be successful. It will, however, exist as a constant reminder that success is a journey, and that where you end up is always a function of your next step.

How to Use This Book

As I mentioned earlier, I believe success is a process that can be learned. In order to extract the greatest benefit, it may be important to know how we learn.

We learn by asking the right questions. At the end of each chapter are suggestions and questions entitled "The Right Questions To Ask." These mental exercises condition your mind to go ever deeper into its infinite pool of resources to find solutions to the challenges you face.

We learn by doing. Once you know the right questions to ask, the next step is to create a "to do" list based on those questions. All great achievers work from lists. If you gain nothing else from this book other than the habit of creating lists from which to tackle the challenges of your life, you'll be among the world's great achievers. This book is meant to be interactive and experiential. I encourage you to perform the suggested tasks in the follow-up file at the end of each chapter.

We learn skills through repetition. Go through the exercises over and over. Each time you do, you'll find yourself moving closer and closer to your goals.

Finally, we learn best by teaching others. Imagine that you'll be required to give a seminar on what you've learned. Share this book with others. Explain what you've learned. Explain the process. Explain the main points. Explain those sections with which you have the most difficulty. You'll find that in teaching it to others it becomes a part of you that you can tap into at any time.

The Secret Power of Life Rhymes!

This book also offers inspiration in the form of what I call *Life Rhymes*. Life Rhymes are "positive, situational, success-oriented, lyrical, rhyme-based poetry designed to inspire new ways of thinking." They are part affirmation, part advice column, part inspired observation, part proverb, part prayer and 100% life lesson all rolled into one. They are meant to guide your thoughts so that you see the world differently, interpret your situations effectively, think critically, and then make choices and act in ways that help you reach your goals and support your greatest aspirations.

Their secret power lies in the fact that, as poetry, they activate your "right brain"-- the more creative, intuitive part of your brain. It is in achieving a balance between the left (analytical) and right (creative) sides of our brains that we achieve the most success. Check out the *Lyrics for Living* series for the complete collection.

Don't Judge The Messenger

Always remember that where you are in life right now is a direct result of all the knowledge you have accumulated and all the thoughts you've thought up to this point. Therefore, if you are not exactly where you want to be, perhaps the thoughts you're thinking aren't working? Why not try things a little differently? Be willing to step outside of your comfort zone.

This book offers a philosophy and a formula inspired by information and ideas from such varied sources as Scientology, Hinduism, Vegetarianism, Eckankar, Astrology, Caribbean culture, and from people as ideologically different as Elijah Muhammad, Deepak Chopra, Les Brown, Buddha, and a wacky engineer friend of mine in New Jersey.

It's the same life lesson once again
I'm learning not to judge
But habits are like mules sometimes
and just refuse to budge

When preconceptions take control
I don't accept all as I should
But everyone deserves a chance
so I'll focus on their good

I'm prone to discount others' worth
and judge by what I see
but each man's worth mirrors my own
so I'm really judging me

My world is made by gifts of thought
that return that which I give
I'll judge not lest I too be judged
and learn my lesson of how to live!

> *"Information, inspiration and ideas may arrive dressed in the strangest of garbs."*

Judge Not
Walt's Life Rhyme #117

No More Excuses

As you proceed on this journey, you may find yourself challenged by doubts and fears. While this is a natural part of being human, giving into them doesn't have to be. Here are suggested counter arguments for "The Top Ten Excuses People Give Themselves For Not Following Passion"

Reason #1: Will people really want to pay me for this?

If you believe that the only place your good can come is from your employer, then that's the reality that you will create. If you accept that your good and all the blessings of the universe come from other sources, and that you can create and receive wealth for yourself from any channel, then you'll understand that you can make enough to thrive, not just survive!

Reason #2: I don't have the credentials.

Most successful entrepreneurs don't have a formal education or degree.

Reason #3: Will it continue long enough for me to be successful?

See the answer to reason #2 above. The question is not whether IT will continue long enough for you to be successful, but will YOU?

Reason #4: I don't know where to begin.

You feel this way because you feel overwhelmed by the task. Make your list of things to do and simply take one step at a time.

Reason #5: I have kids and a family to feed.

Yes, and soon the kids will have more expenses, like college tuition. It's been at least 20 years since one or even two incomes has been enough to meet the average family's rising cost of living. Rather than working more and more hours to make more money, wouldn't it be easier to put something in place to decrease your dependence on a single stream of income?

Reason #6: I'm not a good business person.

That's not a requirement. Many of the most successful entrepreneurs are "idea people" who were smart enough to find people who are good in the areas they aren't.

Reason #7: If I leave my job, I'll lose my pension and benefits.

If it's predicted that 97% of the population will retire dependent on family, friends and the federal government to survive, and they're doing pretty much the same thing you are, what assurances do you have that your fate won't be the same? Besides, no one's saying you have to leave your job, but why not think about creating something that can create your own pension and benefits.

Reason #8: I'll think about that when I'm older.

And in the meantime? There really is no such thing as the future.

Reason #9: It'll take too long for me to be successful at it.

Ask yourself: "How old will I be in 10 years?" Then ask, "How old will I be in 10 years, if I don't do this?" Then ask, "How old will I be in 10 years if I do this?" The fact is, the years will pass regardless of what you decide to do. By not doing, you've simply decided to pass the years unhappy and frustrated rather than in pursuit of fulfillment.

Reason #10: I'll start when I have the money to invest.

Many people assume that no actions can be taken unless and until they have a certain amount of money. In fact, just the opposite is true. Paperwork can be completed. Products can be designed. Calls can be made. Estimates can be acquired. Marketing strategies can be mapped out. And it's been my experience that if you proceed as if you have the money, faith will bring what you need. The creative power of the universe is brought to bear by commitment and serves men and women who go after their dreams.

Now none of this is meant to minimize the reality of your current situation, or to imply that the challenges you face aren't real. Yes, it is challenging to raise three kids, and hold down a job, and pursue a passion at the same time. However, what you need during those moments that threaten to overwhelm you are simply reminders that you can do it. You need to be reminded that others have done it, and you can too. You need to be reminded that the alternative to trying is the same unhappiness that drove you to do something different in the first place. You need to be reminded of the fact that you can be, do and have anything you want if you're simply willing to pay the price. It may not always be easy, but it will always be worth it. Remember, you can always find excuses not to do something you're afraid of. The question is can you find the courage to act even in the face of fear?

It's not about credentials
regulations or degrees
It's not about some board
that validates your expertise

    It's not about the cash flow
    or that "money's kinda tight"
    It's not about your rent
    or getting finances just right

It's not about you needing proof
and knowing this scheme works
It's not about your pension plan
job benefits or perks

    It's not about your debts
    or paying back the student loan
    It's not about your age
    or waiting 'til the kids are grown

And NO, it's not a time thing
so just stop THAT idle chatter
We all know people find the time
for things that really matter

So what is it that stops you?
Well, the truth is that you're scared
But rather than admit it
you just say you're unprepared

    When children want they're fearless
        for there's nothing they want more
        But as adults choose safety
        the predictable and sure

And skill and time and money?
You know what I'll say is true:
You know those who do more with less
who're not half as bright as you!

    Yes, all you need's desire
    forget all that other stuff
    And simply ask one question:
    "Do I want this bad enough?"

Walt's Life Rhyme #316
Excuses, Excuses

Permission To Dream

Laura is an eighth-grader whom I had the pleasure of tutoring in Math. As we finished our tutoring session, Laura and I started talking about personal interests. After much probing, I discovered that Laura really loves to sing. She told me, however, that her love of singing, and the unique thrill she gets doing it was something she had to hide from her parents, as they thought in terms of traditional paths of education and employment. As I encouraged her to tell me more about her passion, Laura became a different person once she realized that I was an adult who wanted to hear about her dreams, and who would actually encourage her to think about being a singer.

I've since lost touch with Laura, but I truly hope that she continues to honor her passion. I truly hope, as well, that you too can reconnect with your dreams with the same excitement of a 12-year-old who's been given permission to dream!

MAIN POINTS OF CHAPTER 1
"Permission to Dream"

• As one who seeks to turn your passion into profit, you are about to embark on a unique journey of discovery. However, the price of the freedom you seek is that you must give up your attachment to your present reality and some of the people, ideas and habits that are a part of it. Change is the price of freedom.

• This book, which contains the world's first philosophy and formula for transforming passion into profit, is itself a manifestation of one person's passion for teaching.

• The Passion Profit Life-style is a life-style of choice, freedom, control, financial independence, personal fulfillment and continuous personal growth.

• The secret to success in any endeavor is in asking the right questions. This book will pose many questions that you may never have taken the time and energy to answer. This book can also answer many questions, introduce you to new concepts, principles, habits and strategies for achieving the Passion Profit Life-style.

• At the same time, this book will not think, dream or act on your behalf, or exempt you from the ups and downs that it may be necessary to experience in the process of growth that change will require.

• Everyone is qualified and capable of turning his or her passion into profit. Every desire, motivation, talent, skill, reason and rhyme you need to make it happen is already a part of you. The information, inspiration and ideas contained within will help you to succeed. Perform, repeat and teach the concepts, tasks and habits suggested in this book. That is the way to make them a part of you.

• The information, inspiration and ideas provided in this book have come from many different world views, belief systems and practices. Allow yourself the benefit of an open mind. Don't judge the messenger.

• Don't allow a belief in your current excuses to rob you of the opportunity to do what you love to do. Find the courage to face the fears that hold you back! You now have permission to dream!

FOLLOW-UP FILE FOR CHAPTER 1
"Permission to Dream"

INSPIRATION: Passion Seeker Profiles

"Passion for Patching"

Ever since he was 8 years old, Kaile Warren loved to fix things. Through an unfortunate turn of events, Kaile soon found himself disabled, unable to work and, eventually homeless. He woke one day with a divinely inspired idea to take his passion for being handy around the house and create a business offering the same service to households which didn't have the time or "man power" to do it. He called his new business "Rent A Husband." Sales are well over 8 million two years after he started. Kaile's advice: "Once you find your passion, intoxicate yourself with it. A life without passion is a very sobering and difficult journey."

IDEAS: The Right Questions to Ask

• What specific things can I do to prepare for the changes I expect?
• What am I prepared to give and to give up in my life?
• What dreams have I stopped believing are possible for me?
• What are my own 20 frequently asked questions about turning passion into profit?
• Read the stories of people whom you admire for pursuing their passions.

Their stories will have the common element of triumph over adversity and will inspire you to greatness. People like Michael Jordan, Oprah Winfrey, Tony Robbins, Sylvester Stallone, Ray Croc, or even local heroes profiled in newspapers, magazines or on the internet exist as examples of the courage you need to create the world of your desires.

Chapter 2: The Passion Prophecy
"A wake-up call"

New Passion Times

Passion Prophet Predicts America's Return to Pre-Industrial Economy!

NEW YORK--Corporate layoffs. Outsourcing. Automation. Downsizing. Paycuts. These are all fancy words for the same phenomenon: Americans are losing their jobs. What will the newly jobless do to secure their future? Walt F.J. Goodridge, a New York-based career coach, and speaker known as the "Passion Prophet", may have the answer: America may have to return to an economic model that existed over 100 years ago!

"Before the Industrial Revolution, 80% of the population were entrepreneurs," Goodridge explains. "You either worked the land you lived on, or had a skill that you bartered or sold to survive. It was only with mechanization and industry, which required labor in factories, that people moved away from being self-sufficient, to working for someone else."

In the face of changing economic realities and disillusionment, many people are questioning the ways they currently make money and seek to create additional incomes. But, instead of getting more jobs or opening franchises, many are looking inward and asking, "What am I good at?" "What's my passion?" Indeed, traffic and orders have increased on Goodridge's www.PassionProfit.com website, which offers books, workshops and courses for people seeking to discover, develop and profit from their passions. His unique formula is based on the philosophy that everyone has a passion, and every passion can be turned into profit.

"Today's trends are all pointing to a move back to the way things were," Goodridge prophesizes. "As the corporate landscape becomes more uncertain, people will need viable options for increasing their streams of income just to survive....[continued in *Lifestyle* Page 23]

A Changing Landscape

In a recent cover story article in *Business Week Magazine,* it was reported that as a result of a shrinking labor market (the people available to be hired), greater opportunities and global competition, companies are being forced to find ways to get the job done without paying employees more. Hence, a new pool of workers is being wooed to their positions with stock options, bonuses and other performance-based perks rather than big salaries. These incentives are all ways to compensate exceptional employees without incurring fixed costs which might cripple the company in the event of an economic downturn. If the economy gets shaky and employers have to cut corners, it's easier to stop paying bonuses than it is to reduce a person's "locked in" salary. The companies save money, and still get the job done.

Among the other tactics companies are using to keep their costs down are: insisting on longer hours without overtime pay; laying off higher paid employees; hiring temporary workers and immigrants; and forcing higher productivity out of its existing workforce. One hotel operator reportedly places dirty laundry behind the front desk so that check-in clerks can wash the linen in their down time. *[Business Week. Dec '99]*

The latest predictions for our workers' economic future suggest that the social security benefits that we've been led to believe will be there to take care of us in our golden years, won't be there when we retire. Inflation, the soaring national debt, and global competition have made this a very different playing field than that on which your parents played. There is growing concern that if current trends continue, there simply will not be any money available to pay social security benefits to future generations.

All this leads to a more unstable future for you if you are an employee. And while you're not guaranteed the big bucks if you jump out on your own, you'll at least be wise to have a plan B, C, D and E in the works as your own insurance policy. I always remind people who seem committed to big companies to their own detriment that these companies make decisions based on their own bottom lines, and nothing else. Your bills, your children and your devotion and loyalty have no place to be entered on your employer's balance sheet. The landscape is changing and you need to prepare for what may happen.

Are You Living A Lie?

In our society, we are told to go to school, get good grades, graduate, get a good job, get married, have children, buy a home, work for a company for 40 years, and somehow, slowly but surely, we will rise to higher and higher levels of prosperity and happiness. Burke Hedges, in his book, *Who Stole The American Dream*, which persuasively promotes the merits of Network Marketing as an alternative paradigm of success, explores the disillusionment that comes with the discovery that the American Dream of success is a misconception that holds no promise for the future.

The truth, as more people are beginning to realize, is that the rules of the game have changed. What may have worked well for previous generations, is now a recipe for disaster when applied to the unique economic reality of present-day society. No longer can the average person rely on the security of working for a large corporation. No longer can a single income comfortably support the average family. The truth is 97% of working people will retire broke and dependent on family, friends and/or the federal government for survival. The truth is more and more retirees are having to get jobs just to survive.

In addition to the economic lie that most of us are living, there is also the lie of self-actualization that has been fed to us. We are taught that our primary concern when it comes to choosing a profession should be that of practicality. After all, we are told, we have bills to pay, and responsibilities that require a stable income with benefits. We are led to believe that artistic pursuits will never be able to provide that income. As a result, we spend our working days--our productive years--engaged in activities for which we have no passion. We mistakenly think that we can find happiness despite this misguided pursuit. The truth is that the pursuit of practicality has never led the searching soul to happiness. Honest expression is the cornerstone of happiness.

For many years, John, a successful stock broker, lived a vicarious existence through his friend Steven, a painter who, though always struggling, was determined not to compromise his passion. John would occasionally lend Steven money to help him pay his rent, or to buy supplies. As a child, John himself had developed an interest in art and had even won a few awards for it in high school. His father, however, discouraged him from pursuing an artistic career, and even refused to pay for John's college education unless he pursued a degree in business. As a result, John's opinion of his talent waned. He started to believe less and less that what he created could have any value such that people would pay him for it. Meanwhile, he amassed an expensive collection of beautiful art that adorned his home. It was years before he developed the courage, with Steven's urging, to actually try his own hand at painting again. Slowly, John got back into his art and, with Steve's help, has even sold a few pieces....for money!

We are taught the lie that there is less monetary value in our creative expression than there is in other "more practical" activities. And that's simply not true.

You Can Handle The Truth

Some time recently, I was discussing the topic of relationships with a dear friend. She commented on the drama she always seems to encounter when dealing with the men in her life. She wondered aloud why even the men she thought were just friends, had expectations of her that were more in line with an intimate relationship. From where I stood, it was obvious that there was something wrong with the picture she was painting. Though she said she and her current topic of conversation were "just friends", I knew that she was not addressing the real issue. I knew from previous conversations that both she and her friend really wanted something more than just friendship, but had decided it unwise given their individual situations. They decided to move forward and build a relationship built on a lie.

Until she addresses the real issue of the type of relationship both she and her "friend" really want from each other, everything they do will be just a facade. I explained that any relationship entered into under false pretense is doomed to difficulty.

Attempting to solve any difficulty while avoiding the bigger picture simply compounds the deception and creates drama. I told her that operating under the wrong premise and missing the big picture was like being on the Titanic during its last hours and asking people for directions to the shuffleboard contest!

Many of us will, in fact, miss the lifeboat of happiness because we don't realize that the big-picture-truth is that we're on a sinking ship. The lie that many of us labor under comes from what others have defined us to be. We haven't been told the truth about ourselves, so we cannot be true to the truth of ourselves. Consequently, we live our lives chasing an illusion of happiness within a life that's going nowhere but down. The greatest lie that you live is that of someone else's perception of who you are.

Have you ever thought about what your life would have been like if your parents and teachers had encouraged you to follow your gift of sports prowess, or your penchant for art, or your love of animals rather than push you to be an accountant or an engineer or a lawyer? It's an interesting thought to ponder. However, it really doesn't matter. There's no such thing as a wrong decision. There are no mistakes. There are simply choices and opportunities to grow and learn. Every single decision you've made, or that was made for you, has contributed to you being here at this very moment with this book in your hand, ready to make a change. Everything you've learned along the way--even the unhappiness and frustration--will help you to discover your passion and turn it into profit. In fact, by the time you've completed this book, you may want to thank your parents and teachers for giving you the opportunity to discover who you want to be by having successfully shown you who you are not. Sometimes your greatest growth comes after experiencing a situation that simply confirms for you the reality that you don't want.

So don't beat yourself up over the decisions you've made. As a wise man once said, "pity not the man for the challenges he faces, but for the lessons not learned in his responses." The tragedy is not that in the past you were steered in a direction that was not towards your passion. The tragedy will be if you allow yourself to keep going in that direction once you recognize the power you have in the present. Everyone will learn their lessons eventually. For some people it will take a little longer (maybe several lifetimes). Others will recognize the lessons in an instant, get themselves out of there, and move on.

The Truth: A New Survival Strategy

Hopefully you are now ready to look at the real issues and to discover your own personal truth. In addition to the personal fulfillment of living a life of truth, there is another compelling reason why you'll want to look seriously at turning your passion into profit. That reason is basic survival. Your survival on a financial and mental level is in the balance. As stated before, the game has changed. In order to prosper in the new era, a new strategy is needed. Here are some tips for what your strategy should include.

Build assets

In his book, *Rich Dad, Poor Dad*, author Robert T. Kiyosaki shares the secret of why the rich get richer and the poor get poorer. What keeps the poor battling in poverty is their failure to create assets which generate money. When most average people get some extra money, be it a pay raise or lottery winnings, they immediately seek to buy things which end up increasing their liabilities. They buy gas-guzzling cars, tax-draining homes, and indulge in expensive habits which deplete their earnings and put them in a worse position than before. The key to wealth is to focus on building assets that generate wealth so your money works for you to create more money. Kiyosaki lists as his choice of assets to invest in: stocks, bonds, mutual funds, income-producing real estate, notes, royalties and your own business. A business that can generate money without your presence is one of the best and most liberating and lucrative assets to own.

Create multiple streams of income

In times past, it was possible to sustain a family on a single stream of income. As society changed, the era of the two income household was ushered in. Both mom and dad now had to work just to maintain the same standard of living. As things continue to change, unless mom and dad create more streams of income in addition to what they're currently making, their standard of living will start to slip away. Economic uncertainty brought about by technological advancements, a declining labor market, and inflation makes it more necessary than ever to have one or several "plan Bs" in place. Diversification doesn't only apply to your stock portfolio anymore. To survive you need to create additional streams of income each strong enough to support you should any one dry up.

Seek sanity and stay healthy

It's often said that the definition of insanity is "doing the same thing over and over again and expecting different results." Many people continue to deny their passions every day, showing up to a job that offers them no fulfillment, while expecting some day that something miraculous will happen to bring them happiness. It's the ultimate in self-deception and insanity to expect an outcome of truth from a life lived as a lie.

Now, I can't actually prove this, but I'm sure you intuitively know this to be true as well that people who are doing what they love live longer and happier lives. Studies do show, however, that stress (the regular stress of being in a job you hate, perhaps?) can dampen the immune system's ability to fight off disease. Studies have shown, also, that having regular social interaction with others may be as important to your health as good nutrition and exercise. And, guess what? Making new friends is often easier if you are doing something you love and interacting with others who share your interests.

Why It's So Much Easier Today to Turn Your Passion Into Profit

These days there are less excuses for not following your passion. One reason it's easier today to turn your passion into profit has been the development of the single most powerful business tool of the 20th Century: the Internet. The Internet is the great leveler. It is the level playing field that we've all wished existed. It offers the consumer more choices, it offers the business owner a global pool of customers, and it offers the entrepreneur a means of competing with bigger businesses.

The main reason the Internet makes it so much easier is the concept of the "wide thin" market. In a recent article, Rich Karlgaard, Publisher of *Forbes Magazine*, states: "Sufferers of rare diseases, start-ups in Africa seeking funds, instrumental surf-music enthusiasts--each is an example of a market that is skinny in the local market, but, globally, inflates to a profitable mass" [*Forbes, May 17, 1999 Issue*]. In other words, if you were to set up a traditional retail outlet selling your particular product to a niche market, you would be limited by geography to just those people within a reasonable traveling distance. With the Internet, however, everyone from Cancun to Canada with access to a computer and a modem can browse your website and order from you. Your potential customer base is everyone, everywhere at any time!

Even former United States President Bill Clinton, declared himself a bona fide e-shopping (electronic shopping) convert. "I intend to join them (cyber-shoppers)," Clinton said, "because online shopping has significant benefits, not just for consumers and large established retailers. Online commerce also opens a world of opportunity for local artisans and small entrepreneurs." He added, "One of the key reasons our economy [will] continue to thrive is that we're making the most of new technologies."

The unifying effect the Internet will ultimately have on our society may be beyond our comprehension. According to visionary Andrew Zolli: "We are on the first letter of the first word of the first sentence of the book of global interconnectivity."

Another reason it's easier today is that support systems exist that can help you achieve and maintain the passion profit life-style. The Small Business Administration (SBA), The Service Corps of Retired Executives (SCORE), the Young Entrepreneur Organization (YEO), and dozens of other organizations exist to provide information, guidance, and even counseling. See appendix for additional resources.

Reality Reconstruction: Are You REALLY Ready?

I would be remiss if I didn't prepare you for some of the consequences of the path you're about to embark upon. There is going to be a price to pay for acting on thoughts that go against the norm. In addition to the ridicule and rejection you may face from friends and family, there will also be some cosmic forces at work.

Many of us don't recognize how the universe works. Quite simply, if you are living in a house and wish to build a bigger better house, it may be necessary to demolish the existing house down to its foundation before you start building anew. In much the same way, once this creative universe we live in gets its orders from you that you want to change your reality, strange forces are set in motion that begin making the necessary changes in your life. If you've been living with people who think negatively and are going nowhere in their lives, you may find yourselves arguing more frequently, or it may suddenly dawn on you that this person whom you thought you knew, has grown in an entirely different direction from where you now find yourself. You may have to make some hard decisions about who to keep with you on your journey, and who to leave by the roadside. They may hold you back from reaching your dreams. Go on without them, and if later you decide you still want their friendship, you can always come back and get them.

Similarly, if you've found yourself in a nowhere job, and you wish for the fulfillment and freedom of pursuing your passion, don't be surprised if things start happening which lead to a (forced or voluntary) separation from your present place of employment.

It's a phenomenon I call "reality reconstruction", and it usually happens right after a new reality is wished for and committed to in a significant way. I witnessed this phenomenon firsthand in one of my business ventures. Within a few days of signing someone into my network marketing business, some "catastrophe" would befall them. It might be an illness, a fight with a spouse, a car accident, or some seemingly random event. At first I thought I was jinxed, or worse, that I was jinxing my new business partners. I soon came to realize, however, exactly what was going on. Their realities were being reconstructed.

Interestingly, "reality reconstruction" doesn't affect everyone. Some people meet their dreams at a point in life *after* they've gone through the necessary preparation. For those people, it can be a smooth transition into their dreams. However, of those it does affect, many fall by the wayside, overwhelmed by the unexpected changes in life, while others see it and embrace it for what it is, a reality reconstruction in progress.

At the same time, I often inform people that following a passion can mean ups and downs, uncertainty of regular income, having to make late payments, having your lights turned off, having your telephone disconnected, and maybe even homelessness.

In *Lessons In Success Volume I*, I recount the months where I was basically homeless and living on my friend's couch and running my business from his living room. I knew that this was a temporary reality that I needed to experience to get to the success on the other side. Nothing motivates like desperation. And for some of us, experiencing dire straits is the only way we'll ever develop the inner strength to really do what's necessary to succeed as entrepreneurs. Are you prepared for any of the possible reconstructive realities that you may experience while you build your life anew?

I know of people who say they could never go through those kinds of experiences. If they happen to be married with children, they add that being single would make such changes easier. In response, I encourage people not to let their reason for doing this be their excuse for not doing it. Think about it. Many people crave the Passion Profit Life-style so they can spend more time with their children, but use the "responsibility" of providing for their children as the reason for not taking the risk to succeed.

I know of one woman with three children and a husband who quit her high-paying job to pursue her passion. She ended up homeless and on public assistance (kids and all) just before her big break came along. She didn't let the downs get her down, and realized that all things "come to pass." That is, they have come so that they can pass. She knew that sunshine follows the rain; that there's always the seed of victory within every defeat; and that sometimes it's necessary to hit bottom, before you can bounce back up.

Like a prophet I rise
after bearing my cross
resurrected from a tomb
of my own backward thoughts

Like a ball I bounce high
after hitting the ground
reaching up to the skies
with the new strength I've found

"Nothing motivates like desperation!"

Like a phoenix I soar
up from ashes of me
nothing left but to do it
and be all I can be

On My Way Back Up
Walt's Life Rhyme #34

So, which example would you rather set for your children? That of a bold, courageous individual who follows his/her dreams despite the ups and downs, taking a chance (and possibly succeeding)? Or that of a person who allows him/herself to be paralyzed by fear and doubt? The choice is yours. Your children will face a very different world from the one you currently do. How will the example you set prepare them to succeed?

The Dawning of A New Age

There is indeed a new age upon us. Mankind is emerging from outmoded ways of life and into new and innovative ways of thought and being. The shift is from the predictive to the creative; from the visible to the intuitive; from fate to free will; from centralized external power to self-empowerment; from respect of things scientific to a reverence of things natural; from segmented concepts of medicine to a wholistic approach of healing; from an external concept of divinity to one which values the divinity in all of us.

Astrologers call it the age of Aquarius--the age of equality, personal responsibility and self-creation. It is the age of spiritual adulthood in which direction and guidance comes from group consensus rather than a father-like spiritual leader. It's the age in which the new values are community and global access. Scholars call it the Information Age, heralded by the decentralization of government, drastic changes in corporate America, and which is now being pushed ever forward by the rapid growth of the Internet.

This global shift in consciousness will affect how we seek ultimate expression of who we are. Following one's internal compass and passion rather than the preprogrammed dictates of externally imposed tradition will be the mantra of the spiritual adults of this new world. This is an exciting time which supports your decision to follow your dream.

MAIN POINTS OF CHAPTER 2
"The Passion Prophecy"

• If you've found yourself questioning the meaning of life, and realize that you are living a lie and not being true to yourself, then perhaps it's time to start following your passion.

• Massive changes are affecting the way people earn money. Some of the economic forecasts paint a dire picture for the future. Companies are cutting back. Social Security is in jeopardy. And, the security once possible working for large companies is no longer guaranteed. The rules of the game have changed, but many people are still living and working outmoded plans.

• The new millennium will bring tremendous changes in the way we do business, in our understanding of personal growth, in spiritual awareness and in people's ability and willingness to earn their livings in nontraditional ways. They will seek more and more to do things that fulfill them. At the same time, many will be forced to seek alternative means of income out of sheer necessity. This will be the decade (and beyond) of the entrepreneur.

• A new strategy is needed in order to maintain financial sufficiency in this new millennium. Create assets, develop additional streams of income, seek sanity by staying true to your dreams and pursue your passion. These are the major aspects of that strategy. More people are seeing the wisdom in finding value in their talents, hobbies and interests.

• Because of the Internet, it's easier today to turn your passion into profit. It provides the means to take advantage of "wide thin markets " that in previous eras would not have been profitable.

• As you learn to think differently, your life may go through some drastic changes as things are broken down to be built anew. This reconstruction is not your new reality, but simply a necessary step to create it.

FOLLOW-UP FILE FOR CHAPTER 2
"The Passion Prophecy"

INSPIRATION: Passion Seeker Profiles

_____

"Just Plain Passion"

At 3 years old, Lorraine Johnson-Coleman proclaimed to her mother, "I want to make books!" Since then, writing has always been her passion. However, she allowed her father's urging to do something "more practical" to influence her decisions. In college, though she majored in English, she also had a minor in economics. She ended up in a high-profile, well-paying job on Wall Street, which, though it appeared to have all the trappings of success, made her absolutely miserable.

Still nurturing her hidden passion for writing and communicating, she found occasions to share her work with others. After reading one of her poems in public for the first time, amazed strangers and friends asked her why she wasn't doing that for a living.

She decided to quit her high profile job, and move to Georgia to follow her passion. Things didn't immediately work out, and Lorraine and her four children and husband found themselves homeless. She always knew, however, that if she followed her heart, that things would work out. So, even while living in a shelter, she managed to publish "*Just Plain Folks*" which won her critical acclaim and eventually a 7 figure publishing contract.

You might have seen Lorraine on an episode of the *Oprah* show in which she shared her advice to the world. She says, "Recognize that the difficult times don't define you, or limit you as to what you can be. It's just for the moment. It's just a passing thing."

The other great lesson she's learned from her experience, as she poetically puts it, is her wish that "these four African American children that I call my own can look at my life and truly realize that anything is possible. And, I hope they go for it."

_____

IDEAS: The Right Questions to Ask
• What lies am I allowing myself to live even though I'm not happy with them?
• What specific things do I wish to change about my life?
• How many streams of income do I have?
• How would I earn money if I couldn't find a job?
• What options do I have if I were to lose my home?
• Do I know anyone who worked all their lives for someone else and retired wealthy?

> *"You can tell how much you love yourself by noticing what you allow yourself to experience."*

Chapter 3: Thinking Differently
"A crash course in personal growth!"

Decide

Once you've given yourself permission to dream, and believe that a new world is possible for you, the next step in your journey is simply to decide. Decide that you fully intend to discover a passion around which to build a business. Decide that you are willing to leave your present reality behind. Decide that you want to be free from living the lies that others have forced upon you. Decide that you will seek out others who are doing it, and who can provide support and inspiration. Decide that you will commit to this journey until you reach your destination. This will be the journey of a lifetime. And like many journeys, there is a price to pay. Yes, your entry into this brave new world and the Passion Profit life-style requires a nominal fee. It requires that you think differently.

The secret to creating any lasting change in your life is to change the thoughts you have about yourself as well as the world in which you live. It is only in adopting new ways of thinking that you will experience success in turning your passion into profit.

"Who Are You, Really?"

You are the product of your thoughts. Despite what you may have heard to the contrary, you are not the product of fate or fortune. You are not controlled by circumstances, or by other people's actions, but by the content of your own mind. You are not your job, your income, or your roles EXCEPT to the degree that you *think* you are. Self-image--what you think about yourself-- controls much of what you achieve in life. Your self image is the sum total of all the ideas about yourself that you have been told, shown or that have been expressed to you or about you, and that you now accept as true. These ideas may have come from parents, other family members, friends, enemies, teachers, strangers, books, television or movies. If you were exposed to these ideas often enough during your early years of development, your concept of yourself has been shaped by them. These are the thoughts that molded how you see yourself and the world, and will continue to create self-perpetuating realities and experiences.

However, you *can* change your reality and stop the cycle simply by changing the nature and content of your thoughts. Once you believe differently about something, you act differently in relation to that thing. When you thought that Santa Claus existed, you acted in one way. Once you thought otherwise, your actions changed accordingly.

The first new thought to accept, is that the universe is a knowable place. In other words, it can be figured out and understood. And although we may never learn all the mysteries the universe has within it, we can learn just enough of the basics to make it less confusing. We can know enough about it to start to feel in control of, or at least, in harmony with the natural order of things. Once you understand the basics of the universe, you'll be one step closer to creating the reality you desire. Following are the major universal concepts that it will be necessary to adopt for you to create the life you wish.

1. Only Fear And Love exist
2. Thoughts Create Reality
3. You Can Only Control Your Reactions
4. "Be, Do Have" Is The Order Of Creation

MAJOR CONCEPT #1: There's Only Fear and Love

> Everything we do in life
> and every thought we voice
> it's love or fear and nothing else   *Which one rules you?*
> from which we make our choice   *Walt's Life Rhyme #78*

While taking nothing away from the power of the other emotions of anger, grief, envy, and so on, the truth of reality is that there are only two causal emotions which govern our actions: fear and love. These two represent the cosmic dichotomy, and all spiritual awakening is based on the realization of this truth. This is important because once you accept that there are only these two causal emotions, then it becomes easier to determine the motives behind everything you do or plan to do. If you can honestly say that the reason you are doing something stems from love of yourself or of others, then by all means you should feel empowered to do it. If, however, you are acting out of fear, then you may wish to examine your beliefs. Love-based actions create a better life for you. Fear-based actions perpetuate fear, lack despair and other negative emotions.

Fear of not having enough makes you pursue professions for money but for which you have no passion. Fear of ridicule, embarrassment, and shame prevents you from attempting to earn a living in nontraditional, but more satisfying ways. Fear of failure is what cripples you from even trying. Fear of success is what keeps you living a life of mediocrity rather than confronting the greatness within.

Love, on the other hand, is the palate into which you dip when you begin to paint a life worth living. In any relationship, the more you love someone, the more committed you are to not hurt them. The same should be true in your relationship with yourself. Unfortunately, many people don't exercise the same standards when it comes to how they treat themselves. If they did, their day to day decisions would be quite different.

When you love yourself, you believe that you're worth more and that no sacrifice is too great for you. In fact, it's impossible for any real act of love to be a sacrifice. Love of the gift of life you've been given is what makes you want to experience it to its fullest by being and doing all that you can, regardless of what others think.

Here's how to tell how much you love yourself. The level of love you have for yourself is demonstrated by what you allow yourself to experience. In other words, consider all the pleasure and pain you now experience. If you had the power to give someone you loved a new life to live, would you give them one just like yours? To the degree that you would wish your life on someone you love, that is the degree to which you love yourself. Because you would only wish upon someone you love, the best that life has to offer. So if you are living such a life--one worthy of offering to another-- it's because you decided you're worth it.

A life in pursuit of passion and the conquest of fear is the greatest gift you can give to someone you love, including yourself.

Entrepreneurophobia: Conquering the Fear

Speaking of fear, there is one common fear that is at the root of many people's reluctance to pursue their passions for profit. It's Entrepreneurophobia--the fear of becoming an entrepreneur!

Naming the fear:

For many of us, the thought of being an entrepreneur carries the glamour of being in charge, calling the shots, setting our own hours, more personal freedom, and just possibly the chance of making it really big with that new idea, service or product. On the down side, we've heard there are long hours, uncertainty, and of course, risk. Success is not guaranteed, and money may not come with the regularity of a paycheck. It's this very reward-risk duality that has more people jumping out into entrepreneurial waters with the goal of improving the quality of their lives, while others who have an equal desire to be free, can't seem to rid themselves of the "employee mentality" that's weighing them down. The fearless ones go on to fulfill their dreams. The fearful choose to suffer in silent desperation making others into millionaires. We live in the most advanced, richest and most opportunity-filled society in human history. So, what is stopping more of us from taking advantage of these opportunities?

What keeps many of us shackled to the nine-to-five grind is plain, simple FEAR. Fear of the unknown. Fear of failure. Fear of success. Don't be too alarmed. Even successful entrepreneurs experience fear. It's part of being human. The trick is not to let it scare you into inactivity. The first step in the task of conquering this fear is naming it. What you are experiencing is a common malady known as Entrepreneurophobia, the fear of being an entrepreneur. And while you won't find it listed in any of the medical or psychiatric journals, I've encountered it often enough to know that it's real enough to deserve its own diagnosis and cure.

How to tell if you suffer from Entrepreneurophobia:

Here are a few questions to help you make a quick self-diagnosis. Does the thought of being CEO (chief executive officer) of your own company make you break into a cold sweat? When you think of starting a business, do you become paralyzed with fear? Do you think that being an entrepreneur takes some magical powers, or a level of intelligence that you believe you don't have? Is the security, and regularity of a constant paycheck more appealing to you than the potential rewards of being on your own? When you hear of others who are jumping out into entrepreneurial waters, do you think deep down that they're destined for failure? Or, do you think that the constant pressure they must be under would be too much for you? If you answered yes to any of these, you might be a victim of this common malady. Fear not. Many others share your apprehensions. In fact, many successful entrepreneurs experience the same fears each and every day. Is there something about being an entrepreneur that is really so intimidating? Or, is there something else going on in your situation?

Fear of failure or fear of success?

Most of us have been programmed all of our lives to believe that the path to "success" requires going to school and getting a good job. While these are admirable goals to pursue, they don't encompass the entire realm of ways to live our dreams. Unfortunately, the programming is so powerful, that any endeavor which we consider that's not based on those norms feels threatening to us and to those around us. Starting one's own business is a bold move which little of our life's teaching actually prepares us for. It is often seen as an impetuous and difficult undertaking reserved for special people. As a result, we are likely to suffer discouragement and even ridicule from family and friends who view such plans as silly and destined for failure. In addition, we often have to overcome our own insecurities: What if I can't sell my product? What if my business fails? What if I get sued, or end up in more debt? How will I pay my rent or mortgage? What will my family and friends think of me if I fail? What will I think of myself?

Overcoming these self-doubts and negative influences doesn't mean you'll be successful either. In fact, overcoming fear of failure may be just the beginning of your "troubles." Because, while many of us suffer from a fear of failure, an equal number suffer from what we can only call a fear of success! It's true. There are many individuals who don't know how to handle success and, when things are going well, appear to do everything in their power to destroy everything they've worked hard to achieve. The story of the superstar who "had it all" and then threw it all away on drugs, sex or gambling is the classic example. The fact is: even after we have achieved success, our own low self esteem may come back to haunt us. What happens is that the public image we've created--the one that everyone else sees--doesn't quite match the one we have of ourselves. Consequently, we subconsciously do what we can to get the two to match. We sabotage our own success in an effort to bring the two images into agreement. Eventually, the facade of wealth, confidence, and success comes tumbling down, replaced with the old self-image of poverty, lack and negativity. At that point, what's now on the outside matches what we've always believed about ourselves on the inside. That's what fear can do to you. And while the bad news is you may never get rid of your fears completely. The good news is that you can learn how to manage them, and succeed in spite of them.

Fear Management

When you're in business for yourself, you become a manager. Sales, employees, expenses, taxes, growth and everything related to your business all require effective management. Fears too, are as much a part of being an entrepreneur, and also need to be managed. Many potential entrepreneurs fail even before they write their business plan, simply because they don't practice fear management well enough in advance and, just as importantly, during the life of their venture. To help you get a handle on your fears and practice fear management, here are a few basic facts you should know.

1. *Fear is at the basis of most of human activity.* It's one of the two reasons why we humans do ANYTHING. (The other reason is love). From working our job, to waging war, to religion, to politics, to sex, practically every aspect of what we call civilization is in response to some fear or another. Fear of starvation leads to the development of agriculture; fear of poverty leads to the pursuit of wealth; fear of the elements leads to construction of shelter; fear of death leads to the development of religion. Fear of losing freedom, independence and territory leads to war.

2. *All fears are learned.* Behavioral psychologists say that the only fears we are born with are the fear of falling and the fear of loud noises. All other fears are learned, and like bad habits, can be unlearned. So there's hope!

3. *Fears are not real.* Fears are illusions. Fears do not exist. They are your responses to ideas that you've created from unreal beliefs. They have power only because you give it to them. Remember the first time you spoke or performed in front of an audience, or the first time you dove into a pool? The fear at those times was so overwhelming that you thought you wouldn't survive into the next day. Well, you have survived, hopefully with the knowledge that the fears themselves are usually more powerful than the thing you feared. In other words, fears rarely equal consequences. As you face your fears, ask yourself: what's the worst that can happen? If your idea doesn't sell, will the death penalty be imposed? Doubtful. Many of us would probably realize that our deepest fears are actually unfounded if we did a realistic assessment. Many of us never do because it's often easier to magnify our fears than admit that the thing holding us back ..... is us.

4. *Fears signal opportunities.* The only way to grow in life is to take yourself out of your "comfort zone." As long as you keep doing only what you're comfortable with, you will never grow. If something you're considering doing causes fear, the fact that you feel the fear is probably an indication that it is something you NEED and MUST do to grow into the next stage of your life. As a child, you couldn't walk until you conquered your fear of standing. You couldn't run until you conquered your fear of walking. You can't ride a bicycle until you conquered your fear of falling. Fears are the body's and mind's way of identifying areas in your life that you need to work on. And as you do, you may sometimes stumble, or even fall, but you ALWAYS learn and grow.

ICE-ing your fears:

Like most entrepreneurs, I struggled to make my business more and more successful. At times, I encountered numerous obstacles which I feared were threatening my dreams. There were times I knew exactly what I had to do, but just couldn't bring myself to do it. For instance, I remember at one point being afraid to send out too many advance copies of my first book, for fear that some more established person or company would simply steal my idea and run me out of business. However, once I learned the truths about fears, I developed my own technique for conquering them: I call it ICE-ing.

To ICE your fears, first (I)dentify, then (C)onfront, and finally (E)liminate them.

Identifying your fears. The first step in conquering your fears is to be honest with yourself. Once you've admitted to yourself that fear is the reason you are not doing what you should be doing, then ask yourself, what am I afraid of? Try putting into words exactly what the consequences are that you fear. Write them down. Don't be surprised if at first you can't come up with any real reasons. (Doesn't it seem silly to be paralyzed by something you can't even name?) With practice, however, you'll become more aware of what's really going on in your head and heart, and you'll be able to put it into words. You then need to find out what's really going on. Often the first fear we identify is not the one that is paralyzing us. Keep asking yourself "why am I afraid of that?" As you keep questioning each answer, you'll get to the bottom line. Forcing yourself to put your feelings and fears into words helps you to make sense of them, and to understand yourself.

Confronting your fears. Confronting your fears means accepting that you have them, and accepting what they say about you. In other words, you may not like that you are the type of person who is frightened by what others think of you, and so you'd rather remain a definite failure than a possible success. However, unless you accept these truths about yourself, you won't be able to get to the next level. Remember:

> *"A fear avoided lingers for eternity. A fear confronted, dies in a heartbeat"*

Our fears are based on false beliefs
our ego's vested in
We strive to be what we are not
and see what we are as sin

A truth opposed will linger still
For what's denied will last
Resist it and it pushes back
Accept and it will pass

> *"You become more
> of you each time you
> conquer you."*

It's what you say does not exist
that lingers on for years
What's railed against is given life
What's seen will disappear

The man who sees things as they are
can then be free to grow
For 'til you hold a thing in hand
you cannot let it go

Untitled
Walt's Life Rhyme #119

Eliminating your fears. The final step in ICE-ing your fears is eliminating them. The basis of fear is uncertainty. Fear is how we react when we "don't know." You are fearful of what you perceive might happen, but you do not actually know what will happen. Your goal in conquering your fears is to find the answer to the "what will happen if?" question. Once you realize this, you'll also realize that only one thing can eliminate the not knowing: Action!

Action nullifies fear. "Knowing" eliminates it. Notice I said nullify. To nullify is to render ineffective. You may still feel fear, but your action has the effect of nullifying it. The knowledge that comes from doing, then removes the uncertainty factor. Remember, we said that your fear is based on the fact that you don't know. So, once you take action, you'll immediately "know" what the consequences are. You may fail, or you may succeed, but at least you'll know the answer to the "what will happen if....?" question.

If you don't take action, you'll live the rest of your life with that single burning question: What if I had? In my own experience, I've found that regret is more painful than the fear of trying.

Of course, if the memory and pain of rejection, or failure, or whatever is holding you back from taking action is greater than the pain of living in regret, then you may never act. If you decide, however, that the relief of knowing, and the growth that comes from facing your fear, and avoiding a life lived in regret is a greater incentive, then in time you may remove this fear altogether. The fear may come up again the next time you need to act, but it becomes less paralyzing over time, if dealt with repeatedly.

Now none of this is intended to imply that it's going to be easy. Being an entrepreneur is about taking risks. Risk taking requires courage. It's often said, however, that courage is not the absence of fear, but action despite the fear! Action is the key. I'm reminded of the powerful title of a book which deals with this very subject. It's called

Feel The Fear, And Do It Anyway by Susan Jeffers. The fears never stop coming. However, you always have the option of action. As you conquer one, the same one, or another appears to take its place. What you *can* change, however, is how you react to fear. Eventually, what others will consider your fearless approach to life, you'll know simply as a commitment to action in the face of fear. You won't be eliminating your fears, you'll be eliminating your fear of your fears! And that, dear future entrepreneur, is the key to success!

MAJOR CONCEPT #2: Thoughts Create Reality

Everything in life, it's true, was first once just a thought
Everything that's seen, and sold, and everything that's bought
Thoughts are what you'll use to grow, there is no other means
Yes thoughts are like the bricks you use to build your house of dreams

Thoughts are like the wings that lift to new heights that you fly
Thoughts are like the cash you choose when things from life you buy
Thoughts are things, my friend. Therefore, although this may seem strange
To get to where you wish to be, the thoughts you think must change

Watch Your words

"The WORDS you hear in your thoughts are your beliefs. Your beliefs color your expectations. Your expectations create your reality. Change the words in your thoughts and you change the world." That quote is the premise upon which my life rhymes have been created. The words you use in your everyday conversations with others and with yourself are the basic components of the thoughts you think. These thoughts create images in your mind which the universe then uses as a template from which to create your world. Therefore, the first step in changing your reality is to recognize the power of the words you use, and to choose to use only the words that create the images of the reality you wish to live.

Every word is a command. Everything from "I'm not good at Math" to "It's hard to start a business" are orders given to the universe. Be careful how you describe the circumstances in your life. For example, you'll notice that nowhere in this book do I use the word "problem" to describe an obstacle (unless I'm quoting someone). When you think of "a problem", especially if you weren't a good math student, you may be discouraged by something you feel may not have a solution. Instead, use words like "challenge", "situation", or even "opportunity" as more empowering ways of viewing the same thing. So the next time you call a staff meeting, or set up a brainstorming session, start by saying, "Ladies and gentlemen, we have a unique opportunity to deal with a situation that has come up." You'd be surprised how that perspective changes the mood and outcome of the meeting. Remove the words "can't", "hard" and "try" from your vocabulary. Notice when you use them, or ask a friend to point out to you when you do, and replace "I can't" with "I intend to"; replace "it's hard" with "here's my challenge"; replace "I'll try" with "I will." Never say anything that you don't want to be true. The words you use are the most important part of turning your passion into profit.

You are exactly what you think

As shocking as it may be to accept, you are living exactly the kind of life you feel someone like you deserves. Your thoughts about yourself can empower you to be more, or condemn you to be less than you are. Your *can-do* thoughts hold the power and promise of possibilities of a life of passion. Your *can't do* thoughts feed you the fruits of fear and lead to failure and frustration.

Unfortunately, we often allow more of the self-limiting thoughts, words and actions to decide who we are. And, when it comes to jumping out and living lives of passion and making money doing what we love, our familiar refrains include "*I'm too old*", "*I have mouths to feed*", "*I'm not creative*", "*I'll be embarrassed if I fail*", or "*I'm too broke.*" We are even rewarded by society for keeping negative thoughts about ourselves. Have you ever noticed that a person who says "*I'm overweight*" is considered "realistic", while someone who says "I have a gorgeous body" is thought to be conceited?

It's true that as a man thinketh, so is he. And it's true that as a woman thinketh, so is she. You create the world of your thoughts because your beliefs about yourself are the constant thoughts you hear. Those thoughts influence your actions. Those actions repeated over time become your habits. Those habits sow the seeds of a reality which grows and becomes your destiny. Everything you think and believe decides who you will become. You are free, however, to become whatever you desire simply by choosing different thoughts. Everything you say expresses something about you, but you yourself are an expression of something that is beyond words. Everything you do defines you in part. However, you are much, much more than the sum of those parts.

If thoughts do indeed create success, how does one change failure thoughts and replace them with success thoughts? That is the question upon which the entire self-help, industry is based. If you are not fortunate enough to have a rich uncle, mother, father or friend who can teach you step-by-step how to think and what to do to create the life-style you desire, what are you to do? If the only talk that circulates around your dinner table is negative, depressing and failure-focused, where do you go for new thoughts? If you have no millionaire friends who are successfully turning their dreams into reality, what role models do you have? Fortunately, there is hope. If the thoughts you need to succeed are not readily available, then books can be your lifesaver on the sinking ship of mediocrity. There are books, audiotapes, videos, CD-Roms, websites offered by people who have become successful, which contain their thoughts recorded and offered for others to use. Take these thoughts and make them yours. There's simply no better way to own the thoughts of others.

Dean was a frustrated office worker who dreamed of doing more with his life. At age 19, the death of his father left him the responsibility of providing for his mother, three sisters, and a younger brother. For years, Dean felt inadequate, and overwhelmed by the mounting pressure. Unknown to his family, he felt so defeated and depressed that he contemplated suicide as a quick solution to his challenges. However, the thought of leaving his burdens on the shoulders of his younger brother, and the thought of what that would do to him was the only thing that had him consider an alternative. Late one night, while watching infomercials, he saw a "try before you buy" no-risk offer for Anthony Robbins' *Personal Power* tape series. Dean had become quite a skeptic, and had always thought that this sort of "pie in the sky" stuff was ineffective at best, and just a scam at worst. Figuring he had nothing to lose by giving it a try, and fully intending to return it within the 30-day trial period, Dean sent for the tapes. What he discovered, however, quite literally changed his life. Today, he is a successful salesman on his way to living his life of passion. Without embarrassment, he credits those "silly audiotapes" as being a critical turning point in his life, which helped bring him from the brink of suicide.

With the tapes he bought, Dean was able to change his reality by changing the way he thought. You too can count on similar results when you pursue new thoughts because of *The Law of Attraction.*

The Law of Attraction

Do you sometimes notice that the things you fear most sometimes come upon you? Thoughts and the events they create are like birds of a feather that flock together. Similar thoughts have a way of attracting each other. Have you ever noticed that even if the phone has been silent and unused all day, that you sometimes receive a flurry of calls the minute you make one? That's the law of attraction at work. *The Law of Attraction* states that you attract into your life the effects of your dominant thoughts. In other words, whatever you think about, that is what grows in effect in your life. You also attract people who are similar to you in beliefs, income level and education.

Again, your thoughts are your beliefs about the way things are. These beliefs affect your expectations. Your expectations determine your actions. Your actions create your reality. In the following sections, we are going to explore the thoughts that you currently have which may be keeping you from doing what you love, and offer you new thoughts with which to replace them so you can attract a new reality.

Our Thoughts=Our Attitudes

Most of us, whether we are aware of them or not, have certain thoughts that go through or minds that determine how we see life, and certain behaviors that go along with them. These thoughts may have come from our parents, or from our own observations of life. By the time we are old enough to start taking our lives in a direction of our own choosing, these thoughts and behaviors are such a part of us that we take them to be the only reality that exists. We don't even question whether things could be other than how they've always seemed. This view of reality determines what we expect of ourselves, and of other people. In addition, as we go through life, most of us want to be "right." We don't like to be shown that we are "wrong." In other words, we like to live in a reality that matches our expectations, even if those expectations are negative. We like to be able to say: "See, I told you so" to our deeply held beliefs that *all women are* _____, or *all men are* _____, or *everyone in business is shady,* or *I'm so unlucky,* or whatever our favorite line is. We are often unhealthily addicted to these expectations, which take the form of biases, stereotypes and fears. It's hard work and a bit unsettling to change these biases, stereotypes and (especially the) fears. Therefore, most of us don't even try. We find it easier to notice the things that confirm our expectations and ignore the things that don't. It makes life comfortable, predictable, stable and safe.

Even the person who's not getting what he says he wants out of life because "people can't be trusted", believes and is comfortable in his belief that that's the way life is. He will become better and better at finding situations that confirm that belief than those that contradict it. If things *did* start to suddenly go his way, he probably wouldn't know how to handle it, or he may become suspicious and paranoid and end up losing it all anyway. One advantage to this negative way of thinking is that he never has to take responsibility for his situation. He can always point towards some circumstance or individual who is the cause. Likewise, the positive-thinking individual who goes through life thinking that "I always meet the right people at the right time" brings that energy into her interactions and approaches every encounter as possibly confirming her view that "things always go my way!" Both of these individuals may one day meet the same person who could hold the key to their dreams. The first person is suspicious and has a distrustful attitude along with negative expectations of how the interaction will go. The other is more self assured and has a pleasing persona and positive expectations. I don't need to tell you who will have a better chance of succeeding. Your attitude and expectations in any situation will affect what you say, how you say it, how you react to what the other person says and all the little subtleties of interpersonal interaction. And if all other things are equal between our negative thinker and our positive thinker, then that personal touch, that ability to open up and make friends with the world could make all the difference!

The Success Attitude

Our thoughts are the basis of the attitudes we have towards success. These attitudes fall into 5 categories: negative, passive, positive, active and creative.

The Negative Success Attitude (Keyword: PESSIMISM)

The Negative Success Attitude is characterized by the following thoughts:
I can't succeed. I can't succeed because of all the obstacles. Why even try?
The individual operating in this stage has a list of ills which are responsible for his situation, and a list of people he blames for his failure. He views himself as a victim and sees success as something unattainable. He sees other people's success in terms of how many people they probably had to step on to get to the top. He is usually very critical of other people. He becomes embittered by life's setbacks. He may become frustrated and try to escape into gambling or some other type of get-rich-quick schemes. Since he feels the whole world is full of deceit, his own sense of business ethics and practices may mirror his expectations. The root cause of this way of thinking may be deep self hatred, but, that's another book altogether.

The Passive Success Attitude (Keyword: LIMITATIONS)

The Passive Success Attitude is characterized by the following thoughts:
I might succeed. I might succeed if someone helps me. I need someone to help me so I can turn my passion into profit. All I need is to meet the right person.
The individual operating in this stage is usually always seeking the benevolence of others. She probably feels defeated by setbacks. She views success as a matter of being well connected. She uses this dependence on others to shield her own insecurity. Fear of failure and feelings of inadequacy rule her actions.

The Positive Success Attitude (Keyword: POSSIBILITIES)

The Positive Success Attitude is characterized by the following thoughts:

I can succeed. I can succeed if I work hard towards my goal.

The individual operating in this stage is heading in the right direction. She realizes that there is a connection between personal commitment, hard work, and the realization of dreams and goals. She has the ability to motivate herself to take action. While this attitude is more desirable than both the passive and negative attitudes, without the proper focus, the end result might be the same.

In other words, just because you are engaged in the pursuit of your passion doesn't mean that you have totally graduated from the passive or negative stages of thought. A good example of this is the entrepreneur who may seem to be actively pursuing his dream by brainstorming, creating brochures, organizing meetings, photo shoots, etc. However, upon closer examination, it's seen that "after all is said and done...a lot more was said than done." He somehow can't seem to get to the point of creating a product, or move to the point of marketing it. His "follow through" may be lacking. He may get sick just before a major meeting or always seem to find an excuse why things aren't quite ready yet. He appears to be motivated because of the constant activity. When it comes down to the wire, he chokes, since on the inside, he is still passive. For the active-on-the-outside-passive-on-the-inside entrepreneur things always seem to be "just about to happen." There is a never ending flurry of excitement and possibilities, but never anything concrete or definite. He always seems to have just met this guy who can "get us the money we need", or who's "connected with" this or that famous person, or a company that's interested in placing a big order. Whatever the multitude of excuses that one can come up with, the bottom line is still the same--he didn't deliver. Remember, when evaluating a business partner's or anyone's effectiveness, the only question that needs to be answered is "Did he get the job done?" No abundance of excuses or reasons why not will change the answer. For those individuals accustomed to living in the shadow of excuses, this may seem to be a harsh way of looking at things. For those in the bright lights of success and accomplishments, it is the ONLY way.

The Active Success Attitude (Keyword: PLAN)

The Active Success Attitude is characterized by the following thoughts:

I will succeed. I will succeed despite the obstacles. I view setbacks as challenges and opportunities to excel. Despite racism I can control my destiny. Despite other people's issues, I will succeed!

The person operating in this stage is positive and focused. Most successful individuals have achieved this level of thinking to some degree. Keep in mind, however, that these people may have the same fears of failure and low self-esteem issues as anyone in any of the previous stages. The difference is that they've developed the ability to transform it into something constructive. Never make the mistake of thinking that successful individuals are any more emotionally, mentally or spiritually healthy than the rest of us. They've simply learned how to act in spite of their dysfunction, and often because of it! Again, though, that's a different book altogether!

The Creative Success Attitude (Keyword: CREATION)

There is another group of successful entrepreneurs who have taken the attitude adjustment one step further. These rare individuals exist in a reality all their own. For them, the normal rules of life don't apply. They have turned things upside down and their thoughts may sound something like this:

BECAUSE of racism, BECAUSE of setbacks, and BECAUSE of other people's issues, I will succeed!

These types of people are driven to perfection. They appear to be undeterred by bad news, rejection and setbacks and keep their heads while others around them are losing theirs. Operation within this attitude may be more familiar to the rest of us as bursts of inspiration or unusual dedication to a particular dream or task. These bursts are usually unexpected and unexplainable. It's not coincidental that I've called this attitude "creative." When many artists, musicians or writers are creating their works, they often enter a mode where their inspiration and energy can come from anything, be it good or bad, anyplace whether real or imagined, and anyone be they loved or not loved. These people, places or things which influence artists' creativity, or where they go to do their creating is often difficult to describe since it is often just as mysterious to the artist. You too can take full advantage of it by practicing going there. You don't have to wait for it to find you. As you go deeper and deeper into this attitude, you will be re-creating your reality through re-creating yourself. Remember, there is no reality except the one you accept.

No event or situation is a failure unless you make it so by giving up. Up until the point that you give up, all the seemingly failed or disappointing efforts are merely experiences for you to learn from on the road of your eventual success. You can "create" a reality where what's bad is good, what's white is black, what's down is up and then you can react to it in any way you choose. You can look at situations and rather than find all the ways in which the situation has defeated you, spend your time thinking how it has helped you. Let's explore the creative success attitude a little more.

Putting the creative success attitude into practice

In my youth, I remember well how my currently held perception of reality was developed in me. For example, if I missed a bus, or an event or some meeting, rather than being chastised by my parents (though I received my fair share), the interpretation would be that it "happened for a reason." We children were told stories of people who missed planes, only to find out hours later that their plane had crashed. We heard stories of people who, because of traffic conditions, were forced to take a different route home from work only to find out that there had been some catastrophe on their usual route which may have affected them. I could go on and on about these stories, but you get the point. Rather than cursing life for dealing us a bad hand, or spending time thinking how we could have made things go the way we originally wanted, we emphasized our belief that whatever did happen happened for a reason which would eventually reveal itself as being "for the best." I never asked if all of the stories were true, but in my later years, I realize that it didn't really matter. The end result was that the seed of the creative success attitude had been planted. Later in life, I found the same sort of teachings, somewhat modified, in books on success. The underlying premise of the creative success attitude is that you always benefit from every experience whether you realize it or not.

In order to take full advantage of the creative success attitude, the first thing you need to do is convince yourself of its validity. In other words, you have to decide whether the "everything happens for a reason" attitude is actually worth adopting. If you've grown up in a suspicious environment, where the "everyone's out to get me" attitude was practiced, this may be difficult. You may even have a lot of personal experiences and bruises to support your belief that the world is an evil place operating on the predator-prey system. However, I am not suggesting that you now go through life with your guard completely down and become everyone's victim. I am asking you to realize that in life there are two options: 1. Focus on the negative, or 2. Focus on the positive. Of the two options, only one has the potential to get you what you want. The world may really be a harsh place, but focusing on how bad things are won't get you anywhere. In still other words, when the game knocks you down you have two options: stay down or get up. You can easily see that only if you choose the second option do you even have a chance of ever winning the game. To continue this analogy: in most physical sports, players realize that getting knocked down, though it may hurt, is really only a part of the game. If you stay down, you may get trampled. If you retire onto the sidelines, the game will definitely go on without you. The successful athlete never questions whether he should get up and try again or stay down. The successful entrepreneur, and passion-seeker doesn't either.

The second thing you need to do is to put into practice your belief that anything that happens to you can help you rather than hurt you. This doesn't mean that you should believe that the world is a rosy place with nothing but good in it, and behave as if everyone is acting with your best interest always in their minds. What it does mean is that even life's disasters contain something which may prove helpful and are not indications that you are destined for defeat.

Here are a few more beliefs that are consistent with the Creative Attitude:
• What others call setbacks are actually opportunities to excel.
• When one door is closed, another is open.
• Every defeat has within it the seed of an equivalent benefit.
• Luck is what happens when opportunity meets careful preparation.
• Failure only happens after you stop trying.
• Nothing ventured, nothing gained.
• If you always do what you always did, you'll always get what you always got.
• Everything happens for a reason

To practice the success attitude, you first need to interpret events appropriately. You then need to adopt the appropriate behavior in response to the event. This practice will help you in two major ways. First, in believing that your goals are still becoming real and coming to you, you continue to focus your energies forward. If you keep dwelling on what has already happened, not only do you live with unnecessary regrets but you are focusing your energies backwards. Second, practicing looking for the "silver lining" develops another skill, the ability to actually read, listen to interact with and react to life. And your reactions to life are very important.

MAJOR CONCEPT #3 : You Control Your Reactions. That is All.

As you go through life, remember this: People aren't always going to act the way you want them to. Situations aren't always going to occur the way you want them to. And, things aren't always going to be what you want them to be. Early in life, you may have realized this, but you may still have wanted a certain amount of control over matters that affected you. As you experience life even more, you realize that no matter how hard you try, you can't completely control people and how they act, things and how they are, or events and how they occur. At this point, many people then resolve to spend their lives waging complex battles for control while ignoring the simple truth: the only thing that you have complete control over are your reactions to the things you can't control!

If you make changing others your mission in life, then throughout your life you'll have hundreds, maybe thousands of people to work on. If, however, you make your goal changing yourself to be more tolerant and less judgemental, then you only have one person to work on. Knowing this, then, it is important for you to develop the right attitude towards the things that happen to you in life, and to the things that will happen as you look about the business of turning your passion into profit.

Many of us have been conditioned for some simple reactions. When things go our way, we react happily. When things don't go our way, we react badly. This simplistic way of reacting is fine when you are a child. Real success in life and business, will require a change. The first major change in attitude that you will need to make is in how you react when things don't go your way. Real control in life lies in taking the reins of your emotions and behavior out of the hands of other people and events and into your own hands. This is particularly important because we live in a world of "isms."

Reacting to Racism/Sexism/Classism

Think about it. "Isms" exist full force in our society. Racism is at the basis of the United States' rise to world power. Sexism defined voting rights in this country for decades. The very constitution of the country supports it. As a result there are people in this society who are routinely excluded from "the mainstream" for a variety of reasons. Rather than being a setback, however, this shameful reality may just as easily be viewed as an opportunity. Here's how I used it to my own advantage.

When I wrote my first book, I realized that many of the books on the music industry routinely excluded Rap fans, Rap musicians and Hip Hop entrepreneurs from discussions, analyses, and observations. This presented a unique opportunity for me to speak directly to this group and find my own niche in the industry and at the same time help the people who were being excluded. The products which a company called W publishes are sometimes in direct response to this separateness which society creates. However, it is not a separateness that I simply cursed. The trick was to accept that it existed, understand it, even work to change it, but also find ways to use it to my advantage while avoiding the pitfalls it presented. In much the same way, you can choose not to curse your hand and discard it, but make it work for you. Whatever the "Ism" you may feel is active in your experience, you can succeed despite it.

Perhaps your passion involves making a difference for single mothers. Perhaps, as a single mother yourself, you have a unique perspective you bring to the table. This can definitely be a selling point for you and your company. It means ultimately, that there will always be a unique set of skills and energies to be harnessed, needs and desires to be met, and perceptions and beliefs to be exposed.   So rather than trying to modify your reality to fit in to the mainstream, realize the vast resources which it contains and use them to their fullest for your benefit.

Real success happens after you realize that the number of possible reactions to life are actually infinite, and are all under your complete control. Instead of the limited number of reactions many of us allow to be controlled by outside circumstances, the successful individual develops a whole arsenal of reactions to use throughout life.

Reading the signs and messages along the way

If everything happens for a reason, then in order to get the most out of life, you should be able to find out what that reason is. Everything that happens to you in life is sending you a message. Every rejection letter that you receive has written between the lines some clue that you need before you take the next step forward. Every bad review that your book gets is sending a message that you need to listen to and act on to be successful. How will you know when a message is being sent? You will feel it. Don't worry, you've felt it before, you just didn't have the right name for it.   You will feel frustrated. You will feel rejected. You will feel that you or your passion and its worth are being attacked. You will feel that if society were a fair place, that things would be better. You will feel that you have tried everything you possibly can and that nothing works. Like I said, these feelings are probably familiar to you.

From now on, however, instead of calling those feelings "failure", "defeat" or "depression", you will realize that those old names come from the few simple reactions that we've all been taught. From now on, you'll call it "the pain of success." Realize that the reason you feel pain is that you're beating your head against a door that you want to go through, while ignoring the door that success is holding open for you. From now on you'll realize that although success doesn't always provide specific directions on how to find it, there are signs along the way to guide you. Just as you wouldn't head blindly down a highway without slowing down every now and then to read the signs, so too must you heed the warnings, detour signs and speed limit notices along the highway of success. One of the rules of the road that everyone on the journey must follow is: NEVER GIVE UP. Some of the other signs that life posts for you are often quite subtle and vary accord-ing to the road being taken. Read correctly, you'll find an infinite range of possible actions to take. At various times in your life, the messages might be saying:

Don't do this right now.

Proceed more cautiously next time.

Proceed more quickly next time.

This is not the best route to take.

This may not be the right group to share your success with.

This may not be the right person to share your success with.

Your commitment needs to be stronger.

Your effort needs to be doubled.

If you read enough of these signs, you will start to notice patterns or certain messages that seem to be repeating themselves. You'll also start to see some similarities between the messages life is sending you in your personal life and those that you receive in your business endeavors. This is a sure sign that you're on to something important. If you notice, for example, that you're always arriving a day late and a dollar short in both your business and personal dates, that's obviously a character flaw that you need to make some adjustments to. Since many of our flaws are deep-seated habits, there's no easy trick to making the necessary adjustments. However, some of the motivational books I recommend in the appendix can put you on the right track.

Practicing the creative success attitude means you can create your own reactions, interpretations and responses to the signs that you'll pass along the way.

MAJOR CONCEPT #4: Be, Do, Have is The Order of Creation

This is where my Scientology course came in handy to emphasize the correct order to approach the creation of reality. Most people believe that if they **have** more money, they would be able to **do** certain things and they would then **be** happy. They've put having, before doing before being. The truth, however, is that you must first assume a "being-ness", in order to accomplish a "doing-ness" in the direction of "having-ness". Our happiness is a state of being that we must create for ourselves first. We must then act and do the things we would do were money in our possession, in order to bring it into our possession. As spiritual author, Neville says, signs precede, they do not follow. To create the signs of wealth and happiness keep your thoughts steeped in the positive.

> Live from the joy of desired experiences
> not from the pain of your last
> See from the heights of your loftiest dream
> and not from the depths of your past
>
> Judge and be judged from the best you've achieved
> not from what you didn't do
> Your power in life comes from which thoughts you keep
> and which ones you let pass on through
>
> *Which ones to keep*
> *Walt's Life Rhyme #23*

So how do you live in the thoughts necessary to become the thing you wish to be? Fortunately, there are tools you can use to form new thoughts and habits.

The Tools of Creation

The entire key to turning your passion into profit will rest on how well you use the tools which exist to help you create your reality. Most have always existed. Others are new, but are simply ways of building upon the old. To help you on the journey of developing the courage you need to act in the face of fear, here are some other tips:

Faith

Acts of faith are the most powerful creative tools.

Your success using the power of the universe rests in the degree of your BE-LIEF in the power. In other words, it relies on your faith. Faith, as the saying goes, can move mountains. You can harness the unlimited power of the universe by daring to take ANY risk in life with the conviction of fulfillment as a net. Here is an affirmation I use as a reminder of the necessary level of faith.

"The conviction and belief of assured success is my only net as I jump off into the unknown. In just the same way that I walk, or speak with full expectation that I will accomplish these things, I must now hold on to my vision of the new world I am creating even in the midst of an 'uncertain' future. I must, however, realize that the future is NOT uncertain. It is as assured and as dependable as the rising of the sun. I can predict the future, because I can create it. Only my total immersion in a sea of unquestioned belief will make the sea real. I see myself on a diving board. I cannot see the water below. I cannot hear the water below. I simply believe it is there so I hold my breath and leap. My action in complete faith is what makes the reality. The future is assured because I will it to be so. I act in complete faith that the universe will provide."

Goal-setting

Studies have shown that those with clearly defined and written goals tend to do better in life and accomplish more than those without. The act of writing your goals impresses them into the subconscious more firmly than if they are just recalled mentally. State your goal in the present tense, first person and in a positive way. (eg. "I own a mansion and a yacht." "I sell 5,000 or more of my product each week.")

TIP: Quantify Your Goals--Whether your goal is a new home, a car, happiness or freedom, you'll achieve it faster if you can translate it into a concrete, quantifiable goal. If reaching your goal can be thought of in terms of a specific number of sales, or clients, it's easier to gage your progress. Let's say that your goal is to acquire a home that requires a $20,000 downpayment, and the product you're selling yields a profit of $10 per item. You would need to sell 2000 units to earn enough to make the downpayment. If you can match your goal to a figure in this way, you'll be a goal-achieving machine!

Affirmations

Affirmations are powerful tools you can use to create your desired reality. An affirmation is a present-tense statement of your desired reality, stated as if it is already happening. It is a creative command given to the universe for it to act upon. It is based on the fact that in the universe there is only now. In ultimate reality, there is no past, and no future. Therefore, a statement of desire stated as a wish for the future, will always remain a wish for the future. A statement of desire stated as a want will always remain a "want." For example, if you say "I want a new car", what you will create and continue to create for yourself is the present reality of "wanting a new car." You will always be wanting a new car. If, on the other hand, you state that "I am the owner of a new car", then that is the reality you will create.

Combined with your tool of absolute faith and belief, you will be unstoppable. You must not only affirm the thing, you must believe the thing and act as if the thing affirmed is real. Affirmations, then, cannot really be a statement of a desired reality, affirmations must BE your reality.

Affirmations are also effective in replacing limiting beliefs with ideas and thoughts of your own choosing. You may wish to replace beliefs about yourself, about others, about the world, and about what's good, what's bad and what's possible. A thought persisted in, and acted upon with belief hardens into fact. With affirmations, you harness the power of the word for your own acts of creation.

In composing your affirmations, remember that "I am" is one of the most powerful creative commands known to man. Anything that you put after those two words is given tremendous creative power. Affirmations can be the reality of yourself being, doing or having anything you desire. Don't affirm means, affirm ends. In other words, don't affirm how something will happen, but just that it is happening. On the other hand, don't be vague either. Affirm what you intend to have with as much specificity as you can. Instead of "I own a car", try "I own a black, 4-door, automatic BMW with a sunroof." Don't affirm what you don't want, only affirm what you do want. So, instead of "I don't spend money foolishly anymore", try "I always make wise decisions about my money." Don't worry about how to achieve it. Simply focus on the what, and the how will take care of itself.

Here are some affirmations to use that include ways of being, doing and having.
- I am turning my passion into profit.
- I am confident and calm as I proceed towards my goal.
- I am selling thousands of my product each week!
- I am earning thousands weekly for my services.
- I act in complete faith that the universe will provide.
- I have the ability to achieve all that I desire.
- I make decisions quickly.
- I am focused even amid criticisms, doubts and all negative influences.
- I am financially independent.
- I earn money on my own terms.
- I always act in the face of fear.

Visualization

Like affirmations, visualization uses the mind's eye to create the desired outcome in order to bring it into physical reality. With visualization you condition your mind to live in the space of the desired outcome even before it appears. In so doing, you bring it into existence using the same law of attraction that we discussed earlier.

Positive Associations

Misery and failure both love company! Stay away from negative thinkers and align yourself with people who are on their way to or are already where you want to be! The people you keep in your circles have a tremendous effect on who you will become.

Associate with people who challenge you. Seek out those whose ideas help you think differently, and whose lives give you something to aspire towards. It's known that:

The people who affect us most
are those who make us think
For growth comes from the forceful thoughts
that push us to the brink

Their thoughts are how we find ourselves
if lost or on a quest
from thoughts is where the visions come
that make us act our best

Think long and hard on who you are
and what you've come to be
and trace it back I'm sure you will
to those who helped you see

They made you think in different terms
their lives made your life shift
they changed your thoughts of who you were
direction was their gift

These people were your signposts
offering what can't be bought
Life's turning points are people   *Turning Points*
who change the level of your thoughts!   *Walt's Life Rhyme #104*

Gratitude

It's been said that the act of gratitude--of simply saying thank you--is a powerful creative command that the universe acts on. Most people only say thank you after they've received something. However, if you practice giving thanks at all times--before, during and after--and for all the things you have and have yet to receive, you'll be creating a reality of such abundance that it may shock you. Gratitude is an indication of a process that has been completed. By simply saying "thank you" to the God of your understanding, you'll be putting into the universe a statement that says in effect "the deed is done, I have received that which I have asked for." And, as we know from Thought Concept #1, our words and thoughts create our reality. So a statement of having combined with the feeling of gratitude creates the reality of receiving.

Another way to express gratitude is to tithe. A tithe--which literally means "tenth"--is a practice dating back thousands of years, which has developed into the giving back of 10% of your income usually to a source of spiritual guidance. There are millions who have experienced the abundance that can result from this simple practice.

Because the practice has been associated with ancient forms of taxation, many debate whether the practice is truly spiritual in nature, or simply a coercive act by materialistic rulers to extort wealth. Without getting into the debate of the origins of the word itself, view tithing simply as an act of *giving* which is in harmony with divine law. Just like inhaling and exhaling, receiving and giving are necessary parts of basic survival. And, it's more important how you give than how much and what you give *to*. Don't give simply as a way to get something in return, but give from an understanding that it is a fundamental practice of natural law to give. Like the farmer who gives back a portion of his harvest to the earth so as to ensure future crops, give as a way to plant the seeds of your own future success. Give ten, twenty, fifty percent or any amount you choose. Practice giving as an act of gratitude.

Meditation

Inspiration, information and ideas favor the relaxed mind. Meditation is a way of allowing yourself to quiet the mind so that all your tools can be put to use in an environment of calm and clarity. The technique you use is less important than the results you achieve. Experiment with different techniques until you find one that works for you.

Your "gut", or intuition, is an important tool for success. Your feelings of fear are gut messages that you need to recognize. They indicate lessons to be learned; new ground to be covered; challenges to be met. Seek out those feelings and move in their direction. With enough practice, your gut will send you messages of situations to avoid, as well as dreams you should pursue. For just beyond the feelings of fear are equally powerful feelings of excitement that indicate your dreams are about to come true.

I'm learning how to hear it;
it's often faint and gets drowned out.
Like a guide who tells me where to go,
but chooses not to shout

It sends me signals from another plane,
and shows me things I might not see.
Who to avoid and who to embrace
it clears my path and sets me free

At times I might feign deafness
and vainly choose another course
But usually look back in regret
when the road I take gets worse

So now I practice getting silent
to hear the falling of a pin
Yes, I'm learning how to listen well
to the still small voice within

"Listen."

The Promptings Come In Whispers
Walt's Life Rhyme #56

AudioTapes/Books

Audio tapes, books and videos, are modern tools that can assist the creative process. They provide you with the information and assistance to help you fully incorporate the previous natural tools into your life, and they provide it in formats that make them convenient for you to access. They can help with your affirmations by providing you with other people's suggestions of powerful affirmations. They can help with visualization and meditation by guiding you through those processes. They can help your faith and gratitude simply by reminding you to keep having faith, and saying thank you. I like to think of them as positive friends who are always available to say the things I need to hear on a regular basis.

As you go through life, it's normal that your energy level will fluctuate. Several good books exist which can help you keep the motivation high. They can usually be found in the self-help or psychology sections of your local bookstore. Check out the appendix for a list of books, including *The Psychology of Achievement* by Brian Tracy, *Unlimited Power* by Tony Robbins, *Live Your Dreams*, by Les Brown, *The Master Key to Riches* and *Think and Grow Rich* both by Napoleon Hill.

BONUS: The Health-Wealth Connection

For many people, the world is a confusing place. For some it's a maze with no map to guide them successfully through. For others it is a puzzle where the pieces don't seem to fit, or worse yet, where some of the pieces appear to be missing! For many still, life is a mass of contradictions, inconsistencies, untruths, failures and disappointment. There often seems to be no connection between the things they do and the results they achieve. "Why is it," they often ask, "that I want success, and I think success, but I seem to attract failure?" The answer is that even though our thoughts create our reality, our thoughts are often going off in many different directions at once. Our thoughts are sometimes logical, sometimes emotional, and sometimes intuitive. Each of these types of thoughts will create realities that are vastly different and sometimes in conflict. Your success in your endeavors will happen as the world starts to make more sense. The world will start to make more sense when the things you know logically, emotionally, and intuitively start to align. The best way to do this is to start to question the things you believe and be willing to think differently about them.

Thinking Differently About Health

Many business books avoid discussions of health and dietary choices. This is understandable considering that the topics of religion, politics and food are such emotionally charged topics. However, practically every talk I've given about business always makes its way inevitably to some discussions about health. People intuitively seek to create balanced success in life. People naturally get it that we are not just entrepreneurs making business decisions that affect our bottom line, but that we are humans making decisions which affect our families, our children, our emotional and physical health and our sanity. They understand that we can't hope to live lives of passion if major parts of our lives are being operated under wrong assumptions, and thus out of alignment.

Many people make decisions on how and what to eat based purely on emotion and habit. They simply eat what their parents ate, and what everyone else eats. It makes no logical or intuitive sense to eat food that has repeatedly shown to cause disease. We do because the bases of our beliefs are lies, and so our abilities to make sensible decisions is compromised. People don't know what to eat, when to eat, or how to eat.

The New Rules

You can't play a game if you don't know the rules. You can't make sensible business decisions if you don't understand the basic premise of being in business. Similarly, you can't choose the correct food to eat, and make healthy choices if you don't understand the basic rules of food and health. The world becomes a simpler place to live once you start to see the connections. If you start to see that the same laws of the universe that apply to business decisions, also apply to health and food choices, as well as other areas of your life, then things start to make a bit more sense.

The fundamental law of nature is that of cause and effect. For every action, there is an equal and opposite reaction. Once it's understood that all actions have consequences, it should follow then that certain food choices must also lead to certain effects.

Once I understood and accepted this, I began to question what I believed about the things I was putting into my body. A friend introduced me to a book by Elijah Muhammad entitled *How To Eat To Live*. It was the first step in making the connection between what I was eating and how I felt. Until then, the world of health was not making sense. If I was supposedly doing all the right things healthwise, why wasn't I feeling better and better instead of worse and worse? Once I read that maintaining the flow in and out of our bodies is the key to health, then I recalled a spiritual lesson I had learned that the flow of money in and out of our lives is the basis of wealth. I made the connection, and making decisions about my health became easier. My constant headaches and fatigue were effects. Once I made the connection between those effects and identified my diet as the cause, I eliminated the headaches and fatigue from my reality. I was able to "cure" myself simply because I made the cause and effect connections.

Similarly, a friend of mine was becoming increasingly frustrated that she too was doing all the right things, but was always getting sick. Even more frustrating, was that her children were following in her footsteps. For all of her life, she was raised to drink milk. She was raised to believe that humans needed cow's milk to be healthy. Once she learned that milk and dairy products have been shown to aggravate sinuses and allergies, cause headaches, increase mucus in the system, lower resistance, and was the culprit of other ill effects, she reevaluated her choices, and by simply cutting it out of her diet, has been able to live at a level of comfort she never did before. She's gone on to question other aspects of her life, making connections that empower and free.

As we've learned, success is sometimes a matter of asking the right questions. In matters of health, therefore, here are some questions for you to consider:
• *What if you could create the effect of good health simply by eating foods that didn't contain preservatives, food coloring, and other non-food "stuff"?*
• *What if what we currently thought of as food was not food at all, but simply some corporation's idea of a product to sell to make money?*
• *What if humans aren't meant to consume the milk of another species?*
• *What if the best food for humans is actually fruits and vegetables that grow in natural settings without steroids, pesticides, antibiotics, and other poisons?*

• What if any illness you are currently experiencing is caused by the accumulation of these steroids, and pesticides and antibiotics and other "stuff" in your system that hasn't had a chance to come out?
• What if illness is just varying degrees of congestion caused by poor dietary choices?
• What if we are created perfectly and that the human race and life on the planet didn't need to await the arrival of man-made chemicals to achieve health?
• What if the body could heal itself if it were simply given the chance?
• What if health and wellness came from food and not from pills?
• Suppose the growing interest in herbs as cures is not quackery but a growing awareness that everything we need to be well is already right here for us?
• Suppose we didn't need doctors since everyone understood the basic premise of health and wellness and could keep themselves healthy by making better choices?

A Natural Order

So how does all this relate to turning your passion into profit? Simple. On a practical level, making different food choices might simply make you more physically able to meet the demands of pursuing your passion. On a deeper level, being willing to think differently about your food choices, as well as anything else that you're blindly attached to and respond to reflexively, may help you to see the world a bit differently. You may notice certain truths and connections between what you do, and what you get. These natural cause and effect relationships exist in every area of your life. On a spiritual level, it may bring you in line with an intuitive appreciation of the simplicity of the way things are that can help you run your business more effectively.

From the Feeling of the Wish Fulfilled

Again, once you decide on the new reality you wish to live, You must live your life as if the things you desire are already part of that reality. As Neville says, you must "live from the feeling of the wish fulfilled." You must become the person you desire to be. You must feel that you are already living in the space you wish to occupy. You must think, and speak and act exactly as you would were your goals already manifest.

> What would I see from a millionaire's view?
> How would I act if my dreams now came true?
>
> What would I do if I simply believed?
> How would I feel if my goals I achieved?
>
> Where in the world would my happiness lead?
> Who would I lift up in word, thought or deed?
>
> To make that world real here's the formula how:
> The only sure path is to be that way now!

The Millionaire's View
Walt's Life Rhyme #15

New Thought Practices

Here, then are the behaviors that are in alignment with the new thoughts.

BELIEFS *If you believe that:*	BEHAVIORS *Then, you should*
What the mind can conceive it can achieve	Visualize desires; Dream; Think in the now
The only way to create reality is to live it first	Act as if your dreams are already real
Your words create your reality	Think and speak only what you desire
You attract what you believe and dwell upon	Affirm the desired reality
You attract your fears	Think on positive outcomes only
The subconscious is a goal-seeking tool	Set goals frequently
Writing goals impresses them into the subconscious	Write down ideas; make lists
You get what you give	Support others; give what you wish to receive
Wealth is a flow in as well as out	Tithe; give to others
Positive energy is infectious	Be with those who are where you want to be
There's enough for everyone	Wish others well; don't envy others' success
Anything is doable	Focus on reasons why, not reasons why not
Everything has an answer	Focus on solutions, not "challenges"
Everyone who is in your life has a lesson for you	Respect everyone; listen and don't judge
The feeling of fear is an indicator of potential growth	Move towards your fears; do it anyway
Everything happens for a reason	Look for the lesson in every situation
Miracles happen	Go forth with confident expectations
There's only fear and love	Assess motivations behind all actions
The Universe is friendly	Don't whine in the face of apparent adversity
Inspiration favors the relaxed mind	Meditate often

All of these behaviors are ways of being that come with new ways of thinking. Be willing to think differently about your fears, life's challenges, other people and what they do, and especially about yourself and what you believe, and things will never be the same again!

It's not my intention in this short chapter to convince you to change all of your views overnight. It's not my intention to tell you what to believe about the reason for our existence; justice; abortions, the legal system, the environment; evolution versus creation; or about diet, deity and death. I will, however, suggest that your willingness to ask if current beliefs are really working for you, and to call them into question and modify them if they aren't, may hold the key to how successful you are in all your endeavors. As you start to question the things you currently believe, you should test which ones work for you, and then decide which you'll make your own.

What it Will Require

In my experiences in business ventures, and in various organizations, I've seen hundreds of people come and go. I've seen people rise to the top in record time, and I've seen others jump ship in utter frustration. I've had a chance to meet people from a wide range of backgrounds, skills, motivations, and talent. It's true that we may never know why some people are more successful than others. We may not be able to pinpoint the single pivotal moment, or the unique sequence of events in that individual's development that are responsible for their success. However, we do know some of the traits the successful exhibit. We hear of successful people's "work ethic", their willingness to help others and their persistence despite setbacks.

In order to succeed, you simply need to be committed to success.

Being committed to success means you have to set yourself to a higher standard than most. It's said that 97% of the people in the United States will retire dependent on family, friends or the federal government for survival. If that's true, then you need to consider yourself what I call a "3-percenter." That being the case, you're going to run into people from the other 97% more often than you will meet others like you. Therefore, to determine who you need to be in order to succeed as a 3-percenter, you cannot rely on what the 97% of the people you run into do. As a 3-percenter, you don't complain when things don't go your way. You learn from the situation and move forward. As a 3-percenter, you realize that every opportunity to quit is either a chance to identify with the 97-percenters, or to set yourself apart. As a 3-percenter, you have to love challenging yourself to do more. As a 3-percenter, you've got to be able to roll with the punches. You have to be able to adapt to situations that would break others. You have to operate at all times from the position of "I can and will do this, and I will keep doing it UNTIL I am successful." You have to be able to sacrifice some things in the now in order to have the life-style and the things you want in the future. You have to be open to new ideas and new ways of being. You can't be too attached to yourself the way you are, if it's not getting you what you want.

Remind yourself that whatever goals you set for yourself are attainable, even with all the challenges that you will encounter. Others before you have survived, succeeded and prospered. It all rests inside of you. The nature of your thoughts must change. Change is the only constant in life. If you're not where or what you want to be, you have to break out of the patterns of thought and behavior no matter how comfortable they are. As one writer put it, "if you always do what you always did, you'll always get what you always got." The choice is yours. Think differently.

MAIN POINTS OF CHAPTER 3
"Thinking Differently"

• Everything you know as real was once just a thought. Everything starts as a thought. Thoughts, therefore, are the basis of all change. If you are not where you wish to be in life, then the nature of your thoughts needs to change.

• The new way of thinking and all that goes with it, is the single most important requirement you'll need to enter and prosper in the new world. That will be your price of admission.

• There are two causal emotions in the universe, love and fear. Which one rules you?

• Conquer your fears. The only things that are holding you back from achieving all that you desire, are the fears you fail to confront, and the inactivity that results.

• One of the first fears it will be necessary to overcome is "Entrepreneurophobia." It is simply the fear of the unknown when it comes to earning money in nontraditional ways. To overcome Entrepreneurophobia, and any fear you encounter, it will be necessary to ICE them. ICE is an acronym for Identify, Confront and Eliminate.

• There are specific things you can do to be successful in any endeavor. There are ways of being which will almost guarantee that no obstacle will prevent you from reaching your goals. These Success Practices should become a habit with you if you endeavor to turn your passion into profit. Affirmations, visualization, goal-setting, "living from the feeling", and viewing everything that happens to you as aiding your growth, are tools of creation that help make your life the product of your passions not the fruits of your fears.

• Thoughts do create success. Specific thoughts create specific attitudes, which create specific actions which create specific outcomes. The Success Attitude is a collection of ways of thinking and acting that will ensure that anything you attempt is successful. Your success at turning your passion into profit will be determined by whether you choose the Negative, Passive, Reactive, Positive, Active or Creative attitudes toward life.

• Be willing to think differently about everything in your life from the way you view obstacles, to the way you eat, to your thoughts about God. All these things are connected to your success in any endeavor.

FOLLOW-UP FILE FOR CHAPTER 3
"Thinking Differently"

INSPIRATION: Passion Seeker Profiles

———————————————————————————

"The Players' Personal Passion"

The three founders of id software are John Carmack, John Romero, and Adrian Carmack. They are the developers of a line of wildly popular video games which have brought their company to over 16 million dollars in sales. To turn their passion into profit, these three video game enthusiasts simply created games that they themselves would want to play. "Ultimately we market to ourselves. We slide right into the demographic mold of the people that we are trying to sell to." They got occasional informal input from friends and family, but abandoned traditional market research in favor of their preferences. I repeat: 16 Million in sales!

———————————————————————————

IDEAS: The Right Questions to Ask

• What specific fears are holding me back from turning my passion into profit?
• What books/tapes/seminars can I read/listen to/attend to help me ICE my fears?
• For what specific things do I wish to change my reactions?
• What negative words/phrases do I use that may be creating my present reality?
• What specific steps will I take to put the tools of creation to use in my life?
• What things would I change about my life before I would wish it on someone I love?
• Who do I know who is where I want to be in life-style, thought or deed?
• What specific things am I thankful for?

Chapter 4:
Your Wow Factor*
"Your personal secret formula for success"

The Wow Factor

"Your Wow Factor is the goal-oriented, response-driven creation, develop-ment and controlled exposure of the private and public perception of your unique assets. This is the key to your success in anything you do."

What makes you special? What will guarantee your success turning your pas-sion into profit? Why will people purchase your product? How will what you eventually create as your passion-centered business stand apart from the competition? The answer to these questions is what I call your Wow Factor.

As a formula, it looks like this:

[(Assets + Perception) x Exposure] + Response = Wow Factor

The Wow Factor formula is the same for everyone on the planet. What changes from person to person will be the components which comprise the variables of the equa-tion. For example, no two individuals will have the same set or awareness of their assets. No two people are perceived in exactly the same way. No two people can gain exposure to exactly the same set of people. And, no two people will desire or achieve the same response from the world. This is where the Wow Factor differs from any other key to success. For when you analyze yourself through the lens of the Wow Factor formula, you come away with something that no one else on the planet has: your own customized secret formula for success!

*NOTE: The original version of this chapter, and more guidance
on becoming a Wow Master are available in The Tao of Wow *by Walt Goodridge*

Finding Your Wow Factor

Before you can maximize your Wow Factor, you must first define its individual components. Let us examine each variable in the equation.

Finding Your Assets .

*[(ASSETS+ **Perception**) x Exposure] + Response = Wow Factor*

An asset is a thought, belief, word, action, person or object that you or others perceive that, when associated with or attributed to you, affects your own as well as the world's perception of you, and can make the world go wow.

The following assertions, assumptions and conclusions form the basis of this new understanding of what an asset is. Please read them carefully and repeatedly until you understand them thoroughly. The entire Wow Factor theory is based on them.

1. Anything can be an asset. Everything is, in fact, an asset. Therefore, any "thing" and every "thing" is an asset. There are, therefore, 5 categories of assets: thoughts, words, actions, persons, and objects.

2. Every quality of human existence may be defined as a being, a doing, or a having. In other words, all humans "are", "do", or "have" some "thing" in relation to themselves and the rest of the world. *(i.e. I AM a poet. I DO windows. I HAVE money.)* There are, therefore, 3 qualities of human existence: being, doing and having.

3. Everyone has access to every thing.

4. Therefore, the 15 categories of assets that all humans have access to are the thoughts words, deeds, people, and objects associated with being, doing and having.

Who You Are

Who you are has 5 assets (thoughts, words, actions, people and objects) associated with it. The **thoughts** about yourself are your *self-perception* (i.e. your *identity*). The thoughts which others have about who you are are called *public perception*. These perceptions may take the form of beliefs, opinions, judgements or ideas. The **words** which describe who you are are called *feedback* and, whether in written or spoken form, represent assets. The **actions** which correspond to who you are are your mannerisms and behavior, and are called your *personality* . The **people** who correspond to who you are are your *friends*. The **object** which corresponds to who you are is your *body*.

What You Do

What you do has 5 assets (thoughts, words, actions, people and objects) associated with it. The **thoughts** which you and others have about what you do, again, are called *perception*. These perceptions may take the form of beliefs, opinions, judgements or ideas. The **words** which correspond to what you do are called *education*. The **actions** which correspond to what you do are your *expressed talents, skills, or your profession*. The **people** who correspond to what you do are your *associates, students, or masters*. The **objects** which correspond to what you do are your *creations*.

What You Have

What you have has 5 assets (thoughts, words, actions, people and objects) associated with it. The **thoughts** you and others have about what you have, again, are called *perception*. These perceptions may take the form of beliefs, opinions, judgements or ideas. The **words** which correspond to what you have are called *descriptions*. The **actions** which correspond to what you have are called *accomplishments*. The **people** who correspond to what you have are your *fans, employees, or servants*. The **objects** which correspond to what you have are your *possessions*.

Again, everything that you are, everything that you do, and everything that you have, all have thoughts, words, actions, people and objects associated with them. All of these resulting thoughts, words, actions, people and objects are your assets.

Assets Everywhere

When you really understand the nature of reality, you'll realize that absolutely everything is an asset that can help you reach your goals. And, every point of contact with the world is an asset.

Remember, an asset is something (a thought, word, action, person or object) that you or another person can perceive that, when associated with or attributed to you, affects your own and the world's perception of you and can make the world go wow.

Therefore, how you speak, where you live, what you see out your window, how you smell, the way you walk, the way you sneeze, what you believe, what you don't believe, what you've experienced, what you've never experienced, how you write, your possessions, your musical tastes, your butterfly collection, your comic books, your friends, your enemies, your body, what people say about you, what they don't say about you, the languages you speak, the size shoe you wear, the arrangement of furniture in your living room, your ability to whistle a tune on key, your children, your pets, as well as the way you and others perceive these things, all have value in moving you further towards your goal, and may represent some specific perception, language, action, person or thing that you can use to make things happen the way you wish.

With so many potential assets at your disposal, then, how do you determine which ones are to be harnessed to create a Wow in the minds of the masses? The critical step in choosing and harnessing your assets lies in making the right connections.

Making connections is a skill that takes practice. Fortunately, there are two realities that will help you-- 1.the interconnectedness of the universe, and 2. your brain.

1. Connections exist everywhere because there's an underlying unity to all things in the universe. There's a cross-connection that a bird flying in the Andes Mountains has with a man crossing the street in downtown Los Angeles. There's a connection that your experiences of 10 years ago have with your goals of tomorrow. There's a connection that everyone you have ever met has with whom you have since become. Scientists are also discovering that the universe is not a collection of separate things as we perceive it to be, but rather that all things are extensions of the same fundamental something. That at a deeper level of reality that we cannot readily see—but for which there is growing evidence—everything interpenetrates everything else.

2. Your brain is a remarkable tool. It's been estimated that you have the ability to memorize up to 10 billion bits of information during your lifetime, or the equivalent of five (5) sets of the Encyclopedia Britannica. The brain's ability to hold and store tremendous amounts of information, and its remarkably efficient filing system that allows you to instantaneously call to mind 20 different correlations when you hear the word "automobile", gives you access to an overwhelming storehouse of possible connections when pursuing a particular goal. Think about it. How many different directions can you head in as concepts like "gas-powered", "pollution", "airbag", "factory assembly line", "crash test dummy", "wheels", and "engine" come to mind?

Therefore, once you know that such links exist among everything, and that you have the ability to process and identify those links, all you need to know is what questions to ask, and how to view the world, and it becomes easier to make the connections.

If, for example, your goal is to become a famous actor, then you should first expect that everything you have ever seen, done, heard, said or owned offers some way to turn that dream into a reality. You might ask, "How can my past experience as a clerk in a bank help me to become a world famous actor? Well, it qualifies me to be able to convincingly portray certain roles. It gave me access to information about the banking system. It introduced me to employees, supervisors and customers who might play roles in my future success. Did anyone I met there have a connection to the movie industry? Perhaps I'll go back there for a visit and mention to whomever I speak with that I'm serious about my acting career. Who knows who I'll meet on the way there?"

Or, perhaps your goal is to find a mate. You might ask, "What do people say about me that is an asset that can help me meet the man/woman of my dreams? What places do I frequent that might prove helpful in exposing me to more people? What music do I like? How can that lead to me meeting people with similar interests? What physical, emotional or personality attributes can I highlight that can make the world go wow?"

The possible connections are almost infinite.

In fact, as a personal example of making such connections, consider this. It's now less than a week before this very book you hold is scheduled to go to press, and as I'm putting the finishing touches on it, I happen to be reading an interesting article on the holographic nature of the universe. Though seemingly unrelated, I know that everything I know is an asset. So I ask myself, "How can what I've just read help me to achieve my goal of explaining a key concept of assets to everyone who reads this book? What connection exists between the concepts in this article, and my ability to recognize and identify assets all around me?" And sure enough, with just the right perspective, and the right questions, I was able to add the "Assets Everywhere" section you just read, which, I believe, reveals a critical technique for uncovering the many assets to which we all have access. To find the best use of your assets, ask, answer and act on these questions.

• What specific assets do I have or have access to that I can use to achieve my goal?
• What creative ways can I come up with to harness the power of these assets?
• Who do I know? What do I know? What do I believe? What Do I own? What have I created? What am I good at? What am I known for? What have I done?

The Assets Chart will help you to ask even more questions in a structured way.

10 BILLION ASSETS

	WHO I AM	WHAT I DO	WHAT I HAVE
THOUGHTS	perception	perception	perception
WORDS	feedback	education	descriptions
ACTIONS	personality	profession	accomplishments
PEOPLE	friends	associates	employees
OBJECTS	body	creations	possessions

How to use this chart:
1. Set your goal.
2. Make a list of assets by asking the following questions.

Row 1: What are the thoughts, beliefs, ideas, opinions, judgements (perceptions) that I and others have about who I am? About what I do? About what I have?

Row 2: What written or spoken feedback, education, or descriptions have I received about who I am, what I do, and what I have?

Row 3: What are my personality traits, skills and accomplishments?

Row 4: Who are my friends, associates, fans, employees and family members?

Row 5: What are my physical attributes, creations and possessions?

Perception

[(Assets + **PERCEPTION***) x Exposure] + Response = Wow Factor*
The next variable in the Wow Factor equation is perception. Once you have your list of assets, your next task is to determine how each of these assets is perceived. By perception we are not only referring to the public's perception, but your own perception of your assets.

Notice that in the descriptions of the assets in the previous section, that the one constant throughout is perception. It is in the understanding, awareness and manipulation of that perception that the power of Wow exists. Once you can control the assets of public and personal perception, you can move yourself and the world to action.

The most empowering aspect of life is that you are able to tell people what you want them to think about who you are, what you do, and what you have.

In business, for example, you can control public perception by creating the advertising campaigns, brochures, press releases, interviews and all the means by which the public will learn about you, your company and your product. In relationships, you can control perception by how you carry yourself, how you treat others, how you allow others to treat you, what you say about yourself, and what others say about you.

In order to create the perception you desire, you must ask, answer, and act on the right questions. Here are some suggestions.

• What perception will a new person I encounter have of who I am, what I do, and what I have? How am I being perceived?
• What perception do I wish every new person I encounter to have of who I am, what I do, and what I have?
• What thoughts, words, actions, people and objects (i.e. assets) best convey the perception I wish to create?
• What creative ways can I come up with to harness the power of these assets to create the perception I desire?

Exposure

*[(Assets + Perception) x **EXPOSURE**] + Response = Wow Factor*

The next variable in the Wow Factor equation is exposure.

Once you have developed your list of assets, and determined how they are perceived, as well as how you wish them to be perceived, your next step is to gain exposure. In other words, it's time to let the world know about you or your product, your assets, and what to think about them.

Included in the process of exposure is the decision of whom to expose the perception. In business, for example, exposure may take the form of advertising, marketing and promotion. In relationships, it may take the form of simply being seen or heard in all your glory. In order to gain the level of exposure necessary to create the desired Wow, you must ask, answer and act on the right questions.

Here are some suggestions.

The Key Questions for Exposure
• Which specific people need to be exposed to me, my assets and the perception I desire?
• What specific steps can I take to achieve the level of exposure I desire?
• What new and creative ways can I develop to expose my assets to ever-increasing groups of people.

Response

*[(Assets + Perception) x Exposure] + **RESPONSE** = Wow Factor*

The next variable in the Wow Factor equation is Response.

Response refers to the reaction and feedback you wish others to express in relation to the exposure of your assets. In other words, you need to request a specific action from those whom you wish to wow. This call to action is an often overlooked component of the Wow Factor. Whether you are launching a new product or looking for a mate, you must be clear on the desired response you wish to elicit from those to whom you gain exposure.

Many people fail to request an action to their exposure and thus are disappointed by the response or lack of it. Remember, you control almost every part of the Wow Factor process. You develop the assets. You create the perception. You control the exposure. And you can also determine the response. So, state clearly, therefore, exactly what that response should be. Of course, you will not always be able to control every response you receive, but unless you ask for one, you may never receive any at all.

Asking for a specific response is vital for another important reason. Within the response is the means to perpetuate the response. In other words, the creation of the initial response will lead others to respond in a similar manner. It's a unique fact of human nature that people follow other people. People learn what response is expected of them by seeing what responses others have. This creates a snowball effect that perpetuates the Wow Response. It doesn't matter whether you're launching a new business or pursuing a mate, you will find this to be true. (In fact, in the dating scene, many people have noticed that people's response to them often seems more pronounced and more frequent once they're already attached!) In order to achieve the response necessary to create the desired Wow, you must ask, answer and act on the right questions.

- What response do I desire?
- What do I wish to have happen next?
- What specific steps can I take to achieve the quality of response I desire?

By applying this unique formula, you can create your desired reality and achieve whatever goals you wish.

Using Your Wow Factor

Imagine that you possessed the power to create reality. What if you had the undisputed ability to make things go your way 100% of the time? Well, you do. Such a power exists and it's contained within the formula of the Wow Factor.

Regardless of your social status, income, occupation, type and place of residence, or educational level, your Wow Factor can help you to achieve, acquire and cultivate success in any area of your life.

The reason why the Wow Factor works to get you what you want is because of The Basic Truths of Wow.

Basic Truths of Wow

• New ideas, things and people are distinctly different from ordinary ideas, things and people. From that distinction comes the manifestation of uniqueness. In uniqueness there is cause for Wow.

• Every truly unique creation, once recognized, elicits a Wow. Wow is the world's response to what you say, what you do and what you have become.

• It is the law of nature that every Wow requires an action. The actions of others in response to the Wow you elicit set in motion another set of creative forces. These forces alter the streams of thought upon which all good things sail on their way to those who think them.

• Wow elevates you. It inspires respect. It begets trust. It creates positive expectations. It oils the transaction machine. It encourages others to share you with their circle of influence. People are attracted to those who wow. People will do anything for you if they are wowed. People will buy from you if they have been wowed.

Every time you meet a new person, you have a new opportunity to impress that person with yourself, your product, your service, what you've done, what you can do, what others have said about you, and what other impressed people have done for you.

The Wow Factor is not just about the image you present to the world, it is also about the image of yourself that you develop for no one else but you. When you become in thought and in deed that which you aspire to be, the world must respond accordingly. Their response may take the form of support, compensation, friendship, love or worship.

Once you know how to wow, you will have the ability to get anything you want.

Wanting What You Get

Getting what you want is easy on this plane of existence. Of equal importance, but of greater challenge to the masses, however, is wanting what you get. This too, requires practice. Here is why it is important to develop this ability.

As you strive towards a particular goal, you will create results based on your thoughts, words and actions. Until you reach the level of mastery of the principles of Wow, however, what you intend to create is not always what you end up creating. This is true because the creative process takes place on the subconscious level of mental activity--the level of belief. Therefore, you should be open to the seemingly unanticipated occurrences that come your way. For example, if you plan and work towards "A" but end up getting "B", do not be alarmed and distressed, but simply learn to accept it. Unhappiness is caused by unmet expectations held too firmly in mind. The more attached you are to a particular outcome, the unhappier you'll be if you do not achieve it at first. Therefore, seek your outcomes, but don't be too attached.

Know that whatever reality occurs, that it has been created because it is necessary for it to exist so that the right awareness and responses will be developed in you. These responses move you to the next level of accomplishment.

Wanting what you get, therefore, does not mean to be satisfied with what you get. It means simply that you accept it as your own creation, grow from that awareness of it as such, and then continue to create from an ever-evolving state of mind.

The Wow Factor In Action

The power of what you have just read will be evidenced by your own use and application of it. However, you can see it being used and applied right now by others whom you know to be successful.

Think of any successful individual whom you know. Think of what you know to be their assets. What makes this person special? What is their claim to fame? Think of what you know to be their perception of themselves as well as what you know to be the world's perception. What do people believe and say about them?

Think also of the means and manner of how they expose themselves to your awareness. How do you know of them? What media do they use to increase their customers, clients and followers? Think, too, of what response they demand of their followers. What subtle and overt ways do they request specific actions from us as their target audience? What do they ask that we buy, or that we buy into?

Are they not goal-oriented individuals, controlling the creation, development and exposure of the perception of their assets, while eliciting a response from us?

You will find in every instance that this is so. And now, you too are in possession of their secret to success.

Impress and Grow Rich

In a capitalistic society, one of the most sought after applications of the Wow Factor is the creation of wealth through business success. Through years of research into the secrets of success, I've created a working understanding of how, why and under what conditions the Wow Factor aids in the creation of business success. I call it the

Science of Impress

The Science of Impress is based on the following principles.

1. All things flow from those who have them to those who expect them. Money, for example, flows from those who have money and desire something, to those who provide that something and expect money.

2. The exchange of one object for another is called transmission. It occurs between a sender and a receiver.

3. No transmission can occur unless the sender and receiver are synchronized. No transaction can occur successfully unless sender and receiver are in agreement as to their mutual expectations. There must be a single path for the transmission.

4. Wow provides that path. It tunes both sender and receiver to the same frequency of expectation. It aligns two sides of a transaction. It creates the path upon which money, happiness, love and power travel from one individual to another.

5. Humans have certain observable needs, wants and expectations.

6. If you meet certain needs, fulfill certain wants, and exceed certain expectations, you can elicit the Wow Response.

As mentioned earlier, the Wow Response is the primary response which must and will always precede any action. Therefore, if you can control the Wow Response, you can control the nature and number of the world's response. The response may be a thought, a word, or any action including the transmission of compensation for that which you offer the world. Your compensation can take the form of money, things, recognition, power, a following, worship, esteem or love.

Through the Science of Impress, therefore, you can use the Wow Factor to sell your wares, gain power, lead a nation, or attract wealth into your life. In other words, you can impress and grow rich!

Who Will Be Wowed?

In applying the Wow Factor to business, there are two types of people you'll meet: customers and gatekeepers. Customers are people who buy your product. Gatekeepers are people who, by virtue of their position and status, have access to and influence over the people who buy your product. Examples of gatekeepers are magazine/newspaper publishers, writers, public speakers, organization presidents, etc. Each has their own set of needs, wants and expectations. And each will require a different use of your Wow Factor.

The operative question you must answer in your potential customer's mind is "Where is the personal benefit for me?"

The operative question you must answer in your gatekeeper's mind is "Is this product, service, or information of value to those to whom I communicate?"

The recognition, encouragement, and exploitation of these needs, wants and expectations will be the primary task of anyone who wishes to succeed in business. Your success will be determined by your thoughts about yourself, your thoughts about the laws of reality, and your thoughts about other people. The *Tao of Wow* will help you to develop the right thoughts.

The 12 Rules of Wow

In order to use the Wow Factor for business success, you'll need to know and apply the 12 Rules of Wow. They are proven techniques based on the understanding of basic human nature and people's responses to each other. You can be assured that success in any business endeavor is based on one or more of the following rules. Once you understand the psychology underlying them, you too can use them to impress and grow rich in your life!

1. *Better always impresses*

Competition is the basis of our society. Those who can run faster, deliver quicker, jump higher and sell cheaper will outperform those who cannot. However, a true "Wow Master"--to use a term in the *Tao of Wow*--does not compete. He or she merely recognizes and exploits the power of the inherent differences to create the Wow Response.

2. *Consistency and completion impress*

It's a fact that most people don't have what it takes to get a job done. Therefore, if you build a reputation of doing what you say you'll do, and doing it consistently, you'll automatically create a Wow Response in the minds of others.

3. *Beauty always impresses*

In our increasingly materialistic society, that which is pleasing to the eye is accorded more attention. Use this to your advantage when you present yourself and your product to the world.

4. *The new and unusual impress*

Great wealth has been created selling old things to new customers, and new things to old customers. Marketing experts know that a thing only has to be 10% different from something else to perceived of as radically innovative. Therefore, there's great wealth right in your own backyard repackaging ideas so they appear new, and reselling them to old customers!

5. *Unexpected accomplishments always impress*

The deaf or blind who perform music, the physically handicapped who participate in sports, the elderly who climb mountains, the very young who perform as virtuosos, are all examples of people exceeding expectations to create a Wow Response.

6. *Intelligence impresses*

We're living in a society that values athletic prowess and beauty over academic proficiency. Therefore, those who nurture their mental abilities, will possess the ability to wow. Read, write, speak, add and subtract well, and combine it with the ability to think critically about the world around you, and you will wow the world. There's Wow in wisdom!

7. *The invisibly obvious impresses*

Have you ever seen a new product on the market, and found yourself exclaiming, "Why didn't I think of that?!" The best inventions always create that response, and their appeal is almost always intuitively obvious to us.... once we see it!

8. *Success impresses*

When attempting to become successful, one must live from the feeling of the wish fulfilled. In other words, because success only visits the familiar, you must *become* success before success will be coming to you. Walk, talk, think and act the part, and the world will have no choice but to confer prizes and honors to match their perception of you. Then use all the awards, and prizes to impress the world even more!

9. *Power impresses*

The greatest power is not political power, but the personal power that people refer to as charm. Many of the world's successful people, rely on the strength of their personal charm to make the world go wow! Remember, people will elevate you to the level of your own self-image. Your charm, your wit, your words, your wisdom, and how you wield them, is in direct proportion to your self image. That, and all the qualities of a pleasing personality, attract others into your life and make the world go wow!

10. *Creativity/talent always impress*

We all have a creative spark within us. Do you paint, write or sing? Whatever your talent, discovering, developing and sharing your special gift is the surest way to impress the world.

11. *The praise of others impresses*

People will trust in, and be more impressed by what others say about you much more than what you say about yourself.

12. *Passion impresses*

There is something that you, and you alone were put here to do. There are activities that thrill you when you do them, and for which the doing is its own reward. That is your passion. Find it, share it with the world, and share it with passion! For it is the depth of your enthusiasm about a thing that will enroll others in your dream. Great leaders move the masses not just with words, but with the strength of their inner conviction of their beliefs. Whatever your interests, people are always impressed by passion!

These 12 Rules of Wow, practiced in all areas of your life, allow you to create the path for all good things to come to you.

The Journey Continues

In summary, everyone has a unique set of assets, which, when perceived and exposed correctly with the intention of eliciting a specific response, can result in phenomenal success in any undertaking. This is called your Wow Factor.

However, simply knowing your Wow Factor is not enough to secure a place of greatness for you. In order to gain the maximum benefit from your Wow Factor, you must "go for the Wow" in all that you do. In other words, you must become a Wow Master.

In order to become a Wow Master, you must adopt a workable set of thoughts, beliefs and understandings about yourself, the world, and others that will serve you as you encounter the challenges that the self, the world, and others will present to you. The *Tao of Wow* will expose you to those ways of thought and being. They are the context within which the Wow Factor must be understood and applied in order to maximize its effectiveness. For example, the *Tao of Wow* teaches that Wow Masters do not compete with others. You must know this to be true before you can maximize your Wow Factor. Failure to truly incorporate the ways of Wow into your belief system will result in frustration as you apply what you have learned. These and other ways of thought and being are an essential part of the journey to mastery.

No matter what your particular goals are at this moment, harnessing the power of your Wow Factor can help you achieve them. In addition, as you proceed on this specific journey of turning your passion into profit, you will now have a new vocabulary, as well as a new way to perceive of success and how to achieve it that will help you manifest your dreams as you make the world go wow! So, let the journey continue.

For more guidance on becoming a Wow Master, see The Tao of Wow *by Walt Goodridge*

MAIN POINTS OF CHAPTER 4
"Your Wow Factor"

• Your Wow Factor is the "goal-oriented, response-driven creation, development and controlled exposure of the private and public perception of your unique assets." This is the key to your success in anything you do. As a formula, it looks like this:

[(Assets + Perception) x Exposure] + Response = Wow Factor

• Anything can be an asset. The thoughts, words, actions, people and objects associated with what you are, what you do and what you have can be assets.

• The most empowering aspect of life is that you are able to tell people what you want them to think about who you are, what you do, and what you have. You can control the world's perception of you.

• Exposure means telling the world about you and your passion.

• People learn what response is expected of them by seeing what responses others have.

• You control almost every part of the Wow Factor process. You develop the assets. You create the perception. You control the exposure, and you can determine the response.

• You can use your Wow Factor to achieve anything you desire because of the basic truths about wow.

• Once you know what impresses the world, you will have discovered the secret formula for using your Wow Factor to impress and grow rich!

• The 12 Rules of Wow, practiced in all areas of your life, allow you to create the path of for all good things to come to you.

• Knowledge, understanding and application of this unique concept will improve your chances of success turning your passion into profit.

FOLLOW-UP FILE FOR CHAPTER 4
"Your Wow Factor"

INSPIRATION: Passion Seeker Profiles

_____

"The Sculptor's Passion"

By the age of 14, Donald Brown drew national television and media attention for his sculptures. His first university degree application was rejected on the grounds that there was no one at the university capable of teaching him anything new where his technique and ability was concerned. He is self taught and even from that tender age chose to ignore those who discouraged him from making, what they viewed as an unwise career choice. However, he pursued his dream of becoming a sculptor. With numerous celebrity endorsements, purchases by Morehouse College, The Nigerian Embassy in Washington D.C., The NAACP and the ANC in South Africa, the international demand for his works have excelled even his expectations!

_____

IDEAS: The Right Questions To Ask

for assets
• What specific assets do I have or have access to that I can use to achieve my goal?
• What creative ways can I come up with to harness the power of these assets?
• Who do I know? What do I know? What do I believe? What Do I own? What have I created? What am I good at? What am I known for? What have I done?

for perception
• What perception will a new person I encounter have of who I am, what I do, and what I have? How am I being perceived?
• What perception do I wish every new person I encounter to have of who I am, what I do, and what I have?
• What thoughts, words, actions, people and objects (i.e. assets) best convey the perception I wish to create?
• What creative ways can I come up with to harness the power of these assets to create the perception I desire?

for response
• What response do I desire?
• What do I wish to have happen next?
• What specific steps can I take to achieve the quality of response I desire?

for exposure
• Which specific people need to be exposed to me, my assets and the perception I desire?
• What specific steps can I take to achieve the level of exposure I desire?
• What creative ways can I develop to expose my assets to more people?

The Cycle of Success
"A Preview"

Where are you in The Passion Profit Cycle of Success?

The Passion Profit Cycle of Success describes the phases of the process of turning one's passion into profit. Starting in the upper left of the diagram above and going clockwise, the sequence includes Purpose, Passion, Product, and then Profit. In other words, according to the cycle of success, to turn your passion into profit, you must

  1. Find your purpose in life
  2. Discover your passion
  3. Create a product (or service), and then
  4. Sell it for profit.

At any given point in your life, you may find yourself in any one of the phases. Have you just started the journey and are looking for your life's PURPOSE? Do you already know your purpose, but don't quite know what your PASSION is? Maybe you know your passion and need to create a PRODUCT. Perhaps you have a product but don't know how to sell it to make a PROFIT. Or, perhaps you're already making a profit from your passion, but need a new or defining PURPOSE in life?

Following is a preview of the process we'll be exploring from this point on.

PURPOSE

According to the Passion Profit philosophy:

Your passion is an expression of your purpose

Have you ever asked, "Why am I here? "What am I here to offer the world?" or "What's the meaning of my life?" That--and similar questions--is at its core a spiritual one. The answer is the first and most critical part of turning your passion into profit. Everyone is here to experience, to grow and to become. Without an understanding of the spiritual component of your journey here on earth, you may find that everything you do leaves you unfulfilled.

In my book, the *Tao of Wow*, based on lessons learned from my continuing quest into things spiritual, I explore a concept based on the teachings and insights from a variety of spiritual perspectives. The "45 Ways of Men (and Women)" explores the "life themes" that are believed to exist for everyone on the planet. According to the life theme concept, each and every one of us is here to live out a particular theme. In analyzing your life, have you noticed that certain situations and circumstances seem to reveal consistent themes? Based on the opportunities, decisions and circumstances that take place in your life, are you here as a *builder*? Are you living out the *poverty* theme? Are you an *artisan*? Are you an *experiencer*? Do you seek *harmony*? Are you a *survivor*? Is the theme of serving others, or of being an advocate, seeking justice, or of making a difference one that comes up often? These are just a few of the 45 themes that offer keys to what your purpose here on earth may be.

Additional questions you can ask in this search are: How will I help the world? What change am I here to enact? What solutions can I offer? Who am I here to help? What contribution will I make to life on the planet? Questions like these lead to more profound analyses and greater insights into using your life to fulfill a specific purpose.

Don't overlook this important aspect of the Passion to Profit Journey. In addition to the chapters in this book, I've created special online reports, coaching opportunities, workshops and services to help you focus on the search for your life's purpose. I sincerely believe that turning your passion into profit is really a spiritual journey at its core.

PASSION

According to the Passion Profit philosophy:

Everyone has a passion

The fact that everyone has a passion means that we all have something that we're good at; something that we're experts in; something that provides us an inner sense of freedom, happiness, fulfillment and personal expression.

There's more to life than working for someone else for 40 years and then retiring. Life should be fun, meaningful, satisfying while offering some benefit to the world. What do I love to do? What are the activities that give me my greatest sense of purpose and fulfillment? These are some of the core questions to be asked during this phase.

Don't know where to look to find your passion? Your passion may be hiding in your hobbies; it may be in your desire to make a difference; it may be a childhood wish. I've created exercises as well as a secret formula for discovering your passion. Wherever your passion is, the Discovery Exercises can help you find it.

Don't know how to choose your passion? Don't worry. The choice of which passion to pursue is LESS important than simply choosing. I find that when people believe they are choosing one passion at the exclusion of all others, that they often choose not to choose. Remember, you are not making a FINAL choice, just the FIRST one. In other words, whichever passion you decide to pursue is just the first step in a journey that may lead through different expressions of your passion. Like me, you may choose to pursue say, a passion for music, which might then lead to you becoming a writer, which may lead to public speaking and eventually coaching. I couldn't have predicted where I would end up (I wasn't always called a passion "Prophet"). I do know, however, that I wouldn't have gotten here had I not taken that FIRST step.

According to the New York Times, "80% of all working Americans are unhappy about their careers..."   I sincerely believe that you never fully ENJOY life to its fullest, nor REALLY have the sort of FUN life was meant to be unless you're actively pursuing your passion!

PRODUCT

According to the Passion Profit philosophy:
Every passion has value
The fact that every passion has value means that everyone can be rewarded for the pursuit of something that has special meaning in their lives.

In order to create a winning idea, you need to know what questions to ask in order to isolate the hidden value of your passion. You need to be able to determine what physical form or conceptual angle to attach to your passion in order to communicate that value to the world. (In other words, you need to know what people will pay for--those are the Magic Questions!) And you need access to the means to manufacture, print, create or assemble your product, or the means to offer your service to the world..

PROFIT

According to the Passion Profit philosophy:
You can make money doing what you love
You NEED Money!! Don't let anyone fool you. As long as you're living in a capitalistic society, much of the good that you'll do for others, the fun that you'll have, and the security you'll achieve will come from the money you earn. Surely, you can do a lot of good without money, but it sure does help.

There are only two ways to make money in business. Charge more, or spend less. In this phase you'll learn how to do both, as well as how o create streams of repeat-business income from your current customers!

I'm sure you've also heard, that it's not how much you make, but how much you keep. In order to keep more of what you make, you need to maximize your profit. In order to do that, you'll need to set up a legitimate business, launch it simultaneously on the Internet, and market your business, product and service creatively and effectively.

From part-timers who make a few extra dollars, to MILLIONAIRE passion seekers who get nominated for prestigious awards, the sky's the limit as to how much money you want to make from your passion! REALLY! It's all possible! The Cycle of Success will show you how!

Other Applications of the Cycle of Success

People have asked if the cycle of success has other applications in other areas of life. The answer is an unequivocal yes. The cycle can be applied to any pursuit that one engages in, from cleaning one's apartment to the quest for romance.

Let's apply it to the pursuit of romance. Your purpose/goal (your reason why) in such a pursuit might perhaps be marriage. Your "passion" is what you do (charm, wine & dine) to win that person over. Your "product" is the value that your intended partner sees in you. Your "profit" is the payoff—the realization of your dream and the myriad benefits (love, security) that you achieve as a result.

purpose =	goal of the activity	marriage
passion =	actions towards the goal	the pursuit/wine & dine
product =	the value	what your intended buys into
profit =	payoff	love, security, etc.

Seen in this way, the Cycle of Success can be a powerful lens through which to view the pursuit of your dreams in many areas of life.

The Cycle Never Ends

The Cycle of Success represents a continuous journey. You may find yourself at different points of the cycle at various stages in your life. Your purpose at age 25 may differ significantly from your sense of purpose at age 75. Your passion when you are single may differ significantly from your passion after you've raised children who are now adults. After you've expressed yourself and derived profit from ventures you started in your youth, you may be ready once again to find a new purpose when you're older.

There's no right answer, or right place to be in the cycle. Just the opportunity to ask more questions as you grow and expand your awareness of who you are. The Cycle of Success simply represents a framework within which to organize the questions you ask. So, let's start asking questions!

Chapter 5: Purpose
"What's the meaning of life?"

The FIRST Law of Passion Dynamics:
"A person NOT in alignment with his or her purpose, will remain unfulfilled, living out someone else's purpose unless acted upon by outside forces."

***

The Ultimate Truth: It's a spiritual journey, silly!

I've always felt that this direction I've taken in my own life was not a business decision, but actually a spiritual one. It was not a decision to become rich financially, but one to become more of who I was meant to be.

Similarly, your own desire to turn your passion into profit comes from a basic and fundamental need to become more of who you are meant to be. The act of *becoming* is a spiritual evolution. Therefore, your decision to turn your passion into profit is ultimately a spiritual decision. The actual act of turning your passion into profit is, at its core, a creative act. It is you doing your part in a much bigger cosmic act of creation.

A small serving of water from a large pitcher has all the properties of taste and texture of the larger body from which it was poured. You, too, as one of the billions of different entities that comprise our universe, are but a single serving from the "infinite all" which seeks forever to express itself in more and more ways. The universe's expansion and movement towards greater expression does not stop simply because you exist. The little serving that you are, with all the taste and texture of the source from which you were poured, seeks similar expression as well. Your desire to do what you love to do is the universe calling out for further expression through you. The fulfillment of that calling results in your willfull participation in a cosmic act of creation. The gifts you offer the world as you turn your passion into profit continue the universe's never-ending act of creation. In other words, it is you fulfilling your reason for being here. It is your purpose.

The reason many of us are unhappy in our current jobs, marriages, relationships and life-styles is that we are denying who and what we are. We are living the ultimate lie. Our true nature is one of life, love, freedom, unlimited expression, eternal being-ness, and of God. Practice putting and saying "I am.." in front of all of these words ("I am life. I am love. etc.) and note how you feel. This is who you are. Anything that restricts you from being these things is unnatural and will feel like a prison for your spirit. We seek life through our jobs, but soon find that they are not constructed to provide that experience. We look for love in our marriages, but find too often that they impose conditional limitations on who we wish to be. We seek to find freedom in our relationships, but find that they become the expressions of obligations rather than of choices. As children, we enjoy the unlimited expression of who we are, but are soon taught to suppress our vitality. The reason the weekend holds such great sway for the masses of people is because it represents freedom from some of these limitations. Weekends are the time we can finally live, finally love, finally taste freedom, and finally get in touch with our God-selves. We can finally, in measured doses, be who we are and wish to be. Thank God it's Friday, indeed!

Can starting a business really bring happiness? I believe the answer is *yes,* if that business is an expression of your passion. In starting a passion-centered business, you will change the relationship between your "self" and your "money". Turning your passion into profit will create for you a life of expression not limited to certain days of the week. You'll be able to experience that weekend feeling of life, love, freedom unlimited expression and eternal being-ness every day of your life.

You have unlimited power, limitless potential, and more value than money. However, living in our society, you have forgotten this and have assigned more value to the pursuit of money than to yourself. Intellectually, you will say that this is not true. You will say that you value people, honesty, and happiness more than money. However, all of your actions reveal just the opposite. If it were not true, you wouldn't trade your freedom and time--your most valuable assets--for it. In addition, people are awarded more recognition based on their financial achievements than their contributions to society. There is great disparity between the rewards given to teachers and that given to sports figures.

Practically everything about who we are has been placed in a subordinate role to money. As children, we are told to control our desires because there is not enough money to satisfy them. As teenagers, we are told that our artistic leanings are frivolous and that being sensible means pursuing a profession that will bring us money. As adults, we find that job security requires we become someone else, creating someone else's dream, while suppressing our own in exchange for a paycheck. Every day we are forced to make the choice between the pursuit of money and being who we are. And the pursuit of money wins every time.

This is our society's skewed value system. Because of it, we grow deeper and deeper into a set of beliefs that devalues us relative to money. We are imprisoned by these beliefs unless and until we think ourselves out of them. Ideally, we should each reach a point where we realize that we are entitled to all the things life has to offer, including money, simply because we exist. For many, however, the journey of getting to that place involves first bringing the two concepts of self and money to a place of equal footing. Then, and only then, can we start to move to the place where we know ourselves to be much more.

That is why turning your passion into profit can be one of the most spiritually liberating accomplishments you can achieve. It reconciles the imbalance that exists between who you are and the things you create, and the value of things in our society using the agreed-upon yardstick of money. When you can finally start to attract money into your life as a direct compensation for who you are, and what you do, rather than for what others want you to be, it begins to set things right in your mind.

Turning your passion into profit, therefore, is about bringing yourself first on par with, and then beyond money. You can't ever rise above the grip that money has on you as long as you see yourself inferior to it.

Life Themes: Roles with Goals

Why am I here on the planet?

Even though mankind has pondered that question for centuries, and has seemingly failed to come up with an answer that adequately satisfies everyone, we are about to solve the mystery for you within the next few paragraphs!

I must ask you first, however, to suspend a few beliefs. Suspend your attachment to what you know, what you think you know, and even what you think you don't know, and let's suppose for a moment that the answer to "why am I here on the planet?" is actually knowable. Let's suppose, for the sake of argument, that the reason you are here on the planet is to live out one or more "life themes." And let's further suppose that a life theme is defined as a particular role, quality or experience with a unique challenge or goal that is intended to teach you something.

The 45 Life Themes are

Activator	Harmony	Patience	Shouter
Analyzer	Healer	Pawn	Spirituality
Artist	Irritant	Peacemaker	Survivor
Builder	Jester	Perfection	Temperance
Catalyst	Justice	Persecution	Tolerance
Cause Fighter	Law	Persecutor	Victim
Control	Leader	Poverty	Warrior
Emotionality	Loner	Predator	Winner
Experiencer	Loser	Psychic	Wisdom
Flaw	Manipulator	Rejection	
Follower	Master	Rescuer	
Giver	Passivity	Responsibility	

How helpful would it be to know your life theme? It might offer a level of clarity to the seemingly random situations in your life. It might explain why certain types of experiences seem to follow you throughout your life. Think about it. A person living out a life theme of teacher might find themselves drawn to situations and people which bring out their natural desire to impart knowledge. Someone living the "builder" theme, on the other hand, might find himself drawn to professions and situations in which he can express his natural desire to build, invent, construct or make things.

For a more in-depth exploration of the concept, pick up the *Tao of Wow.* F o r now, however, simply take a guess as to what your life theme might be. Most people have one dominant and one secondary life theme at work in their lives. So, as you read through the list, ask yourself, "Is this a recurring theme in my life?" "Have my experiences in life been influenced by this particular role or experience?" "And, if so, to what degree?" Discovering your life theme can be a critical first step in turning your passion into profit. Many people find their lives seem more aligned, and fulfilling when they are consciously aware of and working with what they believe their life theme and purpose is in life.

The 4 "Passion Professions"

In order for your passion-centered business to provide you with the most fulfillment possible, it must be in alignment with your life theme.

The Passion Profession provides the necessary link that allows you to honor your life theme while creating market value that you can profit from. It allows you to align what you *choose* to do in a business venture with what you're *here* to do from a spiritual perspective. It allows you to express your life theme in ways that create value for others. The following "Passion Professions" form the basis of any pursuit of passion.

CREATOR--Creators are the artisans in our society. They include sculptors, painters, graphic designers, song writers, novelists and inventors. They include software designers and game inventors and those skilled in crafts, construction and carpentry. This group also includes athletes, singers, dancers and comedians too. *Key action word: CREATE.*

SAVIOR--Saviors are the healers and fixers. They include doctors, health practitioners, massage therapists, as well as those who fix people and things in any capacity. This group includes social workers, firefighters, counselors. *Key action word: FIX.*

GURU-- Gurus are the teachers. They include workshop/ seminar hosts and motivational speakers. *Key action word: TEACH.*

GUIDE--Guides are the leaders and gatekeepers. These are the philosophers, collectors, and any who provide access to ideas and things. They are the publishers, editors, politicians, and heads of cultural and political movements. *Key action word: LEAD.*

Finding Your Passion Profession

Not quite sure of your Passion Profession? The Passion Personality test will help to isolate and quantify certain habits, preferences, motivations and ways of being typically associated with each Profession. Adapted from a larger body of work, it uses single word descriptions to identify specific behaviorial tendencies.This will help to determine which Passion Profession might be the best fit for turning your passion into profit.

Disclaimer: The results of this test are an effective means of understanding a bit more about yourself and others. However, as multifaceted beings, we are always growing and changing, and no one an be adequately described or understood by the answers to forty questions.

THE PASSION PERSONALITY TEST (adapted)

Instructions. Place "X" next to the one word per line that BEST describes you.

Strengths

1.	___Animated	___Adventurous	___Analytical	___Adaptable
2.	___Persistent	___Playful	___Persuasive	___Peaceful
3.	___Submissive	___Sacrificing	___Socialite	___Strong-willed
4.	___Considerate	___Controlled	___Competitive	___Conviction
5.	___Refreshing	___Respectful	___Reserved	___Resourceful
6.	___Satisfied	___Sensitive	___Self-Reliant	___Spirited
7.	___Planner	___Patient	___Positive	___Promoter
8.	___Sure	___Spontaneous	___Scheduled	___Shy
9.	___Orderly	___Obliging	___Outspoken	___Optimistic
10.	___Friendly	___Faithful	___Funny	___Forceful
11.	___Daring	___Delightful	___Diplomatic	___Detailed
12.	___Cheerful	___Consistent	___Cultured	___Confident
13.	___Idealistic	___Independent	___Inoffensive	___Invigorating
14.	___Demonstrative	___Decisive	___Dry Humor	___Deep
15.	___Mediator	___Musical	___Mover & Shaker	___Mixes Easily
16.	___Thinker	___Tenacious	___Talker	___Tolerant
17.	___Listener	___Loyal	___Lion-hearted	___Lively
18.	___Contented	___Chief	___Chart Maker	___Cute
19.	___Perfectionist	___Permissive	___Productive	___Popular
20.	___Bouncy	___Bold	___Behaved	___Balanced

Weaknesses

1.	___Brassy	___Bossy	___Bashful	___Blank
2.	___Undisciplined	___Unsympathetic	___Unenthusiastic	___Unforgiving·
3.	___Reluctant	___Resentful	___Resistant	___Repetitious
4.	___Fussy	___Fearful	___Forgetful	___Frank
5.	___Impatient	___Insecure	___Indecisive	___Interrupts
6.	___Unpopular	___Uninvolved	___Unpredictable	___Unaffectionate
7.	___Headstrong	___Haphazard	___Hard to Please	___Hesitant
8.	___Plain	___Pessimistic	___Proud	___Permissive
9.	___Angered easily	___Aimless	___Argumentative	___Alienated
10.	___Naïve	___Negative attitude	___Nervy	___Nonchalant
11.	___Worrier	___Withdrawn	___Workaholic	___Wants credit
12.	___Too sensitive	___Tactless	___Timid	___Talkative
13.	___Doubtful	___Disorganized	___Domineering	___Depressed
14.	___Inconsistent	___Introvert	___Intolerant	___Indifferent
15.	___Messy	___Moody	___Mumbles	___Manipulative
16.	___Slow	___Stubborn	___Show-off	___Skeptical
17.	___Loner	___Lord over others	___Lazy	___Loud
18.	___Sluggish	___Suspicious	___Short-tempered	___Scatterbrained
19.	___Revengeful	___Restless	___Reluctant	___Rash
20.	___Compromising	___Critical	___Crafty	___Changeable

Scoring Sheet

To Score: Now place a check next to the responses that you selected in the previous section

STRENGTHS

	CREATOR	SAVIOR	GURU	GUIDE
1.	___Animated	___Adaptable	___Analytical	___Adventurous
2.	___Playful	___Peaceful	___Persistent	___Persuasive
3.	___Socialite	___Self-Sacrificing	___Self-Sacrificing	___Strong-willed
4.	___Convincing	___Considerate	___Controlled	___Competitive
5.	___Refreshing	___Reserved	___Respectful	___Resourceful
6.	___Spirited	___Satisfied	___Sensitive	___Self-Reliant
7.	___Promoter	___Patient	___Planner	___Positive
8.	___Spontaneous	___Shy	___Scheduled	___Sure
9.	___Outspoken	___Obliging	___Orderly	___Optimistic
10.	___Funny	___Friendly	___Faithful	___Forceful
11.	___Delightful	___Diplomatic	___Detailed	___Daring
12.	___Cheerful	___Consistent	___Cultured	___Confident
13.	___Invigorating	___Inoffensive	___Idealistic	___Independent
14.	___Demonstrative	___Dry Humor	___Deep	___Decisive
15.	___Mixes easily	___Mediator	___Musical	___Mover & Shaker
16.	___Talker	___Tolerant	___Thoughtful	___Tenacious
17.	___Lively	___Listener	___Loyal	___Lion-hearted
18.	___Cute	___Contented	___Chart Maker	___Chief
19.	___Popular	___Permissive	___Perfectionist	___Productive
20.	___Bouncy	___Balanced	___Behaved	___Bold

Subtotal: _____ _____ _____ _____

WEAKNESS

	CREATOR	SAVIOR	GURU	GUIDE
1.	___Brassy	___Blank	___Bashful	___Bossy
2.	___Undisciplined	___Unenthusiastic	___Unforgiving	___Unsympathetic
3.	___Repetitious	___Reluctant	___Resentful	___Resistant
4.	___Forgetful	___Fearful	___Fussy	___Frank
5.	___Interrupts	___Indecisive	___Insecure	___Impatient
6.	___Unpredictable	___Uninvolved	___Unpopular	___Unaffectionate
7.	___Haphazard	___Hesitant	___Hard to Please	___Headstrong
8.	___Permissive	___Plain	___Pessimistic	___Proud
9.	___Angered easily	___Aimless	___Alienated	___Argumentative
10.	___Naïve	___Nonchalant	___Negative attitude	___Nervy
11.	___Wants credit	___Worrier	___Withdrawn	___Workaholic
12.	___Talkative	___Timid	___Too sensitive	___Tactless
13.	___Disorganized	___Doubtful	___Depressed	___Domineering
14.	___Inconsistent	___Indifferent	___Introvert	___Intolerant
15.	___Messy	___Mumbles	___Moody	___Manipulative
16.	___Slow-off	___Slow	___Skeptical	___Stubborn
17.	___Loud	___Lazy	___Loner	___Lord over others
18.	___Scatterbrained	___Sluggish	___Suspicious	___Short-tempered
19.	___Restless	___Reluctant	___Revengeful	___Rash
20.	___Changeable	___Compromising	___Critical	___Crafty

Subtotal: _____ _____ _____ _____

Totals

Your Score

Add the number of responses in each column for a final score for each type. Shade the number of boxes corresponding to your score for a graphical representation.

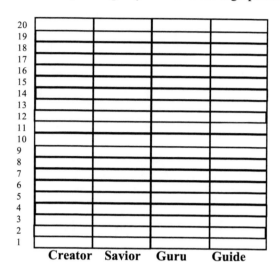

The Creator's Personality Profile (The Exciter)

Motivation: The operative word for Exciters is *fun*! They are moved to action by the promise of entertainment, and social interaction. To get an Exciter to take action in the face of fear, reframe the necessary action as fun, or one that will lead to enjoyment.

Strengths and Weaknesses: Exciters are outgoing and spontaneous. Exciters are people-oriented. The spontaneity, humor and popularity that are natural expressions of who they are can be of value to those who seek the same in their lives. Providing people with ways to experience joy in their lives can be very profitable.

Because they are usually jumping from one fun activity to the next, and focusing on everything else but the task at hand, Exciters may miss the success that comes from patience, and the ability to commit to tasks until their dreams come true.

Exciters may have a short attention span and tend to be a bit too impulsive in their behavior. To be better Exciters, therefore, they should work on balancing fun with work. They should work on creating their long-term good rather than simply instant gratification. They should work on controlling emotions when things don't go their way.

Ideal Professions: Exciters do better in professions and situations which allow them freedom, interaction with others, travel, and a changing environment. Exciters make great salespeople. They tend not to do well in jobs that are repetitive, factual, or laden with paperwork, charts, graphs and numbers. However, Exciters can succeed in these types of professions if they develop their Informer traits.

The Savior's Personality Profile (The Supporter)

Motivation: The operative word for the Supporter personality type is *help*. They are inspired by the desire to be of service, to care for and to comfort others. To get a Supporter to take action in the face of fear, reframe the necessary action as one that will make a difference in the lives of others, and is helping a greater good. Use words like "help", "honesty", "people", "caring", "love", "deserve" (as in: "you deserve this because of all you've done for others").

Strengths and Weaknesses: The Supporter's sense of personal value is determined by the value they can create for others. They are tolerant, diplomatic, caring and are of tremendous value to those whose lives are out of control or ruled by chaos.

  Helpful to a fault, Supporters can allow themselves to be used by others. They should be wary of others who may motivate them to extremes of service for their own goals. Since they tend to be quite people-oriented, Saviors need to focus on being more like the task-oriented Informer and more like the self-oriented Competitor, or they may run the risk of "finishing last."

Ideal Professions: Supporters do better in professions and positions that provide care such as doctors, nurses, day-care providers, social workers etc. They tend not to do well in situations where the focus is on personal advancement or monetary gain through competition. Supporters can succeed in these types of situations if they balance their desire to help others with satisfying their own needs.

The Guru's Personality Profile (The Informer)

Motivation: The operative word for the Informer is *information*. They are inspired by understanding, ideas, facts, data, knowledge and order. To move an Informer to action, use words like "facts", "documentation", "proven", "absolute certainty", and "intelligence." Informers respect and are inspired by intelligence in others. Informers feel more inclined to embark on a new journey when they are as informed as possible. To get an Informer to take action in the face of fear, what you're saying must be factual and accurate. Reframe the necessary action as one that will lead to knowledge or certainty.

Strengths and Weaknesses: Informers project an image of calm, collected and in absolute control. Many people see strength in the Informer's ability to stay emotionally detached while others around are losing their heads. Informers are confident when they speak since they rarely speak on matters on which they are uncertain. They are usually well-spoken and inspire others with their eloquence and command of the language. When an Informer gets involved in a business venture or organization, they are the ones who know exactly what's going on at all times. They are the ones who others come to for information and insight.

  Informers are conservative in both nature and dress and tend to be conformists. Analytical in their approach to life, people and situations, they have little tolerance for people who are ignorant or ill-informed. They value being right over being popular.

Informers however, can tend to be aloof, detached and intellectual rather than intuitive in their approach to life. They tend to be extremely task oriented individuals who put the project ahead of the people. Therefore, they need to get in touch with their feelings, and the feelings of others if they are to grow and be successful. They need to be more people-oriented in their interactions and embrace confrontation and communication as means to achieve understanding and growth in relationships.

Ideal Professions: Informers do better in professions and positions which reward knowledge, detail and accuracy. They make great accountants, engineers, computer programmers, bankers and statisticians. They tend not to do well in jobs or businesses which require people skills. Informers can succeed in these profession if they develop their interpersonal skills. The information, order, analysis, perfection and attention to detail that characterizes the Informer can be of value to others who seek these qualities in their own lives. The Informer's passion offers knowledge and order to others' lives.

The Guide's Personality Profile (The Competitor)

Motivation: The operative word for the Competitor is leadership. To motivate a Competitor , use words like "best", "competition", "money", "control", "excellence", "power" and "the finer things in life." If you're speaking to a Competitor, you've got to be aggressive and strong. Competitors relate to strength and they respect others who are where they want to be, even though they're probably already thinking of ways to outdo them! To get a Competitor to take action in the face of fear, reframe the necessary action as one that will be challenging, and will set them apart from others.

Strengths and Weaknesses: Competitors are born leaders driven by wealth, prestige, and independence. Achievement has value to them, and therefore they can offer it to those who seek the same in their lives. When a Competitor gets involved in a business venture or organization, they are the ones who inspire others by setting the goals and motivating others to do their best, often just to keep up with them! In the presence of a Competitor, others are moved to be the best they can be!

Competitors can tend to be too aggressive in their pursuit of success to the detriment of others' feelings and others' needs. They tend to be viewed as egotistical and selfish. They are known to take advantage of others in order to achieve their goals. To be a better Competitor, therefore, they need to work on being supportive of others' dreams and desires. They need to view people as collaborators rather than always competitors.

Because they tend to focus on self to the exclusion of others, Competitors may miss the success and profit that comes from helping others to achieve their dreams.

Ideal Professions: Competitors do better in professions which reward the pursuit of wealth and status. Competitors make great leaders and money makers. They tend not to do well in businesses which require sensitivity or the taking on of supportive roles like social worker or nurse. However, Competitors can succeed at these professions if they develop their supportive nature.

Summary

Your Passion Personality Profile reveals your strengths and weaknesses, what inspires you, what ways of being represent your comfort zone, how you view the world, how you deal with stress and challenges and how you interpret information. It also tells what moves you to action, which you can use to fuel your passion.

The passion-centered business you eventually create should capitalize on your strengths, and incorporate other people who can compensate for your weaknesses -- while you work on those weaknesses.

NOTE: For an online version of The Passion Personality Test, which automatically computes your results, visit www.passionprofit.com, and click on "Personality Test".

 # The Cycle of Success Step 1:

Identify your Passion Profession

Your first step in turning your passion into profit is to determine what Passion Profession or Role you believe you are here to fulfill.

Choose: Creator | Savior | Guru | Guide.

My Passion Profession is

MAIN POINTS OF CHAPTER 5
"Purpose"

• The reason many of us are unhappy in our current jobs, marriages, relationships and life-styles is that we are denying who we are and what we are here to do. We are denying our purpose.

• Th First Law of Passion Dynamics states, "A person NOT in alignment with his or her purpose, will remain unfulfilled, living out someone else's purpose unless acted upon by outside forces." Therefore, the first step in discovering your passion is to discover yourself by finding your purpose.

• Turning your passion into profit is ultimately a spiritual journey of becoming who you are. In doing so, you will change the relationship between your "self" and your "money" bringing yourself on par with, and then ultimately beyond the value of money. You can't ever rise above the hold that money has on you as long as you see yourself beneath it.

• Starting a business can bring happiness if that business helps you to fulfill your purpose.

• One or more of 45 life themes might offer clues to your purpose.

• The 4 Passion Professions of Creator, Savior, Guru and Guide can allow you to honor that purpose while making money at the same time. Knowing your Passion Profession, and the personality strengths and weaknesses associated with it, can help you focus on what you're best at. The Passion Personality Test can provide additional clues.

• The operative action word for the Creator is: **Make**. The dominant Personality type is Exciter. The motivational factors are freedom, flexibility and fun.

• The operative action word for the Savior is: **Fix**. The dominant personality type is Supporter. The motivational factors are help, support and making a difference.

• The operative action word for the Guru is: **Teach**. The dominant personality type is Informer. The motivational factors are information and order.

• The operative action word for the Guide is: **Lead**. The dominant personality type is Competitor. The motivational factors are money, status and competition.

FOLLOW-UP FILE FOR CHAPTER 5
"Purpose"

INSPIRATION: Passion Seeker Profiles

"Walt's Story"

Perhaps the best way to illustrate the power of purpose, recurring themes and experiences in turning passion into profit is to share my own personal story. Like to hear it? Here it goes:

Flatland

Within the first fifteen minutes of my first assignment on my first day of work at my first job, I realized beyond the shadow of a single doubt that I hated being there. What I saw on that day scared me to the core, and haunted me until I left seven years later. I saw mostly men, and a few women, who were living lives of quiet desperation. People who, at age fifty and above, had spent their lives allowing their dreams, and thus their spirits, to stagnate. I met men who long ago had given up dreaming about doing more, and who had resigned themselves to live out their most productive years in the claustro-phobic confines of cubicles engaged in personally unfulfilling work just for the sake of a paycheck. I met others who, at my young age of twenty-one, were already planning their retirement. I met people who had bought into someone else's roles and expectations and were acting out the script without question or concern that there was something more.

They reminded me of the characters in *Flatland* by Edwin A. Abbott, a book I read in high school geometry class. The inhabitants of Flatland are paper-thin geometric shapes living on a flat surface, who think only in one dimension since the concept of height is one that has no meaning in their world. I felt like that lone inhabitant who discovers the existence of a third physical dimension. He is met with resistance, ridicule and scorn, but perhaps, most frustratingly of all, there was simply no one else he could relate to or who could understand him.

As I met more and more of my co-workers, I felt more and more alone, for I had less and less in common with them. They all relished the comfort of working at what veteran employees called "the country club": a worker's paradise known for its great benefits, little real stress, and which rarely, if ever, laid people off. Many felt they had truly made it, and that all there was left to do was fit in, make as few waves as possible, draw a steady paycheck, earn their yearly 2% raise, and enjoy the ride. They were one-dimensional figures living in a mental flatland, unaware or unwilling to conceive of more.

My soul felt imprisoned, and I was determined to set it free.

Unlike most of my "flatland" coworkers, I dreamed of more. I dreamed of doing something that I could really get excited about. I dreamed of a life-style where, instead of being locked away from the world for a third of my life during the daylight hours of every day, I would have the freedom to decide when to rise, when to have lunch, when to work and when to relax. One of my fantasies was simply having the freedom to go see a movie in the middle of the day. I spent the next 7 years doing everything within my power to realize that dream!

The Prisoner

I can trace my desire to be free to an early episode in my childhood in Jamaica. Unlike most of the kids in my neighborhood, my older brother and I weren't allowed to leave our home after school, until our mother came home. It was her quite sensible way of keeping us safe from harm. Once we arrived home each day, we would pick up the house keys from our next door neighbor, lock ourselves in, and watch with longing at what was happening on the outside.

At the time, *Colditz*, a British television series about prisoners of war (POWs) during World War II, was airing on Jamaican television. Everyone on the island who had access to a television set watched *Colditz*. (With only one station on the island at that time, there wasn't much choice, actually). Because we weren't allowed to go out and play, the other kids would tease us and, using a variation of the show's terminology, would call us "POHs", i.e. prisoners of house. Yes, kids can be cruel.

While admittedly, not an earth-moving, traumatic experience, I now realize that from an early age, freedom became a recurring motivation. At 7 years old, however, I didn't have many options. I had to bide my time.

The Littlest Teacher (Enter the Guru)

Perhaps the first clue that I got that I had something unique I could share with the world that had the power to change my situation, happened on the first day of class in the first grade. At seven years old, dressed in my shiny new khaki school uniform that all Jamaican schoolboys wear, I found myself at the front of the classroom, sharing the teacher's desk to help her correct the other students' papers for a math test we had just taken. I can't tell you how I got up there, or how it came to be that I was grading the work of other 7 year-olds, but there I was.

My teacher was so impressed with how advanced I was that she walked me over to a 2nd-grade classroom. She left me there to continue my education in a more challenging setting. In all, I spent a total of 2 hours in first grade, and my career as the littlest teacher ended for a while. That act, however, set the stage for the rest of my life as far as what my teachers, parents, and others expected of me, and more importantly, what I perceived and came to expect of myself. I discovered I could get myself exempted from taking certain tests, from getting caned by the teachers and free from the other restrictions and control. All I had to do was express my gift of intelligence. That strategy worked well for a while, until our family moved to America.

Coming To America!

Once my family came to America, things changed. My brother and I were enrolled in a Catholic school in Queens, New York, and though I continued to impress the teachers, it seemed I was making enemies among the other kids.

Adolescence is a time when there's a higher premium on socializing, fitting in, and being like everybody else than on being smart. So being intelligent, *and* a foreigner didn't bode well for me. I was a prisoner again, but this time for different reasons. I was ostracized to the social prison for nerds and geeks!

Freedom came my way through my art. I started drawing when I was about 8 years old. My brother, Nicolae, had introduced me to the concept while we were still living in Jamaica. He would often draw soldiers as a means of expressing his own passion for things military. He was a war and history buff who knew more about every battle waged between man than anyone I've met. It wasn't the drawing that really interested him, however, so he did it just long enough to inspire me. I practiced drawing the people in my mother's fashion catalogs until I got quite good at it. Drawing was a means of escape that allowed me to create a world of characters into which I could fit in, be accepted, and one that I controlled entirely. Drawing was also a claim to fame that seemed less intimidating to the arbiters of adolescent acceptance. In high school, I contributed drawings to the school yearbook, and even turned that passion into profit by free-lancing for a neighborhood community center. I would later call on that creativity to design album covers, brochures, and ultimately webpages.

Tutoring

I didn't, however, lose my interest or aptitude for academics. It was still a gift for which I was praised and recognized throughout my school years. I even won the senior award for "most intelligent male", a dubious distinction during a period when, quite honestly, I would have preferred "most popular" or "best dressed." Unfortunately, those honors were reserved for people who were, in fact, more popular and better dressed than I was! In any event, I was asked to participate in the Peer Tutoring program at my school and was often praised as having something a little special about the way I did things. The little teacher had returned. The students I tutored improved dramatically. To this day, I still get a unique thrill from being able to ignite the spark of understanding in others' minds. It was an early foreshadowing of the self-help, and business how to books that I would later write. I also turned that passion into profit making a few dollars each week tutoring neighborhood children.

It was that gift for Math and Science that prompted my guidance counselor, Ms. Charlotte Huey, to insist I pursue a degree in engineering. She insisted as well that that degree be from New York's Columbia University. I applied and was accepted.

The Columbia Years: My Double Life

By my second year at Columbia, I became recruitment chairperson and later president of the school chapter of the National Society of Black Engineers.

However, not wanting a repeat of the same separation I felt in high school, I decided not to define myself solely by my identity as an engineer. This was a good decision, since it was beginning to dawn on me that I didn't really want to be an engineer. I joined the Caribbean Students Association, where I befriended others who shared a cultural bond. I also showed up one night at WKCR-FM, the college radio station, where I met Courtney Munroe, host of the "Carib Riddims" show. After sitting in on several of Courtney's shows, I got the chance to develop my on-air presence and soon joined the ranks of the station's music staff. I took over the show from Courtney a short time later when he felt confident that he was leaving it in good hands. I had found another passion! By day I was an unassuming engineering student, and every Thursday night for the next 5 years, I was "Sir-Walt", the Reggae DJ!

My passion for music had started back in high school. After attending my first reggae concert with my friend Clarence, who had me realize it was OK to be who I was rather than try too hard to fit in. I soon started collecting records and joined the Caribbean students Association as a way of reconnecting to my Caribbean roots.

In college, along with a few of my friends, I was also part of a rag tag group of partyers who called ourselves *Unity HiFi*. We put on the best (or was that the 'only'?) Caribbean parties on the Columbia campus. I can't remember if we made any money, but we had a lot of fun. I even made a few dollars turning my music passion into profit when I launched *Walt's Reggae Record Club*, making tapes for Reggae-hungry students.

As I look back, I'm glad that I made the decision to nurture that other side of me. While I didn't have an official second major, music turned out to be my plan B.

It was also during the Columbia years, that I met Christine Karmo, a dear friend who changed my way of thinking. She showed me how to look inside for the answers to the pressing questions in my life. Under her tutelage, I started on the path of a lifelong interest in personal growth. These two passions--music and personal growth--would figure prominently throughout my life and eventually provide the freedom I craved.

The Working Years

It was the Spring of 1987. I was about to graduate with a Bachelor of Science in Civil Engineering. By February of that year, I had already received two job offers. One was from New York's Con-Edison, the local utility company with whom I had interned during the summer of my junior year, and the other was from the state Port Authority (PA). I had already chosen to go with the PA, not on the basis of salary--as the PA was offering about $1,000 less--but on the basis of freedom. For while Con-Ed wanted me to start working the very week after graduation, the recruiter at the PA had said that the decision of when to start was mine. I could start whenever I wished. (Thanks Catherine!) I chose the path of most freedom, and chose to take the summer off.

My secret plan was to use the summer months to start my own business, strike it rich, then, call up my would-be employer and "regretfully" inform them that I wouldn't be reporting in for work since I was now a millionaire. Well, things didn't quite work out as I planned. I ended up reporting for work in August of 1987.

I was now in the belly of the beast; a salaried worker in corporate America. I was growing unhappier each day. I was more desperate than ever to break free.

The Day the Music Died

A year after graduation (even though I was not longer a student), I was still doing my Thursday night radio show from 11:30 p.m. until 1:00 a.m. I would share my taste in music, my knowledge of the artists, with a sprinkling of personal growth thoughts in between songs. I would return home by 2:00 or 3:00 in the morning, get about 2 hours of sleep, and head out to work by 6:00 a.m. This weekly ritual was an oasis in an otherwise passionless existence. I was doing something I truly loved. Then, one day, it all came to an end.

One night, after my show, the station manager and another board member called me into the lounge area just outside the studio to "talk." They reminded me that since one of the missions of the station was to provide broadcasting to students, they requested that I give up my show to another student. I was crushed. They were right of course. I had benefited from that mission...but, what would I do now? The show was my life.

Fans and even radio staff encouraged me to fight the policy, citing the fact that there were others at the station who were hosting shows who were no longer students. Others suggested I circumvent the policy by signing up for a single course which would make me an official student. I decided, however, to move on. I felt that this might just be the push I needed to experience something even greater. What that something greater would be, I still didn't know, but I was optimistic. And eventually, the answer appeared.

Strata Records

While at WKCR, I had met an up-and-coming recording artist named Wayne Wright. One evening, following an on-air interview, at about the same time that I was being handed my walking papers, Wayne and I discussed the state of the music industry, his goals and his desire to release an album of his music. Seeking to jump into the industry in some way, I offered to design his album cover. He agreed and we became fast friends. That led to me managing his group and eventually to us forming Strata Records, a short lived venture created to promote his music.

Wayne helped me to understand the workings of the music industry, how records are pressed, how they are distributed, and how money is made. I participated in the recording process, the album design process, picking up the records from the pressing plant and even handled early trunk-of-the-car distribution of our first product.

Eventually, however, we started to differ in our individual visions for the direction of the company. In the winter of 1991, I left to start my own record company. It was called "*a company called W*".

The Rise and Rebirth of a company called W

Now at the helm of my own company, and using the knowledge I had gained from the Strata venture, I released the music of a college buddy. I soon signed four artists to the label, and released a total of 5 singles. We had some national press coverage, video exposure, national distribution and a modicum of success. However, after a year and a half, I realized that I wasn't going to be the music industry mogul I had envisioned, so I started looking for other ideas.

One day, a friend called with someone on the line who was in need of business information and guidance. I had always found myself sharing my music industry knowledge and experience to help others do what I was doing. So this call was no different. What *was* unique about this call was that after talking for about an hour, this particular individual thanked me and said, "I really appreciate the information you gave me, Mr. Goodridge. I would have been willing to pay you for it." I jokingly asked him how much he would have paid. He said (and I remember this figure), "About $179." At that moment, a light bulb went on in my head, and I became inspired. At that time, no books existed that showed young Hip Hop entrepreneurs how to start their own record label and release and promote their own music. I decided to write one!

The Return of the Guru!

It took me the next 3 weeks of sleepless nights to complete the 250 pages of information which became *Rap; This Game of Exposure: Promoting Your Rap Record/ Artist* (now called *Change the Game*). I was rushing to debut the book at an upcoming music industry event. I completed the spiral-bound prototype at a 24-hour copy center at 5:00 a.m. the morning of the event. I got an hour's sleep and was then off to catch a flight to Atlanta for the convention. I distributed fliers at the event, and even made an announcement during one of the workshops that made me the center of attention at the back of the room. I was mobbed by throngs (or was it 3 people?) who were interested in taking the book home with them right then. By the time I got back to New York three days later, there was a check in my mailbox from someone who had received a flier.

With ads placed in targeted industry magazines, more orders soon started pouring in. I created several more books and then incorporated other authors' books and videos to create a catalog of "success tools for Hip Hop Entrepreneurs." I was soon making the same amount of money selling my books, as I was as a Civil Engineer, now earning a combined annual income of about $90,000. I could taste my freedom! However, try as I might, I couldn't bring myself to break free from my job to follow my passion full time. Something was missing. I soon discovered what it was.

ACN. Freedom Comes My Way!
The final piece of the puzzle of freedom came shortly after I joined a Network Marketing company called American Communications Network (ACN). I was introduced to ACN by the same college friend whose music I had released several years earlier when I was actively running my record label. He invited me out to a presentation during which I saw a unique opportunity to take part in the growth of the telecommunications industry, so I jumped aboard.

Though it doesn't always receive its due respect, network marketing is a great industry that teaches great sales techniques, advocates success through personal growth, commitment, and by helping others. It's helped many to overcome the fears that hold them back, and of course, offers the opportunity for creating unlimited income.

It was the training system that taught me the new reality that wealth of mind must precede wealth of pocket. Five months after joining, I attended a leadership training designed to do just that. The leap in awareness I achieved at that training, and the energy of being in a roomful of people just like me who wanted the same things I did, and who were there for support, gave me the courage to do what I should have done within that first 15 minutes of my engineering job 7 years earlier. I took the next day, a Monday, off from work. I wrote my single line resignation letter that evening, and on Tuesday, I handed it in and walked away from corporate America forever! I was free!

The Journey Begins
Little did I realize what I was in for! Being a full time entrepreneur hasn't always been a smooth ride, but as I share with you later in this book, I've found that the ups and downs we experience are often necessary reconstruction periods that occur when we make major life transitions. I've learned that everything in life happens to take us closer to our goals, whether we recognize it or not.

The journey, with all its challenges, has resulted in constant growth as I redefine who I am, and who I wish to be. It's allowed me to be creative and to express my passions within different business ventures. I've created multiple streams of income through ACN, and the sales of the books I wrote several years ago continue to enrich my life.

In 1997, I started *NicheMarket.com*, a community-based website offering information, products and networking for visitors with interests ranging from health, MLM, Hip Hop, Black film, poetry, the Caribbean and more. The "niches" on the site reflected my own interests and passions, which were then built upon and added to as others shared their own. My passion for personal growth led me to launch *Walt's Friday Inspiration Life Rhyme weekly email*. What started as a single success-oriented gift to friends and family has grown into a worldwide phenomenon reaching tens of thousands weekly. Then came *PoetsNiche.com*, an online community suggested by followers of the Friday Inspirations. We helped members of the group publish their work and have given them an opportunity to turn their passion into profit through commissions from the sales of books. *HipHopEntrepreneur.com* took the success tools for the Hip Hop Entrepreneur online. Today, I continue to write more books and launch more sites.

Living the Passion Profit Life-style

It took me several years to do it, but I've created my own perfect Passion Profit life-style. I'm earning money in ways that allow me the most freedom. I create new products using my talent for writing and my skill at teaching to *share what I know so that others may grow*. The products are advertised in classified ads run in specific trade magazines, and by word of mouth, giving me the benefits of a 24-hour sales force. They are also marketed over the Internet, which provides me with a 24-hour storefront operation which doesn't require my presence. Customers order my products online or by mail, and a fulfillment company ships out the orders. I can run my business from a laptop on a beach, and don't ever need to be tied down to any particular place. I've turned my passion into profit, making money doing what I love, helping others to do the same, and, true to my personal vision of freedom, I finally have control of my days to go see movies in the middle of the afternoon!

_____

IDEAS: The Right Questions To Ask

- Why am I here on the planet?
- What roles have been consistent themes in my life?
- What's my purpose?
- What was I sent here to do?

Chapter 6: Passion
"Eureka!"

pas'sion (pash´en) n. **1.** boundless enthusiasm; **2.** the object of such enthusiasm

What is a Passion?

According to the dictionary, *passion* is both boundless enthusiasm, as well as the object of such enthusiasm. Anything can be a passion. Passions span a wide range of interests as well as every conceivable type of person, place, thing or idea from the mundane to the esoteric. From the shallow to the profound. From the ordinary to the rare. There are people who are passionate about certain types of food; music; a particular life-style; a period in history; fruits; pets; dancing; singing; humor; cars; religion; boats; fishing; celebrities, helping others, you name it! In fact, there are as many possible passions as there are words in the dictionary. So as I scan further down the page, I can't help thinking there are people who are passionate about pasta, pastels, pastiche, pastilles, pastry, pattycake, patchwork, paté, patellas and patents!

There are also many ways to express a passion. You may express your passion for words by writing novels or poetry. Your passion for certain ideas may lead you to be a teacher or consultant. You may express your sports passion by playing, coaching or simply being a fan. Your people passion may find you traveling, volunteering, or opening a restaurant. Your passion for certain times of day may inspire you to paint sunsets, climb mountains at noon, or rise before sunrise every day. You might live your passion for certain places doing just about anything as long as it's by the sea, or in Alaska, or in Zimbabwe. Your passion for certain objects might find you collecting clocks, fixing cars, or selling jewelry. Your passion for certain periods in history might make you a collector of antiques, or a tour guide for historical landmarks. Passion makes the world go 'round.

If you're not sure what your passion is, this chapter will help you discover it. If you already know your passion, then get ready to see it in a completely different way!

What's NOT a Passion

While the title of this book is *Turn Your Passion Into Profit*, a passion is not just any entrepreneurial business idea that makes you money. There's a big difference between turning your passion into profit, and simply turning a profit. Any business can make you money. And there's certainly nothing wrong with finding a lucrative business and using it to create the reality you dream of. In fact, if more people would simply do that, the level of happiness in the world would increase tenfold. However, a passion-centered business answers to a higher calling. Even profitable business vehicles will often fail to sustain your interest, and eventually fail simply because they are not meeting your needs. You may have some success, but may still end up looking for something else later. It's that something else that we seek in this chapter.

A passion is also NOT someone else's idea of what you should be doing. Even though you can and will use other people's observations about your talents and strengths in figuring out your passion, the final choice should be something that you decide is important to you. "My dad thinks I'd make a great doctor" is not a valid reason to pursue that profession. A passion cannot be an obligation or someone else's vision for you. It must be yours and yours alone.

A Job By Any Other Name

One of the most common tendencies people have when they start thinking about doing something they love is to start looking to standard professions. They hold out the hope that changing professions will offer them a means of escape from the monotony and lack of fulfillment of their present form of incarceration, er, I mean employment. Unaccustomed to thinking about making money in ways other than those with names like lawyer, social worker and accountant, they make choices within those boxes.

It's time, however, to think outside the box. As you search for your passion, don't make the mistake of simply trading one form of employment for another. While it's true that some jobs may be more satisfying than others, and that you can get degrees of fulfillment from various forms of employment, what we're doing here is something completely different. We're not looking for an existing box within which to fit ourselves. We're starting with our dreams, and making our own box from scratch.

Your Desire is Your Degree

To live the Passion Profit life-style, no resume is needed. There are no pre-qualifications, just your natural gifts, talents and interests. The lack of formal education or degrees will not exclude you as long as you have a willingness to learn. Your desire is the only degree you'll need.

In addition, there's no job description to adhere to because you are creating a life that allows you the freedom to follow your heart from one day to the next.

There was no name for what "Jane A" did before she started massaging horses for profit in Canada. There was no want ad for people who wanted to make teddy bears out of dog hair, and sell them for profit, as a lady I know does. As far as I know, there's also no job description for "passion prophet" my own pursuit of choice. If you're lucky, there'll be no box that currently exists that will adequately encompass all the things you want to include in your ideal day as a passion seeker. You're going to create one!

Your Passion As Therapy: How Your Passion Heals You

I've found that the desire to turn passion into profit is never simply about making money, but achieving something worthwhile. Invariably, the people who actually jump out in the direction of their dreams learn more about themselves, their strengths, their weaknesses and their motivations than they ever expected. Discovering, recognizing, indulging, respecting and yes, even profiting from your own passion has a therapeutic effect that can heal a lifetime of neglect, low self-esteem, feelings of inadequacy and a thousand other ailments of the spirit.

It's been said that you find your ministry in the place where you need the most healing. Your passion is your ministry. It is what you will share with the world to heal others, and will be a source of healing for you as well.

Your L.I.F.E. P.A.S.S.I.O.N.

The thing that is your passion and which will eventually find expression as your passion-centered business and provide you with the satisfaction you seek, will be what I call your LIFE PASSION. Life Passion doesn't mean you'll spend the rest of your life doing this. It simply means that it is *one* of many passions that has significance in your life. It is "A" life passion not "THE" life passion. L.I.F.E. P.A.S.S.I.O.N. is an acronym you can use to remind yourself of the qualities of your passion.

L-love	Your passion is something you love to do.
I-interest	Your passion is something that interests you.
F-fulfilling	Your passion gives you a sense of fulfillment.
E-empowering	Your passion usually empowers and energizes you.
P-personal	Your passion has personal significance to you and you alone.
A-abilities	Your passion capitalizes on your assets, attributes and abilities.
S-service	Your passion will usually provide a service or fulfill a need.
S-spiritual	Your passion and its pursuit represents an area of spiritual growth.
I-inspiring	Your passion is inspiring to you and therefore will inspire others too.
O-obvious	Your passion, once found, is usually something obvious to you.
N-natural	Your passion is often unstudied and comes naturally to you.

What If I Have Too Many Passions?

I often hear this question during my workshops and consulting sessions. Here is my best advice for those who are overwhelmed by the many things they like to do. In choosing a passion to pursue, it's not important what you choose, but simply *that* you choose. You are not obligated to stick with this decision for the rest of your life. Go forth boldly knowing that you can change your mind and your direction at any time. Following your passion is like taking a journey. Each decision is a station along the way. Each choice is a single step in a thousand mile journey. That's why it's vitally important to simply head in the direction of your passion, because the journey is the most important thing. Six months from now you may be an entirely different person with different needs, desires and motivations which require completely new passions to express. Don't be paralyzed by thinking that your decision is written in stone, or that you are excluding all the other things that interest you. You are simply taking the first step.

I also believe that the multiplicity of passions you enjoy might be linked in ways that no one has ever though of. I once coached a woman at a workshop who found a unique connection to her love of music and her desire to help others. She left with an idea to use music as therapy for healing.

However, if such connections exist among the many passions *you* enjoy, you may not recognize them unless you make that initial choice of one to explore. Again, think of it as a journey. As you move forward on your path, what you'll see ahead of you--the forks in the road, the intersections and the landscape--will all be constantly changing. Opportunities and new directions which exist further down the road won't be visible to you at the beginning. of your journey. You'll have to be travelling to recognize them. That's why it's important to be moving forward on this journey. So pick a passion. Any passion. It doesn't matter which. Keep your eyes open to how the landscape changes and look for ways to incorporate the many things you love to do.

What If I Don't Have a Passion?

The answer to this, another popular question, is EVERYONE has a passion. The fact that you exist is your guarantee that you do. Your passion is who you are. Descartes' "I think, therefore I am" loosely translated into "passionese" (the language of passion!) becomes: "I am, therefore I have a passion". Everything about you is an expression of your passion. Your love is the expression of your passion. Your enthusiasm is the expression of your passion. Your fear is an expression of your passion. Your desires are the expressions of your passion. Every thought you've ever had of new ways to express yourself is your passion speaking to you. Every feeling that has ever passed through you that beckons you to be, do and have more is an expression of your passion. Your passion is the reason and rhyme for why you are here. It reveals the underlying theme of your life and the role you have chosen to play in this drama called life. Your passion is what guides your decisions in all of your choices. Your passion communicates its existence through that still small voice within you when you choose to listen.

The opposite of a life lived with passion, is a life of desperation, misery, frustration and unhappiness. It is a life that appears confusing, chaotic and out of control. It is a life perfectly described by Henry David Thoreau, who said "the mass of men live lives of quiet desperation." So, if you're experiencing any of those feelings, it's a sure sign that you do in fact have a passion that is seeking attention and expression.

So, the question is not whether you have a passion, but how do you discover yours.

You can discover your passion if you know which questions to ask, and then answer them honestly. That is what the exercises in this chapter are designed to accomplish. Any one of the exercises may hold the key to helping you find your passion. Many people report experiencing breakthroughs simply by asking themselves the question in the first exercise: "What Do I Want"? For many people, that question alone is one they have never really answered. Allowing their own desires to be brought to the forefront of their minds, opens up limitless possibilities that, quite literally, changed their lives.

***

Finding Your Passion Part 1:
"What You Love"

Behind the veil of ordinary thoughts
greatness lies concealed
Within the whim of wishful words
truth waits to be revealed

Where the Passions Are

If your passion exists, the question then, is how do you discover what it is and where is it hiding? The answer is that your passion is already inside you in the form of the thoughts you think. It is hiding in the compliments you give to the people you admire. It is disguised as regret at not pursuing certain paths in life. It is concealed by the unspoken vision of who you wish to be. It is in the plots and personalities of your favorite films and books, as we often use novels and movies to experience worlds and ways of being that we are afraid to claim as our own. It may be found wrapped up inside the emotions evoked by the words of your favorite song. Yes, your thoughts are your passion in disguise. Those thoughts can take the form of:

• *Childhood memories* - What are those things that got you excited as a child? These can provide the most revealing clues into to what your passion is.

• *Personality* - Are you outgoing? Introverted? Warm? Methodical? Your character traits indicate inborn strengths that can influence where you look for fulfillment.

• *Habits* - Are you always daydreaming? Love to tap out rhythms with your pencil? Doodle when you're bored? Perhaps your inner inventor, musician and artist are trying to get your attention.

• *Dreams* - Interpreted correctly, these can be an open window into the subconscious workings of your mind.

• *Style* - What you think is stylish, how you dress and how you decorate your apartment may say more about what you really value than you realize.

• *Hobbies & interests* - Most hobbies are the societally accepted ways to express that creative side that is your true passion.

• *Pet peeves* - What are the things about people's behavior, the system or the world that annoy or upset you? Your annoyance may be an indication of something you passionately want to change.

• *Jobs* - We often take jobs that are closely related to what our real passions are.

• *Ideas* - Whatever became of that idea you had for a new way to clean toilets? Value your ideas. They are the often overlooked bridges between passion and profit.

Your mission, therefore, is to lay all the thoughts, dreams, knowledge, hobbies, peeves and ideas out in plain sight. And, like an archeologist unearthing an ancient treasure, brush away the dust and hardened ways of thinking to reveal the grandeur beneath. Or, like a sculptor creating a priceless work of art, simply chip away the outer until you reveal the grand vision that lies within.

The Discovery Exercises

The Discovery Exercises which follow will help you to stir up the thoughts under which your passion may be hiding. These exercises contain the questions we need to encourage our children, family, students, parents, customers and clients to ask and answer on a regular basis. They develop the thinking that empowers people to follow their own dreams rather than others' expectations of them. They need to be explored if you are ever to break free from the lies you may be living. When answering, include anything and everything that comes to mind. Remember, no one is watching or judging you. Use additional paper as needed, and use your responses as content for your daily journal. The twelve exercises are:

1. What Do I Want?
2. My Ideal Day
3. Me, at eight
4. Me, at Eighty
5. In The News
6. If I Ruled The World
7. Enter The Twilight Zone
8. A Few Of My Favorite Things
9. What Others Say About Me
10. My Must-Join Conversation
11. My Three Wishes
12. If I Could Not Fail, I Would...

Exercise 1. What Do I Want to Happen Next in My Life?

Assignment: Describe in detail what you want to happen next in your life?
1. First, sit comfortably in front of someone. If you can't rustle up someone whom you trust, then sit in front of a full length mirror. (Yes, do it even if you feel silly!)
2. Have your partner ask you: "What Do You Want?"
3. Quickly reply with the first thing that comes to mind. Then have them ask you the same question again, and again. Do not think about your answers. Be completely honest with yourself. Do this for at least 10 minutes.

As a follow-up to this exercise, record every thought or personal discovery that comes to you, including memories, images of people, and ideas. They may prove important later.

_____

_____

_____

_____

_____

_____

_____

_____

Exercise 2. My Ideal Day
Assignment: Describe your ideal day.

What would you do if you had all the money you needed, and didn't have to work? If you had unlimited time and resources, what would you choose to do? In describing your ideal day consider the following: Where do you live? When do you rise? Do you wake early and meditate? Or, do you rise at noon and watch soap operas? What do you spend each hour doing? Describe the day's activities. Describe what you do, and with whom. How do you make your fortune? Does it come to you in a single large check, or in thousands of individual checks for your product? Whom do you work with? Is your day filled with leisure activities? Is it hectic or relaxed? How does your day end? How do you feel at the end of the day?

Think big! Don't limit yourself to known realities. Invariably, when I ask people to do this exercise, someone will answer that given all the money in the world, they would spend their days sleeping, traveling, watching television, listening to music or making love. All enjoyable pursuits, I agree, but, even for the most overworked among us, there are only so many hours you can sleep, watch television, fish, eat, or even make love before you decide to include some other activities in your day. So look beyond the immediate gratification that's foremost on your mind at the moment and think more long-term.

eg. *"In my ideal day, I get up in the morning before sunrise. I step out into the yard of my estate and breathe in the fresh morning air. I live in the mountains or close to natural surroundings like a lake or woods. There are fruit trees and grass which I pass during my stroll around the grounds and through the neighborhood. I sit on a rock and meditate by a stream as I clear my mind and think about all the things I have accomplished and all the good fortune which came my way in order for me to be at this place in my life.*

My overall feeling is one of serenity. I am enjoying being alive here and now. Everything is as it should be. There is nothing in the future that owns me. There is only this present moment, and I am happy to be alive and happy to be making a difference in the lives of others.

My company is being run by competent individuals whose experience has enabled it to grow to a multimillion dollar enterprise. My campaign to turn my passion into profit was very successful. Millions around the world are benefiting and I earn millions each month.

Exercise 3. Me, at Eight

Assignment: What things were you passionate about as a child?

Whether you were 8 months or 8 years old, what can you remember getting so excited about that you had to share it with someone? Was it music? Was it animals?

_____
_____
_____
_____
_____
_____
_____

Exercise 4. Me, at Eighty

Assignment: Describe your life from the perspective of yourself at eighty.

It's your eightieth birthday. You are at a "middle of your life celebration". Think about what you have accomplished from eight to eighty. What have been your roles? Describe yourself as a mother, father, son, daughter, teacher, lover, friend, boss, entrepreneur and in as many roles as you've had during your ideal life. How have you affected others' lives? What do your friends and family think and say about you in each of these roles? If you're already 80, think about what you wish your life to be like in the *next* 80 years!

_____
_____
_____
_____
_____
_____
_____

Exercise 5. In The News!

Assignment: Write a newspaper article about you and your passion.

Imagine you are a reporter who has been given the task of writing a front page or cover story article about you and your passion. The article will reveal to the world all of your accomplishments and successes as if they were real. Include the who, what, when, where, why, how and how much of your passion and accomplishments. (See the sample press release in chapter 10) Sample headline: *Mary Makes it Big Turning Passion Into Profit!*

*HEADLINE:*_____

*ARTICLE:*_____
_____
_____
_____
_____
_____
_____

Exercise 6. If I Ruled The World
Assignment: What would you do if you ruled the world?

Imagine that you have been elected ruler of the world or mayor of your town. You have been given the power to enact change simply by decree. Who would you help? What wrongs would you right? What little or big thing has always bothered you about the way things are? Identify the 3 to 5 groups you would help first, what they need, and what solution you would propose. They can be ethnic groups, citizens of a particular country, smokers, actors, etc. These will be the "chosen people" you'll need for a future exercise. eg. *"If I ruled the world, I would stop people from spitting in public. If I ruled the world, I would make it easier for people to purchase homes without having to go through all the hassles they do now. If I ruled the world, I would require people to take courses on parenting ..."*

_____
_____
_____
_____
_____
_____
_____

Exercise 7. Enter The Twilight Zone
Assignment: What 3 to 5 new identities you would take on if you could?

If you're a fan of the *Twilight Zone* television series you'll remember that a recurring theme involved characters waking to find themselves living in different realities. Imagine for a minute that when you wake up tomorrow, you'll be living a different life. However, it will be a life of your own choosing. What person, real or fictional, what profession, life-style, country, time period, or age would you choose? Choose 3 to 5 new identities.

_____
_____
_____
_____
_____

Exercise 8. These Are A Few Of My Favorite Things
Assignment: What do you like?

Like the character Maria Von Trapp sang in *The Sound Of Music*, sometimes it helps to think about the things that make you smile. Anything goes. List people, places, things, thoughts, words, deeds, ideas, emotions, books, movies, etc, that you enjoy.

_____
_____
_____
_____
_____
_____
_____

Exercise 9. What Others Say

Assignment: Make a list of the talents, skills or personality traits people have noticed that you possess.

Sometimes your talents and skills are more obvious to others than they are to you. What things about you have people noticed in their compliments and comments?

_____

_____

_____

_____

_____

_____

Exercise 10. What's Your Must-Join Conversation?

Assignment: In what types of conversations are you compelled to participate?

Imagine you're sitting at a bus station, or airport waiting for the next bus or flight out. A group of people is excitedly engaged in a conversation a few feet away. You listen in and realize that they're talking about the one subject that really interests you. What are they talking about that has you eager to join in? What subject is it that you would feel you just HAD TO join in and give your opinion, observations or expertise. (Of course, if you're one of those people who just likes to jump in to anyone's conversation, then this exercise may simply reveal that you're just plain nosy!)

_____

_____

_____

_____

_____

_____

_____

_____

_____

_____

Exercise 11. My Three Wishes

A genie is waiting to grant you three wishes. What will you wish for?

1._____

2._____

3._____

Exercise 12. What Would I Attempt If I Knew I Would Not Fail?

Assignment: *What would you attempt if you knew you would not fail?*

Fear of failure is what stops many of us from attempting the things that would bring us fulfillment. What thing would you dare to do if you knew you could not fail?

_____

_____

_____

_____

_____

_____

_____

What bold thing would I do today
if I knew I could not fail?
If it mattered not what people thought
would I let my heart prevail?

What secret wish would I act upon
if success were guaranteed?
Which actions would I then give life
with all mental shackles freed?

Would I speak my mind and then some
say the words I should have said
become the person I've always wanted
but acted out fears instead?

If my days were caught on camera
for the world to watch and view
would my performance inspire others
who wish that they could too?

Well I'll never know from wishing
for the thought alone won't do
The life I crave is brought to bear
by the things I choose to do

Like supporting cast without lead actor
your dreams await director's cue
The results you seek wait in the wings
but won't ACT until you do!

Lights, Camera, Action
Walt's Life Rhyme #97

What did these exercises help you to discover about yourself? Did you recall any memories or interests you had long forgotten? Which exercise was most significant for you? Why? In Part 2, you'll discover the skills you have acquired that can add another dimension to these interests and bring your passions to life!

The Cycle of Success Step 2:

Identify your passion

Your next step in turning your passion into profit is to identify your passion.

My Passion is:

Finding Your Passion Part 2
"Mining Your Inner Gold"

Second Law of Passion Dynamics:

You are never given a passion without also having the talents, abilities and people in your life to turn it into profit if you desire.

As a result of the previous exercises, you've hopefully discovered a connection between what you're *here* to do, and what you *love* to do. *The Second Law of Passion Dynamics* goes further and provides the link between what you *love* to do and what you've *learned* to do Your talents, skills and training are a gold-mine of potential waiting for you to tap into. Remember,

> *ANYTHING that you can do,*
> *can be a source of wealth for you.*
> *EVERYTHING you choose to be,*
> *can be what others pay to see*
> *ALL the many things you know,*
> *can cause the streams of cash to flow*
> *ANY person that you meet*
> *can help bring fortune to your feet*

The following exercise will help you to recognize or remember the many resources (skills, knowledge, personality and people) you have access to and that are at your disposal to bring your passion to life.

Skills

Complete a sentence about your abilities in each category.

[ ] SPEAKING SKILLS *eg. I have a nice speaking voice; I can speak in a professional and authoritative manner; I can speak without fear in impromptu settings.*

_____

[ ] WRITING SKILLS *eg. I can write clearly and effectively.*

_____

[ ] COMMUNICATION SKILLS *eg. I get my ideas across. I can make women/ men feel special; I can communicate well in business situations;*

_____

[ ] MANAGEMENT SKILLS   *eg. I can manage sales teams.*

_____

[ ] MOTIVATIONAL SKILLS   *eg. I inspire and bring out the best in others.*

_____

[ ] USE/OPERATION SKILLS *eg. I can use and operate computers; I can drive a car; use a typewriter, a 35mm camera, a sanding machine*

_____

[ ] CREATIVE SKILLS *eg. I can draw, paint, sculpt and cook.*

_____

[ ] SPORTS SKILLS *I can play table tennis; I can play soccer.*

_____

[ ] PROGRAMMING SKILLS *eg. I can write programs; I can design websites.*

_____

[ ] REPAIRING SKILLS *eg.I can repair mechanical objects.*

_____

[ ] INFORMATION GATHERING SKILLS *eg. I research information.*

_____

☐ ORGANIZATIONAL SKILLS *eg. I can create order, organize an office.*

_____

☐ LISTENING SKILLS *eg. I can stay focused on what others are saying.*

_____

☐ TEACHING SKILLS *eg. I can teach others to drive or use the Internet.*

_____

☐ COACHING SKILLS *eg. I can coach others in basketball, football.*

_____

☐ ANALYTICAL/DECISION MAKING SKILLS *eg. I assess situations and act quickly and appropriately.*

_____

☐ LOGIC SKILLS *eg. I apply logic to find solutions.*

_____

☐ DIET SKILLS *eg. I can stick to diets. I can inspire others to change their diet.*

_____

☐ HUMAN RELATIONS *eg. I am sensitive to others; I can build rapport with people quickly; I can make love creatively; I am considerate and can make others feel special; I can inspire others with my words; I can give others hope; I can remember peoples' names the first time I meet them; I can make people laugh.*

_____

☐ MACHINES *eg. I can follow technical directions to fix things.*

_____

☐ COMPUTERS/SOFTWARE *eg. I am proficient in popular software.*

_____

What other skills do you have?

_____
_____
_____

Personality Traits

Another area of wealth for you are those personality traits that you know to be true about yourself, and/or that others have commented on. *eg. "I am charming, witty, outgoing and patient."* *"People tell me I am a good listener, good with kids etc."* I know that I am: People tell me I am:

_____   _____
_____   _____
_____   _____
_____   _____

Specialized Knowledge

Specialized knowledge are the bits of information, facts, aptitudes, trivia and book smarts that you acquired along the way. Don't worry if some of them overlap with what you wrote in the skills section. If they do, simply list them again. To get your mind working in the right direction, start your sentences with any or all of the following: "I have knowledge of...", "I know...", or "I studied...", "I once took a course in...", "I went to school for...", "I was taught, or I taught myself to...", or "I learned how to...", or "I have observed that ..."

I know/studied/learned:

_____   _____
_____   _____
_____   _____
_____   _____
_____   _____

Relationships: *Who Do You Know?*

The people you know may play a role in turning your passion into profit. They may possess skills, talents and personality traits themselves which may complement your own. Who do you know who has impressed you with their accomplishments, skills, strengths and even their weaknesses? Who are the people you would want on your company's Board of Directors? Who are the people who have done what you intend to do? Who would you want with you for their ingenuity, outlook or even their humor, if you were trapped in an elevator, stranded on a deserted island or in a financial bind?

Name of Person   Strengths   Weaknesses

_____   _____   _____
_____   _____   _____
_____   _____   _____
_____   _____   _____
_____   _____   _____

The Cycle of Success

Step 3: Identify your skills

My Skills, Talents and Contacts:

Use the memory joggers on the previous pages and list your skills, talents, personality traits, education and contacts.

_____

_____

_____

_____

_____

_____

MAIN POINTS OF CHAPTER 6
"Passion"

• Your Passion is that expression of you that gives your life meaning. Everyone has a passion. A passion can be an activity you enjoy, a place you like to be, an idea or just about anything.

• Finding and following your passion can actually be a form of therapy for you. Once you find it, you may be surprised to find that it may not be something that you spend the rest of your life doing. In fact, it may be just one of many things that you do throughout your life as you grow emotionally and spiritually. Let your passion heal you.

• The thing that is your passion and which will eventually find expression as your passion-centered business and provide you with the satisfaction you seek, will be what I call your LIFE PASSION. Life Passion doesn't mean that this is what you'll spend the rest of your life doing. It simply means that it is *one* of many passions that has significance in your life.

• The Discovery Exercises can help you uncover your life passion.

• According to the Second Law of Passion Dynamics, you are never given a passion without also being given the skills, talents, training or relationships you need to transform it into value. Knowing the skills, talents, training, and relationships you have at your disposal can open you up to a wide range of ways to turn your passion into profit.

FOLLOW-UP FILE FOR CHAPTER 6
"Passion"

INSPIRATION: Passion Seeker Profiles

"Their Passion-Fruit Passion"

Tom First and Tom Scott met in college and found that they shared a similar passion for a particular place: Nantucket Island. Both loved the island and wanted simply to maintain a life-style there. Both moved there after graduation and ended up in businesses which catered to the island's marine and boating industry. They created a small business called Allserve that sold groceries and convenience services to the boats that visited the harbor in Nantucket.

One night, inspired by a beverage he had tasted during a vacation in Europe, Tom First created his own version using a blender, some fruit and juice products. The two partners were then inspired to bottle and sell the juice to their Allserve customers. This product concept is what ultimately became the Nantucket Nectars enterprise which even spawned a new market called "New Age Beverages." Within six years, Nantucket Nectars products were carried in retail outlets in over 30 states, and reached revenues of over $20 Million dollars.

And while the headquarters of Nantucket Nectars' new company is now in Boston, Massachusetts, it was by following their island passion that led them to their "passion fruit passion" and entrepreneurial success.

IDEAS: The Right Questions To Ask
• What specific things do I enjoy doing?
• Which of my passions do I feel I will express in my lifetime?
• What skills do I believe I may need to turn my passion into profit?
• What knowledge, skills and talents do I possess that are valuable?
• Which skills might I need to find in others to turn my passion into profit?
• Who can I surround myself with who thinks like I do?
• Who do I know who is turning their passion into profit?
• What specific things did I do today to bring me closer to living my ideal day?

Chapter 7: Product (or Service)
"In search of great ideas!"

The Third Law of Passion Dynamics:

"For every creation, there exists an equal desire for that creation. Anything that has been created from your passionate interest and attention contains inherent value which others will recognize and pay to have in their own lives."

In Search of Great Ideas

Now that you've identified your purpose, your passion, and your proficiency, your next step is to use them all to create a product or service that people will pay for.

Throughout history, men and women have profited from great inventions, business ideas, fads, and services the inspiration for which seem to be completely random. While some of the best ideas are, in fact, those that creep up on us in that inspired "Aha!" moment, I believe you can, in fact, go in search of great ideas!

Your success in this next phase of the cycle of success is based on the *Third Law of Passion Dynamics,* which states that what has value for you automatically has value for others too. The trick, therefore, is to determine the unique value that your passion has in your own life and then marry that with the value people are searching for in theirs! Let's find that hidden value!

Value Everywhere

The real secret to turning your passion into profit cannot be captured in a box, a kit or a 3-ring binder for business operations. Success requires that you think differently and become obsessive about seeing value in everything.

I once heard of a woman who, when asked what she loved to do, said she loved to hug people. So passionate was she about hugging people and making them feel welcomed, that she became the official "greeter" for her church. Every Sunday morning, people would line up before each service just to get one of her hugs. Her energy was a real boost to people who could feel the genuine love and positive energy in her embrace. Could she have parlayed that volunteer position and passion into profit? Certainly!

At a party I once attended, a friend of mine held a small group of us spellbound as he explained the finer points of winning at casino gambling. We discovered that it wasn't just about putting money on the table and hoping for the best. As he explained it, there was a flow and a rhythm to the cards and to other people's actions that made it all seem more exciting than any of us had ever imagined. Could my friend turn this knowledge and passion into additional business profit? Undoubtedly!

I could go on, but, as we discovered in the previous phase of the cycle of success, many of us have talents, skills, perspectives, and ways of being that are what a mentor of mine calls under-producing assets.

The process for converting those assets into winning ideas by matching their value with what the world wants involves three important steps.

1. Listening to what people want
2. Asking the right questions, and
3. Awaiting the Divine Idea.

> No one has a monopoly in the free market of ideas.

Listening to What People Want

Essentially people want things and experiences. They want things and experiences that help them to achieve positive feelings and avoid negative ones.

To help them create these feelings, your passion-centered business will be selling things in the following clearly formats: an email, a book, a compact disk, videotape, DVD or other sound/image transmission medium, an invention, food, art or some artistic or funtional creation. If your passion-centered business is marketing a service, you will be providing: consulting, coaching, lecture, therapy, a performance or access.

The Value Tree illustrates that any product or service you sell starts as a unique combination of your creativity and expertise. It then becomes marketable in the forms indicated (cd, book, etc.). These products and services fit into the Value Categories of Functionality, Entertainment, Comfort, Education, Access, Guidance, Survival, Kinship | Status and Self-Fulfillment.

THE VALUE TREE

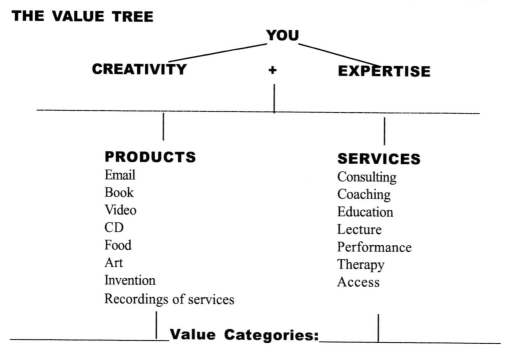

Value Categories:

**Functionality | Entertainment | Comfort | Education | Access
Guidance | Survival | Kinship | Status | Self-Fulfillment**

People want:

affection, beauty, comfort, companionship, convenience, ego satisfaction, enjoyment, entertainment, friends, good health, happiness, knowledge, love, money, peace of mind, pleasure, praise, recognition, security, self-actualization, self-confidence, self-esteem, self-improvement and spiritual well-being.

People also want to:

accomplish, achieve, acquire possessions, be accepted, be appreciated, be attractive, be fashionable, be liked, be successful, belong, enjoy a good standard of living, express their creativity, express their individuality, get ahead, have fun, laugh, play, relax, save money, save time, and have sex.

People also want to avoid:

confusion, danger, deprivation, embarrassment, failure, fear, grief, hunger, hurt, illness, loss, pain, sorrow, tension, thirst and worry.

***

That's what people want. And they'll buy a wide range of things and experiences in order to get it. Let's now discuss what people will actually pay for.

Asking the Right Questions

Great ideas come in answer to great questions. The key is knowing which questions to ask. Here are 3 types of questions and ways of asking them that you can use to turn your passion into profit.

A. Magic Questions
B. Passion Party Brainstorming Questions
C. Questions to the Universe

A. The Magic Questions

Asking the Magic Questions about your passion can help you to see the value it can offer to others. The Magic Questions are hidden within the rhymes of *Why People Pay*. Each verse is followed by an interpretation with the specific magic questions.

> *People pay to have possessions.*
> *People pay to reach perfection.*

Can I create a product that captures the essence of my passion that people will want to buy? Can my passion be collected? Is my passion an animal or thing that others want to own? Is there a phrase I can coin to capture my passion and which I could put on a T-shirt, coffee mug, etc.?

Can I help others become better at my passion? Is it a sport, or other activity that requires practice to perfect? Can I offer the guidance or the setting for this practice?

> *People pay for times of pleasure.*
> *People pay to relieve pressure.*

Can my passion be offered to provide physical, or emotional pleasure?
Can my passion relieve stress in any way?

> *People pay for what you know.*
> *People pay to see a show.*

Is there information that people want to know about my passion? Can I write a book, produce a video, audio cassette, website, lecture, or workshop to share what I know about my passion?

Is my passion something that can be performed or recorded in some way to provide people with entertainment? Is there a feature movie, situation comedy, talk show or game show idea hiding within my passion?

> *People pay to save the past.*
> *People pay to have things last.*

Is my passion something with ties to the past? Does my passion capture or represent a bygone age? Is my passion something for collectors of memorabilia?

Does my passion involve preserving or maintaining things that others value?

People pay to make things run.
People pay to get things done.

Does my passion involve fixing or repairing things that others value?
Can my passion help people accomplish things?

People pay to be led.
People pay to be fed.

Can my passion guide, teach or direct others to value that they desire?
Is my passion a food that can be sold? Can I charge them for this?

People pay to treat their teams.
People pay to live their dreams

Is there an organization or corporation which might be interested in me, what I know or what I can do? Can my product or service be a gift or program they can provide to their members or employees? Can I charge them for this?
Can my passion fulfill a fantasy? Can I create a unique experience for others?

People pay to see.
People pay to be.

Is my passion fun to look at? Can I charge admission for the chance to look?
Can my passion allow people to experience being alive in a unique way?

People pay to live with ease.
People pay to cure disease.

Does my passion make life more convenient? Can I charge for this luxury?
Does my passion have health properties? Can my passion heal others?

People pay for things embellished.
People pay for things they relish.

Can I create a character or logo that embodies my passion and which I can put on everything from keychains to lunch boxes?
Is my passion simply something that people have always liked? Is it a new or old fad that generates desire on its own?

B. The Passion Party Brainstorming Session

One of the best ways of coming up with a winning idea is to have a Passion Party! Unlike the informal "pity parties" that many of us engage in with our friends in which we lament our lot in life, a passion party is a formal, goal oriented event. The goal is to help each participant discover his/her passion and to come up with ideas on how to turn it into profit. At the end of the Passion Party, each person should come away with a plan they can use to take the first or several steps towards turning passion into profit.

Passion Party Brainstorming sessions can be conducted alone, but they're more effective when two or more like-minded, supportive people are involved in the process. Start by posing a clearly worded and framed question or challenge. Then simply engage in free-association to come up with as many answers and solutions as possible.

In a Passion Party brainstorming session, the quality of the answers and solutions is of less importance than the quantity. The goal is to come up with as many ideas as you can, and then sift through them later. You can use any of the Magic Questions as the idea generator for your Passion Party, or develop your own. One of my favorites is: *What Specific Things Can I Create or Do To Make Money Doing What I Love?*

C. The Overnight Question

The third type of question is the type you ask to God. The Universe operates on very simple principles. One of the simplest was explained over 2000 years ago by a wise teacher who said "Ask, and it shall be given unto you." The process works this way: Simply pose the question to yourself before you go to sleep, and during the night, your subconscious mind will set about working out the solution. Ask for clarity, understanding, guidance, or simply "What should I do about _____?" It's important to ask the right question. If you're lucky and you've had practice listening to the answers from the universe, you may find that sometime during the night, or by the next morning, you'll feel the excitement of an idea just bursting to be set free. Sometimes, you may need to do this several times over the course of days or weeks. In either case, posing questions in this way has given the world some of its greatest inventions and breakthroughs. (Remember to sleep with a pen and paper close by.)

How The Ideas Come To You
The Subconscious Mind: Your Tool for Exploration

Whether in a brainstorming session or overnight, you have access to one of the greatest computers known to man: your own subconscious mind. Your mind is like a great computer that pulls together disparate pieces of a vast puzzle using influences from the past, the present and the future constructed in ways that often defy logic. It makes connections and associations that no man-made computer has ever been able to match. In your mind, a smell can ignite a childhood memory, which can bring to mind a person, or a word spoken to you years before, which has meaning only for you, and which then connects you to activities and ideas that may be the perfect expression of your passion.

As a computer, your subconscious mind taps into its own storage areas of

Current Events
Observations
Memories
Preferences
Understanding
Talents
Experience
Relationships

and combines them in ways to come up with winning idea that no other person on the planet can predict, or duplicate. Once you pose your question to the Universe, the ideas will surely come. The question is not whether you'll receive them, but will you be able to hear them?

Listening for Messages

Maybe it's just me, but I believe that there are no accidents, that EVERY event, from a headline on a newspaper being read by someone in front of me, to the words I hear in a passing conversation, to the page my book falls open to provides a message for me to use. It's like the universe is dropping clues on my path to let me know I'm headin in the right direction. I receive validation of ideas and encouragement of my goals from the strangest places. Sometimes even the typographical errors I in my letters and books are giving me clues! Was that really a wrong number? Or maybe it was a chance to learn some valuable information or make a friend I just might need? Hmmm. So when I see or hear echoes of my life on the news, on the radio, or in a song, I know that it's the universe telling me I'm on the right track!

> coincidence? a dejavu?
> perhaps that's how
> it speaks to you
> slip of the tongue? a TV ad?
> could be advice
> you'll wish you had
> a stranger's words? lyrics in song?
> might be a hint
> of right and wrong
> a nagging hunch? a random thought?
> a signal sent
> a lesson taught
> a misdialed call? perhaps more true:
> "Universe calling"
> and it's for you!   So pay attention

How the Universe Speaks to You
Walt's Life Rhyme #91

The Zone

Athletes often speak about being "in the zone"--it's a state of peak performance and timelessness where thoughts and actions seem to originate from somewhere else other than within them. Athletes in the zone speak of having limitless energy, of always making the right decisions, and executing them flawlessly.

The Zone is not the exclusive hangout of athletes. Many of us find ourselves there while engaged in activities like writing, speaking or painting. Sometimes we enter the Zone during the calm of meditation, or while engaged in simple activities like taking care of children, plants or pets. People have described the zone as a feeling of being energized and inspired where they feel someone or something else is in control doing the painting, or speaking and that they themselves are simply a channel through which the activity is taking place. I believe that everyone, at some point in their lives, has experienced a degree of being in "the zone." You can find great ideas for products while there.

The Right Frequency

It's been shown that at any given moment in time, great inventions and scientific breakthroughs are resulting from similar experiments occurring among different groups in different countries. These groups are acting independently with no knowledge of each other's activities. This is possible because the ideas these scientists are working on are universal truths on which no one individual or group can have a monopoly. Think of all ideas, great and small, as floating around like radio waves in the atmosphere just waiting for us, for anyone, to tune in to the right frequency to access them.

Coming up with ideas is a process of "tuning in" rather than "venturing forth" in search of them. It is an act of receiving, not of construction. Ideas are uncovered not made. Do not struggle to create something that doesn't exist, but allow yourself to be the channel for something that already exists to make itself known. And they'll make themselves known through "the still small voice within." That is, your intuition.

Miracle Moments, Inspired Thoughts and Divine Ideas

The voice of intuition speaks to you during what I call "the miracle moment." The miracle moment of consciousness sets the stage and invites the intuitive or inspired thought which, if followed, leads you to the divine idea, which, if nurtured, grows into an act of creation which fulfills the universe's desire for self-expression.

The miracle moment is the perfect setting to hear your uniquely inspired thought. Miracle moments can occur at anytime. However, they seem to favor certain times of calm or unconscious focus in our lives; times in which our minds are clear and free of self-conscious thoughts. They visit us in the morning moments before the din of rush hour activity, or in that minute of eternity that you experience during meditation. They visit us when we are engaged in repetitive activities in which our minds are only partially involved. They can be encouraged by indulgence in activities and states of mind and body that allow us to enter The Zone. Driving a familiar route, playing games, showering, running, combing your hair or even dancing, set the stage for miracle moments.

An inspired thought is a whisper in that moment that passes as quickly as it comes. It is a thought in your mind that is connected to the universe by that slight twinge in your heart. It is an intention that is relevant only in the moment that it is felt, but dissolves into insignificance if not written down or acted upon right away. It's the eureka moment of a vision in your mind's eye in which you see with absolute clarity the connection between it and the realization and successful accomplishment of a long desired goal, right before the cloud of doubt obscures it from view. It's the fleeting feeling of excitement that lights a fire in your heart before the cold rain of reason dampens it. It's the "If-I-wasn't-watching-TV-right-this-second-I-would" idea that grabs your attention but is then lost in the instant between the end of one commercial and the beginning of another. If you followed that inspired thought to its destination, you might discover the divine idea.

Divine ideas are the children of a moment created by the marriage of time and space. Since they have been conceived in a place other than your own mind, they can transcend your state of awareness, surpass your level of education, bypass your blocks and beliefs, ignore your history and personal experience, and appear at your door, nonetheless to be raised by you. Whom they choose as parents is independent of status. Divine ideas are born to prince and pauper alike. You don't have to be wealthy, or even consider yourself successful to have an idea of value to share. William, a good friend and musician, producer, composer with an impressive list of credits, felt unworthy of writing a book about his experiences, knowledge and accomplishments, because, as he put it, he hadn't really "made it" (i.e. become successful) yet. Rest assured that wherever you are in your journey, the knowledge you've gained is of infinite value to someone just a few yards behind you who has not yet walked your path. And even those ahead of you can find value in your unique interpretation of the scenery they may have missed on their own journey.

Divine ideas defy rational explanation, though many of us instantly recognize them. They are often ignored though they are the most valuable gifts we will ever receive. They are ageless even though they have existed for all time. They are the old ways and methods resurrected to greatness by unclouded eyes. They are worn, useless objects given new-found brilliance through a change in disguise. They are the answers to old questions offered without the weight of old beliefs in tow. And finally, they are the sum of your talents, multiplied by your passion, divided by intentions of service and squared by the power of love. So don't take them for granted, for like our own precious children, divine ideas have the promise of hope within them and are gifts from above.

And with that, all that's left to do is to remain open to the arrival of the idea that will light the path for your next step. Your idea is searching for you and seeks expression in the world of things, if only you would listen.

(Yeah, Walt. Whatever.)

Ok. For those of you who would like something a little less philosophical to wrap your mind around, here's an easily recognizable part of the process of coming up with ideas that I call "The Switch."

The Switch

The "switch" has two interpretations. You can think of it acting just like the switch that controls a the flow of electricity to a light bulb. It may also be conceived of as the mental switch in perception that allows you to see things in a slightly different way. In either case, it can provide the key to coming up with the perfect product or service upon which to base your passion-centered business.

The switch can be a question that someone asks like "how much would you charge me to _____?" It might be an observation by others who notice that you have talent in a particular area. It might be an unexpected payment of money by someone you've helped in some way. It might be an expression of frustration by someone, which if heard and responded to correctly, might result in an invention or service as the solution.

Whatever the actual trigger, the switch represents a pivotal moment in awareness in which something old becomes new, something hidden is uncovered, or something long obvious is finally seen. It is that "eureka" moment which is usually followed by the idea which elicits statements to the effect of "It was there all along!" or "Why didn't someone think of that before?" Remember too that such ideas favor the open mind.

The process of coming up with a winning idea cannot be hurried. It's a process, however, that can be helped along by your ability to see things differently. So, to get your mind in the habit of seeing things differently, use the Passion-Finder Chart.

THE "PASSION FINDER" CHART™

The Passion Finder Chart takes what you've discovered about yourself so far and gives you action words, customer needs, concepts, product ideas and target audiences to consider when coming up with your product or service.

PASSION FINDER CHART

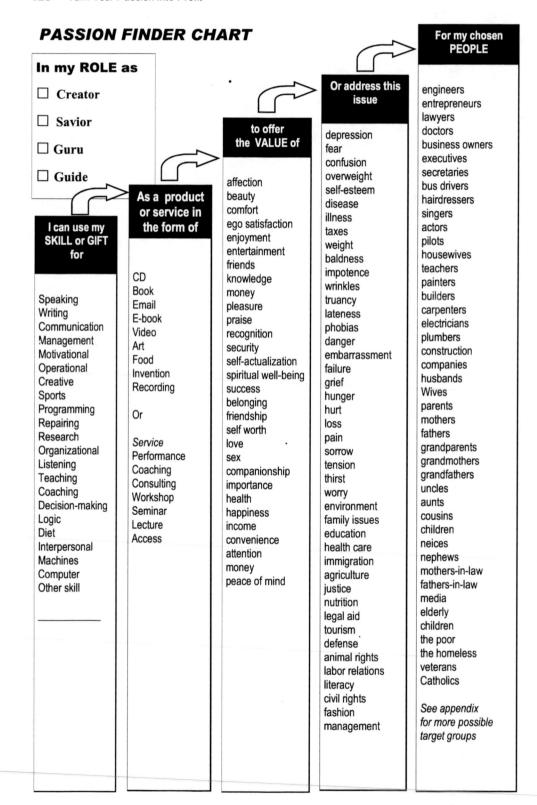

In my ROLE as

☐ Creator

☐ Savior

☐ Guru

☐ Guide

I can use my SKILL or GIFT for

Speaking
Writing
Communication
Management
Motivational
Operational
Creative
Sports
Programming
Repairing
Research
Organizational
Listening
Teaching
Coaching
Decision-making
Logic
Diet
Interpersonal
Machines
Computer
Other skill

_____

As a product or service in the form of

CD
Book
Email
E-book
Video
Art
Food
Invention
Recording

Or

Service
Performance
Coaching
Consulting
Workshop
Seminar
Lecture
Access

to offer the VALUE of

affection
beauty
comfort
ego satisfaction
enjoyment
entertainment
friends
knowledge
money
pleasure
praise
recognition
security
self-actualization
spiritual well-being
success
belonging
friendship
self worth
love
sex
companionship
importance
health
happiness
income
convenience
attention
money
peace of mind

Or address this issue

depression
fear
confusion
overweight
self-esteem
disease
illness
taxes
weight
baldness
impotence
wrinkles
truancy
lateness
phobias
danger
embarrassment
failure
grief
hunger
hurt
loss
pain
sorrow
tension
thirst
worry
environment
family issues
education
health care
immigration
agriculture
justice
nutrition
legal aid
tourism
defense
animal rights
labor relations
literacy
civil rights
fashion
management

For my chosen PEOPLE

engineers
entrepreneurs
lawyers
doctors
business owners
executives
secretaries
bus drivers
hairdressers
singers
actors
pilots
housewives
teachers
painters
builders
carpenters
electricians
plumbers
construction
companies
husbands
Wives
parents
mothers
fathers
grandparents
grandmothers
grandfathers
uncles
aunts
cousins
children
neices
nephews
mothers-in-law
fathers-in-law
media
elderly
children
the poor
the homeless
veterans
Catholics

See appendix for more possible target groups

Top 10 Tips for Finding Your Passion Idea

1. Don't Limit Yourself to Just One For All Time. Keep your mind open to new ideas.
  The passion you decide to pursue may be one of many that you indulge throughout your lifetime. Don't feel that any decision you make today is written in stone, or that you are obligated to pursue this single passion for the rest of your life.

2. Use Currently-held Jobs As Clues
  Did you take the job at the record store as a way to be close to the music industry? Is your current gig as host or maitre d' hinting at your own restaurant passion?

3. Beware the Aptitude Trap
  I was good in Math and Science, so off I went in the direction of my aptitudes. I ended up doing what I was trained to do, but which provided me no enjoyment. Pursue your passion, not just your proficiency.

4. Create Your Own
  There's greater personal fulfillment and profit in being at the top of the creative totem pole. Create your own product. It's easier than you think. Experts say you have to be just 10% different from the competition to be perceived as radically innovative. Many seemingly new products are simply the clever repackaging of things that already exist.

5. Beware the Gold Rush
  Beware the "lemming effect" of rushing headlong off the side of the cliff simply because everyone else is doing it. There are many new "flavor of the month" concepts and products that may be lucrative, but not viable as a passion-centered business.

6. Look Closely At Things You're Already Doing
  Many of the things you're already doing for free can be easily "profitized.'

7. If The Need Doesn't Exist, Create It
  Sometimes effective selling is about finding a need and filling it. At other times you'll need to create the need, and force people to ask themselves "how could I have survived this long without this?"

8. Don't tell the world right away
  Keep the energy of your new idea within the incubator of your mind. Give it time to grow in the energy of your commitment before you introduce it to the world and the possible ridicule, judgment and speculation of well- intentioned, but limited visionaries.

9. Go with your gut
  If it feels good in your gut, go with it. And perhaps the most important tip....

10. Choose the Right Activity.
  This one is so important that we'll give it its own section.

Beyond the Obvious Connections: Choosing the Right Activity!

This, in my opinion, is one of the most critical components of turning your passion into profit. When looking for ways to express your passion, some of the connections may seem quite obvious. A person whose passion is cooking may decide to open up a restaurant. Someone who's good at decorating may decide to start an interior design service. Don't be too hasty, however. There are other factors to consider. What if you love to cook, but hate interacting with people? A restaurant or catering business might be the worst business to start. You need to think beyond the obvious connections.

It's the ignorance of this component that has many people simply trading one form of unhappiness for another. They wind up in a passion-centered business that ultimately fails them, because they've failed to take into account the different aspects of their being that need nourishment. The next set of questions, therefore, focuses on certain qualities of the passion activity.

What do you actually enjoy doing?

What's the activity you actually like engaging in? What is that gives you your greatest sense of competence, fulfillment and satisfaction? As a cook, for instance, is the value in the creation, the completion, the feeding or the feedback?

What's your defining scene of success?

How will you know when you've created your ideal day? What single act or accomplishment will say to you, "You've done it"? This defining scene is different for everyone. For some people, it's the review in a certain magazine. For others it's a certain bank balance. For me it was being able to go to movies in the middle of the day. What's your defining scene? It is important to structure your business in such a way that you can eventually experience the defining scene of your ideal life-style. Keep your defining scene as a goal that you work towards a little at a time. Don't tie yourself to a desk if you really enjoy being out meeting people. Make the time to travel or develop relationships if your defining scene involves you seeing the world, or sharing your success with a significant other.

What's the review that you crave?

Authors, actors and performers know that the right review from the critics can do wonders for their careers. Passion Seekers too, have a particular "review", an observation, a compliment, or particular actions that we associate with having done a good job at something. Everyone likes to feel special, creative, smart, effective or of value. Imagine that you've just completed your passion activity and a satisfied customer or client walks up to you with a big smile, grabs your hand and says something that makes you proud. What would that statement sound like? Examples of ideal reviews include:
"I couldn't have done it without you!" "You changed my life!" "You changed my way of thinking." "I really like what you're doing." You're the most talented and creative person I've ever met!"

Who needs to give the review?

When you imagine receiving your review, who is speaking? Is it one person? Is it a crowd? Is it mostly women? Men?

What Makes a Passion-Centered Business Different

Depending on the answers to the previous questions, your Passion Activity will end up taking shape in many different ways. If you enjoy creating with your hands, then stay away from using a factory. If the defining scene involves you sitting on a beach free to relax, then you may want to set up, say, an Internet-only business that doesn't require your physical presence. If it doesn't matter who gives your review, your passion may end up being something that's sold to the public on a global scale rather than something that you provide in one-on-one sessions with individuals.

What you're doing here is redefining what it means to be in business. Being in business must now include being rewarded for doing what you love. It must now include being able to make deeper personal statements through your work. It must include being able to fill needs within yourself that you may never have thought a business could.

Judy: A Case Study

It's time to bring all the theory into practice by walking through a real example. Keep in mind, however, that there are no hard and fast rules for predicting how a person's passion will express itself. Two people with the same passion but with different life themes, skill sets, chosen people ideal days, reviews etc., will end up creating two entirely different businesses. The following example, therefore, is meant solely as a broad generalization of the Passion to Profit process and to illustrate certain principles.

"Judy" represents a composite of many clients I've coached over the years. Judy loves to cook. People have told her all her adult life that she should go into business sharing her gift with the world. Let's contrast how Judy's passion for cooking might express itself if she were a savior, creator, guru or guide.

Judy the **Creator** finds that her joy comes from the presentational aspect of cooking. She likes hosting big banquets with many courses, and likes the sense of completion she gets from the act of preparation. She's leaning towards opening a restaurant.

Judy the **Savior** finds that she loves to help and support people. Her greatest joy comes from helping people succeed. She's got great communication and human relation skills and loves to interact. We discover that playing a supportive role as the caterer of events is the most appealing expression of her passion.

Judy the **Guru** likes to empower people with knowledge. She decides to incorporate her writing and research skills and write a cookbook. She decides, also, to do workshops to teach others to cook, thereby setting the stage for launching her own cooking school.

Judy the **Guide,** a natural cook with a flair for the exotic and unique, cooks to impress. She's always winning competitions. She wants to be the best at what she does. She decides to bottle her secret recipe and sell it on a large scale in supermarkets, restaurants and specialty shops around the country. Her leadership and competitive nature leads her to form an organization for cooks. She stages competitions, and markets the best of the winners' products through her own company.

If Doves Can Fly...

As you can see, there are many ways to express a passion. Let's look at another example. Say you have a passion for birds that you'd like to turn into profit. The exact direction you go will be determined by what aspect of birds really intrigues you. Do you like to watch them? Do you like to raise them? Do you breed them? If you recall from the Magic Questions, *people will pay to buy* birds. So perhaps you might consider opening up a bird shop. *People pay to reach perfection.* So perhaps people will pay for your expertise on bird habitats to help them create the perfect environment for their birds. *People will pay to see a show.* So perhaps you might create a show featuring the world's most talented birds. *People pay to know* about birds. So perhaps you'd enjoy sharing your knowledge about birds in the form of a book, video, workshop or private consultation. People will pay to have their birds looked after professionally. So perhaps you'll start the first bird day care center. *People will pay to save the past.* So perhaps you'll become a professional bird photographer for birds that are part of the family.

The possibilities are out there. And no idea is silly. One woman I've heard about took her love of the sight of birds flying and created a business staging "dove releases" as part of wedding ceremonies. People pay her to bring a flock of birds to their weddings, and set them free so they can watch the sight and go "ooooh, aaahhh!" Who knew?

Adding More Value

I always encourage my clients--particularly those who provide services-- to create a physical product to sell. Creating a product allows you to earn money online, in retail outlets and in other passive ways without you needing to physically sell your time, energy or presence. So, let's again use Judy's cooking passion as an example of how a passion might be enhanced by the creation of some sort of product that can maximize the value and create additional income or leads.

Email: subscription to a recipe of the week club.
Book: create a collection of recipes, cooking schools, marketing tips, or a start-up guide
E-Book: sell the above in e-book format
CD: audio tape or interactive cookbook
Video/DVD: a cooking "How to" guide
Food: sell the actual food by overnight delivery, restaurant, bottled/canned product
Art: pictures of great meals, sculptures of fruits, etc.
Invention: Is there some handmade tool you've made that makes cooking easier?
Consulting: one-on-one guidance for new brides who want to learn how to cook certain foods.
Workshops: ethnic food cooking workshops
Lecture: Speaking engagements on the history of cooking and things culinary
Recordings of services: Why not sell recordings of consulting, coaching, workshop and lecture sessions?

Act in the Gap!

Whatever your idea is, once it comes to you, you must act quickly within the gap between inspiration and doubt. When ideas come they are often quickly followed by doubt which leads to inaction. The successful entrepreneurs--the so-called geniuses we all know and love--are simply people who have learned to act before the doubt takes over. They act, get a little encouragement and positive reinforcement for that action, and the doubt is pushed further back, giving them time to act again. When they take the next step, they may receive positive reinforcement, or even a setback, but the encouragement from their first action is enough to sustain them through the setback and gives them still more time to act again. The process continues until success is achieved.

The rest of the world, on the other hand, gets an idea which is then immediately surrounded, mercilessly attacked and beaten into submission by the gang of doubts that is always cruising around in their minds waiting for the lonely wandering inspiration!

 **The Cycle of Success**

Step 4: Identify your Product/Service

Using all the tools at your disposal--The Personality Profile, The Discovery Exercises, The Magic Questions, and Passion Finder Chart--describe what you'll be selling.

My Product or Service will be :

_____

_____

_____

*****

 The Cycle of Success

Step 5: Sleep on it!

Stop reading here. That's right. I said close the book and put it down. (Well, O.K. Read this page first.) Do not proceed past this point until you've had at least one night's sleep. Before you retire for the night, write your Passion Idea for a product or service on a piece of paper and read it 10 times before you go to bed. Pleasant dreams, and I'll see you in the morning!

WELCOME BACK!

If you've done what I've suggested--and I hope you did--you may be reading this book with one of two thoughts going through your mind. You are now either really excited about bringing your passion to life, or, in the light of the new day, you've convinced yourself that it'll never work.

What sorts of thoughts were you thinking as you drifted off to bed? Were you seeing things that haven't been and saying they could never be? Or, were you seeing things that aren't as yet, and asking why not me?

The nature of your thoughts will be a key factor in how successful you'll be at turning your passion into profit. If you had some negative or fearful thoughts, it doesn't mean you won't be successful. You may simply need to work harder to overcome them.

Bringing Your Product To Life

After the initial euphoria of your new idea has worn off, sometimes even before, you may start to have doubts. It's natural. Even the most positive thinkers face occasional doubts. Once your failure programming kicks in, you may find yourself talking yourself out of this whole crazy idea. As I've said, the trick now is to take action before the gang of doubts shows up to beat down your dream. You've got to take your idea from the realm of wishes and dreams into physical reality. Therefore, you should immediately do something to make it real.

Whenever I decide to write a new book, I always create a physical prototype. I design the cover, and then decide the exact size that book will be. Then, if I don't have a book of the same size in my possession, I'll go to the library armed with a ruler and find one. I do this to create a model of the book so that I can start to visualize it in finished form. I'll use the book that's the size of the one I intend to create, I'll wrap my newly designed cover around the front and back, and voilá, I've created a prototype. I can now walk around with it, hold it in my hands, and experience the feeling I will have when it is actually completed.

Whether your passion idea is a book, an invention, a service-oriented company or a singing career, you can do something similar to make it real. In the case of a service, you can create letterheads, business cards, or simply arrange your desk in preparation for doing business. For a passion that's a speaking or performing career, try setting up a stage with a microphone placed in front of the mirror, or consider creating ads that announce your upcoming performances. For a passion that involves an invention or physical product, create a cardboard, wood or wire model, a drawing of the finished product, a clay figure, anything that helps you feel the reality of your creation. This is an important step in the creative process. For as all great creators say, you must start with the end in mind.

Brainstorm For Ideas

Your next task is to come up with ideas on how to bring your passion to market and make it sell. If this is something you've done before--if you have the knowledge of how to patent and market an invention, self-publish a book, or open a retail store--then this process will be a little easier. If, on the other hand, this is the first time you're even attempting such a thing, fear not. Success, as you've heard before, is simply about asking the right questions. The right question in this case is "What specific things do I need to do in order to sell $50,000 worth of product or generate $40,000 in business within the next 12 months?" Or, you can try: "What specific things do I need to do to get my product created and in the stores?" Or, "What specific steps will I take to launch my business and generate paying clients by December?" Any one of these questions can serve as a good idea generator for a brainstorming session. Yep! It's time for another Passion Party!

This Passion Party will produce a wide range of answers covering every conceivable thought, word or deed that you think is necessary to bring your product or service to life. And while the question asks for specifics, include whatever ideas come to you, whether general or specific. For example, if the idea, "get my product in local toy store" comes to you, write it down. Later, that idea will lead you to more specific actions like "call toy store owner to make appointment." In addition, when you make your list, don't limit yourself only to things you feel are in your immediate power. The number one mistake many people make is thinking too small. Think Big! If one of the things you think you need to do to reach your goal is to meet with the president of the United States and convince him (or her) to endorse your product during the next nationally televised State of the Union speech, then put that on your list! (I respectfully suggest, however, that you add some other options to your plan!)

Your Plan

The tasks on your list will fall into one of the following categories.
1. Ideas
2. Research
3. Creative (Design)
4. Marketing (Promotion/Publicity/Advertising)
5. Sales

To categorize your list of ideas place "I" next to those items that are simply more ideas of new products/inventions, etc. Place "R" next to those items that involve getting more information, website research, investigation of similar products, etc. and so on.

Idea items include things like:
>"create new kind of golf club"
>"offer new massage course"
>"invent product for car drivers"

Research items include:
>"find out how the movie distribution process works"
>"see if someone else has a patent on my idea"
>"find a local distributor of kids' clothing"
>"contact *USA Today* for advertising rates"

Creation items include:
>"send book manuscript to printer"
>"develop wood prototype of invention"

Promotion/Publicity/Advertising items include:
>"draft brochure for item X"
>"develop sales letter for product"
>"design *USA Today* advertisement"
>"contact newspapers about invention"
>"send samples to key people to wear"

Sales activities include:
>"Call *ToysRUs* about placing an order"
>"call potential customers"
>"mail brochure to mailing list"

Prioritize the Items on the List

The next step is to prioritize your list. Prioritizing helps you to focus your limited time on the essential while avoiding the unnecessary. Essential items are those activities that cut to the chase and move you forward to making sales. The following question can help you decide which tasks are more important. *If I were leaving town for a month, which of these tasks COULD NOT wait until I got back?*

To help you prioritize the items on your task list in sequential order, you need to ask yourself the right questions. The following question can help you put your tasks in the right sequential order. Start with any sales item on the list and ask: *Can I do this task right away? If not, what do I need to do first?* If a particular sales item cannot be immediately done, then work backwards from that task looking for the necessary prior task that must be done.

One of the most powerful lessons I've learned is that it's not always necessary to start at step 1 to get to step 3. In fact, it's possible to focus on sales right away even before you've researched, designed, created or publicized anything about your product.

How you ask? Say you've just come up with a new idea. If you have a clear idea of exactly when the product will be ready, you can start to collect advance orders even before your product is done. I often send out brochures to my mailing list announcing forthcoming books and start to generate sales even before I write a single line! Now this strategy isn't for everyone. You've got to be able to work under pressure and really commit to meeting any deadline you set so you don't disappoint your customers.

Quite simply, if you want to make money in your venture, you've got to spend the appropriate amount of time focusing on each category. Many entrepreneurs tend to focus on the areas they enjoy and neglect the areas they dislike. In using this technique on my own projects, I realized that as a creative person, I tended to focus more on creation tasks than sales. Once I had a product created, I immediately set about to find another creative project to sink my teeth into. Needless to say, sales of my product suffered because I wasn't focusing on the right things. If you think you may have the same challenge, you may want to implement the assembly line concept to keep your business growing.

At the outset of your venture, you'll be doing more research and creative tasks. As you progress, marketing will become most important, then eventually sales tasks will dominate. Every product requires a certain amount of each type of activity in order to be successful. The key is not to spend any more time than necessary in any one type of activity to the exclusion of others. Each has its appropriate time, sequence and duration.

Work Your List

To accomplish the items from your brainstorming session, get in the habit of making lists. All great successes swear by them. I use a simple lined, spiral notebook in which I have a list of the things to be done on each day. Each day gets a new page. When an item is accomplished, I simply check it off. On this list I'll put everything from ideas and tasks to reminders to myself. As I'm driving, on a bus, plane or boat and an idea comes to me, I write it down. I even sleep with my notebook by my bed so that if I'm awakened by a bolt of inspiration, I can capture it on paper before the idea moves on to someone else.

Monday, November 3
-confirm fax to John
- Buy supplies at Office Supplies R Us
- create flier for handing out at expo
- deposit check
- Call manufacturer re: delivery
- register site with search engines

Make your new list at night, so the subconscious mind can work on ways to bring it to life. Add non-completed items to the next day's list.

Keep in mind that lists, planners and charts are only as good as your desire to implement them. Having a list doesn't guarantee that the tasks will get done. Making a list doesn't ensure that you'll look at it every day. If you are not already in the habit of working from lists, remember that you are creating a new habit. Lasting change of any kind comes from your own desire and resolve to make it happen. Of course, everyone will have different techniques for getting things done, and the key to making any technique work is the "follow through": the ability to continue to do something you've committed to, even after the feeling under which you made the commitment is gone.

Your Passion Plan

With the creation of your idea for a product or service, you now have enough information to pursue your passion. However, to be truly successful in this pursuit, your purpose, passion, mission and motivation must be aligned and synchronized.

your purpose	is	the role you are here to play
your passion	is	the vehicle you choose (one of a possible many)
your mission	is	the destination
your motivation	is	the fuel that keeps you going (your "why")

The combination of these 4 elements comprise your Passion Plan. As we've already explored purpose and passion, let's now examine mission and motivation.

Mission

Your personal life's mission is an important part of your journey. If you don't already have one, then it's important to take the time to find it. Your mission is what sets the direction of your life. You may already be living out your mission even though you haven't put it into words. You may already have an idea of what your mission is by what you've been driven to do most of your life. To help you in creating your mission, here are a few of the right questions to ask:

What's the operative word of your purpose?

What action word best defines your skill? Is it create, manage, communicate, coach, inspire, teach, or some other word? What word from the Discovery Exercises best describes the action from which you gain the greatest sense of empowerment?

What's your core value concept?

What idea is it that means more to you than anything else? What concept or cause is it for which you would fight? What is it that you believe in and stand for which you would not compromise? Is it family, justice, honesty, opportunity or spirituality? Is it human rights or freedom? What concept or cause, consequently, would you also passionately provide for others? Think back to the *"If I Ruled The World"* exercise for hints.

Who are your chosen people?

Think back again to the *"If I Ruled The World"* exercise. Who was your target group? Was it children, families, your community? Was it immigrants, the unemployed, the mentally retarded? Was it simply anyone and everyone?

Combining these three concepts, you can create a mission statement for yourself. *eg. My mission is to promote a sense of family within my community. My mission is to improve opportunities for immigrants.*

The statement of your mission should be short, easily understood and easily remembered. Your mission will be perfectly suited to the personality you determined in the previous section. It should be broad enough in scope to allow you a wide range of expressions. My own mission statement is "*I share what I know, so that others may grow.*" As I look back on my life, this broad statement has been the underlying theme of many things I've done including tutoring, writing, teaching, inventing and lecturing. As the scope of your mission expands, so too does the number of possible passions. The average person may have many passions, but usually one mission. Passions are not the end, but simply the means to an end.

Motivation

The ability to follow through is what separates the winners from the "also-rans" in life. This intangible quality that makes people follow through is also called motivation, desire and hunger, and hinges on having the right "why." Your "why" is the compelling reason that drives YOU to do the things you need to do. Is it to provide for your spouse and children? Is it your desire to give back to the community? Is it your craving for freedom? Whatever it is, you must identify it, and frame it in such a way that you can access it at any time in order to fuel your follow through.

Here is an example of how your purpose, passion, mission and motivation combine into a Passion Plan.

eg. To help me fulfill my [role as a Guru] and create the [motivation] freedom I desire, I can combine my [passion for rare books] my [talent/skill at organizing] and turn it into an [information service] selling [adults who collect books] the [knowledge] they desire.

In Other Words...

In other words, you will use your passion, fueled by your motivation to achieve your mission and live out your life's purpose.

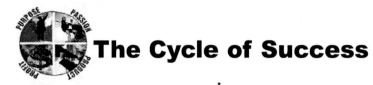 **The Cycle of Success**

Step 6: Write Your Passion Plan Statement:

I am a _____ (Purpose/Role).

I love _____ (Passion).

I am also good at _____(skills, talents).

Therefore, I can use that skill to help _____(chosen people) to
_____ (fulfill a need). I can market my talent in the form of
_____(product/service).

Here are the steps I will take to bring this plan to life.

_____

_____

_____

_____ _____

_____

_____

_____

_____

_____

_____

MAIN POINTS FOR CHAPTER 7
"Product"

• According to the *Third Law of Passion Dynamics*, *"For every creation, there exists an equal desire for that creation. Anything that has been created from your passionate interest and attention contains inherent value which others will recognize and pay to have in their own lives."*

• The Value Tree illustrates the unique relationship between the value you offer and the value others are seeking. All value that others seek is either a thing or an experience that provides Functionality, Entertainment, Comfort, Education, Access, Guidance, Survival, Kinship, Status and Self-Fulfillment.

• There's value everywhere and you can find a way to create something of value that others will buy if you learn to listen to what people want, ask the right questions, and open yourself up to the Divine Idea. The Magic Questions can get your mind thinking in ways that recognize value in just about everything you think, know and do.

• There are ways to open up your mind to insights and inspiration which can help you to discover or turn your passion into profit. The Passion Finder Chart can help you with some brainstorming ideas of possible ways. It will be important to learn how to listen for the clues from the universe that are always around you. So pay attention.

• There are many combinations and permutations of interest and skills that can result in quite unique expressions of the same passion. There's deeper value beyond the obvious. Always seek to add more value to your passion by maximizing the types of products and services you can offer.

• Always do something immediately to bring your passion idea to life so that you can advance the momentum and maintain the excitement of the discovery.

• The Passion Party is your new terminology for an idea-generating brainstorming session. At the end of the Passion Party, each participant should come away with a plan they can use to take the next step towards turning their passion into profit.

• The Plan for transforming your passion idea into a product or service that you can offer for sale is nothing more than a list of tasks put in sequential order. It's important, however, to commit this list to paper to take advantage of the power of goal-setting.

• To be successful, your purpose, passion, mission and motivation must be aligned.

FOLLOW-UP FILE FOR CHAPTER 7
"Product"

INSPIRATION: Passion Seeker Profiles

_____

"Passion for Peaceful Patrons by Pepper Pacification"
     Did you hear the one about the owner of a Mexican restaurant who got so frustrated with drunk college kids coming in late at night and messing up his restaurant, he created a hot sauce which he hoped would calm them down and encourage them to leave? The hotter he made the sauce, the quicker his boisterous patrons left. So he set about on a quest to make the hottest sauce ever. He soon created Insanity Sauce, a sauce so hot that it was banned at a Fiery Foods Show for causing respiratory difficulties. Banned, but selling well!

_____

IDEAS: *The Right Questions To Ask*

• What unique product or service can my passion offer to the world?

Chapter 8: Profit
"Money and me!"

The Law of One:

"The profitability of a passion increases in direct proportion to the level of belief in the value of its creator. If you can sell one, you can sell one million!"

Think about it. The more a movie studio believes that a particular leading actor can create box-office success, the more they are willing to invest in that actor's talents in the form of a hefty salary. A star athlete's or a performer's endorsement contracts, a singer's album sales, and a software company's market share all increase the more the team owners, sponsor companies, and buying public believe in the ability of the player or performer to provide the return on investment. That belief, however, starts with the belief the individual star, athlete or entrepreneur has in herself and talents. So your belief level is a critical component of your profitability.

What this means, therefore, is that if you can sell one copy of your book, one sample of your invention, or sign one client for your services, you can sell two, then three, and ultimately sell one-million. It's simply a matter of raising the original belief level. As I've always said, the dollar that makes you a millionaire is not the last dollar you receive, it's the first. It's simply a matter of discovering the unique mix of words and placement that result in your first sale (what I call "cracking the code"), then repeating the process over and over to increasing numbers of people.

The challenge to profitability comes after that first sale. It's what you do *after* you start making money that has the greatest impact on your profit. You've no doubt heard of lottery winners who go broke and superstars who file for bankruptcy. All the sales in the world will not make you rich if you sabotage your success by mismanaging your wealth. Fear not. It doesn't have to be this way. If you're ready to move beyond the limiting beliefs that have kept passion and profit on opposite sides of your reality, now is when you will learn to marry the two. In this chapter, I hope to help you discover a few of the secrets of money so that you can really turn your passion into financial profit.

Money. Can You Handle It?

Are you always in debt? Do you find it difficult to save money? Do you always find yourself borrowing to pay your bills? Do you often come into a great deal of money, and find that you spend it quickly with nothing to show for it? Are you hiding bills from your spouse? Are you constantly bouncing checks? Do you find that no matter how much you make, that it's never enough? If you've answered yes to any of these questions, it may be an indication of a relationship to money that you established years ago, and that will continue to cripple you until you take steps to end it. The first thing to do to end your current relationship with money is to examine your beliefs.

Many of us have certain beliefs about money that create fear, ambivalence, guilt and a range of other emotions whenever the subject is discussed. These beliefs are what keep money coming to us, or what keeps it constantly slipping through our fingers. As we've already established, thoughts create reality. It follows then, that thoughts about money will create the reality we experience when it comes to money matters.

Think of money as a servant that does as it is told. What you say about money, therefore, becomes the instructions which money listens to in deciding how to relate to you. Is money, or the love of it, the root of all evil? Does money not grow on trees? Is it necessary, as singer Donna Summer says, to *work hard for the money*? Is it true that money can't buy happiness? Or, that money isn't everything? You've probably heard beliefs like these repeated throughout your life. These beliefs become a part of who you are and determine whether you make money a trusted friend, or an evil spectre stalking you and lurking just beyond reach. Money often becomes the forbidden fruit enticing with its desirability and utility, while at the same time holding the threat of punishment if you indulge.

Many of us operate from a basic assumption of an inherent scarcity of money. We feel that for us to have a dollar, that someone, somewhere is being deprived of that dollar. Similarly, we feel that another person's success is somehow limiting our own opportunities to be equally successful. We then feel guilty at any financial success that we achieve because we feel that we're creating a state of poverty for someone else, or that our own success may be taken away by someone else. Having money does not diminish another's potential to create wealth in their own life. As Ghandi said, there really is enough for everyone's need.

Many of us also operate from an assumption that there always has to be some direct work performed in order to justify the acquisition of money. In fact, some people shy away from ways of making money, like investing in the stock market, because they see it as somehow cheating. I like to remind people that money is just one means the universe uses to achieve balance. True to the law of cause and effect, every deed, whether good or bad, is rewarded in kind. However, you don't always receive your reward from the person or place to which your deed is directed. You might help someone today and receive your reward from a completely different source two years from now. Who knows? Perhaps the wealth you receive today is the reward for a good deed you did back in high school. Who are you to shun your blessings simply because you can't see the good being balanced? Accept all wealth that comes your way in the knowledge that the universe is perfect and is working to stay perfectly balanced. Don't screw it up!

Remember, also that money is a tool. It is a means to an end, not the end itself. So, just like your time and your talent, it is simply another tool you can use to create more wealth. Just as you invest your time at a job to make money, and you invest your skills in a project to make money, you can also invest your money as a way to make money.

Many people I talk to also believe deep down that they have to be smart to make money, or, that in order to make money, they have to take advantage of others; or that the process of making money is so arduous and time consuming, that they'll have to give up a lot in order to do it. If these are your beliefs about money, then you are being controlled and kept in poverty by the very thing you wish to change.

Remember, money is just another expression of the abundance that exists. It is just another expression of gifts we can use to make our own and other's lives more enjoyable. It takes no special talents and requires no special worthiness to acquire it. It simply awaits your willingness to accept it.

The concept of money and how to attract it into your life is a key topic in turning your passion into profit. We often operate in fear of money and what we think it says about us, and what we fear it does to us. Until you change what believe and say about money, its absence in your life will continue to say volumes about you. For money only says about you and does to and for you what you say and do to and for it. You'll never attract something you despise or think of as evil. You'll never have enough of something you don't see as abundant like the leaves of a tree. You'll never keep something that you don't feel is your right to possess. You'll never become greater than you are if you believe having money makes you less of who you are. And you'll forever want the very thing that can help turn your passion into profit, but which your beliefs will not allow you to have.

How can you create a profitable business if, while you're trying to sell your product to make money, you're also sabotaging yourself and doing things that create a reality of lack and scarcity. It will be difficult. Anything you associate pain or negativity with, you will avoid, and anything you associate pleasure with you will move towards. If your negative associations with money are just a bit greater than the positive ones, the negative associations will dominate your consciousness, and create a lack of wealth.

God, Money, and Me

Your image of God
is how you pattern your self
your God's views on money
is what determines your wealth

How does God feel about money? How much money does God have?

When I ask people to answer those questions, I get a wide range of answers. Some people who've been working on their belief systems about money will readily answer that God wants us to be abundantly provided for, and that money is a means to an end that God put here for us to use. At the same time, there are others who answer that in God's eyes money is evil. Or, that according to scripture, "it is easier for a camel to pass through the eye of a needle than for a rich man to enter the kingdom of heaven", and that this represents a condemnation of money and wealth. These conflicting views we imagine to be God's views on money. You may ask, however, why this is important.

If you believe in a deity, your perception of God sets the standards for the ideal you. We all secretly aspire to be God-like in our behavior. If so, it's unlikely that you aspire to have qualities, beliefs and behaviors that are opposed to those that you attribute to God. The reasoning is "If God thinks less of money, then I should too." "If God doesn't need money, then neither do I." How can you aspire to accumulate something that you believe makes you less than holy? The answer is you can't. Therefore, unless and until you see money as something that God created, and moreover, that God wants you to have, then you've already doomed yourself to poverty even before the journey begins.

If you see money as an expression of the abundance of the wealth that God has created, and that you are entitled to share in, then you will be on your way to wealth. If, on the other hand, you feel money is one of man's evil inventions that is far removed from the realm of the Godly, then you'll surely have a difficult time attracting and accumulating it in your life. For which person wants to be un-Godly in anything they do?

I'm suggesting here that your ultimate success in turning your passion into profit may have deeper influences that require more than business techniques and tools to adequately address. Excellent books have been written which address the issue of money and the connection to your spiritual and emotional growth. Three of my favorites are *The Trick To Money is Having Some* by Stuarte Wilde, *Spiritual Economics* by Eric Butterworth and *The 9 Steps to Financial Freedom* by Suze Orman.

Money And Self-Worth

> *"For some, the love of money is the root of all evil,*
> *but for all, the love of self is the root of all money"*--Walt Goodridge

They say that the love of money is the root of all evil. However, if you want to turn your passion into profit, you need to replace that belief with the understanding that the love of self is the root of all money. You may envision great success and wealth for yourself, but if at your core you have a limited view of yourself, then you will never do what's necessary to create that vision of success.

Money is a means of exchange. It is a means of measuring value. As such, it not only measures the value of the things you create, but it measures the value you place on yourself. This is not to say that your value to yourself is measured in monetary terms, but on some level, we all have a value assigned to what we do, what we deserve as a result, and thus, who we are.

If, as a result of your current opinion of what's possible for you, you don't see yourself earning money in other ways, or at higher levels than you do now, then it will not happen with any degree of satisfaction.

If someone offered you a job for $10,000 per year *less* than you were currently making, would you take it? All other things being equal, you probably wouldn't because you have an opinion of the market value of what it is you have to offer, and you know that you have bills to pay. Therefore, you have a bottom line income that you'll always insist upon. At the same time, if someone offered you double what you were making for the same work, though you might take it, you might also feel guilty for being overpaid, and might even do things to bring your pay down to a level that makes you more comfortable.

Sound crazy? It's been shown that even when given the chance to earn substantially more, people's opinions of what they're worth will often override, and they'll talk themselves back to a figure that is more in alignment with their self-worth.

There once was a salesman who impressed his higher-ups by generating enough sales to make $50,000 in yearly commission for himself. His higher-ups were impressed because the geographical area in which he was selling had never before yielded that amount of sales. The next year, he was assigned to a high volume area, and strangely, did just enough sales to make $50,000, yet again. It was discovered that he thought of himself as a "$50,000-a-year salesperson". It didn't matter whether he was placed in a traditionally high sales area, or a historically poor sales area, he always managed to do $50,000 per year in commissions. He produced a reality that matched his opinion of himself regardless of the potential or the limitations others thought were there.

Many of us do the same thing. They key is to constantly work at raising your self-concept of what you're worth. Practice affirmations. Interact with others who are earning more than you are. Find a mentor. Go back to the chapter on *Thinking Differently* for tools you can use to help you with this.

Compensation is Appreciation

If you have difficulty accepting money for what you do, or if you're tempted to give products or services away for free, think about this: refusing to accept money for the things you do sours the experience of doing the activity. You will feel resentful while engaged in your passion because you'll know that you are slowly going bankrupt. Offering your products and services for free creates no value for them in the minds of the people for whom you think you're doing a favor. Furthermore, the sobering irony is that they won't share you with others because who would give away their "golden hen"? They think to themselves, "*If I know that John takes my photos free of charge, then if I recommend others to use him, he may get too busy to have time for me. Or, maybe others will pay him what he's really worth, and he'll start charging me too.*" At the same time, if they do recommend you to others, how much of your value can they communicate to others if they aren't paying what you're worth?

Many people feel that charging others (especially people they know) somehow makes them a bad person. They say "I have a hard time charging my friends", or "It just doesn't feel right", or "It makes me uncomfortable to ask for it." I often ask, "Would you perhaps find it easier to charge your enemies? If so how many of your enemies do you presently do business with?" The truth is that although some of your friends may indeed expect discounts because they know you, the ones who respect what you do will understand the value of supporting you.

Don't feel guilty about earning money for your passion. Remind yourself of the following when you are plagued by the fear of charging for your services:

Compensation is appreciation
that's the first thing you should know
when others love you and what you do
that's just one way for them to show

Fear not that others think
through sale that all good will is lost
devalued worth brings low regard
in that which has no cost

Our world is such that money's thought
the child of evil spawned
yet rules our lives through absence 'til
truth's light from darkness dawns

See, money does good and bad alike
whether crook, king, villain or star
the wealth you earn won't make you bad
justmore of what you are!

> *"There is nothing that
> we encounter outside of
> ourselves, that isn't an
> echo of something from
> within ourselves."*

Compensation is appreciation
Walt's Life Rhyme #61

People can show their appreciation for the things you do in many ways. They can smile, they can say thank you, or they can give you something else in return. What they choose to give you can measure the relative value of what you've given them. Money is just one form of measurement. Money is simply one of the many things they can choose or which you can request as a measure of value. So that's all money is, a method of exchange and a means of measuring the value of items being exchanged. You can surely choose and agree upon other methods and measures. In our capitalistic society, based on a system of free enterprise, we've all agreed that money has a set value relative to other things in our society. Now why would you want to mess all this up?

Charging Appropriately for your Product or Service

Another volatile topic among new entrepreneurs is determining what to charge for their product or service. Later we'll explore the specifics of actually setting prices. For now let's just address the psychology behind it.

When was the last time you walked into a store and saw something you just had to have? What did you think to yourself the moment you looked at the price tag? If it was much *less* than you expected, did you think to yourself that there must be something wrong with it, or that it was defective or damaged? That's a common thought. On the other hand, if the price was much *higher* than you expected, did you think that it must be very valuable? Did that just make you want it even more? It may not even have occurred to you that it was too expensive. You wanted it so badly that your desire made the price tag all the more justifiable in your mind. Or, if it was just about what you expected to pay, did you simply put it in your cart and make your purchase without a second thought? Think about it. Haven't you bought something that was expensive simply because you wanted it? Haven't you left things sitting on the store shelves that seemed too cheap to be of quality? And haven't you simply bought things for what they cost? Everyone does. Everyone, including your potential customers.

Many entrepreneurs, however, feel they'll scare away customers by charging certain prices. They really aren't convinced of the value of what they are offering.

They've forgotten a simple truth: people will buy the things they want. It's that simple. Most people understand how the world works. Things cost money. People will pay you what you charge if they value what you're selling. So set your price, stick with it and know that you're in business to sell to the people who see value in what it is you have to offer. You can't sell to those who don't. No amount of price cutting will get you customers who don't recognize your value. And ironically, if the price is too low, some people won't buy because you've lessened the perceived value in their minds. One of the strangest facts about human nature, is that many people actually like to pay *more* for products and services. It makes them feel special. It says that they can afford to, that they love themselves, and that they're getting something of value. Why would you want to deprive them of that feeling? In fact, sometimes adding a little extra to your price may actually help you sell more! Remember:

Until I respect my time,
the world will always impose.
Until I value my talent,
my masterpieces go unsold.

Until my best means as much to me
as I would that others feel,
then no one else will come to trade
or feel uplifted by the deal.

The terms of sale are simple then,
for you always get what's due:
If who you are has worth to you
It will for others too!

> *"People want things. Things cost money. People will pay for the things they want. It's that simple."*

What's it really worth?
Walt's Life Rhyme #54

The Meaning of Debt

Debt is a statement of insufficiency. It is a manifestation of a belief in scarcity. It is an expression of fear. It says that there's not enough time, not enough money and not enough good fortune in the present or the future. I'm sure you know of people--maybe even yourself--who never seem to have enough. No matter how much they make, they always need more and consequently go into debt to get it. There are often many emotional issues at the core of the behavior of these habitual borrowers. However, living beyond one's means is just another way of saying "I am worth less than the things I value." If we are to pursue our passions to earn a profit, it will be necessary to move beyond the self-depreciating beliefs that keep us tied to debt. Debt counseling is an excellent way to address the practices that are keeping you in debt. Contact Debt Counselors of America at www.dca.org, or The National Foundation for Consumer Credit at www. nfcc.org. Keep in mind, however, that beyond the practices themselves, are deeper emotional issues. Your commitment to personal growth may help you get to them in time.

Saving

Saving, on the other hand, is an act of abundance. It is a statement of your faith in the future. It says, "I don't have to spend this dollar, or try to make it do everything I need to get done. I have enough. I can put it away and begin to build something that may come in handy, for an opportunity, an investment, or something I know is in my future."

The Final Analysis

And so it is also with you. This new exciting idea you discovered in the previous chapter might be the answer to your dreams. However, you must begin to see yourself as someone who can earn more than you're earning now, and in different ways.

You must also see yourself acting in ways that create and sustain wealth. You must start eliminating debt, saving money and charging appropriately for your products and services if you are to successfully turn your passion into profit.

Your money is a reflection of you and the things you believe. If you believe there is more than enough for everyone, you'll attract your share. If you believe that it's difficult to earn and hold on to, that will be the reality that finds you. View money as the well-deserved reward for the value you add to the world, and it will seek you out. View it as evil and un-Godly, and it will bring chaos and disorder into your life. Treat it as a trusted friend, and it will go out of its way to please you, as any good friend would. Start to think differently about money and it will start to behave differently around you. Accept it as an expression of the love you give to others, and it will be like a doting lover whose only purpose is to make you happy!

Now let's move beyond the metaphysical and basics of generating profits.

The Basics: What Exactly is Profit?

> **prof'it**, *n.* **1**, advantage, benefit. **2**, monetary gain; excess of returns
> over costs; interest, gain, earnings, return
> *v.* **1**, improve, make progress; **2**, gain; become richer

By definition, the profit one can experience in the pursuit of passion can be emotional, spiritual as well as financial. For the remainder of this book, however, we'll be focusing primarily on the *"monetary gain,* and *"excess of returns over costs"* definition. In other words, money. Financial profit is what keeps the wheels turning in a capitalistic society. Without it, and the leverage it provides, your effectiveness in creating the life-style you desire will be substantially diminished. Profit is what you will use to grow your business. It is what you'll use to invest in assets that make you more money. It is what you'll use to treat yourself and those you love to life's luxuries.

Profit is what's left over from a dollar of income after you've accounted for all your production costs and expenses. Let's pretend you're in business to sell 1 hat. You sell your hat for $10 and are beaming with pride at your sale! Let's say it cost you $2 to actually make or have the hat made for you, $1 in gas to go pick it up from the post office, $2.00 for the box and wrapping paper, $3.20 to actually ship it to the customer. That adds up to $8.20 in expenses. So of that $10 you made, $1.80 (i.e. $10 - $8.20=$1.80) is actually profit. But wait! We haven't included a percentage for rent, phone bills, box rental fee, paper for the receipt, website hosting charges, the stamp on the brochure you originally sent to the customer, or the cost of the label and staples on the box. So, you see then, that even as you hold that $10 in your hand, much of it has already been spent. This example illustrates that profit is not what you get, but what you get to keep.

Therefore, you should have in your mind at all times a figure that represents the profit that remains for each dollar of income. The question is not simply 'how much did I earn today?" The right question is "how much of this dollar is actually free to be used to invest, grow my business or spend on a luxury?" Once you have that figure in mind, you'll have a clearer more realistic idea of how your business is doing.

Understanding Profit Margins (Finally!)

What do you think of when you hear the word *margin*? If you're like most people, you think of setting the margins in a word processing document, or you think of the margins of a book. Well, just like the margins of a book, your Profit Margin is how much is left over, or "not used up" in every dollar of sales you earn. When you make your first sale, a portion of that dollar represents the cost to you of making or acquiring the product you sold. In other words, if the hat you're selling for $10 cost you $6 to make or purchase, then the (gross) profit margin is $4, or 40% (4/10 expressed as a percentage). However, that's not your "real" profit. It's called "gross" profit margin because you haven't subtracted other expenses and determined what actually ends up in your "net." It's called a margin because somewhere inside that amount is where your actual, final profit is going to be. When your gross profit margin is 40%, it means that for every dollar you earn, 40% of it is what's left over to pay the expenses AND provide a net profit.

Understanding Markup

Markup is what you do to your costs in order to arrive at a selling price. In the hat example, above, you spent $6 to purchase or make the hat and then added $4 (marked it up) to arrive at a selling price of $10. Your mark up, therefore was $4, or 66% (4/6 expressed as a percentage) of what you paid for it.

Why is this important? Even though you marked up your product by 66%, your gross profit margin worked out to be only 40%. It's the same $4, but when you actually make the sale, that $4 represents much less than it first appears. Don't assume that just because you added $4 to arrive at a price for the item, that you're actually making $4 profit every time one of them sells. I repeat: *Don't assume that just because you added $4 to arrive at a price for the item, that you're actually making $4 profit every time one of them sells.* That 4 dollars now has to cover all your fixed costs like rent, office equipment and salaries, as well as your variable costs like telephone and advertising.

Understanding Break-even

The next important concept is "break-even point". This is the quantity of sales at which your variable and fixed costs are covered, and you begin making a profit.

A typical Breakeven Analysis requires that you:
1. Determine the Variable Cost Ratio,
2. Determine the Fixed Costs, then
3. Determine the Breakeven point,

1) Variable Cost Ratio.

First, you need to determine your variable costs. In the hat example, let's say you buy your hats in batches of 100. You determine that for each batch of 100 hats, you incur the following costs:

— hats $ 500 (100@$5 each)
— shipping at $ 26.00
— insurance $20.00

All these variable costs (costs that vary depending on how much you sell) total: $500 + 26 + 20 = $ 546.00$ for 100 hats

Next, you set the price for 1 hat at $ 10.00. That's $ 1000.00 income for 100 hats. Therefore, your variable cost per batch is $546 with a selling price per batch of $1000

The variable cost ratio is:
= Variable Cost divided by Selling Price
= $546.00 / $1000.00
= 54.6% (or 0.546) (i.e. every time you sell a hat, 54.6% of the income is covering variable costs. These costs, therefore, will keep going up as you sell more hats.)

2) Breakeven Points.

Next, determine the amount of your fixed costs per year. Let's say, for this ideal scenario, that rent is your only fixed cost and is $700/month. That's $8400 for the year. With a fixed cost of $8400 per year, and a variable cost ratio of 54.6%, (0.546) and a selling price of $1000 per batch,

Your Breakeven Dollar Sales = Fixed Costs / (1 - Variable Cost Ratio)
= $8,400.00 / (1 - .546)
= $ 8,400.00 /(.454)
= $ 18502.20 of sales must be achieved for turning a profit.
And your Breakeven Unit Sales =
= Breakeven Sales / Selling Price
= $ 18502.20 / $ 10.00
= 1,850 hats must be sold to make a profit.

In other words, you'd have to sell 1,850 hats for your business to break even. You can manipulate the numbers to create the specific scenario you desire. For example, to make a profit earlier than 1,850 hats, you can increase your selling price, or you can reduce your variable costs.

These three concepts of profit margin, markup and break-even ratio are important to turning your passion into profit. Practice doing break-even analyses for different combinations of selling price and fixed and variable costs.

Setting Your Price for Profit and Prosperity

Whether your passion is a product or a service, you now need to decide how much you're going to charge people. This is often a major challenge for new entrepreneurs. As we learned earlier, issues of self-worth often play a detrimental role in how much money people allow themselves to earn. Ultimately, the price that people will pay for your product will depend on the value that *you* place on it, and then on your ability to communicate that value. At the same time, there are certain factors which will determine what you can and will have to charge in order to make a profit.

From a business perspective, your price must accomplish several things. Not only must you charge enough to cover your expenses and maximize your profits, but that price can't be so high that it will discourage sales. To help you set your price for profit and prosperity, here are four things to consider along with the right questions to ask.

1. The market

What are others in your industry charging for similar products and services? Are you entering an industry in which retail prices have already been set by tradition? If so, you can set your price using "competitive pricing."

2. The demand

Is your product a currently popular , or hard-to-find item that people are willing to pay a premium for? Will you or are you selling so much of your product that you can create or purchase your inventory at a lower unit cost? If so, you can set your price using "demand pricing." Set your prices higher if people are willing to pay a premium. Set prices lower (to beat the competition) if you can purchase at lower unit cost.

3. The cost to you

What does it cost you to purchase or create your product? If you know this, you can simply add a percentage, or use a multiplier to arrive at the cost to the consumer. This method is called "markup pricing."

4. The perceived value

Is your company's image such that consumers will pay more for your product than they would for a competitor's? Is your packaging, reputation, customer service, guarantee or overall quality so special that customers expect to pay more? Is your product one-of-a-kind? How much you can charge using perceived value is unlimited. It's simply a matter of how much value you can establish in the minds of consumers.

There are certain situations in which you might intentionally set the price of your product or service at less than optimum. When you "upsell", for example, you encourage sales by offering a lower-priced introductory product, with the intention of selling a higher-priced follow-up product. You may also want to set your prices lower simply to win customers from your competition, and to announce to the world that you have arrived.

Remember, setting your price is not an exercise in random number generation. In other words, you shouldn't simply pull a number out of thin air (or some other place), and attach it to your product and hope it will sell. There are concrete considerations (margins, markup, etc.) you must take into account in order to make a profit.

Tips on Pricing a Service

Pricing a service presents a unique challenge. The services you provide through your passion can be in the form of consulting sessions, workshops, personal appearances, catering, etc. As a result, you have many options of how to present the cost of your service to your clients. You may charge people by the hour, by the day, by participant (as for a workshop), by customer usage of your service, or by the project. You may also charge a flat fee per job, or charge a retainer fee.

In each instance, however, what you are doing is placing a value on your time. Therefore, it is essential to know how many hours you actually spend in providing the service regardless of how you present your final price to your client. Once determined, you can multiply by your hourly rate to determine the amount you should charge.

Here's one way to determine your hourly rate. It's based simply on how much money you want to make in a given year.

Step 1. Determine how much you wish to earn each year

$2,000	to operate your business each month
$4,000	family expenses per month
$1,000	miscellaneous expenses each month
$7,000 =	Total you wish to earn each month
$84,000 =	Total you wish to earn for the year ($7,000/month x 12 months)

Step 2. How many hours you will actually work

The next step is to determine how many hours you will actually be billing your customers. Taking an average of industry standards, we'll use 5 hours per day. That translates to 25 hours per week, or 1250 hours per year.

$$\$84,000 \text{ income desired } / \text{ } 1,250 \text{ billable hours} = \$67.2 \text{ per hour}$$

Therefore, if a customer requests a session or a project that will require 3 hours of your time, you now know you'll need to charge at least 3 x $67.2=$201.60. I say *at least* because you may incur other costs in performing the task. There may be supplies, phone costs, fax charges, postage, mileage, tolls, gas, parking and other hidden costs that you'll need to bill to your client.

If you are not doing the work yourself, you can charge based on what you need to pay your employees or consultants or subcontractors. Take into account all your expenses like materials, rent, equipment, and supplies, and include a markup for profit.

Types of Income

Once you're ready to start accepting money for the things you do, it's wise to acquaint yourself with the many ways you can actually acquire it. You can beg for it, borrow it, steal it, earn it, buy it, find it or inherit it. It's completely possible that someone will read this section, realize they've been suppressing a legitimate passion for gambling, and simply toss this book aside and head off to turn their passion into profit in Las Vegas or Atlantic City. For the purposes of this book, however, we're going to focus on ways to trade it for the value we provide to others. In other words, we're going to earn it.

The chart below shows different types of income and ways of generating them. In the first column, *you* work for money. In the second column, *your creations* work for it. In the third column, *others* work for it. In the fourth column, *your money works for you*. And, in column five, neither you nor money is doing a stitch of real work!

Linear	Residual	Passive/Leveraged	Investment	Other
Job	Royalties	Network Marketing	Stocks	Grants
Consulting	Licensing	Employer	Bonds	Gifts
	Syndication	Franchise Ownership	Mutual Funds	Lottery
	Real Estate	Mail Order	Antiques	Gambling
		Internet		Inheritance

Linear Income

Linear income is employee income. To earn it, you trade the hours of your life for dollars. The transaction starts with the commitment of an hour of your time and ends when you are paid for that hour. There's nothing inherently wrong with linear income, except you are limited by how many hours you can devote. To earn more money, you must work more hours or get a pay raise. You may not have control of these options.

Residual Income

In the Residual income model, you do something one time, and get paid for it over and over again! If you're Michael Jackson, you're getting paid royalties today for music that you recorded in your childhood. If you're Maya Angelou, or Stephen King, your books sell and create income for you even though you did the writing one time many years prior. With your ideas, creations and possessions working for you in this way, what you can earn is exponentially greater and can continue even after you're gone!

Passive/Leveraged Income

Passive/Leveraged income allows you to earn money not from your efforts, but from the efforts of others. Employers and Network Marketing professionals have staffs, or teams of people who are out getting customers and generating income even if they are out playing golf. Leveraged income allows you to focus your time and energy on other things.

Investment Income

Investment income is a form of passive income as well. Your investments can be stocks, bonds, homes, jewelry, precious metals and any other asset that increases in value and creates income in the form of "gains."

Other types of Income

Grants, gifts, lottery winnings, inheritances and found money are examples of other types of income that don't fit neatly in the other categories.

If you are currently earning only linear income, don't despair. You can use it as a springboard to create residual, passive and investment income. Turning your passion into profit will allow you to create alternate streams of income as well as a surplus that can be used for investments. That is the plan upon which our journey is based.

The Cycle of Success

Step 7: Set your Price for Profit

Type of income I will generate is [ ] Linear [ ] Passive [ ] Residual [ ] Investment
[ ] Other_____

The price of my product/service is:

Product
My unit cost is   _____
My markup is   _____

The gross profit for my product is:

The BreakEven Point for my product is   _____ units
My monthly expenses are   _____
How many units will I need to sell each month   _____ units

Service
I charge   [ ] by the hour   [ ] by the project [ ] Other_____
My monthly expenses are   _____
How many clients will I need per month? _____ clients

The gross profit for my service:

MAIN POINTS FOR CHAPTER 8
"Profit"

• The Law of One states *"For every creation, there exists an equal desire for that creation. The profitability of a passion increases in direct proportion to the level of belief in the value of its creator. If you can sell one, you can sell one million! "*

• What you say and believe about money determines how money responds to you.

• Some people associate money with immorality, evil and a host of negative emotions, and thus keep themselves from enjoying it.

• Issues of self worth affect how much money you earn, and will determine how successfully you turn your passion into profit.

• Practice a few new ways of being. Eliminate debt and save.

• You have exactly the amount of money in your life that you feel you deserve. Charge appropriately for your services. Money is simply a measure of your service to the world. Remember that compensation is appreciation.

• There are some fundamental concepts about making a profit that you need to know. Become familiar with *profit margins, break-even points* and *markup.*

• One of the reasons more people do not jump out on their own is that they simply don't know the many types of income and ways to earn it that exist. You could be earning linear, residual, passive, leveraged, investment or several other types of income as a way of turning your passion into profit.

FOLLOW-UP FILE FOR CHAPTER 8
"Profit"

INSPIRATION: Passion Seeker Profiles

"Joey's people passion!"

Joey Crugnale, the owner of Bertucci's Restaurant says he loves retail and loves people! He turned down offers to grow and expand so that he could pursue his passion. "I liked walking into my stores and seeing my customers and trying new flavors as opposed to going to a plant. I don't like that, it was a position I didn't want." His first business, the Steve's Ice Cream business he bought from its creator, turned out to be a huge success. He himself ran the original Steve's location. When retail space opened up next door, he quickly bought it simply "as a way to keep other restaurants and businesses next to [mine] out, a way for me to have some fun, and a place to bring my friends to drink wine and play boccie." This fun place was the first Bertucci's.

The restaurant's location, the relaxed atmosphere, and Joey's own passion for authentic Italian cuisine all combined into a winning chain of restaurants that he eventually took public several years later.

IDEAS: The Right Questions To Ask

• What specific beliefs about money was I raised with? Are they helping or hindering?
• What specific things can I do to start earning money in a variety of different ways?
• Who do I know--who I will contact--who is earning money in different ways?
• What types of income can I create with my passion?
• What specific things can I do to reduce my monthly expenses without feeling deprived?

Chapter 8:
The Philosophy and Formula
"A Review"

"I am proud to offer the world a philosophy and formula for turning passion into profit. I encourage its use by parents, teachers, coaches, as well as within institutions of higher learning. It is my hope that it will foster a greater understanding and appreciation of each individual's inherent value as a spiritual being and the expression of that value within the global marketplace. It is my wish that these ideas lead a revolution in thought and in deed and usher in a new era of entrepreneurial expression, financial independence, and personal freedom." **--Walt F.J. Goodridge, The Passion Prophet**

The Passion Profit Philosophy

Your passion is part of your life's PURPOSE.
Everyone has a PASSION.
ALL passions have value as a PRODUCT or service.
ANY passion can be turned into PROFIT.

The Cycle of Success

PHASE 1: PURPOSE

Key Question: Why am I here?
Governing Principle: The FIRST Law of Passion Dynamics:
"A person who is NOT aware of his/her purpose, will remain unfulfilled, living someone else's dream unless acted upon by an outside force through new ways of thinking."
Tool: Passion Profession Personality Test

PHASE 2: PASSION

Key Question: What do I love to do?
Governing Principle: The SECOND Law of Passion Dynamics:
"Everyone has a passion. You are never given a passion without also having the talents, abilities and people in your life to turn it into profit if you desire."
Tools: Discovery Exercises; Asset Finder

PHASE 3: PRODUCT

Key Question: What's the value that I can offer?
Governing Principle: The THIRD Law of Passion Dynamics
"Every passion has value. Anything that has been created from your passionate interest and attention contains inherent value which others will recognize and pay to have in their own lives."
Tool: The Value Tree; The Magic Questions

PHASE 4: PROFIT

Key Question: How can I communicate the value?
Governing Principle: The Law of One:
"For every creation, there exists an equal desire for that creation. If you can sell one, you can sell one million! The profitability of a passion is directly proportional to one's level of belief in the value of its creator."
Tool: The Code Cracker

THE UNDERLYING SECRET OF SUCCESS

Governing Principle: VALUE NO ONE CAN STEAL:
"If you create and market a product or service through a business that is in alignment with your personality, capitalizes on your history, incorporates your experiences, harnesses your talents, optimizes your strengths, complements your weaknesses, honors your life's purpose, and moves you towards the conquest of your own fears, there is ABSOLUTELY NO WAY that anyone in this or any other universe can offer the same value that you do!"
Tool: The Passion Profit Secret Formula

THE PASSION PROFIT
_____SECRET FORMULA_____

The Passion Profit Secret Formula is a sequence of questions designed to guide your thinking as you turn your passion into profit. Some questions require deeper probing to come up with the final answers. Some questions require brainstorming and creating lists of possible answers.

PASSION = [What do you love to do? + What's the value in it? + What's the value in it for you? + What's the value for others? + What's the need that is filled? + What is the pleasure that is offered. What is the pain that is avoided? + Is the value in the knowing? + Is the value in the possessing? + Is the value in the experiencing? + Is the value emotional, spiritual, or physical? + Is the value real* or symbolic*? + Is it direct or indirect? + What emotion or feeling is being symbolized directly or indirectly? + Can you transmit or recreate that feeling in words, thoughts or deeds? + What different ways exist to transmit those words?+ What different ways exist to transmit those thoughts? + What different ways exist to transmit those deeds? + Of all of these ways, what is the best way to transmit or recreate those thoughts, words and deeds? + Can those words, thoughts and deeds be put into a physical form? + Using your skills and talents and aptitudes, what physical form or activity can you create or organize that best embodies and recreates the feeling, experience or possession or service that is valued? + Can those words thoughts and deeds be put into the form of a service? + How can you provide that symbol of value repeatedly to others? + (Insert Magic Questions here) +What would people be willing to pay to have access to that symbol? + How can you create it and offer it in such a way to attract more money than it costs you to create it?] = PROFIT

*real values come in the form of shelter, protection, money, health, sustenance, knowledge.
*symbolic values come in the form of memories, feelings provided by pictures, images.

So there it is! You now have a proven philosophy and formula for finding your purpose, discovering your passion, developing a product or service, and turning it into profit.

The next several chapters will expand on the mechanics of "profitizing" your passion. We'll explore in more detail the legal structure, income reporting requirements, and marketing techniques which are all necessary aspects of turning one's passion into profit.

Please note that some specific information, (eg. business structure, and tax reporting) may be more applicable to territories governed by United States Tax Law.

> *"A passion-centered
> business, unlike a job,
> empowers, fulfills and
> frees!"*

Chapter 9: Starting Your Business
"This is easier than I thought!"

A New Word

Tonya is an administrative assistant who has been working various temporary assignments for some time. She came to see me because she longed to be a full-time passion seeker, but felt that something was holding her back. I asked her why she wanted to start her own business, and as she shared her reasons, I found myself a bit confused by her explanation. She revealed that she always loved her "job" and wanted to do it ever since she was fifteen. It wasn't until I realized that she was using the word "job" to refer to her passion for planning weddings, that my confusion subsided. I asked if she had a job right now. She said yes. I then asked if she enjoyed her job. She said no.

I explained to Tonya that the words we use create the reality that we associate with them. I suggested to her, therefore, that if she thought of her passion as "a job", that she might end up creating for herself yet another unsatisfying experience rather than something exciting and new.

In *passionese*--the language of passion--a "job" restricts, controls and suppresses. A "passion", on the other hand, empowers, satisfies and frees. You get to decide who to sell to, how much money you'll earn, and you can give yourself a raise or a promotion any time you wish. You get to choose aspects of how you spend your days, and above all, you get to offer unique value to the world that has meaning for you.

To accomplish this, however, the thing you love to do--your passion--can no longer be just a hobby, an "on-the-side" thing, passing fancy, and least of all, a job. There must be a structure through which you will offer your unique value to the world, and through which the income, and eventually profit will flow to you. In other words, your passion must become a living, breathing honest-to-goodness business!

What Business Are You In?

The first thing to decide when starting your own business is what business you're actually going to be in. If you sell shoes by mail order, are you in the shoe business, or in mail order? It's important to understand the distinction because if you consider yourself in mail order, for example, then you may shut yourself out of other streams of income since mail order is really just one way of *marketing* a product or service.

On the other hand, if you consider yourself in the fashion industry and that shoes are the thing you sell, and that mail order is simply a means to sell that shoe, then you open yourself up to a multiplicity of income streams by exploring different marketing methods. Business experts always say that the key to success is to focus on one thing and then sell the heck out of it.

Here's how the terms *industry*, *business*, *product* and *sales method* would apply to the above example:

industry	fashion
product/service	shoes
business model	retail/wholesale
sales/distribution method	direct marketing/mlm/mail order/Internet/ franchise/licensing/ job / consulting

If you decide to branch out into other products within the same industry, know that for each new product—hats or shirts, for example—you can and should develop a unique marketing strategy that may or may not include the same sales methods.

Who to Sell To?

In developing your passion, you'll also need to decide to whom you'll be selling. You may not always use the traditional business-to-consumer model for your business. Here are some additional options:

Business To Consumer -	traditional retail stores follow this model.
Business To Business -	you can sell products to other businesses. Consulting services and temporary staff services follow this model.
Consumer to Consumer -	auction sites capitalize on the growing consumer to consumer trend.
Consumer to Business -	the next big trend, perhaps? What ways can you think of to facilitate transactions from consumers to businesses other than as an employee?

Choosing the Best Business Model

The business model you choose encompasses the sales and distribution strategy you select to get your product to the masses. Here are some models to consider.

Multi-Level Marketing (MLM) [also known as Network Marketing]

It was the power of network marketing that freed me from the shackles of corporate employment. It's also, I believe, one of the purest forms of business that rewards people for hard (and smart) work, commitment and most importantly, helping others to succeed.

In network marketing, independent sales representatives become your sales force earning commissions for every sale. They also earn commissions on the sales of anyone they "sponsor" or recruit to be sales representatives. This gives every representative a financial incentive to sponsor as many people as possible, thus increasing your sales force exponentially! You earn money from the sales of hundreds, possibly thousands of independent representatives all going out selling your passion! You could be the owner of the next Amway, Nuskin or MaryKay!

MLM has had a short, but challenging history. There have been sad tales of companies which misled the public with promises of wealth, and with scams that turned out to be nothing more than "pyramid schemes" milking money from naive consumers. Consequently, MLM companies are often heavily scrutinized by Attorneys General in all states for compliance to certain ethical codes of conduct. Contact the Multi-Level Marketing International Association (CA) at (949) 854-0484, or online at www.mlmia.org for more information, and definitely retain legal advice if you choose this route.

Franchise

As a franchisor, people (your franchisees) pay you for the right to sell products using your trade name. Their success, and yours is based on the power of your reputation, your concept and/or a proven system of selling and marketing. It's a powerful way to leverage the efforts of others in the creation of your wealth.

If your passion involves a product or service that has a unique method of selling then you might want to consider a franchise. Franchises work best if your business can be set up as a "turn-key" operation that others can use to offer the same consistent level of quality of your orginal location. That's what the founders of Starbucks, Blimpies, McDonalds, Redi-Maid, Maaco all did. You could be next.

Contact The International Franchise Association, (DC); at (202) 628-8000, or online at www.ifa.org for more information.

Licensing

If your passion is in the form of an idea, a logo, images of cartoon characters, or some other unique design, you can license your idea to others. Others will pay you for the right to sell products featuring your logo. The licensees do the work of manufacturing and marketing the product, and you, the licensor, simply collect ongoing royalties. Contact the International Licensing Industry Merchandisers' Association in New York City at (212)244-1944 for more information.

Where You Do Business

You have several options of where to operate your business. You can work from home, or buy or lease a location. Your decision will depend on several factors based on the type of business you are starting. Is there a need to deal directly with clients? Do you need storage space for inventory? Does your passion involve heavy machinery? Will you need employees? Will frequent shipping and deliveries affect your neighbors?

Working from Home

Experts indicate that at least 40 million people work from home. Thirty million of those are home-based entrepreneurs. Here are some points to consider.

Advantages	Disadvantages
• convenience	• possible zoning restrictions
• comfort	• isolation/tendency to overwork
• low overhead expenses	• no separation between business and home life
• home-business tax deductions	• interruptions and distractions

Buying or Leasing Space

Buying or leasing an office or building from which to run your business is another option. Before you make that decision, be sure to consider monthly costs, your cash flow, the image of the surrounding community, the structural integrity of the building, zoning regulations, options for expansion, and tax advantages of leasing over buying.

Advantages	Disadvantages
• more professional image	• expense (taxes, insurance, maintenance)
• separation of business and home	• commute
• tax deductions for rent fees	• business may be hurt by poor location

Other Options

Other options of where to do business include sharing office space with other businesses in "Business Parks", renting space in a mall or using a Business Incubator (a service offering shared space, services, financial assistance and guidance for fledgling businesses). See appendix for other support associations to contact.

The Right Name!

Choosing a name for your passion-centered business is a very important step. The success or failure of a business often rests in how appealing or unappealing the name is to potential customers. The name you choose should be short, but it could also be long. The name you choose might convey something about your business, or perhaps not. In other words, there are no rules, but there are some tips which can guide you.

Plan for expansion--Unless you're sure that you want to spend the rest of your life doing one thing, you may want to avoid a name like Susie's Socks. A name like that would limit you and require that you change your checks, stationery, etc., should you decide to expand. (A more general name like "SuzieWear" might be better).

Play on words-- A clever name can bring business to you and make you a profit simply because it makes people smile. Did you hear the one about the man who started a company offering around-the-house handyman services to single women and the elderly who called it Rent-A-Husband? Or the maid service company called Got It Maid? Or the rest room advertising company called Stall Tactics? Or the teddy bear clothing company called Bearly Dressed? Or the furniture stripping shop called The Towne Stripper? Or the silk plant business called Make Be-Leaves? Many of these companies get business just on the strength of their unique names.

Test on friends--One way to start the creative process of coming up with a name for your product or service or company, is simply to make up names using words and phrases that are related to what you do. Then try them out on friends. You're looking for names that are memorable, easy to spell, and that say what your product/company is about with minimal to no explanation. Use a thesaurus or dictionary to come up with unusual names.

Decide on a tag line--The next thing you'll want to do is come up with some slogan or "tag line." This is the little phrase right below your product or company name. The slogan might be a description of your product or company, or a benefit it provides. (*"we do chicken right"*) It often clarifies something that might be confusing about your company. (*"We make the things that make communications work"*). Or it might emphasize your position in the market (*"When you're #2, you try harder"*).

Use software--In this technological world we live in, books and software exist to help create winning names for your product or business. See appendix for more information.

Protecting Your Assets and Ideas

Metaphysically speaking, your passion idea is yours, and what's yours cannot be taken away from you. However, there may be other souls on the planet who may attempt to turn *your* passion into *their* profit by infringing upon your ideas. Patents, trademarks and copyrights exist as a way of protecting your creations and ideas..

Patents

If following your passion results in an invention, a patent will help to protect that invention within the marketplace. A patent is a right granted by the government. It gives the patent-holder the exclusive right to exclude others from making, using, selling, or importing their particular invention, product or process for a period of twenty years from the filing date. According to the actual wording of the law, it is granted to an individual who *"invents or discovers any new and useful process, machine, [method of] manufacture, or composition of matter, or any new and useful improvement thereof..."*

Because of the different fees involved (filing fees, maintenance fees, resubmission fees), as well as the legal costs, a patent application can cost thousands of dollars. The application process (which requires submitting drawings, models and specimens) may take several months or even years due to required searches, as well as the actual approval process. Contact the US Patent and Trademark office at 2900 Crystal Drive, 4B10, Arlington VA, 22202; 703-308-900, or at www.uspto.gov.

Trademarks

Trademarks and Servicemarks protect the words, names, symbols or devices that embody your company, your reputation, or what you offer your customers. These can be logos, characters, designs, slogans or particularly unique ways of writing. These images—or marks—are the symbols under which you trade (do business) or provide service, and with which the public has come to associate your particular brand of quality, expertise, price, or whatever your Unique Selling Point (USP) is. Trademark rights may be used to prevent others from using a confusingly similar mark, but not to prevent others from making the same goods or from selling the same goods or services under a clearly different mark. So, the Coca-Cola trademark prevents others from using that name, but doesn't prevent Pepsi from selling cola as well.

The registration process for trademarks as well as general information concerning trademarks is described in a pamphlet entitled *"Basic Facts about Trademarks."* As of January 10th, 2000, the basic filing fee is $325. There are also fees of varying amounts for renewals, extensions, cancellations and oppositions. Contact the US Patent and Trademark office at 2900 Crystal Drive, 4B10, Arlington VA, 22202; 703-308-900, or online at www.uspto.gov for details.

Copyright

Copyright is a form of protection provided to the authors of "original works of authorship." If your passion involves the creation of literary, dramatic, musical, artistic, or certain other intellectual works, both published and unpublished, then a copyright can help you protect your creations. The 1976 Copyright Act gives the owner of copyright the exclusive right to reproduce (copy) the copyrighted work, to prepare derivative works, to distribute copies or phonorecords of the copyrighted work, to perform the copyrighted work publicly, or to display the copyrighted work publicly.

The copyright protects the *form* of expression rather than the *subject matter* of the writing. For example, a description of a machine could be copyrighted, but this would only prevent others from copying the description; it would not prevent others from writing a description of their own or from making and using the machine. Your greeting cards, brochures, poems, novels, posters, lyrics, can all be copyrighted.

Contact the U.S. Copyright Office Library of Congress, 101 Independence Ave., S.E., Washington DC 20559-6000 Public Information Office: (202) 707-3000; Forms Hotline: (202) 707-9100 or online at http://lcweb.loc.gov/copyright, for more details.

Keep in mind that your rights of ownership exist from the moment you create your product. These rights are enforceable, even without the patent, trademark and copyright, if you can show prior use in some valid way. The patent, trademark and copyright are simply legal ways for you to enforce these rights. They prove that by virtue of the filing dates and dates of first use, that you got there first.

Starting a Business: The Process

In truth, you are IN business from the moment you say you are. However, for the purpose of being a legitimately recognized entity, these are steps you'll need to take:
- Choose a business structure.
- Announce your intention. (publish an announcement--some states)
- File necessary papers and pay fees as required for your chosen structure.
- Get appropriate licenses, permits, insurance as necessary.
- Set up a bank account.

Types of Business Structures

In order to be legitimate, your business must be registered with the government as a legally recognized entity. There are several possible structures for your company:
- $ Sole Proprietorship
- $ Corporation
- $ Subchapter "S" Corporation
- $ Non-profit Corporation
- $ Professional Corporation
- $ Foreign Corporation
- $ Foreign Non-Profit Corporation
- $ General Partnership
- $ Limited Liability Company (LLC)
- $ Limited Liability Partnership (LLP)
- $ Foreign Limited Liability Company (LLC)
- $ Foreign Limited Liability Partnership

With few exceptions, every single business, operation, or other money-making venture--even not-for-profit organizations--fall into one of these categories. Each form has its advantages and disadvantages which may make it appropriate for certain types of businesses and not others.

Sole Proprietorship

If you are launching your passion-centered business alone, you may want to consider starting a Sole Proprietorship. As the name implies, as sole owner, YOU are the company. You can still have employees, of course, but the company itself is owned entirely by you. You alone have the power of the checkbook. While this control is appealing, it also means some other things you should be aware of. As a Sole Proprietor, the courts and the government don't differentiate between you and your company. In other words, if for some reason, someone decides to sue your business and wins, or if the company fails and incurs a sizable debt, or if you owe taxes on the business, then you, the individual, will ultimately be responsible for these judgments or debts. Your assets (anything you own), including your personal savings, may be used to repay the debts. Don't let this discourage you, however. There are between 13 and 14 million small businesses in the United States, and a good 75% of them are Sole Proprietorships. It requires the least paperwork to get up and running and, if you set realistic goals, plan your strategy, and do things correctly, you can avoid most legal and tax headaches.

Form to file: "DBA"/Certificate of Doing Business Under an Assumed Name or similarly titled form. You'll usually need three copies; one for the county, one for your bank, and one for your place of business. Additional copies will be required if your state requires any special permits.)

Where to file: County Clerk's Office/County Courthouse

Fees: Filing fee (anywhere from $0 to $50, depending on the state)

Certification fee (varies widely per state);

NOTE: Some states require you to announce your new business in the local press.

Partnership

If you and some friends are going into this venture, you might want to consider forming a Partnership. A partnership is the relationship between two or more persons who join together to carry on a trade or business. The main reason people form partnerships is to increase the money, labor and skills available to the business. In a General Partnership (the most common form), the partners share control, profit, as well as liability for debt. In the Limited Partnership, there are some partners who invest money or property in return for a cut of the profit, but their control is limited and their liability, as well, is limited to the amount of their investment (Limited partners are sometimes referred to as "silent" partners). In determining how profits are split, or how control will be shared, the partners are free to come to any arrangement they choose without government restrictions. It is similar to a Sole Proprietorship in that the persons involved are generally still considered individuals as far as the government and tax laws are concerned. This structure also involves minimal paperwork to get started. In fact, in some states, the individuals involved don't even need a written agreement among them to be considered in a partnership. However, I recommend always having something in writing. The drawbacks to a partnership are more personal than legal. Conflicts of egos, miscommunication, incompatibility of management and operational styles are among the main issues cited as challenging by entrepreneurs involved in partnerships. Liability should also be a concern for anyone considering a partnership. You should be aware that any decision, agreement or deal made by one member of a partnership is binding on the other members as well, even if the other members were not consulted or present when the decision was made. So, for example, both you and your partner would be held legally responsible for paying for the 10,000 widgets your partner ordered (acting on his/her own initiative) the Friday you were out of town.

Form to file: Certificate of Conducting Business as Partners (from stationery store)

Where to file: County Clerk's Office/County Courthouse

Fees: *Filing fee* Anywhere from $0 to $50, depending on the state.

Certification fee Usually less than $10 per form; you'll need about 3 forms; one each for the county, your bank, and your place of business. Additional copies will be required if your state requires any special permits.

Limited Liability Company (LLC)

The Limited Liability Company (LLC) is the newest form of business entity. Owners of an LLC are referred to as active or nonactive "members." Active members are taxed like general partners whereas nonactive members are taxed like limited partners. All members, however, enjoy limited liability and may report profits or losses on their personal tax returns. What makes the LLC attractive to many entrepreneurs is that it combines the best features of a corporation and those of a partnership. The members have limited liability like a corporation while income and losses are passed through to the individual members as in a partnership. The LLC is not a taxable entity like a corporation.

Although an LLC sounds a lot like an S-corporation (Both LLC and an S-corporation avoid double taxation by allowing the pass through of income to the owners (or members) and they both provide for limited liability), the LLC does have some additional flexibility that may be important for some businesses.

Advantages of an LLC
- Limited liability for all members, unlike a general partnership.
- No taxation as an entity. No double taxation as in a corporation.
- May have more than one class of stock. Profits and losses need not be distributed in proportion of ownership, unlike the S-corporation..
- No limit to the number of members, unlike the S corporation.
- Allows greater flexibility in management and business organization.
- No ownership restrictions of S Corp, so are ideal for foreign investors.

Disadvantages of an LLC
- Fairly complex to setup properly. Each state has slightly different rules.
- No "continuity of life" like a regular corporation. The LLC dissolves if one of the members dies or leaves. Formal agreements, however, can solve this.

Important bits of information concerning LLCs

A business that intends issuing stock incentives to employees or selling shares to the public should consider incorporating instead of the LLC. A few states, (Texas, California) impose annual fees or taxes on LLCs. As of Oct 1998, in California, the District of Columbia, Massachusetts, New Jersey and Tennessee, an LLC must have at least two owners. Most other states allow LLCs to be formed with one person.

How to Form an LLC
1. Choose an available business name that complies with your state's LLC rules.
2. File formal paperwork, ("articles of organization"), pay filing fee (from $40 to $900)
3. Create an LLC operating agreement (rights and responsibilities of LLC members)
4. Publish a notice of your intent to form an LLC (required in only a few states).
5. Obtain licenses and permits that may be required for your business.

Filing Articles of Organization for LLC

After deciding on a name, you must prepare and file "articles of organization" with your state's LLC filing office. While most states use the term "articles of organization" to refer to the basic document creating an LLC, some states (including Delaware, Mississippi, New Hampshire, New Jersey and Washington) use the term "certificate of formation." Two other states (Massachusetts and Pennsylvania) call the document a "certificate of organization."

You'll have to pay a filing fee when you submit your articles of organization. In most states, the fees are modest —about $100.

Articles of organization are short, simple documents which can be prepared by filling in the blanks on a form provided by your state's filing office. Typically, you must provide only your LLC's name, its address and sometimes the names of all of the owners — called members. You will probably be required to list the name and address of a person —usually one of the LLC members — who will act as your LLC's "registered agent," or "agent for service of process." Your agent is the person who will receive legal papers in any lawsuit involving your LLC. Generally, all of the LLC owners may prepare and sign the articles, or they can appoint one person to do so.

Creating an LLC Operating Agreement

Even though operating agreements need not be filed with the LLC filing office and are rarely required by state law, it is essential that you create one. In an LLC operating agreement, you set out rules for the ownership and operation of the business (much like a partnership agreement or corporate bylaws). A typical agreement includes:
- the members' percentage interests in the business
- the members' rights and responsibilities
- the members' voting power
- how profits and losses will be allocated
- how the LLC will be managed
- rules for holding meetings and taking votes, and
- "buy-sell" provisions, which establish rules for what happens if a member wants to sell his interest, dies or becomes disabled.

Corporations

Of the three forms of business, the corporation involves the most paperwork, "legalese", and is the most regulated by the government through state and federal laws. A corporation is formed after an individual or group of individuals applies to the state for a charter. The corporation, which the state approves into existence, has its own identity. It needs to file its own taxes, and have its own bank account. Income and losses are taxed to the corporation. Any income generated by the corporation for the stockholders is also taxed. In other words, if the company makes $100, and your share is $50, the government would tax the $100 at the corporate rate, and then tax your $50 at the individual level. This "double taxation" is one of the more annoying drawbacks to the corporation. The corporation is a separate entity from the individuals who run it. That means your personal assets usually cannot be touched in the event of legal or financial action against the company.

Here a few of the benefits of setting up a corporation.

Reduces Personal Liability

Incorporating helps separate your personal identity from that of your business. Sole proprietors and partners are subject to unlimited personal liability for business debt or law suits against their company. Creditors of the sole proprietorship or partnership can bring suit against the owners of the business and can move to seize the owners' homes, cars, savings or other personal assets. Once incorporated, the shareholders of a corporation have only the money they put into the company to lose, and usually no more.

Adds Credibility

A corporate structure communicates permanence, credibility and stature. Even if you are the only stockholder or employee, your incorporated business may be perceived as a much larger and more credible company. Seeing ",inc." or "corp." at the end of your business name can send a powerful message to your customers, suppliers, and associates about your commitment to the ongoing success of your venture.

Provides Tax Advantages – Deductible Employee Benefits

Incorporating usually provides tax-deductible benefits for you and your employees. Even if you are the only shareholder and employee of your business, benefits such as health insurance, life insurance, travel and entertainment expenses may now be deductible. Best of all, corporations usually provide an increased tax shelter for qualified pension plans or retirement plans (e.g. 401K's).

Allows Easier Access to Capital Funding

Capital can be more easily raised with a corporation through the sale of stock. Investors are more likely to purchase shares in a corporation where there is a separation between personal and business assets. Some banks prefer to lend money to corporations.

Creates an Enduring Structure

A corporation is the most enduring legal business structure. Corporations may continue regardless of what happens to its individual directors, officers, managers or shareholders. If a sole proprietor or partner dies, the business may automatically end or it may become involved in various legal entanglements. Corporations can have unlimited life, extending beyond the illness or death of the owners.

Allows Easier Transfer of Ownership

Simply by selling stock, ownership of a corporation may be transferred, without substantially disrupting operations or the need for complex legal documents.

Provides Anonymity

Corporations can offer anonymity to its owners. For example, if you want to open an independent small business of any kind and do not want your involvement to be public knowledge, your best choice may be to incorporate. If you open as a sole proprietorship, it is hard to hide the fact that you are the owner. And as a partnership, you will most likely be required to register your name and the names of your partners with the state and/or county officials in which you are doing business.

Offers Centralized Management

With a corporation's centralized management, all decisions are made by your board of directors. Your shareholders cannot unilaterally bind your company by their acts simply because of their investment. With partnerships, each individual general partner may make binding agreements on behalf of the business that may result in serious financial difficulty to you or the partnership as a whole.

Types of Corporations: a closer look

General or "C" Corporation

A general corporation, also known as a "C" corporation, is the most common corporate structure. A general corporation may have an unlimited number of stockholders. Consequently, it is usually chosen by those companies planning to have more than 30 stockholders or large public stock offerings. Since a corporation is a separate legal entity, a stockholder's personal liability is usually limited to the amount of investment in the corporation and no more.

Close Corporation

A close corporation is most appropriate for the individual starting a company alone or with a small number of people. There are a few significant differences between a general corporation and a close corporation. A close corporation limits stockholders to a maximum of 30. In addition, many close corporation statutes require that the directors of a close corporation must first offer the shares to existing stockholders before selling to new stockholders. Not all states recognize close corporations.

Nonprofit Corporation

A nonprofit corporation is a corporation formed for purposes other than generating a profit and in which no part of the organization's income is distributed to its directors or officers. A nonprofit corporation can be a church or church association, school, charity, medical provider, legal aid society, volunteer services organization, professional association, research institute, museum, or in some cases a sports association. Nonprofit corporations must apply for tax-exempt status at both the federal and state levels.

Professional Corporation (PC)

A professional corporation is a corporation engaged in providing professional services. The corporations formed by architects, attorneys-at-law, public accountants, physicians, dentists, optometrists, osteopaths, chiropractors, registered nurses, veterinarians, podiatrists, practicing psychologists, occupational therapists, engineers and land surveyors, landscape architects, certified clinical social workers, geologists & foresters are usually considered PCs.

Foreign Corporation *Typical usage refers to definition 2.*
Definition 1: A corporation which was incorporated under the laws of a foreign country; also called an alien corporation.
Definition 2: A corporation doing business in a state other than the one in which it is incorporated; here also called out-of-state corporation; opposite of domestic corporation.

Foreign Non-Profit Corporation

A foreign nonprofit corporation is one that is incorporated under laws other than the laws of this state. A foreign corporation is required to obtain a Certificate of Authority if it is "transacting business" or "conducting affairs" in this state.

Subchapter S Corporation

A Subchapter S Corporation is a general corporation that has elected a special tax status with the IRS after the corporation has been formed. Subchapter S corporations are most appropriate for small business owners and entrepreneurs who prefer to be taxed as if they were still sole proprietors or partners. For many small businesses, the S Corp offers the best of both worlds: the tax advantages of a sole proprietorship or partnership with the limited liability and enduring life of a corporation.

When a general corporation makes a profit, it pays a federal corporate income tax on the profit. If the company also declares a dividend, the stockholders must report the dividend as personal income and pay more taxes. S Corporations avoid this "double taxation" (once at the corporate level and again at the personal level) because all income or loss is reported only once on the personal tax returns of the stockholders.

This may be advantageous for new business owners who would benefit from the low individual tax rates during the early life of the company when profits are usually low (or negative). Later, when profits are higher, the corporation can elect to revert to general corporation status and take advantage of the tax benefits the corporation enjoys.

You can have a lawyer handle the incorporation process, or use one of the many "quickie" services for which you can search online. For an average cost of from $100 to $400 (includes filing fee and lawyer's fee) it may be worth being sure it's done right.

How to File as a Subchapter S Corporation

- Form a general or close corporation in the state of your choice.
- Obtain the formal consent of the corporation's stockholders and note this consent in your minutes.
- Complete Form 2553, Election by a Small Business Corporation

Forms to File: Certificate of Incorporation. Each state has its own form and rules.
Federal Form 2553—Election by a Small Business Corporation.
Fees: Filing fees, minimum taxes, and other requirements vary widely by state. If you choose to do it yourself, your local bookstore should have books under the general title of "How to Start a Corporation in (Your State)". Your State Department of Taxation or Comptroller's Department or State Revenue Department may also have information.

Restrictions:

- To elect S Corporation status, your corporation must meet specific guidelines. All stockholders must be citizens or permanent residents of the United States. The maximum number of stockholders for an S Corporation is 75. If an S Corporation is held by an "electing small business trust," then all beneficiaries of the trust must be individuals, estates or charitable organizations. Interests in the trust cannot be purchased. S Corporations may only issue one class of stock. No more than 25 percent of the gross corporate income may be derived from passive income.

Exclusions (The following entities may not elect S-Corp status):

- a financial institution that is a bank
- an insurance company taxed under Subchapter L
- a Domestic International Sales Corporation (DISC)
- certain affiliated groups of corporations

How To Form A Corporation

There are several steps required to legally create a corporation. The first is filing a short document called "articles of incorporation" with the corporations division of your state government. (known in some states as a "certificate of incorporation," "articles of organization," a "certificate of formation" or a "charter.") To file this document, you'll pay a filing fee of $100 or so. Articles of incorporation contain:

- ✓ the name of your corporation
- ✓ the corporation's address
- ✓ a "registered agent" (the contact person), and in some states,
- ✓ the names of the corporation's directors.

When forming your corporation, you must also create "corporate bylaws," a longer document that sets out the rules that govern your corporation, including necessary decision-making procedures and voting rights. Finally, before you start doing business, you must hold an initial meeting of your board of directors to take care of some formalities, and you need to issue shares of stock to the initial owners (shareholders).

Steps for Starting a Corporation in New York State

Preliminary Step. The first place to start is a stationery store that carries legal forms (The Blumberg line of legal forms is the most popular). There, you can purchase a corporate kit ($50-$100) which includes most of the forms mentioned below that you'll need to complete and/or file. The forms not included in the corporate kit can be purchased directly from the stationer.

Step 1. Choose a corporate name (Certain restrictions apply). Contact Dept. of State and request a name search ($5) to make sure no one else has registered the name. You may also wish to check phone book listings, the Federal Trademark Register (at your library), the county clerk's office, and industry directories to make sure the name you want is not being used by someone else.

Step 2. Complete and file Certificate of Incorporation. Mail to Department of State along with appropriate fees, ($125 + $0.05 per share tax), backing sheet (a sheet with corporate name and person submitting certificate), and a cover letter.

Step 3. File Stock Registration Certificate. (No filing fee required, but the form must be notarized) The purpose is to notify the Tax Commission of the existence of your corporation. This is necessary because every time stock is transferred a small tax is required to be paid to the Commission.

Step 4. Set up your Corporate Records Book. This is simply where you keep all your corporate papers (Certificate of Incorporation, Stock Registration Certificate, Bylaws, Statement of Incorporators, Minutes of Meetings, stock certificates, etc). Many people will simply get a three-ring binder to accomplish this.

Step 5. Get a corporate seal (about $40). You've probably seen Notary Publics use a similar type of embossed seal. Your corporate seal serves the similar purpose of authorizing certain formal documents like leases, stock certificates, mortgages and loan documents as being valid acts of the corporation.

Step 6. Order stock certificates. Your legal stationer can have custom-made for you, or you can use the generic ones included in your corporate kit. These are given to your shareholders in return for their monetary investment in your company.

Step 7. Prepare Bylaws. The Bylaws are the rules for the management and operation of the corporation. Once again there are standard forms with a few blank spaces for you to fill in specific information about your corporation. These are also in your corporate kit.

Step 8. Prepare Statement of Incorporators. This step is a formality that's required before the corporation can legally begin to operate. The person(s) who signed the Certificate of Incorporation are required to officially adopt the bylaws and elect the directors who are going to manage the corporation. The statement is simply a signed letter stating just that. Of course if you are the only board member, getting the require signatures should be quite easy!

Step 9. Prepare and sign minutes of first meeting. This may seem a tedious formality, but if you're going to do this, do it right! There are certain items which must be resolved at a first meeting. So, again, there's not much to do since there are generic "minutes of first meeting" forms with blank spaces to be filled in. (Also in your corporate kit.)

Step 10. Issue shares of stock. The number of shares to be issued and the price per stock were determined at the first meeting. There are federal and state securities laws which govern how stock can be issued. Contact the Securities Exchange Commission (SEC) to have them send you a package.

As you see, none of these steps requires any great outlay of money nor any knowledge that you can't find in the instructions.

4 Reasons To Choose a Corporation over an LLC.

1. Your business needs the ability to issue stock or stock options to attract investors.

2. Your business is so profitable that you can save significant income tax dollars by keeping some profits in the corporation each year. This strategy is called "income splitting" because profits are split between the individual owners and the corporation itself.

3. You own a family business and you want to begin making gifts of ownership to your family as part of your financial or estate plan or to plan for the next generation of owners. With a corporation you can easily make gifts of shares in your company without necessarily giving up management control and, done correctly, without paying gift tax.

4. Others insist that you incorporate your business. For example, if you are an independent contractor, companies you want to work for may ask you to incorporate before they will sign contracts for your services. This is because if you form a corporation, the IRS is more likely to view you as an independent contractor than an employee — a less-risky proposition for those who want to hire you.

Which structure should you choose?

The decision of which form of business to use will depend on a number of factors: the particular financial situations of the individuals involved, tax and legal requirements of the business, record keeping, the need for and number of employees, and other unique circumstances. Also, since each state will have its own set of filing and tax requirements for each form of business, these must be considered as well when deciding which is best for you. After my own personal experience with The Service Corps of Retired Executives (SCORE), I strongly recommend finding the office nearest you and establishing a relationship with an adviser. Having someone to guide you to ask the right questions can save you major heartaches in the future.

For the record: Here's my FINAL Answer!

I'll gladly go on record as saying that I believe your choice will be between the LLC and a Corporation. I say this because of the tax benefits provided. The game that the rich play is knowing how to separate themselves from their money. In other words, the average person feels more secure with everything in their name. The rich, to avoid liability, seek to have nothing in their personal name, but everything at their direct disposal as an asset or perk of doing business. Think about that.

The major advantage to having a corporation is that you can legally benefit from many "perks of doing business" without having the financial accountability and tax burden of having these perks in your own name.

So, for the record, I'm advocating LLC or Corporation as your choice of business structure. And, unless a new entity comes along before I revise this book, that's my story and I'm sticking with it! On the next page is a chart that allows for easy comparison.

*****

Structure	Advantages	Disadvantages
Sole Proprietorship	Simple and inexpensive to create and operate Owner reports profit or loss on his or her personal tax return	Owner personally liable for business debts
General Partnership	Simple and inexpensive to create and operate Owners (partners) report their share of profit or loss on their personal tax returns	Owners (partners) personally liable for business debts
Limited Partnership	Limited partners have limited personal liability for business debts as long as they don't participate in management. General partners can raise cash without involving outside investors in management of business	General partners personally liable for business debts More expensive to create than general partnership Suitable mainly for companies that invest in real estate
Regular Corporation (Also available: Professional Corporation and non-profit corporation)	Owners have limited personal liability for business debts Fringe benefits can be deducted as business expense Owners can split corporate profit among owners and corporation paying lower overall tax rate	More expensive to create than partnership or sole proprietorship Paperwork can seem burdensome to some owners Separate taxable entity
S Corporation	Owners have limited personal liability for business debts Owners report their share of corporate profit or loss on their personal tax returns Owners can use corporate loss to offset income from other sources	More expensive to create than partnership or sole proprietorship More paperwork than for a limited liability company which offers similar advantages Income must be allocated to owners according to their ownership interests Fringe benefits limited for owners who own more than 2% of shares
Limited Liability Company (LLC) (also Professional LLC in which Members must all belong to the same profession) Also LLP (Limited Liability Partnerships)	Owners have limited personal liability for business debts even if they participate in management. Profit and loss can be allocated differently than ownership interests IRS rules now allow LLCs to choose between being taxed as partnership or corporation	More expensive to create than partnership or sole proprietorship. State laws for creating LLCs may not reflect latest federal tax changes

Other Considerations

Every business has different needs. However, here are some of the things you may need in order to get started.

Licenses and Permits

Depending on the type of business, the type of product or service you offer, or the part of town you set up shop, you may need to get a local business license, federal import license, county license, state license, or federal license.

Licenses are an indication that you have the authorization, expertise, or zoning approval for a given jurisdiction. The issuing agency for a given license varies by state. You may need to contact the county clerk's office, city hall, the county registrar, or the recorder's office. If in doubt, contact the local Small Business Administration (SBA) office in your area. They'll put you in touch with the right agency where you can get information on the required certifications for your business as well as the appropriate fees.

Permits, on the other hand, are an indication that you have complied with certain local and state laws affecting safety, appearance or the right to collect sales tax. Again, a call to your state government office, or the local SBA will put you in the right direction.

Resale Certificate

As a business, you do not pay sales tax on the purchase of goods and services which will be resold, or which will be used in creating a product or service for resale. For example, if you buy lumber to make chairs to be sold to the public, you would not be required to pay taxes on the purchase of the lumber. Your payments to your printing company, supplier, manufacturer or other individuals or businesses (vendors) involved in your trade will generally be exempt from sales taxes. To qualify for this exemption from paying sales taxes, you need to be authorized and recognized by your state. You will need to apply for a Sales Tax Vendor ID/Certificate of Authority with your state department of taxation. You will be given a sales tax vendor ID number (in most cases, you will be able to use the EIN which you'll receive after completing form SS-4).

When making purchases on behalf of your company, inform the vendor that you have a resale certificate. You'll need to provide them with a completed copy of a certificate. (The state or your local stationery store can supply you with this form. Be sure to make extra copies). Generally, this form must be completed each time a purchase is made. If you anticipate recurring interaction with a particular vendor, you should request that she or he keep a "Blanket Certificate", on file which will cover any future purchases you make from this vendor, eliminating the need to complete a new form each time.

Sales tax is charged on purchases at the retail level. That is, at the point where it is offered for retail sale to the consumer. Your status as a vendor will also authorize you to collect sales tax on retail sales—that is, sales directly to the public. You are collecting taxes on behalf of the state, and are therefore required to hand over what you've collected at (usually) quarterly intervals. The necessary forms, coupons or deposit slips will be provided to you by your state agency at the time you apply for your Vendor ID.

Insurance

While some experts advise strongly in favor of insurance, others ignore it altogether. The reasoning in favor of insurance is that, as a business, you will come in contact with customers, suppliers and employees who, for any reason might file a claim against you for negligence, bodily injury, product liability, worker's compensation, or because your property may get stolen or damaged. You must, therefore, prepare and protect yourself for that possibility by taking out an insurance policy.

Ultimately, this decision will be influenced by the type of business you operate, the likelihood of such need, industry trends and practices, your comfort level of risk, and the cost of insurance relative to your budget. Contact the Small Business Administration (SBA), the Insurance Information Institute and The Service Corps of Retired Executives (SCORE) for advice and information.

Financing Your Business

If possible, you should start your business without getting into debt. Most people start their business using their own money and often use their present source of employment to provide the necessary funding.

Some passions, on the other hand, may require start-up cash that's greater than what you currently have on hand. For example, you may need large sums of money to buy equipment, purchase inventory, get patents, etc. In figuring out how to raise money to jump-start your business, there are essentially 3 ways to get it. Non-Debt Financing, Debt Financing and Equity Financing.

Non-Debt Financing

1. YOU. You are your own best "lender". If you have the savings, this approach can be quick and easy. Entrepreneurs have started billion-dollar companies with as little as $0 invested.

2. BARTERING. You need money to pay for supplies, starting inventory, advertising, etc. What if you could get those goods and services directly in return for providing some service or product you already have? Bartering allows you to trade your goods and services for those of other companies. Contact the International Reciprocal Trade Association in Chicago, IL, at (312)461-0236, or online at www.irta.org for more information.

3. GRANTS. Many foundations provide funding in the form of grants. The "Foundation Directory" can provide a list of foundations that may have an interest in your specific business idea. The Foundation Center may be reached at (212) 620-4230, or online at www.fdncenter.org. You may also wish to contact the National Endowment for the Arts at (202) 682-5400, or online at www.arts.endow.gov for information on their programs. Another little-known fact is that the US Department of Agriculture, in addition to sponsoring over two dozen money-lending programs, encourages growth in rural areas, with an Industrial Loan Program which provides funds for businesses in towns of less than 50,000 people. Contact the USDA at www.usda.gov.

4. VENDOR FINANCING. If your business is one that relies heavily on certain vendors, it may be possible to obtain financing through the vendor. After all, they want you to use their product or service and therefore have an interest in helping you be successful. Contact the SBA or SCORE for guidance.

5. FACTORING. If you are owed money by customers, there are finance companies, banks and individuals, known as factors, who will purchase the right to collect these debts. Say you have an invoice for $2,000 owed to you by Carrie Customer. ABC factor may purchase this invoice for say, 85% of it's value. You receive $1700 that you can use right away for your business, and Carrie now owes ABC factor the $2,000. ABC factor now has the responsibility of collecting the $2,000 from Carrie.

You can also factor purchase orders. If you receive an order from a large store, chain or other buyer, the purchase order represents a promise to pay which can be sold to ABC factor. You get money up front to use to purchase inventory or manufacture the product. Again, the disadvantage is that you only get a percentage of the total amount of the purchase order. Look in your local yellow pages, or online search engines under "factors", or call the SBA, SCORE, your bank, or The Commercial Finance Association (NY), at (212)594-3490, or online at www.cfa.com for more information.

6. PRE-SELLING. You may wish to consider pre-selling your product as a means of generating capital by taking orders in advance from friends, family, advertisers, etc. Offer a "pre-launch discount" as an incentive. (*i.e. Pre-order NOW and save 10%!*)

Debt Financing-As the name implies, with debt financing, you are financing your passion by going into debt. Someone lends you the money that you need. You are required to pay back this loan with interest. The interest rate that you pay on the loan will vary depending on who gives you the money. The vast majority of small businesses that need more money than they have available use debt financing.

7. RETIREMENT PLANS. Some retirement plans (401K for example) allow you to borrow against vested benefits. Generally, up to 50% may be borrowed as long as this is less than $50,000. If you quit your employment, the loan must be repaid immediately. If you don't pay, the amount borrowed is treated as an "early distribution" and is taxable.

8. LIFE INSURANCE. Some types of life insurance policies (whole life and universal) have cash value which can be borrowed at low interest rates. You are not obligated to pay this money back, but your policy payout is reduced by the amount borrowed.

9. HOME EQUITY LOAN. Interest rates for this kind of loan are generally quite low and the interest is fully deductible for the first $100,000 borrowed. Keep in mind that you are placing your home on the line as collateral with this method of financing.

10. THE SMALL BUSINESS ADMINISTRATION (SBA). The SBA does NOT lend money directly but rather guarantees a loan (normally up to 90% of the loan amount). They, in effect, become your co-signer on the loan. This can make it a lot easier to obtain a bank loan since the bank's risk is lowered considerably. The exception is that the SBA does provide direct loans to certain groups including disabled veterans and handicapped individuals. In general, the SBA will not offer any assistance until you have been turned down for a loan by a commercial bank. Most loans guaranteed through the SBA are between $25,000 and $750,000. However, there is a "microloan" program for amounts from a few hundred dollars up to $25,000. Another loan program, SBALowDoc, under which an entrepreneur can borrow up to $150,000, is a popular new option with a stream-lined loan-application process. Find your local SBA office on the agency's Web site at www.sba.gov, or call the SBA Answer Desk at 800-822-5722.

11. SMALL BUSINESS INVESTMENT COMPANIES (SBICs) The SBIC program was formed by the Small Business Administration (SBA) in 1958 to help small businesses and entrepreneurs secure financing. SBICs are typically formed by a group of people experienced in venture capital financing who have at least $5 million in capital they want to invest. They pool their money together, and apply to the SBA for an SBIC license. SBICs can use the money to offer loans or purchase equity in companies they feel might be successful.

12. FRIENDS and RELATIVES. If they believe in you and your idea, friends and relatives are sometimes willing to fund you. Choose this route with care and execute a formal loan document stating loan terms (interest, terms of repayment). Be advised, however, that many friends have been lost and many relatives alienated because of a small business failure.

13. BANKS and CREDIT UNIONS. Many banks and credit unions (check with your own first and then with local chambers of commerce for alternate possibilities) will loan money for starting a small business. This approach will require that you present a formal business plan to the bank showing justification for the amount you are borrowing.

14. STATE. Some states have small business financing authorities that issue tax-exempt development bonds that can be used to finance land, buildings and equipment for manufacturing businesses. Check with your local government office for details.

15. CREDIT CARDS. Despite stories of credit-card funded start-ups which have gone on to million-dollar success, the best advice is to use this option as a last resort. Credit card interest rates are excessively high.

Equity Financing-With equity financing, you are financing your passion by giving away a piece of the future income of your business. The person or organization that provides you with the money becomes an investor who then has "equity" or a piece of the company "equivalent" to how much they invested. Equity investments involve a certain amount of risk on the part of the investor. Investors make their money if the business is profitable, but lose their money if the business fails. The downside for you is that you are giving up a certain degree of ownership of your company.

There are several sources you can use if you're in need of amounts ranging in the hundreds of thousands to millions. America's Business Funding Directory (ABFD), is a directory for venture-capital funding. They have a searchable database of more than 15,000 potential lenders and investors. Keep in mind that many venture capitalists are usually interested in experienced small businesses in high-growth areas like technology that can provide potentially big returns.

Angels, as these investors are called, look for a clearly identifiable niche with a large market potential, a competitive advantage and, ideally, a product or process that can be protected with a patent. Angels are investing in the people behind the business, and therefore look for people who are passionate about what they do. Angels often expect to get their investment and return after five to seven years. And although they know they probably won't earn much, if anything, along the way, they eventually expect an annualized rate of return of 20% to 40%, perhaps through a buyout of their shares or a sale of the business.

Remember that many of these funding and financing ideas will require you to sign a personal guarantee. This means that regardless of what structure your business is operating under, and regardless of what happens to your business, you are personally liable for the repayment of the loan amount. Think carefully before signing.

Organization Chart

Exercise: create an organization chart for your business.

To help further with the growth of your passion-based business, create an organizational chart. Create a structure for the departments/divisions/subsidiaries you anticipate needing in your company. Some key departments to include are Sales, Production, Marketing, Publicity, Research, Customer Service, Legal and Internet. Some positions you may want to include are secretary, web designer, sales manager, research assistant, accountant, business manager and legal advisor.

Even though at this moment, you might be the one filling all those positions, the purpose of going into business is not to work 10 times harder than you did when you had one job. The goal is to create freedom for yourself by delegating those tasks to others. Ask yourself whom you would hire for your board of directors. Look back on the Relationship List you compiled earlier. Enter the individual's name, their title and who they report to. This is a good way to visualize your company, its structure, and growth, and it will also help you when you're putting together your business plan.

Here is a sample organizational chart. Yours may have additional departments not shown here.

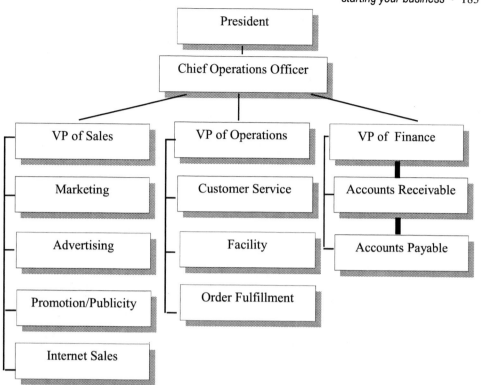

From the Ground Up

The best way to grow a company is to start from the ground up. As you launch your company, you'll most likely be the "chief cook and bottle washer" performing a wide variety of tasks from the menial to the major. As you perform these many tasks, be conscious of the particular position you're working in and document everything you do. Define the goals, procedures and standards associated with each position. For example, as you perform the "mail room/order fulfillment" functions associated with your business, keep a written record of what you do, how you do it, why you do it, when you do it, and to what standards it is done. Keep records of everything from who your suppliers are, key contacts, how copies are made to how you answer the phones.

In effect, you'll be creating an operations manual for each position. This creates a system for your business, streamlines operations, and ensures that these operations continue to a pre-determined level of quality. This information may also come in handy if, as a Guru, you decide to write a book on how to start and operate your particular type of business.

As sales revenues increase, and you are able to hire or sub-contract necessary staff, these tasks will be delegated to new hires as required. You give yourself a promotion by hiring and training someone to fill a position. You immediately become their supervisor, and then begin to work on the operations manual for the supervisor position. When you're ready to move up another level, you hire someone to fill the supervisor role, and the process continues.

A Quick And Easy Business Plan

Used correctly, a good business plan can help you to structure, set goals, and anticipate the future needs of your passion-centered business. Here are the major sections of the typical business plan along with the specific questions each should address:

Executive Summary

What's your company mission? How is your business structured? Where is it located? How long have you been in business? Who are the people running the business and what are their qualifications?

Business Description

What exactly does your business do? What is your product or service? How is it sold? What job positions will you need filled to get this done? How and where does the business operate? How is it going to be managed?

Marketing Plan

Who are you selling to? Who is your audience? How do you plan to market your product to your audience? What are your pricing, distribution, advertising and customer service policies? What do you know about the industry you are getting into? Who is your competition? What sets you apart from them?

Operation and Management

How will you recruit, qualify, hire, train, manage, evaluate, compensate, delegate, reward, promote and terminate your full/part-time employees and consultants?

Financial Plan

How much money do you anticipate making in the next 12 months? 2 years? 5 years? What's your personal financial history? What do your balance sheet, profit & loss statement and cash flow analysis reveal about your business? (Samples of these statements are in Chapter 11) How do you plan to budget any money invested in your company? What returns on investment do you project for someone who invests in your company? This is the most important part of your plan for raising capital. Potential investors are most interested in how much they need to invest, and how much they will earn in return.

Other Information

What's your long-range plan for the business? How do you plan to transfer ownership of the business in the future? Has the sale of your business been planned for?

The business plan is a tool for running your business. And just like any other tool, if it's not doing the job you intend it to, you need to fix it. In other words, you need to update and revise your business plan, just as you would sharpen, oil or maintain any other tool you use repeatedly. Over the course of time, it may change and provide the basis for contingency plans for running your business when customer preferences, technology, the economy or foreign and domestic policy affect your business.

Manufacturing Your Product

If your passion involves an invention or other product, you'll need to locate suppliers, manufacturers and printers to provide or create your product. The ultimate source for this information is the Thomas Register. This 34 volume storehouse contains 156,914 companies, 63,669 product categories, 2,600 catalogs and much more. You can find virtually any company that makes every product from shoelaces to aircraft, paper clips to submarines. Every library in America has a set of these familiar thick green books for you to browse. If you wish to own your own set, contact (212) 290-7277, or online at www.thomasregister.com.

Once you locate potential suppliers and manufacturers, contact them and request brochures, media kits as well as samples of their work. Verify what their payment terms are and any other requirements of doing business. Establish a good relationship with your suppliers. They are a vital link between passion and profit.

A Smooth Operation

You're just about ready to get started running your business. Here are some items you might typically need around the office to make things run smoothly. These items, along with the ongoing expenses which follow must be kept in mind when putting together your business plan and when completing your various business statements.
- Telephone; cellular phone; pager
- Fax Machine
- Computer with printer; scanner; Internet access
- Production equipment (for manufacturing)
- Voice Mail or answering system
- Rolodex ™ or other system for organizing your contact names/numbers
- Subscriptions to trade publications
- Some effective means of time management
- Attractive furniture (image matters if you're in the service business)
- Car or convenient access to transportation
- Express delivery company account. (UPS, Federal Express, etc.)
- Padded envelopes (9 X 12 is a convenient and versatile size)
- Filing Cabinet

You may also have these ongoing expenses running your business.
- Office supplies
- Printing
- Inventory
- Legal fees
- Insurance
- Licenses or permits
- Lease deposits
- Remodeling costs
- Utility deposits
- Salaries
- Shipping/postage
- Advertising and promotion
- Salaries and wages
- Utilities
- Travel
- Telephone
- Rent
- Other miscellaneous costs

Cutting Costs

There are only two ways to make a profit in business. You can sell more, or you can spend less. The best strategy is to do a lot of both. Once you realize that fluctuations of just 5% to 10% in gross sales can cause a business to go into bankruptcy, you'll recognize the importance of cutting costs wherever you can. A small increase in the cost of your supplies, manufacturing, even postage costs, for instance, can have a detrimental effect on your bottom line. Profit margins are what keep your company going and growing. Don't underestimate the power of those small percentages. In a recent year, Boeing Aircraft Manufacturers had a profit of 1 Billion dollars. Admittedly, 1 Billion dollars is a lot of money. However, in terms of percentages, that's ONLY 1.7% of their total sales of 57 Billion. Get a hold of any year-end report of companies in which you have stock and you'll see that their profit is usually anywhere from 1 -10% of total sales. Seen in this light, it makes even more sense to cut costs as much as possible. When I first started my mail order company, I was unaware of this little fact of business accounting, and carelessly tossed away my profit by doing things like not charging for shipping, sending correspondences by overnight delivery, and other no-nos. To save you the heartache of going through what I did, here are 7 principles of great importance .

The 7 Principles of Getting it For Less

1. Competition. "There's Always Someone Cheaper, even Someone Free."
2. The Art of Barter
3. Buying in Bulk
4. Mixing and Matching
5. Out of State? Out of Sight! aka "Buy your fish by the sea!"
6. You Can Get a Better Deal by Asking
7. The Hierarchy of Holding On to Your Money

1. Competition. "There's Always Someone Cheaper. There's Even Someone Free." The basic underlying principle of capitalism is that the next guy is always trying to get more customers than the next guy! As a result, there's always someone selling cheaper or maybe even giving it away free as an enticement, premium or incentive. In addition, there's always someone whose overhead is less, who has got inventory to move, who got a good deal at a wholesale price that they're passing on to you, or has some other circumstance or situation that can result in a better price for you. Always be on the lookout for deals!

2. The Art of Barter.

Even though "cash is king", it's also equally true that trade is just as powerful a means of getting what you want without parting with cash. Join barter organizations like Intagio.com or do a search for "barter" on your favorite search engine.

3. Buy Bulk. Pay Less.

Companies that purchase in large quantities are able take advantage of discounts. That's why it's often cheaper to buy your supplies at office supply superstores. Ask for discounts when purchasing larger quantities of supplies or inventory.

4. Mix and Match

Don't feel obligated to fulfill all your needs at one supplier. You can often save a bundle by, for example, getting your merchant services processing through one company, but the actual terminal from a different supplier.

5. Out of State? Out of Sight! "Buy Your Fish by the Sea!"

It often goes unnoticed that companies in other states and even other countries can provide the same product or service at better prices. Labor costs, storage, shipping, trucking and delivery charges will often boost the price of a particular commodity in a given region. Companies doing business in states and countries with lower labor costs, and with little to no need for shipping their raw materials or finished products to the point of manufacture or sale, can charge less for the final product. That's why book printing in paper-producing states and certain states close to Canada, (Michigan, Minnesota, Wisconsin, Montana, N&S Dakota) is cheaper, and why you get the best deals on fish near the coast. Remember: "paper is cheaper in Canada; buy fish by the sea!"

6. You Can Get a Better Deal Just by Asking

Yes, it's true. It's even truer if you're dealing with the owner of the company, or a representative who gets paid on commission, and who would rather make a slightly lower commission than lose the sale entirely.

7. The Hierarchy of Holding on to your Money

Before shelling out your hard-earned cash, there are several options you can explore which might be able to get you your desired product or service free! We call them "The Hierarchy of Cheap".
A. Request a review/evaluation copy (This works well if you're the head of an organization with enough members who might be interested in future purchases.) We, at the Passion Profit Company, receive many of the books in our library as review copies to us based on the promise of writing a review, or recommending them to our subscribers.
B. Ask for a referral deal where you get yours for free. (Offer to bring them 3 new customers in exchange for one free copy).
C. Ask about barter options. If you find the "no pay" options, don't work, then
D. Shop out of state or internationally for cheaper options. Then,
E. Ask them to beat a competitor's price (another discount tactic)
F. Simply ask for a discount: Yes, sometimes all you have to do is ask! And finally,
G. Ask for older versions, editions and models which may now be excess inventory.

With these new skills, perspectives, mindset and practices, you're now ready to hunt for and eliminate the secret "profit stealers" that exist in most businesses. These are the often-overlooked expense categories that slowly deplete your cash reserves, stifle your cash flow, and eat away your profits.

The Secret "Profit Stealers" of your business

The following are tips you can use to cut corners and reduce costs in several major expense categories. Visit us online at www.passionprofit.com for an updated report.

Secret 1--Shipping/Mailing Costs

• Use Priority Mail Flat Rate-There is a little-known option of the United States Postal Service offerings that there's a "Flat Rate" envelope you can use to send items by 2-3 day delivery. As long as what you're sending can fit inside the flexible cardboard 9x12 envelope, you'll be charged the 2lb rate, which, at the time of this printing, is $3.85. I've sent items of up to 4 lbs in this way, saving as much as $6.00! (see comparison to follow)

• Use Global Priority Flat Rate-Similarly, for $9.00, you can send items to many countries. You can calculate postage on the www.usps.com website before making the trek to the post office.

• Use Printed Matter and Media Mail rate-If you're sending "books (at least eight pages), film, printed music, printed test materials, sound recordings, play scripts, printed educational charts, loose-leaf pages and binders consisting of medical information, and computer-readable media" to customers, (up to 70 lbs) you can also consider using the USPS "media mail" option. The advertised shipping time is between 3-7 days, but I've found that items I've shipped reach just as quickly as first class mail. The savings can be as much as 50%. For example, say you're sending a 3lb package (a book, say) from New York to California. Here's a cost-saving comparison.

Comparison

Regular Priority/First Class	$8.85	
Priority Mail Flat Rate:	$3.85	(save $5.00)
Bounded Printed Matter:	$3.07	(save $5.78)
Media Mail	$2.26	(save $6.59!)

Other Tips:

• Email instead of faxing.
• Presort your mail if you mail to large lists and save. Contact Postal Service for details.
• Remove bad addresses from your mailing list (USPS offers address verification)
• Investigate and use co-op mailing programs.
• Purchase stamps online and save.
• Don't send overnight unless positively, absolutely necessary.
• Cut back on unnecessary packaging items. (Priority envelopes are free)
• Eliminate envelopes. Trifold your letters, and seal with address labels.
• Charge your customers for shipping.
• Have packages to be shipped to customers picked up by the carrier

Secret 2--Communication Costs

• Find a Plan-Many companies are now offering "Flat Rate Plans" which include unlimited Local as well as Long Distance calls. If a per-minute plan is best for you, check out www.lowermybills.com for an instant comparison of available plans in your area.

According to the site, the average American consumer could save up to $400 annually simply by choosing a different plan!

• Don't use Operator Assistance ("411 Information")-Yes, it's convenient, but very time you call the operator for information, it can cost you as much as several dollars, for a single number!! Try www.5551212.com, www.anywho.com, or any of the many directory services at any of the major portals like Yahoo.com.

• Get the lowest long distance rates. Look for single-second, or actual time billing. Some websites are even offering free calling capability using your personal computer and a microphone.

• If you're on a calling plan that has better rates at night, do your "broadcast faxing" during the night hours.

• Get only necessary services on your phone line (call waiting; 3 way calling).

• Use (800)555-1212 to determine if a business you're calling has a toll-free number.

• Ask your local phone company about their unlimited calling plans.

• Review your bills every month. Mistakes do occur.

• Consider the pros and cons of using an 800 number for your business. Is it really necessary? If you use an 800 number, ask about blocking incoming calls from within your state or immediate calling area.

• Free Teleconferencing is available. Search online

• Consider an Order Taking Center to handle incoming calls and catalog requests. *(Use companies in states "where overhead is less, and reps have low stress.")*

Secret 3-Web Hosting and Things Internet
• Search for the lowest rates for Domain Name Registration.
• Find a Flat Rate Web Hosting Service and pay once for the year.
• Buy, don't lease, a shopping cart for your website

Secret 4-Merchant Processing Fees
• When becoming a Credit Card Merchant, purchase, don't lease, your equipment; Check ebay, or do a search engine search for "merchant processing terminals" and shop around for deals. Most companies that offer processing hope to make more money by selling, or leasing you the terminals at exorbitant prices.

Secret 5-Printing & Design Costs
• Free Business Card offers abound. Search them out.
• Print your own checks; Visit www.shareware.com for free check writing software
• Logos; Visit www.gotlogos.com
• Try out a Print on Demand Service for your book/catalog printing;
  The advantage: small runs; quick turnaround;

Secret 6-Reduce Banking/ATM Fees
• Shop around for a bank. Maintenance, overdraft and deposit fees add up.
• Order your checks by mail from independent printers.
• Find "No fee" Credit Cards/Low interest Credit Cards; Visit www.lowermybills.com

• Don't use ATMs for withdrawing money from your account. If you need cash, consider asking for "cashback" when you make purchases at the supermarket, post office and many pharmacies. Yes, there's often a small fee associated, but it's usually much less (say 25 cents) than the increasingly larger ATM fees (often as much as $3.00!) incurred every time you use an ATM.

Secret 7-Save on Office Supplies

• Buy "house brands".
• Compare prices between major office supply outlets as well as dozens of other online companies to find the best prices.
• Cut back on magazine subscriptions. Use the local library.
• Buy office supplies in bulk; If you use paper in your copier or printer, for example, you can save as much as 30% by purchasing cases rather than single reams.
• Use reconditioned laser cartridges instead of new.
• Barter when possible.
• Consider auctioned, second hand or previously owned equipment. Check ebay first.
• Use Shareware programs downloadable for free (try www.shareware.com) from the Internet. You can get programs for invoicing, scheduling, mailing list management, spreadsheets, expense tracking, etc.
• Laminate daily work sheets so you can reuse them by writing with erasable markers.
• Before shopping, find coupons first online.
• Shop at Used Computers/Computer Trade Shows.

Secret 8-Legal & Accountant Fees

• Consider arbitration, mediation and/or alternative dispute resolution (ADR) instead of costly litigation.
• Contact the local Better Business Bureau for other low cost legal alternatives.
• Check local listings for the Lawyer Referral Service nearest you. You can often get low cost advice from lawyers who specialize in your specific area of interest.

Secret 9-Staff, Salaries & Wages and Payroll costs

• "Rent" your employees rather than hiring them full time.
• Offer workers the option of working from home to cut down on your costs.
• Utilize free resources before hiring consultants (contact SBA or SCORE office).
• Use independent sales reps or online affiliates to sell your product or service.
• Pay employees every two weeks, or even monthly, to save on payroll costs.
• Use debit cards to pay employees
• Consider using interns, college students, family members, friends, and work-exchange programs in which the sponsoring organization pays the participants' salaries.

Secret 10--Consulting & Experts

• While there's no substitute for experienced, seasoned help, there are many online sources of experts in their fields that can offer some valuable insights and "out the box" thinking.
• Check with the SBA's Service Corps of Retired Executives (SCORE) for absolutely free business advice from those who've been in the trenches.

Secret 11--Inventory
• Remember the 80-20 Rule: 80% of your income is usually through the sale of 20% of your products. Keep a careful eye on product sales and cut back on slow sellers.
• Barcoding and inventory tracking helps businesses run more efficiently.

Secret 12--Collecting Debt
• Charge interest on monies owed to you.
• Fax letters and invoices in addition to mailing them to debtors.
• Offer discounts for early payment; 1% - 3% for paying within 10 days.

Secret 13--Travel Expenses
• Sign up for "e-saver" email lists and get notified of low-cost last-minute fares.
• Sign up for a courier service (try Int'l Association of Air Couriers at www.courier.org).
• NEVER EVER use the phone in a hotel room. (Did I need to tell you that?)
• Ask for it. If you ask for a lower rate when making reservations, you might get it.
• Sign up for "EZ-Pass" type discount and save on travel time and tolls.

Secret 14--Printing
• Print brochures in quantities that take advantage of price breaks.
• Streamline forms, receipts, invoices etc. Make them smaller to save paper.
• Print rather than photocopy. Sometimes professional printing beats the copy center.
• Consider "two color" rather than "full color" for fliers, brochures and posters.

Secret 15--Marketing (Advertising, Publicity, Promotion)
• Don't spend unnecessarily. Smaller classified ads often outperform bigger display ads.
• Never pay magazine or newspaper rate card rates. Magazine and newspaper publishers would rather get something than nothing, especially since they have to print anyway.
• If a newspaper or magazine ad isn't working, drop it.
• Websites have become more important than brochures. Your business may require both. However, you should asess their relative effectiveness before committing to either.

Secret 16--Events
• If you stage seminars as part of your passion, remember that people attend seminars for the information. Fancy catering is often unnecessary. Don't overdo it.
• Research other vendors' success before investing in trade show or convention booths.

Bonus Secret 17-Operations, Time & Energy & Miscellaneous
• Save time. Since time is money, anything you can do to streamline your operations to be as efficient as possible, will increase productivity, cut waste and increase profits.
• Set preferences and frequently used options on computers, browsers & phones.
• Designate certain days ONLY for certain tasks. For example, in our business, we ship out orders on Mondays, Wednesdays and Fridays. If you have a small staff, you'd be surprised just how much time this frees up!
• Organize your office space by department and function.
• Run your business from home and save with the many tax advantages the IRS allows.

• Negotiate! Advertising, supplies, legal fees and even rent can often be negotiated.
• Use the Internet. These days, just about any information you need is now available online. Everything from rates, advice, contact information, prices, demographic info, grammar, spell check, weather, time and more are now available. So click, don't call.

Setting Up Your Business Online

Speaking of clicking on the Internet, it's now the foregone assumption of every consumer on the planet that every business on the planet has a website on the Internet. People expect to be able to point their browsers to a URL with your domain name, and find out about your company. They want to have their questions answered quickly by email or FAQ (Frequently Asked Questions page) 24 hours a day. Experts agree that a large portion of future business revenues will be derived from online transactions or from offline transactions that were the result of online marketing efforts.

As more consumers make their buying decisions with information they obtain online, any business which does not have a service provider hosting their web pages and providing them with a presence on the World Wide Web is missing out on the thousands of visits and dollars they could be getting from people surfing the Internet. There is very little that can't be sold over the Internet. More than 20 million shoppers are now online, purchasing everything from books to cars to utilities to clothing and more. If you can imagine it, someone will figure out how to sell it online. Internet experts predict that online revenues will range between $180 billion and $200 billion in 2003. They also predict that the number of online consumers will grow at a rate of 30 to 50 percent over the next few years. You need a presence on the Web so that customers, potential employees, business partners and perhaps even investors can quickly and easily find out more about your business and the products or services you have to offer.

What is the Internet?

Even before we answer the question of *what* the Internet is, let's address *why* the Internet is! The answer may dispel any reservations you may have about jumping into this new medium and, may ultimately be of more importance to you than anything else you read. Here's the answer: The Internet exists in order to help you communicate.

The human need to communicate has spawned some of mankind's most life-changing developments. The pony express, postal service, Morse code, radio, walkie talkies, television, the telephone, overnight delivery and the fax machine, have all been ways to get words, pictures and ideas from here to there quicker and cheaper. In fact, the telecommunications industry generates approximately 1 Trillion dollars each year. Communication is a big need and therefore big business!

The Internet is a means of communication, but it's not just any means. The Internet is probably the most awesome means ever developed because it combines two of humankind's most powerful inventions, the informational and computational capacity, versatility, and speed of the computer, and the global reach of the telephone network. From "hoofs in weeks" to "keystrokes in seconds", this latest advancement in communication means you don't need horses, stamps, or even a telephone to reach out and touch others. You can turn on your computer and be connected instantly to everyone in the world, and they can potentially do the same!

The Single, Most Effective Selling Tool

Why is communication important? Well, if you recall, the key question in the Profit phase of the Passion Profit Cycle of Success™ is, "How can I communicate that value?" Once you have a product or service that you intend to sell to the world to generate income, the most critical need is getting the word out to the greatest number of potential customers. The Internet, the single, most cost-effective and wide-reaching means of communication could be the single most important means you will have to turn your passion into profit in a huge way!

Many good books and websites exist which demystify the practices, terminology and development of the Internet. In a later chapter, we'll address how to market your product or service online. For now, however, just know that setting up a web presence can and should be a vital component of your business plan and strategy.

Towards that end, here is some good information that will help you focus on the essential elements to increase website sales.

Frequently Asked Questions and Answers About Profiting From A Web Presence:

Why do people abandon their shopping carts?
41% The Web page was too slow
20% The Web page looked unprofessional
16% The site didn't take credit cards
14% Couldn't find the check out area
12% Couldn't find a return policy
Source: Esearch; from a survey of 1000 consumers

What can I do to increase my online sales?
Duplicate the winners. Check out what sites like Amazon.com, Dell and other sites that you KNOW FOR SURE are making money, and see how they design their pages, as well as how they structure their checkout and ordering processes. Notice where they place their guarantee statements, privacy statements, pictures and white space. Remember, sometimes the simplest item like where you place your "click here to order" link, may have an effect on your sales. So pay attention and follow the leaders.

Any tips for choosing a domain name?
Avoid ambiguity or confusion. Avoid words that may be misspelled. If your ideal dotcom does not exist, choose something else. Avoid going for a dotnet only. Avoid letters that may not be heard clearly over the phone, on the radio, or in front of a crowd. (Is it "f" as in "frank" or "s" as in "sam?" Did she say "d" as in "david" or "t" as in tom?)

Can I have more than one domain name?

YES. You can always have more than one domain name "pointing" to the same site. For example, both my www.hiphopentrepreneur.com, and my www.hiphopbiz.com domain names take visitors to the same site. Having different domain names allows you to experiment to discover which one is easier for people to remember and which one may lend itself to unique marketing ideas.

If I have more than one domain name should I set up multiple pages?

That's not necessary, based on the answer to the previous question. However, if each page has a different content, it might prove helpful in securing multiple placement in search engines.

What if someone owns the domain name I want?

Find another one. If you brainstorm long enough, you can come up with something that suits you perfectly. Here's a tip: just because someone currently owns your desire domain name, doesn't mean you can't have it soon. If someone owns your domain name, but hasn't put up a site yet, they may not really have plans to. Consequently, they may let their ownership lapse by not renewing through the registrar. When you check on the ownership using the "WhoIs" Database, make note of the "record expires" date. If it's scheduled to expire in a few weeks or months, you might get lucky and be able to grab it if they don't renew. Whatever you do, however, DO NOT, I repeat, DO NOT notify the current owner that you're interested in the domain name, unless you DESPERATELY, REALLY want it and are willing to pay for it.

Should I purchase email names on the Internet?

ABSOLUTELY NOT. Stay away from purchased lists unless it's an "opt-in" list where the names of the list belong to people who've specifically requested to be on that list. Otherwise, you'll make many enemies, and may even have your website shut down for sending unsolicited email--a crime known as "spamming" for which more severe penalties are being enacted into law.

What should I include on my site's order form?

-Phone number on upper and lower sections
-Visa/MC/Amex/Discover logo
-The words "Order Now"
-Shipping and handling information
-Sales Tax information; privacy and security information

What other ways can I keep people coming back to my site?

Make your site a portal of information. It encourages your visitors to return and stay. Make your site interactive with a guest book, forum, tell-a-friend link, webring, customizable news, contests, polls and/or related links page.

How often should I communicate with my mailing list?
Unless you have a daily news, entertainment column, or a horoscope feature that people want to read each day, you might be wise to keep it to no more than once per week.

Any tips for naming my Website?
It's been said that brevity is the soul of wit. On the Internet, brevity is the soul of hits! (And for those of you not yet versed in Web terminology, a "hit" refers to a visit to your site.) How many hits your site gets each day will be determined by many things: What you are selling, how well you advertise, your position in the major search engines, and how often people share information about your site to their online friends. You need, therefore, to make it easy for those people to remember your "dot.com" name. In making the transition online, companies created before the Internet rush, simply took their names with them. Barnes And Noble, for instance, became BarnesAndNoble.com. If you already have a trademarked company name with a reputation and image, then it would be wise to use the power of your existing image to woo online customers. These days, however, more and more entrepreneurs are creating their names with Internet friendliness as a top consideration. The ideal Internet company name is short, easy to remember and easy to spell. It may or may not have anything to do with what you are selling (i.e. Ebay, Amazon)

It's been my observation that the sites that have the most successful and profitable MAINSTREAM appeal are those with names that are short (1 or 2 syllables), or which have no product-specific ties. (i.e. Ebay, Amazon, Yahoo, MP3). Of course effective marketing never hurts either. Companies which already have a track record, history and brand-name recognition (BarnesandNoble.com, Dell.com, Borders.com, Nordstromshoes.com, ToysRus.com) can have tremendous success simply on the strength of their names, no matter how long or short.

If you don't have a name that has established itself offline in the consumer's minds, it is important to get something catchy and that sticks in the mind. Even if you are not going after mainstream appeal, it's important to use the same psychological technology that allows your name to be retained in the customer's mind. For example, if you are targeting a particular group, knowing about that group's language, slang, concepts and history will help to establish the chosen URL in those groups' collective consciousness.

Finally, if you use a vanity 800 number as your company name, like 1800Mattress, or 1800Flowers, then the consistency of having your company name, telephone number and Internet URL all the same, gives you a winning combination!

Making Money Through Your Online Presence

Creating a successful online presence is increasingly vital to being in business.

Your mission is to establish an internet presence through which people purchase your products, memberships, subscriptions, and anything else you're selling. Think of your online business as a virtual storefront and a place for people to congregate, not simply as a brochure. Your website is a place, not a thing. The more reasons people have for getting to know more about you, your company and what you have to offer, the more loyalty they develop and the more sales you'll eventually have. Here, then, are some tips to keep in mind when planning, creating and growing your business website:

- make the experience of visiting your site an informative and enjoyable one
- develop a sense of community (use chat rooms, bulletin boards, distribution lists)
- give people a reason to return to your site (update your content occasionally)
- collect demographic information (your visitors' identity, likes and dislikes)
- commerce-enable your site (make it possible for customers to purchase online)
- keep in touch with customers with occasional emails
- provide a place for visitors to sample your product in some way
- link with other sites
- register with search engines

More of the Essentials...

The concept of turning your passion into profit on the Internet is a book in itself. (Hmmm. Now there's an idea!) However, the Web Launch Checklist and Triz and Internet Selling section of the Appendix contain the essential tips and techniques for driving traffic to your site and stimulating sales.

FIRST STEP: YOUR EMPLOYER IDENTIFICATION NUMBER (EIN)

Regardless of your business name, structure, location, internet presence or URL, the first step in starting your business will probably be to get your EIN.

An EIN (Federal Employer Identification Number) is like a social security number for your business. You need one if you are a sole proprietor and you pay wages to one or more employees, or if your business is a partnership, corporation or LLC. If you are a sole proprietorship with no employees, you can usually use your own social security number as your EIN. In this case, the tax department of your state will assign a separate special account number for your state tax returns and business records. However, since it costs nothing to get, I recommend having an EIN--even if you have no employees-- so as to establish a separate identity for your company. To get an EIN you must file federal Form SS-4 (Application for Employer Identification Number) with the IRS. On the back of the form are instructions for receiving your EIN over the phone. A copy of Form SS-4 is provided here.

Tip: If you place "0" in line 13 for "highest number of employees expected in next 12 months", you may be told to use your social security number as your EIN. Therefore, enter "1" in anticipation of future employees.

Form SS-4: Application for Employer Identification Number

Form **SS-4**
Millennium Version
Department of the Treasury
Internal Revenue Service

Application for Employer Identification Number
(For use by employers, corporations, partnerships, trusts, estates, churches, government agencies, Indian tribal entities, certain individuals, and others.)

► See separate instructions for each line. ► Keep a copy for your records.

EIN
OMB No. 1545-0003

1 Legal name of entity (or individual) for whom the EIN is being requested
HEADSTRONG HATS

2 Trade name of business (if different from name on line 1)

3 Executor, trustee, "care of" name
MARY P. ROBINSON

4a Mailing address (room, apt., suite no. and street, or P.O. box)
P.O. BOX 123

5a Street address (if different) (Do not enter a P.O. box.)
401 PASSIONFRUIT LANE

4b City, state, and ZIP code
CLEARVIEW CA 90210

5b City, state, and ZIP code
CLEARVIEW CA 90210

6 County and state where principal business is located
FREEDOM COUNTY CA

7a Name of principal officer, general partner, grantor, owner, or trustor
MARY P. ROBINSON

7b SSN, ITIN, or EIN

8a Type of entity (check only one box)
- [ ] Sole proprietor (SSN)
- [ ] Partnership
- [ ] Corporation (enter form number to be filed) ►
- [ ] Personal service corp.
- [ ] Church or church-controlled organization
- [ ] Other nonprofit organization (specify) ►
- [ ] Other (specify) ►
- [ ] Estate (SSN of decedent)
- [ ] Plan administrator (SSN)
- [ ] Trust (SSN of grantor)
- [ ] National Guard   [ ] State/local government
- [ ] Farmers' cooperative   [ ] Federal government/military
- [ ] REMIC   [ ] Indian tribal governments/enterprises

Group Exemption Number (GEN) ►

8b If a corporation, name the state or foreign country (if applicable) where incorporated
State | Foreign country

9 Reason for applying (check only one box)
- [✓] Started new business (specify type) ►
- [ ] Hired employees (Check the box and see line 12.)
- [ ] Compliance with IRS withholding regulations
- [ ] Other (specify) ►
- [ ] Banking purpose (specify purpose) ►
- [ ] Changed type of organization (specify new type) ►
- [ ] Purchased going business
- [ ] Created a trust (specify type) ►
- [ ] Created a pension plan (specify type) ►

10 Date business started or acquired (month, day, year)
JAN 1

11 Closing month of accounting year
DECEMBER

12 First date wages or annuities were paid or will be paid (month, day, year). Note: If applicant is a withholding agent, enter date income will first be paid to nonresident alien. (month, day, year) ► **JUNE 1**

13 Highest number of employees expected in the next 12 months. Note: If the applicant does not expect to have any employees during the period, enter "-0-." ►
Agricultural | Household | Other
 | | **1**

14 Check one box that best describes the principal activity of your business.
- [ ] Construction [ ] Rental & leasing [ ] Transportation & warehousing [ ] Health care & social assistance [ ] Wholesale-agent/broker
- [ ] Real estate [ ] Manufacturing [ ] Finance & insurance [ ] Accommodation & food service [ ] Wholesale-other [✓] Retail
- [ ] Other (specify)

15 Indicate principal line of merchandise sold; specific construction work done; products produced; or services provided.
RETAIL SALE OF HATS

16a Has the applicant ever applied for an employer identification number for this or any other business?
[ ] Yes [✓] No
Note: If "Yes," please complete lines 16b and 16c.

16b If you checked "Yes" on line 16a, give applicant's legal name and trade name shown on prior application if different from line 1 or 2 above.
Legal name ►   Trade name ►

16c Approximate date when, and city and state where, the application was filed. Enter previous employer identification number if known.
Approximate date when filed (mo., day, year) | City and state where filed | Previous EIN

Third Party Designee
Complete this section only if you want to authorize the named individual to receive the entity's EIN and answer questions about the completion of this form.
Designee's name | Designee's telephone number (include area code)
Address and ZIP code | Designee's fax number (include area code)

Under penalties of perjury, I declare that I have examined this application, and to the best of my knowledge and belief, it is true, correct, and complete.

Name and title (type or print clearly) ► **MARY P. ROBINSON**
Signature ► *Mary Rob___*   Date ►
Applicant's telephone number (include area code) **(000) 123-4567**
Applicant's fax number (include area code) ( )

For Privacy Act and Paperwork Reduction Act Notice, see separate instructions.   Cat. No. 16055N   Form **SS-4** Millennium Version

The Cycle of Success

Step 8: Decide on Your Business Model

Name of Company: _____

Structure: _____

URL: _____

What's your product? _____

Will you be a retail or wholesale business?_____

How will you sell your product?

        in a store? ____

        by mail order? ____

        over the Internet? ____

        through licensing? ____

        Other_____

How will you sell your product?

Will your product offer a multi-level marketing opportunity? ____

Will your product offer a franchise opportunity? ____

What's your service? _____

How will you market your service?

        Will you take a job? ____

        Will you be a consultant? ____

            Will you work at home? ____

            Will you work on site? ____

            Other_____

Will your service offer a multilevel marketing opportunity? ____

Will your service offer a franchise opportunity? ____

MAIN POINTS OF CHAPTER 9
"Starting Your Business"

• Turning your passion into profit is not about finding another job. It is about starting your own business.

• The first thing to determine in setting up your business is what business you're in and to whom you're selling. Are you a business to business, business to consumer, consumer to consumer, or consumer to business operation?

• You can sell your product in traditional ways, start your own multilevel marketing company, a franchise, or license your way to wealth.

• You can work from home or find a business location. Each option has specific advantages and disadvantages to consider before making the commitment.

• In choosing the right business structure, you can choose a Sole-Proprietorship, Partnership, Corporation or Limited Liability Company. Each has its pros and cons and the best choice may depend on the type of business you are starting.

• You may also need licenses, permits, a resale certificate and insurance when you start your own business.

• A frequently asked question among new entrepreneurs is "How can I get money to launch my business?" While it is suggested that you use as much of your own resources to get your business off the ground, there are some sources you can investigate which may provide the necessary funds.

• Patents, copyrights and trademarks can help you protect your passion.

• Use an organization chart to conceptualize your business, and use it to build from the ground up.

• Your business plan can be used to raise capital for your business venture, and can help you to structure and set goals for your business.

• Cutting costs is critical to keeping your business profitable.

• Understanding the Internet and establishing an online presence will be an important part of turning your passion into profit.

• One of the first steps you'll need to take is to complete form SS-4.

FOLLOW-UP FILE FOR CHAPTER 9
"Starting Your Business"

INSPIRATION: Passion Seeker Profiles

——————————————————————————————

"Shopper's Passion"

Tracee McAfee-Gates loves to shop! This enterprising lady took that love and talent for finding just the right gift, to heights most only dream of. As a buying agent for companies like QVC and Home Shopping Network, her Diversified Concepts Marketing Inc. of Canton, Ohio reached sales of nearly 10 million in 2000, and earned her a place in the competition for the Ernst &Young Entrepreneur Of The Year Award.

——————————————————————————————

IDEAS: The Right Questions To Ask

• What specific names can I come up with that might make my product or business stand out?
• What specific things will I acquire in order to help me run my business?
• Who do I know whom I could recruit for my business?
• What specific sources of money do I have to launch my business?
• What are the specific questions I have for my SCORE advisor?
• What websites do I wish to model when building my online presence?

Chapter 10: Selling with Passion
"Cracking the code!"

The Joy of Selling

According to the Third Law of Passion Dynamics, there is no creation that exists without an equal desire for that creation. This means, that you can ALWAYS turn your passion into profit! To do so, however, you'll need to communicate those unique qualities of your creation to the rest of the world. You have to sell your passion.

Yes, if you are serious about turning your passion into profit, then you have to take selling seriously. You'll have to sell to more people than just mom, dad, and the next door neighbor. You'll have to know a bit more about why people buy, how people make buying decisions, how to get the word out about what you're offering, and how to create value in their minds for what it is you are selling. Within this chapter are the powerful basics that you need to empower you to sell your passion..... with passion!

Selling is the Name of the Game

Many people are often confused by the terminology that marketing people toss around when explaining how to make money in business. As illustrated above, the terms involved are:

Selling
Marketing
Branding
Promotion
Publicity
Advertising

Selling is what you want to do; it's your ultimate goal.

Marketing is the process of putting it out there. The goal of marketing is to sell more things to more people. Promotion, Publicity and Advertising are forms or techniques of marketing which help you to sell more. There's overlap among all forms of marketing. Some advertising looks like publicity; some advertising might be called creative marketing, etc.

Branding is the identity you occupy in the minds of the public. Branding is what you accomplish in the process of marketing. It happens whether you focus on it or not. If done consciously and effectively, you'll create a strong brand identity and sell more. If not done effectively, your sales will suffer because of a poorly perceived brand.

Promotion is the marketing of your product to the people who will sell your product. It involves sending product samples, putting on sales, creating and positioning point-of-purchase displays, anything that gets your product better positioned in the places it will sell.

Publicity is the free coverage you get in newspapers, magazines, radio programs, video shows and television. If you, your unique story, your product, or some other aspect of your passion is of newsworthy interest to the world, you have the chance of being interviewed, reviewed or exposed to the readers, viewers or listeners of particular programs. Publicity is the best form of marketing because: 1. It's free, and 2. Third-party validation (what others say about you) is more powerful than what you say about yourself. The task of gaining publicity is called Public Relations, or PR for short.

Advertising does just about the same thing publicity and promotion are intended to do with one difference: Advertising costs money. You may need to advertise in magazines, newspapers, on websites, television, radio or billboards to sell your passion.

Regardless of the terminology you use, the bottom line becomes a single, simple question: "What will I say and do to get people to purchase my product or service?" The solutions you develop to answer that question are what form the strategy of any marketing, promotion, publicity or advertising campaign you launch.

The Code Cracker has been developed to help you answer that question.

THE CODE-CRACKER: Secrets to Selling With Passion

Not finding the right audience? Website not selling? Brochure not producing results? Ad copy not pulling prospects? Sales pitch not wowing them? Prospects not turning into customers? Customers not turning into repeat buyers? Whatever selling challenge you have can be solved by applying one or more of the Code Cracker principles. They represent the most powerful secrets I've learned about selling that have helped me crack codes in just about every venture I or my clients have launched. They include techniques, strategies, mindsets, perspectives and truths about human nature that are critical to everyone who wants to turn their passion into profit.

Effective marketing is nothing more than communicating an idea from within the right mindset. In order to have the right mindset, you need to know who you're speaking to, what they want to hear, and you have to know the words to use to say it to them. Here then, are the Mindset secrets which can help you sell effectively.

Mindsets

MINDSET: Put People First

People don't care how much you know, until they know how much you care. Make customer service an important part of your business and treat your customers, suppliers and employees well. Do whatever it takes to make a good impression with everyone who does business with you. Sometimes it means refunding the money of an angry customer, even if he or she is in the wrong. Sometimes it means shipping out a product overnight at your expense even though it means you make no money on the sale. One unhappy customer can do more to damage your reputation than ten happy customers will do to improve it. Are you sending a message to customers that you're in it just for the money? Put people first.

MINDSET: There's a process to selling: Get Attention, Spark Interest, Elicit Desire, Move to Action (AIDA)

In sales workshops, people are taught to take their prospective customers through a four-step process known as AIDA in order to make a sale. A.I.D.A. stands for Attention, Interest, Desire, and Action. Whether you're selling in person, by mail, over the Internet, or by phone, the process is the same.

The first step in making a sale is to get your customer's attention. If you're dealing with them personally, you probably already have their attention. If you're placing an ad, your headline will be what grabs their attention.

The next step is to arouse their interest. To do this, you may ask a leading question—a question that makes them think and which requires an answer. The quicker and more often you can get your customer to say the word "yes" either out loud or to themselves, the closer you are to making a sale. Ask: "Would your life be different if you had all the money in the world?" "Are you interested in feeling healthy?" "Do you like to have fun?" "Want to lose weight?" "Need more cash?" Chances are good that you'll get a yes to those questions.

The next step is to build on that interest and turn it into desire. Here's where you need to appeal to their emotions by showing how your product or service fulfills their wants and needs and helps them avoid their dislikes. (Remember the Value Tree)

Finally, move your customer to action by overcoming any objections they may have, then asking for the sale.

MINDSET: Get Excited

Enthusiasm sells. When you talk about your passion you need to get excited if you want to sell more. *I'm often asked, "What if I'm not the type of person who gets excited?"* My answer: "Get excited, anyway!"

Plain and simple. If speaking excitedly is not something you are comfortable doing, then get uncomfortable. If it's just not you, then become it. It all starts with you. Even if you hire someone to be a cheerleader for you and your product, you need to communicate your excitement to them, or they won't get excited about it either.

People respond to excitement. As one sales expert says, "people are more impressed by the height of your enthusiasm than the depth of your knowledge." Set yourself on fire and people will come and watch you burn! (And hopefully they'll buy something from you while you sizzle!)

In my workshops and private sessions, I have attendees stand up and practice selling their passion with passion to the audience. It's an effective way to have people step outside of their comfort zones.

I'll also add that you should be nice, smile, greet people, treat others the way they want to be treated, remember peoples' names, and birthdays, deliver what you promise and be honest in all your dealings--and do it all with excitement!

MINDSET: Always have a plan B (or C, D, E, F and G)

NEVER, ever let any ONE person be the only key to your success. As I always say to people who get discouraged by rejection, "no one person has the key to EVERY door that leads to success." Just because one distributor won't carry your product doesn't mean you're doomed. Just because the most powerful newspaper in the country doesn't write a story about your novel, doesn't mean it'll never be read, UNLESS you believe it. There is ALWAYS a way to get things done. When you make your plans, think positively and expect success, but always ask yourself, "what will I do if this plan doesn't work? What's my Plan B?" Even if it means selling your product yourself on the Internet, or out of the back of a van, there's a way. Find a way, even if it means having someone else talk to the same distributor about your product. "Plan B Thinking" means that no one will ever stand in the way of your success. As Bob Marley says, "When one door is closed, another is open!"

MINDSET: Think: Do For Self

When I set my business goals, my basic mindset to achieve it is "How will I use my talents and skills to get this done? I've met too many people whose basic thought pattern is "Who can I get to let me in the door." I've always been more of an independent achiever. As a result, I've always acted as if everything was up to me. Now that doesn't mean you don't rely on others for your success. It means you approach success as something you claim and take for yourself, not something that someone else gives to you. No one wants to distribute your product? Great! Then do it yourself! Can't find someone to represent you? Then represent yourself! Can't find a publisher to sign you? Then publish it yourself! Get the right information, become your own expert, and make your own path to success!

MINDSET: Every Challenge or Situation Has a "Right" Answer

Perhaps it's my math and engineering background and the fact that I used to work out assignments for extra credit in school, but I always act under the assumption that everything has a right answer. I design brochures knowing that there is a perfect arrangement of words and pictures that will sell the most products. My mission, and yours is to find that right way!

MINDSET: Never Accept The First Answer As Final

Whenever I call a company for some information, or to get something accomplished that may be outside of their normal scope of activities, I have a certain rule that I always follow. If I don't get the answer I'm looking for, or the respect I expect, or a speedy response, I always call back and ask the same question to another salesperson or representative. First, I politely thank the first person for their help, wait a few minutes, or until lunch time, or the next day and call back. There have been many times that a "no" has turned into a "yes", or an "I don't know" has become a "here's the answer you're looking for", or a "she's not here" has become a "hold on, I'll get her." That's simply because not everyone is operating with all the information. The person you first speak to might be a new hire (who doesn't realize you're entitled to special treatment), a person from another department who just happened to answer the phone, a temp, or simply a misinformed employee. In any company of greater than 10 people, the law of averages predicts that if you simply call back in a few minutes, you can get a new person who might be better able to help you. This works great for telephone companies or utilities. You can pretty much call back every minute of every day for a year, and never get the same person twice! Now, if it's a small company, and you're sure you'll get the same person again, you might want to call, ask for a different department, the supervisor, or perhaps call with a different question which might lead you to a different person with different information and the authority to grant your request.

MINDSET: It's Not Necessary that Everything be In Place Before Selling.

As we learned earlier, you can sometimes jump directly to sales activities even before you have a product to sell. For many entrepreneurs, this is a way of creating structure in the form of a deadline that keeps them working to get the product out. Don't try this one if you don't like that sort of pressure.

MINDSET: If You Can Sell ONE, You Can Sell A MILLION

I call it the Law of One. Sure, that one sale could be a fluke. However, if you've been able to sell your product to someone other than your mother or your best friend, it's a good sign. If two people buy it, you might have a winner on your hands. You've passed the first test. Most people ask, "Can it sell?" The right question is "What can I say or do to create value in the minds of others to make it sell?" The Slinky, a popular toy for years, was simply a spring from a machine. Value was created for it as a toy, and the rest is the stuff of entrepreneurial legend.

MINDSET: There's Enough For Everyone

When it comes to money, customers, ideas, happiness and even love, many people believe that there's just not enough to go around. They operate from an assumption of scarce resources. Now the world may not really need another book on investing in the stock market, but every person has his own unique way of doing things, so therefore every person has his own unique audience. As many McDonald's fast food restaurants as there are in the world, there always seems to be enough hungry people to support another one, sometimes right on opposite sides of the same street. In matters of money, there is, in fact, enough wealth for everyone. Some people will choose different levels of wealth for themselves. That's not an indication of scarcity. It's simply a fact.

MINDSET: People are not Obligated to Buy Your Product

"Why should I buy my product from you rather than the woman down the street?" "Why should I spend my hard-earned money at your business and not someplace else?" When I ask that question to new entrepreneurs, I often get blank stares. Many people I speak to are stumped when asked to communicate exactly what it is that sets them and their passion apart from their competition. One entrepreneur jokingly replied, "You should buy my product so I can feed my family!"

As humorous as that may be, many people do, in fact, look at their business simply as a way for them to make money. Or, if they have recognized their product or service as something people need, they haven't gone the extra step to set themselves apart from everyone else who offers the same thing. Unless people have a particular emotional attachment and compelling reason to give you their money, they'll probably choose any more convenient option. If they can get what you're offering, or something relatively similar, by expending a little less effort, they probably will. The additional compelling reason you need to give your potential customers is what's called your Unique Selling Point, or Unique Selling Proposition (USP).

In the Wow Factor Formula in Chapter 4, your USP is just one of the assets at your disposal that you can use to impress and grow rich. Your USP is perhaps the very first thing you should determine while you're working on your passion idea. Your USP is what you're actually selling. You'll need to communicate it within your business plan, to potential investors, in your advertising, in your company mission and slogan, and in every place of contact with the public. You may be in the hat business, but unless your hat has a particular USP that you can define, then as far as the world is concerned, any other hat shop will do just as well.

Your USP can be the extra attention you give customers. It can be 1-hour delivery when everyone else delivers in a week. It can be just about anything that sets you apart, and that customers feel is reason enough to do business with you instead of the other guy. However, whatever your USP, make sure you can provide it at all times. It's always better to under-promise and over-deliver than it is to over-promise and under-deliver. For example, if you say you can deliver a product in 3 days and your deliver it in 2, you'll be a hero. If you say you can deliver it in 1 day and it takes 2, you're now a liar with a bad business reputation.

To be even more effective, your USP should appeal to your customers' emotions. To do that, you need to focus on benefits rather than features. In other perhaps more overused words, you need to sell the "sizzle", not the steak. If your USP is quick delivery, then tell your customer that it helps them "save time." If your USP is the unique look of your clothing designs, tell them it will help them "be attractive" or "express their individuality."

MINDSET: People Buy For Specific Reasons

If you recall from the Value Tree, people have many different needs that you can satisfy. These needs are the emotional reasons people buy.

Quite simply, your product or service must address one or more of these needs, and give people what they want or help them avoid what they don't want.

MINDSET: People buy based on Emotion not Logic

People make emotional decisions. Every decision, from whom we marry, what clothes we wear, to what color and model car we buy, is made emotionally. Although we may have a host of logical reasons to convince ourselves that we made the best decision, the truth is the decision itself is usually emotionally motivated. Advertisers have known this for years. That's why they can sell cigarettes without ever showing a picture of one. That's why food ads often show more images of smiling faces than lists of ingredients. That's why athletes and performers are paid tremendous sums of money to endorse products. People identify positive emotions with their favorite celebrities, and will, by association, have positive emotions with the products those stars are linked with.

Your mission, therefore, is to create positive emotional associations in your customers' minds to the product or service you are selling.

MINDSET: If You Put a Price Tag On It, People Will Buy It

This doesn't mean you should sell junk, or that people will buy garbage. What it does mean is that everything has value to someone else. Just think of garage sales, auctions and flea markets when you think that people may not buy what you're selling.

One of the worst mistakes you can make in business is to underestimate the buying power of your customer. You'll learn, if you haven't already, that people will pay for what they want. A statistic that has always stuck in my mind comes from India, which is known to be one of the poorest nations per capita. Did you know that people in India, who supposedly have little money, spend more on the movie industry than any other? Going to the movies provides an escape that people in that country somehow find the means to afford!

MINDSET: You Can Make Money Doing Just About ANYTHING

I truly believe this. The idea is reinforced every time I read another story about an entrepreneur who sells a new invention, or an off-the-wall service that's making a millionaire out of it's originator. I only have to recall the fact that I, too, bought a "pet rock" when I was a child as a reminder that the *Third Law of Passion Dynamics* is alive and functioning in our society.

MINDSET: Ten Percent Difference is All You Need To Be Innovative

This bit of marketing wisdom is based on how the human mind perceives differences. It's simply a reminder that it doesn't take much to stand out from the crowd. However, if you set out to make your product or service 100% different, then you'll be way ahead of the pack.

PRINCIPLES AND METHODS for Fixing "Broken" Sales

If your sales pitch, ad copy, website, or brochures aren't generating the sales you desire, this section of the Code Cracker shows how to apply certain proven principles to fix them. The principles are loosely based on a 60-year old algorithm for solving technical and technological challenges, [see appendix for more on TRIZ].

PRINCIPLE: "SEGMENTATION" (Divide the complex into simple)

THE FIX: Incorporate Others

Set up affiliate programs, offer referral rewards.

Word of mouth advertising is very powerful. A happy customer is your best advertiser. If people like doing business with you, they will refer others. I once launched a very successful referral campaign that rewarded people who referred others to my business with a 10% commission on whatever that new customer purchased!

THE FIX: Do the Two-Step

No, it's not a dance. The "two-step" is a process through which you take your potential customers to improve the chances of making a sale. Let's say that you're selling a book and you place a small ad in a magazine.

Step one: instructs the customer to call and request a free brochure or sales letter.
Step two: The sales letter they receive then asks them to take place an order.

The two-step allows you to make initial contact with those who are interested in your offer with no risk on their part. It then allows you to repeat your message to qualified prospects in more detail, thereby improving the chances of making the sale.

THE FIX: Up-sell, Up-sell, Up-sell

In many business transactions, follow-up is the key to success. Up-selling is following up with an existing customer in order to sell an additional item. For many businesses, repeat customers can represent a sizable portion of income. And, as we learned earlier, selling many items to the same customers is key to success in the new paradigm of business. Someone who buys from you once is more likely to buy from you again. And it costs much less to sell to an existing customer than it does to find a new one. For best results, follow up within 30 days of the initial sale.

THE PRINCIPLE: "TAKING OUT" (Eliminate Distractions)

THE FIX: Keep It Simple

Speak in clear simple language that an eighth-grader can understand. Don't use acronyms unless you explain them. Don't use slang or colloquialisms unless you know your audience quite well. Think about how someone new to this society would interpret the following if the explanations in parentheses were not there. "I called someone at the IRS (Internal Revenue Service), who told me to call the SBA (Small Business Administration) ASAP (as soon as possible) to get a DBA form ("Doing Business As") to start my IT (Information Technology) company." Remove extraneous links from websites. Create single, long-form websites that focus on one product or service

THE PRINCIPLE: "COPYING" (Use facsimiles)

THE FIX: Follow The Leaders

Duplication is often a powerful key to success. Notice the things about other companies' ads that grab your attention. Notice which ads are consistently run in magazines to determine which ones are successful. How are the successful sellers making their sales? Find out and follow their lead.

THE FIX: Adjust Your Image

People often use strange criteria to make purchase decisions. Have you ever decided NOT to buy something at a store because you didn't like the owner? Have you decided NOT to buy something from a catalog because you couldn't hold the item in your hands? In the absence of dealing with you personally, or of being able to touch a product, consumers rely on the image that you project. If you're creating a video, a book, a doll, make sure your product and packaging look as professional as others out there. Look at how and where other successful companies place the fine print, logos, wording, copyright notices, trademarks, barcodes, etc. Details matter.

PRINCIPLE: "HOMOGENEITY" (Use the power of similarity)

THE FIX: Speak to the personalities

When speaking or writing ad copy, use words which speak to the 4 personality types. To appeal to the Exciter, use words like *fun, excitement, adventure, fast-paced, exhilarating* and *new*. To appeal to the Supporter, use words like h*elp, support, deserve, warm* and *family*. To appeal to the Informer, use words like *facts, information, credibility, documented, authentic, professional, respected, reputation, knowledge* and *research*. To appeal to the Competitor, use words like *power, money, wealth, winning, best, success* and *"number one."*

THE FIX: Speak to Demographics

Am I using slang that others are not relating to? Should I be using certain words that my target audience relates to?

THE FIX: Speak to Basic Human Motivation

According to researchers at Yale University, here are some of the most powerful words in the English Language. Incorporate them into your sales pitches.

Discover	Proven	Health	New
Easy	Results	Save	Secret
Guarantee	Safety	You	Power
Love	Money	Free	Tested

THE FIX: Speak to consumers' short attention spans

Studies have shown that people reading a sales letter almost always read the postscript. People who ARE interested, but who don't have time to read the full letter, will scan the headline then the postscript. In fact, people who DON'T want to read a sales letter almost always look at the postscript before they throw it out. With that in mind, a postscript should, in essence, include your entire sales pitch in a single sentence or two. Tip: sometimes putting the P.S. in a different color will draw even more attention to it. *eg. Yours sincerely,*

Walt Goodridge,
P.S. Start living your dream today and make money doing what you love. Call us now to order "Turn Your Passion Into Profit" for just $29.95 plus $3.85 shipping and receive a FREE "Don't follow me, follow your passion" bumper sticker! Limited time offer. Call now and have your credit card ready.

THE FIX: Speak to Those Who Need Clear Directions

No matter how clear you think it is to your audience that what you're selling is a book, tell them, in no uncertain terms, EXACTLY what you want them to do. *"Order this great book now! "Send $29.95 today for this great book and...", or "Use your credit card to order this great book today."* Have you asked for the sale? How can you be more direct, simple, forceful and effective in your communication?

THE FIX: Speak Through Stories

"Fact's tell, stories sell." There was once a dejected entrepreneur who was thinking of giving up his passion-centered business and returning to a job he despised. I helped him increase his sales within 72 hours, simply by adding a short story to his sales pitch. He was so grateful, he named his first born son after my chihuahua! Get it? Add power to your brochures, websites, sales sheets with a story!

PRINCIPLE: "LOCAL APPEAL" (Eliminate distractions)

THE FIX: Add Local Appeal

Create your brochures, websites and sales copy in different languages in regional media to create local appeal. How can you make people feel this pitch is tailored to them? What is happening in specific areas that you can incorporate into your sales approach? Staying current with your market, industry and product is key to selling more.

PRINCIPLE: "ALIGN FOR LIFT" (Align with others)

THE FIX: Use Third-Party Validation

Align your website or company with third parties that provide credibility. The logos of Amazon.com, the Better Business Bureau, or a reputable magazine or organization add a degree of respectability in the consumer's mind.

THE FIX: Use Celebrities

What people say about your product has power. What people with power say about your product is even more powerful. If you can't afford millions of dollars to pay Michael Jordan to say good things about your product, don't despair. You may be able to get some indirect endorsements simply by sending samples of your product to famous people. These people may become passionate endorsers simply by being seen in or using your creations, or they may end up unofficially endorsing it out of sincere appreciation of what it does for them. Sales of my books got a boost and continue to be influenced by rapper Chuck D's public endorsements of them. He does it out of a sincere desire to help others. He's told me that refering my books made his life easier, because he wouldn't have to continually answer all the music industry questions he's constantly asked

You can, in effect, act as your own celebrity if you first establish yourself as an expert. Write and offer articles about your passion to local and national papers and magazines. Place your bio and contact information at the end of each article. These will serve as indirect advertising for you and your business.

THE FIX: Build Relationships

Whether it's getting a newspaper editor to write a story, or getting a store owner to carry your product, other people's help will be vital. What's as important as "who you know" is "who knows you" and "who LIKES you." According to Dale Carnegie, author of *How to Win Friends and Influence People*, people will do things for you if they like you. Cultivate relationships that are not just about "getting", but about mutual benefit and long term interaction.

PRINCIPLE: "PRELIMINARY ANTI-ACTION" (Control harmful actions)

THE FIX: Use Assurances and Testimonials

Use customer testimonials generously, add security measures to your website and offer a money-back guarantee prominently in all your copy.

Some new businesses worry that they'll lose money by offering a money-back guarantee. Trust me, if you're product is good, only a small percentage of people will ever take you up on it. However, you build a world of trust simply by having those words prominently displayed on your product or brochure. Ask yourself, "How can I set my customer's mind at ease about making this purchase?"

PRINCIPLE: "SELF SERVICE" (Make an event serve itself)

THE FIX: Make it Easy

Make it easy for customers to find you, reach you and buy from you. Depending on your business and product, the following suggestions may not all apply to you:

1. Get an 800 number
2. Establish "merchant status" (so customers can order by credit card)
3. Display your address and order information prominently on all items
4. Set up a website
5. Get listed in trade journals, directories, 800 directory, search engines etc.
6. Include an order form, and a return label in your packages

THE FIX: Offer Something free

Offering something free is a very powerful incentive that moves people to action. Make sure it's something useful or somehow related to the main product or service.

THE FIX: Introduce Automation

Allow the customer to serve himself, answer her own questions, sell himself. Incorporate downloadable orders, include FAQs and abundant information on your website. Ask, "How can I leverage technology to assist the customer in serving himself?"

PRINCIPLE: The Principle of More Or Less

THE FIX: Hide it or Expose it

Sometimes improved results can be obtained by doing more of something or less of the same thing. Overcompensate or Undercompensate. Make your "buy" button a bit harder to find OR make it very large and easy to find.

PRINCIPLE: "FEEDBACK" (Introduce Feedback to the Process)

THE FIX: Give People What They Want

People want to feel special. Feelings and emotions are what drive consumer spending. If your product can provide your customer with any of the following, you'll be well on your way to success. People want the feelings associated with: love, power, sex appeal, control, security, importance, excitement, hope, appreciation, improved competence. To provide them with these feelings, you need to stress the benefits your product or service provides, NOT just features. A feature is what something is. A benefit is what it does. *"Our book has information"*, is a feature. *"It saves you time"* is a benefit.

PRINCIPLE: "ANOTHER DIMENSION"

THE FIX: Include Pictures

Whether on the Internet, in brochures, in magazines or on radio and television, pictures sell products. People like to see what they're buying. If you're selling a service, then have pictures of people in your ads, or include pictures of something you want people to associate with your service. Hint: adding color to brochures, packaging and ads sell even more. Having 3-dimensional rotating images on your website might be an effective means of selling certain products.

Summary

Refer back to the Code Cracker whenever you're faced with a challenge jumpstarting sales of your product or service. See Appendix for other tools and resources you can use to sell with passion!

Important Tools for Getting The Word Out

You can't afford to be shy about yourself or your product. In order for people to know you have something to sell, you've got to put it out there. Once enough people know about what you do, you'll still have to sell, but you'll have the help of others as well as your own product reputation selling for you. There are a few standard tools you can use to get the media coverage you need.

Press Release

The Press Release is the standard tool for generating media coverage. It is usually a single page that tells a newsworthy story. You had some practice creating one when you did the "In The News" Discovery Exercise. Press release topics can range from product announcements, human interest stories, promotions, community interest stories to anything innovative, funny, and that readers, viewers, listeners of a particular program would be interested in. Press releases usually follow a traditional format. The opening paragraph should tell the entire story, while the rest of the release gives more details. It should include the relevant who, what, when, where and why of your story. On the following page is a sample of a fictitious, but typically constructed press release.

You'll want to send press releases to radio stations, magazines, newspapers, television programs, and specific websites. Getting press releases into the right hands can be time consuming. You may wish to utilize a PR service to make the job easier.

Media Kit

The purpose of the media kit, quite frankly, is to impress the heck out of anyone you send it to. Its job is to get the person reading it—usually a producer or editor—to say, *"Wow, look at what's going on here! I didn't know that! Really? There's something exciting going on that I need to find out more about. This is a hot story, and I need to expose it to my readers/listeners/viewers."*

The typical media kit includes:
• cover letter/business card
• press release
• bio (for you or the company)
• picture of you and/or product
• other media coverage
• sample of product/brochure
• testimonials
• suggested interview questions

Its purpose will be to provide a more complete story, as a follow up to a press release, to any magazine/newspaper editor or radio/TV producer who wants one.

Your press release and media kit should be able to sell your product, service or company if you're not around. Make sure your product or service is explained accurately and concisely. Through your media kit, you have an opportunity to write your own press. If an editor decides to write a story on you, he/she may simply copy your press release or media kit content exactly as you've written it. The release, therefore, should be written in the third person, just as if the editor were writing about you or your business.

Headline

**Date after which info
is no longer relevant
(ie. for events or other
time-sensitive news)**

For Immediate Release:

no kill date
contact: (301)555-1212

Penniless Professor Profits Peddling Peapod Passion to President!

Casper, WY.   Professor Wesley Winchester used to be an unemployed Physics professor. That is, until 6 weeks ago, when his remarkable new product, a hat made out of peapods caught the attention of the President of the United States. Ever since then, the president has been seen sporting his new Peapod Porkpie, and the world has been beating a path to Professor Winchester's door to the tune of over one million dollars in sales within its first month on the market!

"I never dreamed that my passion for peas would cause such a stir," Professor Winchester explains. "I love peas, and ever since I was a child, I used the peapods to make toys for myself. I use them to stuff pillows, I use them for packaging, and I use them to make hats just like the one I was wearing when the president came to town." It was that fateful meeting on the streets of Casper, WY, during a campaign stop, in which the president asked if he could try on Winchester's unique looking head piece. The rest, as they say, is history.

Professor Winchester's passion has resulted in a website which gets over 1,000 visitors daily. In honor of his success using his passion to become a millionaire, Winchester launched Passionaire.com, which sells hats, sweaters, shoes and other products made out of peapods. Winchester, now affectionately known as "Professor Peapod", is set to launch a world tour speaking on the many ways to incorporate peapods in our daily lives. His new book, *The Unbearable Lightness of Peapods* is due in stores for the holiday.

For more information, contact Peapod Public Relations at (301)555-1212

###

indicates end of release

The How, What, When & Where of Selling

How to Sell

Personal Sales

Better known as the "trunk of the car" method, this has been the starting point of many successful journeys. You should always have samples of your product, or brochures with you at all times.

Warm Market Referrals

Your immediate "warm market"—your circle of friends, family and acquaintances—can be a great sales team. Offer them a monetary incentive and give them commissions whenever they refer new customers to you.

Word of Mouth Marketing

In his book, *Rules for Revolutionaries*, Guy Kawasaki recounts how Apple Computers grew as a result of the passionate loyalty of early Macintosh users. The "Mac" was an early alternative to the personal computer that was favored by artsy types. Converts became "disciples" and spread the word far and wide to their friends. It was the best, and cheapest marketing campaign Apple could have hoped for. Sales of the Mac grew phenomenally. Network Marketing has used this concept for years. The best salespeople for a product are often satisfied, converted customers. Word of Mouth marketing typically gives people an incentive for telling others about a product. In Apple's case, the reward was simply being able to belong to a unique community of users.

WARNING: Many new entrepreneurs naively rely on word-of-mouth alone to get the word out about their business. There are only two conditions under which you should rely on word-of-mouth exclusively to build your business. 1. If you're selling your product via network marketing AND have a compensation plan or some incentive that makes it worthwhile. 2. Your product is so global in it's appeal, and life-changing in its effect that the standard of living of everyone is enhanced by using it. (Cures for cancer, the perfect mousetrap, and replacements for the telephone fall into this category). Be careful, for even Viagra (a male virility booster) needed to be advertised. Perhaps the men who used it were not too eager to boast to their friends via word-of-mouth.

Door to Door

Though this is not the preferred method to make sales, it might be effective in some instances and for some products. However, if you're allergic to having doors slammed in your face, you might NOT want this to be your primary method of getting customers.

Sidewalk Selling

If you have a new product that needs to be demonstrated, then you may want to set up your display on the sidewalk, in the local mall, or in a shopping center inside or just outside a store where your product can be purchased. If you've got boundless energy, enthusiasm and an engaging personality, this method can work to get you some sales and may be effective in starting a word-of-mouth campaign.

The Party Plan

Also called "the Tupperware way" in honor of the in-home events which independent representatives use to sell this company's products, you may also have a sales party in your home to kick off your venture.

Cold-Calling (Telemarketing)

Telemarketing involves calling complete strangers and giving your sales pitch to them. It can be effective for certain products and services.

Mailing Lists (Direct Mail)

You can purchase addresses which have been sorted by occupation, age, race, religion, etc. to send a direct mail brochure or sales letter. See your local yellow pages or search engines under "mailing lists."

CO-OP Mailings

To reduce the often high cost of creating, printing, stuffing and mailing brochures to thousands of people, there are companies and organizations that offer you the chance to be part of a mailing with other vendors like you. Merchant member organizations, Retail Councils and Barter organizations can direct you to these programs.

Email Lists

You can purchase the email addresses of people who might be interested in your product or service. It's considered a cyber faux-pas to send unsolicited email. "Spamming", as it is called, can make you many online enemies, and can even get your website, or email account shut down. To prevent this, use a service that offers "opt-in" lists. These are lists in which the people on the list have "opted in", or chosen to be on them and may have requested to receive emails from companies like yours offering certain types of products.

What Medium Sells

Classifieds

Despite their size, classifieds are one of the best ways to get customers. Millions of people in search of specific objects or services for sale, scour these fine-print ads every day. For this reason, they often out-produce big ads which may get lost in a newspaper or magazine. Classifieds should be short and should move people to action to call a number for a brochure or to speak to a sales person. The best medium to place a classified is in a magazine or newsletter that caters to the particular niche you sell to. If your product has mass appeal, then newspaper ads might do well also.

Online classifieds

Because of the sheer number of websites out there, and the tremendous volume of listings, online classified ads are not as effective as print classifieds. Services that automatically match customer inquiries with vendor offerings, do better.

Online Auctions

If your passion is antiques, collectibles, movies, books or the latest toy craze, posting your product on an online auction site can get you a truckload of customers. While there are now dozens of online auctions, www.Ebay.com remains the leader.

Directories

Getting listed in industry directories is a wise way of letting people know you exist. People who are just getting into a particular field, or those doing research often use directories extensively. If, for example, you sell a product for boat owners, then getting your business listed in, say, a National Directory of Boating Industry Dealers & Manufacturers wouldn't hurt. Trade organizations are a good resource to discover what directories exist. In most cases listings are usually free.

Catalogs

Getting featured in catalogs is another way to sell your product. Check online for comprehensive lists of the more than 12,000 catalogs published today.

When To Sell

Sell on Holidays

Since people make emotional buying decisions, specific holidays like Mothers day, and Fathers day, when emotions are running high, are excellent times to push your passion. Many flower shops do 50% of the entire year's business on Valentines day!

Theme Days, Months, Years and Centuries

The year of the child. Black History Month. Secretaries Day. These theme periods all present the perfect opportunity to create a tie-in to your passion. If you have a passion for animals, you may want to follow the Chinese calendar to find out which animal is featured this year. And by the way, I've heard that this is the "Century of the Entrepreneur", so if your passion appeals to people just like you who are pursuing their passion, then you have the next 100 years of prime marketing time to make sales!

Seasons

If your passion is linked to a particular season, you may want to focus your marketing efforts, or the launch of your venture, to capitalize on that time of year. The key is to realize that in many cases, marketing needs to start several months (or maybe years) in advance in order to be in place for a particular season. For example, if you wanted an ad to appear in a magazine for the winter months, you'd need to make those arrangements in August or September.

Where To Sell

Craft Fairs, Street Events, Flea Markets

If your passion involves selling something that people need to see up close, touch or feel before they purchase, then the outdoor or indoor flea market/crafts fair setting might do well for you.

Conventions, Expos and Trade Shows

If your passion appeals to specific groups of people who gather on a regular basis, then renting a booth, or taking out an ad in the event directory of a convention, expo or trade show might bring you a host of customers.

Sidewalks, Malls, Stores, Libraries, Subway Stations, Bus Stops, Gas Stations

In other words, just about any place where people congregate.

Who to Sell To

Sell to Stores

Chains, discount stores, supermarkets and department stores usually have buyers located on the premises or at a company headquarters who make the decisions on what items to carry. Call the stores you're interested in and ask if they deal with small businesses like yours, or if they prefer to deal with distributors.

Sell to the Government

Local and federal governments offer a great resource for selling products. If the government decides that they need a copy of your book, or invention in the hands of every government employee, you'll have found a lucrative source of sales. There are also many federal programs specifically designed to benefit small, minority, and woman-owned businesses. Ask the SBA about these government programs.

Sell to Large Corporations

Corporations may use various products as premiums, incentives, giveaways and gifts. You can offer a customized version of your product or service just for a targeted company to sell or give to their employees.

Sell to Special Interest Organizations

There are many organizations which might be interested in using your product or service in their fund-raising efforts. Visit your library for a copy of the *Encyclopedia of Associations*, and also *National Trade and Professional Associations*.

Sell to School Systems, Library systems & the Military

A passion which caters to teachers, librarians, students or armed forces personnel that can be purchased in bulk can be a great sales opportunity. While some of these systems are notoriously slow in paying, it may be well worth the wait!

The Bottom Line: Get Creative

There are as many creative ways to sell your product or service as there are products and services to sell. Do you have a passion for running? Is there some product or service that practically every marathon runner, or their families could use? Where can you find a lot of marathon runners all in one place? Hmmm. That's a tough one!

Have you considered advertising in or on newspaper inserts, matchbooks, grocery store bags, inserts in books, milk cartons, paper restaurant placemats, the sides of buildings, the backs of commuter passes or tickets, bumper stickers, supermarket bulletin boards, in-flight magazines, store receipts, campus student centers or t-shirts?

The Distribution Process

Distribution is the process of getting your product in the hands of your customers. You have two choices. 1. Do it yourself, or 2. Have someone (a distributor) do it for you. Using a distributor means that you sell your product at wholesale (about 50% of retail) to the distributor, and they in turn sell it to the stores.

If you distribute your product yourself (i.e. sell it directly to the stores or directly to the customers), you'll keep more of the money you make (as long as you keep your overhead and expenses low). In addition, you'll have a direct link to your customers. In the publishing industry, for example, you, the self-published author can sell 1000 books and make about as much as an author signed to a major publisher who sells 15,000 books.

However, there are pros and cons in both scenarios. When you self-distribute, you make more profit per item sold, but unless you have the time and resources to really push your product, you may lose out on overall sales because you're not selling in large volumes. On the other hand, if your product is handled by a distributor, though you'll make less profit per item sold, you may make out better if the distributor has the resources to sell higher volumes.

So how do you decide which direction to go? It depends a lot on the product, the industry, your resources and other factors. Here are some key questions, provided in flow chart style to take you through the process of deciding what's best for you.

STEP 1.

Forget all the stories about people setting up websites selling sauces. Forget all the *Oprah* interviews with people who sell millions in make-up from their living rooms. If you're selling a new kind of morning cereal, is the perceived value high enough for people to make a separate trip to the phone, or computer to buy it rather than simply reaching for the Frosted Flakes next time they're in Piggly Wiggly's? In other words,

QUESTION: Will people buy your product directly from you? Or is it the sort of product that is more conveniently purchased in a store?

If YES, continue to STEP 2. If NO, go to STEP 2A

STEP 2.

If people will buy directly from you, then you may make more profit per item sold, but you may not sell a sufficient volume if you are not getting your message out in front of enough people. It will take effective marketing to keep your sales going strong.

QUESTION: If people will buy directly from you, do you have the time and resources to get it to them quickly and cost-effectively?

If YES, go to STEP 3. If NO, go directly to STEP 5

STEP 2A.

In some industries, retail stores won't buy directly from the small-time manufacturer/ inventor/designer/publisher. They prefer buying their inventory of toys, say, from one distribution company. They can place one huge order for all their Mattel, Hasbro and Milton Bradley products rather than having to place a hundred different orders to a hundred different toy makers.

QUESTION: If it's more convenient for the consumer to purchase your product in a store, will the stores buy directly from you?

If YES, go to STEP 6. If NO, go directly to STEP 5

STEP 3.

The advantage of some distribution companies is that since they are already connected to and have more influence with the retail outlets, the items they distribute often get better placement in the stores and thus stand a better chance of being seen regularly. You would need an equally effective means of advertising and marketing in order to compete.

QUESTION: Do you have an effective way of keeping your product in front of the consumer?

If YES, continue to STEP 4. If NO, go directly to STEP 5

STEP 4.

Using the same publishing example, a major publisher will usually allocate money in the budget to market your book IF they believe it's warranted. In most cases that means if you are a big name author. In other industries, whether you are a priority in a distributor's marketing plans will be determined by how well your product is selling.

QUESTION: Will the distributor also market your product to its retail customers (the stores) and to the public as well?

If YES, then **STEP 5** = Pursuing a deal with a distributor might be a good idea.

If NO, then **STEP 6**= Distribute it yourself and make it happen!

A good way to decide which way to go is to familiarize yourself with what others in your industry are doing. Are there a few success stories of entrepreneurs who are self-distributed, or does everyone go through a handful of key distributors? To find out which distributors are favored by stores, call the stores' buying offices.

Should I distribute my product myself, or use a distributor?

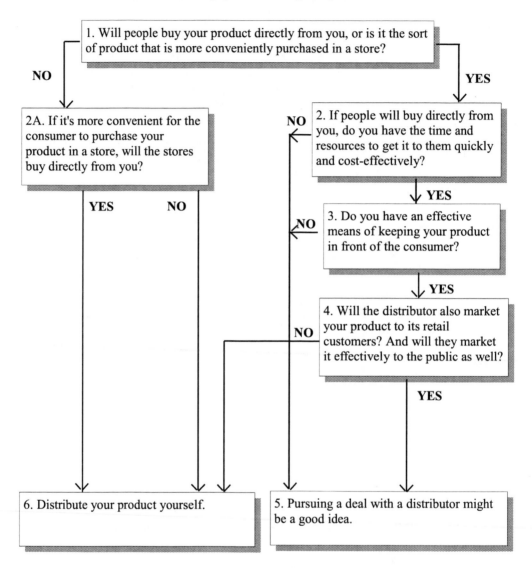

1. Will people buy your product directly from you, or is it the sort of product that is more conveniently purchased in a store?

NO   **YES**

2A. If it's more convenient for the consumer to purchase your product in a store, will the stores buy directly from you?

NO → 2. If people will buy directly from you, do you have the time and resources to get it to them quickly and cost-effectively?

YES   **NO**

↓ **YES**

NO ← 3. Do you have an effective means of keeping your product in front of the consumer?

↓ **YES**

NO 4. Will the distributor also market your product to its retail customers? And will they market it effectively to the public as well?

YES

6. Distribute your product yourself.

5. Pursuing a deal with a distributor might be a good idea.

How Will They Pay?

Now that you know the different ways you can reach your audience, the next step is to make it easier for your customers to give you their money. Here are some key points to consider in the payment acceptance, order taking and fulfillment processes.

The Standard & the New

Cash, Checks, Money Orders, C.O.D. (Cash on Delivery) are all standard ways of accepting payments. The internet has introduced new methods and made others more popular. You'll want to give your customers the option of paying by Paypal™, or into a third-party escrow account,

Terms

Payment Terms are simply a statement of the period of time within which you expect to be paid. For example, if you receive a large order from a chain, or large store, you may wish to ship the products along with an invoice stating that the terms are "Net 30", which means that your customer has 30 days in which to pay you. You may wish to charge a fee as a penalty for late payments.

Before offering payment terms to a customer, you'll want to do a credit check. Contact the customer's bank and 2 or 3 other companies with which your customer does business, or you may contact the Better Business Bureau to see if any complaints have ever been filed against the company.

While there may be conditions under which you'll want to offer payment terms, as a small business, I recommend that you request payment in advance for products sold or services rendered.

Merchant Status

In addition to establishing a checking account in the name of your business, it is absolutely imperative that your business also has "merchant status" to be able to accept credit card payments.

When I first started my mail order company, it was difficult for home-based businesses to get approved for merchant status. While things have definitely changed, if you experience challenges having to do with your size and credibility, you may wish to go through an umbrella organization. For example, many trade organizations offer merchant status as part of their membership packages. I was able to get my merchant status by being part of the state's Retail Council.

These days it's a bit easier, and many options exist. You can search online for merchant services providers who will set up Visa and Mastercard status for your business. Once your account is established, you'll need to contact American Express directly at (800)528-5200, and Discover/Novus at (800)347-7009. Many Internet Service Providers now offer merchant status as part of their website hosting package as well.

Tip: When choosing a payment processing company, be wary of middle men who charge you monthly fees to "lease" the point of sale equipment (terminals, printers). You should own the equipment and pay only a nominal monthly account maintenance fee.

Displaying the credit card logos so that your customers know they have the option, has been shown to increase consumer confidence and increase sales.

Order Forms

Your brochure and/or flier should provide an order form for your customers' convenience. It should be large enough to make it easy to complete, and should provide the price of the item being sold, your mailing address, the "make payable to" information, shipping charges, a telephone number and website address, even if all these pieces of information are provided elsewhere.

Check approval

To avoid being swindled and being charged fees for bounced checks, whether you deal with large suppliers or the public, it's a good idea to run check verifications. To do this, simply call the bank phone number on your customer's check and inform the bank that you're a merchant calling to verify sufficient funds in an account. If there is no bank telephone number on the check, call (800)555-1212, or Directory Assistance in the state the bank is located. You'll need to provide the bank account number, the name on the account, the amount of the check, and possibly the check number. The bank will not divulge how much money is actually in the customer's account, but they will tell you if the amount the check is written for will be covered by the current balance.

What's In The Box?

When preparing your customer's package, be sure to include the product, a receipt or invoice, a return label, an order form or current brochure, a questionnaire or survey, and any announcements of new products.

Returns

It's a fact of business that even if you get your product in stores, there's no guarantee that they will sell. Customers may also change their minds and simply return the items ordered. Establish a return policy which states the maximum time allowed for returns, the expected condition of returned items along with how much of the original cost will be refunded by you. Cheerfully refund your customer's money as quickly as you can. For future reference, you may wish to find out the reason for the return. This will help you adjust your product or service to cater to your future customers' expectations.

MAIN POINTS OF CHAPTER 10
"Selling With Passion"

• Selling is the most important part of turning your passion into profit. Even if you have the greatest product or service, you won't make any money if people don't know you exist. Marketing, branding, promotion, publicity and advertising are all aspects of the selling process.

• The Code-Cracker exists as a way of formulating the mindset and methods you can use to sell to the widest range of customers.

• Press Releases, media kits, brochures, business cards, fliers and ads are tools of selling.

• Deciding on how to distribute your product is critical to your eventual success. You'll need to determine if you have the time and resources to do it effectively. If not, then you may wish to use a distributor.

• Establish different ways to make it easier for people to pay you.

FOLLOW-UP FILE FOR CHAPTER 10
"Selling With Passion"

INSPIRATION: Passion Seeker Profiles

———————————————————————

"Passion for Miles"

According to Judy Collins , "After the birth to my son, Miles, I decided not to go back to working for anyone other than my family or myself. I wanted to mother my child, naturally, but I'd still have to make a living. The desire for flexibility and financial freedom, a fondness for fashion and the need for creative expression led me to the newly renovated T-shirt market. I thought about my new life with all of its changes and started sketching. Before long I had a series of images that represent, well… life. I screened them onto soft cotton T-shirts and personalized them with short blurbs and tales of everyday experience. The revolutionized T-shirt is my new uniform, and why not? They're cheap, easy to wear and speak volumes about personal style."

———————————————————————

IDEAS: The Right Questions To Ask

- What specific publications can I advertise in to appeal to my target audience?
- What are some creative ways in which I can market my product/service?
- Who do I know who has the skills I need to help me sell?

Chapter 11: Accounting and Taxes for the Mathematically Challenged (and the "fact-and-figure-phobic")
"Yes, you need to know this stuff!"

Accounting Tools

This chapter provides the tools you'll need in order to understand where your money is going, monitor income and expenses, and keep track of your profit. If you've followed the discussion up to now, you're more than ready to tackle the next section. Even if you don't fully understand every concept or figure, read through it anyway with the goal of just getting through it. As you get more involved in your business, the terms, procedures and the importance of each tool will become clearer and more apparent.

TOOL #1: BALANCE SHEET Explanation of Terms
The balance sheet is a snapshot of the health of your business.

CURRENT ASSETS are the resources of value that you use every day to conduct business and generate wealth. It includes cash, merchandise, supplies, stationery, boxes, etc.

Cash on Hand includes EVERY form of money that you have on hand. (cash, coins, checks/money orders, petty cash in a jar behind the counter, money in your safe, etc.)

Marketable Securities includes the market value (what they are currently trading at) of all business-owned stocks, mutual funds, and other securities that can be converted into cash.

Accounts Receivable (or receivables) is the money that your customers owe you that they haven't paid yet. Since some people may never pay you, deduct a small percentage (1-10%) from this figure to reflect that fact. In other words, you are taking a 10% allowance for bad debts because in the real world, if you are owed $1,000, by the time all money owed to you is paid, you may only receive $900.

Merchandise Inventory is the value of the products you keep on hand to fill customer orders. You may base it on the cost you incurred to acquire/create these products, or you can use the current market value of the goods, whichever is less.

Supplies Inventory is the value of boxes, letterheads, staples, paper clips, paper, and all the various supplies you keep on hand to run your business.

Fixed Assets are your company's more permanent possessions. Include the value of furniture, office equipment, machinery, trucks, servers, the building and land on which the business sits (if owned) . Depreciation is the gradual loss of value of your fixed assets. So, for example, if you bought your copier two years ago for $1,000 and it depreciates 10% each year, then after the first year, it's only worth $900, the second year it's worth $810 and so on. IRS Publication 534 gives information on how to figure out a realistic depreciation schedule.

Leaseholder Improvements is the money spent by you the tenant on improvements to the building or space leased for the business.

Liabilities means all the money you owe. It includes everything from bank loans, money owed to suppliers, customers, employees, magazines or newspapers, and taxes you owe.

Current liabilities are those monies owed which you'll need to pay back in the next 12 months.

Accounts payable are the monies owed to suppliers and individuals from whom you buy on credit.

Long-Term liabilities are monies your business owes that you must repay in the future, beyond the next twelve months.

Net Worth is simply assets minus liabilities. This is also called Owner's Equity.

Balance Sheet Template   For: Year Ended December 31, 20___

ASSETS

CURRENT ASSETS
    Cash on hand and in bank
    Marketable securities
    Accounts receivable (less allowance for bad debts)
    Merchandise inventory
    Supplies Inventory
      Total current Assets   _____

FIXED ASSETS
    Office Machinery and equipment (less depreciation)
    Furniture
    Improvements on property
      Total fixed assets   +   _____

TOTAL ASSETS (Current Assets + Fixed Assets)   =   _____

LIABILITIES AND NET WORTH

CURRENT LIABILITIES
    Accounts payable
    Notes payable within year
    Accrued taxes
      Total current liabilities   _____

LONG-TERM LIABILITIES
    Notes payable
    Total long-term liabilities   +   _____

TOTAL LIABILITIES
(Current Liabilities + Long Term Liabilities)   =   _____

NET WORTH (OWNER'S EQUITY)

(Total Assets - Total Liabilities)   _____

TOOL 2. INCOME STATEMENT (Profit & Loss) Explanation of Terms

The income statement, on the other hand, shows what was made and what was spent in your business over an *extended period of time* (typically a tax year).

Gross Sales is the total amount of income taken in by your business.

Net Sales is the above amount minus any amounts refunded to customers, any amounts not received because of discounts given to customers, employees, or any other losses.

Cost of Goods Sold is the answer to the question "How much did you spend to create those items that were sold during the year?" To compute that, determine

start	cost of what you started with,
+	cost of what you added during the year
+	cost of getting those items to you (can't forget the shipping/freight charges!)
=	cost of all the merchandise you had on hand during the year, then subtract
—	cost of what you have left at the end of the year

So for example, if you started with 10 hats, then bought/created 90 during the year and ended up with 15 at the end of the year, you actually sold 85 hats. Those 85 hats were the "goods sold." In order to have those hats to sell, you had to buy/create 90, plus have them shipped to you.

Gross Margin is an important number in business. This represents what you really have to work with to turn your passion into net profit. After you figure out how much it costs to buy/create the products you're selling, and subtract that from what you actually made in sales, the gross margin, or gross profit, as it's sometimes called, must be large enough to pay all your operating expenses with enough left over to yield a healthy profit.

Operating Expenses are all the costs incurred in running your business. Every business has a different set of operating expenses.

Operating Profit is computed by subtracting the operating expenses from the Gross Margin. This is the amount of profit derived from running the business. But wait, we're not done yet! We still have to pay taxes, but before we do that, we have to factor in...

Other income is money generated from sources other than the sale of products. Includes savings account interest, royalties, licensing income, mailing list rental, etc.

Total Income (and profit) before income tax is precisely that.

Provision for income tax. Even though you may not have actually paid taxes, you should subtract the amount you expect to pay (see IRS tax tables online at www.irs.gov, or in form 1040 instructions) before calling the above figure your profit.

Net Profit is your "bottom line" (hence its position on the P&L Statement). This is how much after-tax profit your business has earned.

Profit and Loss Statement

For: Year Ended December 20__

1. Gross Sales _____
2. Net Sales. _____
3. Less cost of goods sold:
    a. Opening Inventory _____

    b. Purchases during year _____
        c. Freight charges _____
        d. Total goods handled (line 3a + b + c) _____
        e. Less ending inventory, Dec 31 _____
        f. Total cost of goods sold (line 3d - 3e) _____

4. Gross Margin (line 2 - 3f) _____

5. Less operating expenses
    a. Salaries and wages _____
    b. Payroll taxes _____
    c. Utilities _____
    d. Telephone _____
    e. Rent _____
    f. Office supplies _____
    g. Postage _____
    h. Maintenance expenses _____
    i. Insurance _____
    j. Interest expense _____
    k. Depreciation _____
    l. Advertising _____
    m. Dues and contributions _____
    n. Miscellaneous expenses _____
    o. Total operating expenses (line 5a +...n) _____

6. Operating Profit (line 4 - 5o) _____

7. Other Income
    a. Dividends on stock _____
    b. Interest on bank account _____
    c. Rental of customer list _____
    d. Total of other income (line 7a + b + c) _____
8. Total income before income tax (line 6 + 7d) _____
9. Less provision for income tax _____

Net Profit (line 8 - 9) _____

TOOL 3. CASH FLOW ANALYSIS Explanation of Terms

The cash flow analysis shows the flow of money into and out of your business. For income, it shows when money came into your business, and where it came from. For expenses, it shows when the money was spent and what it was spent on. Because there are columns for "estimated" as well as "actual" income and expenses, broken up into periods of time (4 periods in the example which follows), it can help determine when certain expenses will fall due, and when certain monies can be expected to help you pay them. This is a great tool to help run your business more effectively and less stressfully.

Line 1	**Cash on Hand**- The total money available as readily usable cash
Line 2	**Cash Receipts** is cash that is received in the form of a. Cash sales b. Collections from customers who owe you money c. Loans, gifts or other investments into the business
Line 3	**Total Cash Receipts** (Lines 2a + 2b + 2c) is the sum of all the cash coming in from line 2.
Line 4	**Total Cash Available** is the sum of all cash on hand and cash receipts. (Lines 1 + 3)
Line 5	**Cash Paid Out** This category includes all business expenses.
Line 6	**Total Cash Paid Out** is the sum of all the itemized expenses in line section 5
Line 7	**Cash Flow**, therefore is Total Cash Available minus Total Cash Paid out (line 4 - line 6)

***

Monthly Cash Flow Statement

During your first year in business, you should complete one for each month.

	Start up		Period 1		Period 2		Period 3		Period 4		TOTAL		
1. CASH ON HAND (Beginning of month)													**1.**
2. CASH RECEIPTS (a) Cash Sales													**2.** (a)
(b) Collections													(b)
(c) Loans/other cash in													(c)
3. TOTAL CASH RECEIPTS													**3.**
4. TOT CASH AVAILABLE													**4.**
5. CASH PAID OUT													**5.**
Purchases (Merchandise)													
Gross Wages													
Payroll Expenses													
Outside Services													
Supplies (Office)													
Repairs and Maintenance													
Commissions & Fees													
Advertising													
Travel Meals/Entertainmt													
Legal and Professional Svc													
Rent													
Utilities													
Taxes													
Loan Payment (Interest)													
Other _____													
Other_____													
Other_____													
Miscellaneous													
SUBTOTAL													
Purchases													
Loan Payment (Principal)													
Startup costs													
For Owner's Personal Use													
6.TOTAL CASH PAID OUT													**6.**
7. NET CASH FLOW (end of month)													**7.**

DOING YOUR TAXES

Remember, turning your passion into profit is not about what you get, but what you get to keep. Unless you make the appropriate moves to shelter your income, you could end up sharing too much of it with the IRS. The following two scenarios will show you how the most basic tax forms would be completed in each case. The first scenario reflects a business loss. The second scenario represents how the tax forms would be completed for a profit. For the purposes of our scenario, and to illustrate certain basic concepts, we are going to focus only on the forms that a Sole Proprietor would complete.

TAX SCENARIO #1: LOSS

Mary Robinson of HeadStrong Hats

Mary Robinson is a legal secretary who's always had a passion for hats. Since she was a little girl, she dressed up in her mother's hats to the delight and appreciation of her family. She even worked for a short period of time at a millinery shop and came to learn a lot about the industry and the men and women who frequent hat shops. She noticed, however, that many people often left the shop in frustration after not being able to find a hat that fit their personalities.

Mary passionately believes that every hat has a personality. Every hat imparts it's personality to the person wearing it. Mary noticed that people tended to change themselves to match the personality of the hat they were wearing. What if, she reasoned, instead of having the people change to fit their hats, she could create a hat that could be changed to fit the customer's personality? She started a company called Headstrong Hats and designed her first "convertible hat" she called the Swerve. She marketed it with the slogan *"Get your swerve on!"* Men and women, who were previously unable to find a hat that fit their unique self-image and personality, fell in love with her creation. Eventually she came up with other designs with names like the Variance, Reformat, Chameleon, Transitional, Permutation and Mood. She created a line of reversible hats with names like alter-beret, the modi-fedora, the diversi-derby, and the converto-cap.

TAX SCENARIO #1:

Mary started HeadStrong as a sole proprietorship. In her first year in business, while still employed as a legal secretary, Mary generated $6,500 in sales. Not bad for her first year. However, she spent a bit more than that just getting the company started. So let's see how she handles this on her tax returns.

Her first step is to gather all of her receipts, cancelled checks, income statements and bank statements which she will use to complete the following forms.

Explanations
Form: SCHEDULE C - (PROFIT OR LOSS FROM BUSINESS) Page 1 of 2
Scenario: **LOSS**

Line	Explanation
	Mary enters her name and social security number as the proprietor of HeadStrong
Line B	According to Principal Business and Professional Activity Code list included in the instructions for this form, her business falls under "Retail Trade", sub-category "Clothing and Clothing Accessories" code 448150 for Clothing Accessory Stores
Line C	The official name of the business is HeadStrong Hats.
Line D	Mary enters her employer ID number which she received by completing Form SS-4.
Line F	Cash accounting method used to value inventory
Line G	Mary does, in fact, participate materially in the business. She checks "yes."
Line 1	Mary sold 130 hats during during the year at $50 each for a total of $6,500 in gross receipts.
Line 2	Ten people returned their hats, so her returns were $500
Line 3	Line 1 - Line 2 = $6,500 - $500 = $6,000
Line 4	After completing Part III, it's determined that it cost Mary $1,300 to make the hats that were sold.
Line 5	Her gross profit, therefore, is $6,000 - $1,300 = $4,700
Line 6	She had no other business income, so she leaves this item blank.
Line 7	Mary's gross income for the year, therefore was $4,700
Line 8	Mary spent $2,000 to advertise her hats in various fashion magazines
Line 10	Mary put 10,000 miles on her car for the year. She estimates that 25% of those miles were for business purposes. The IRS currently allows a deduction of 31 cents per mile traveled for business use. Therefore, her deduction is: 10,000 miles X .25 X .31 =$775
Line 17	Mary paid a lawyer and a business consultant $200 to advise her
Line 18	Office expenses for the year were $400
Line 22	Mary spent $500 on additional supplies

Line 24   Mary attended a trade show during the year. She spent a total of $700 in plane fare, hotel fees and other travel-related expenses.

24b   Mary spent $100 on meals during the trade show
24c   She is allowed to deduct 50% ($50, in this case) of this expense.

Line 25   Her utilities expenses include local and long distance telephone bills which total $1200 (Electric bills will be included on form 8829-Business Use of Home)

Line 27   Mary's "Other Expenses" total $2000 (see itemization on page 2)

Line 28   Mary's total expenses for the year, (lines 2 thru 27) were $7,825

Line 29, 31   Tentative profit or (loss) is $4,700 - $7825 = ($3125). This is a loss.

In this scenario, and as sometimes occurs in many new businesses, Mary's company incurred a loss. All is not lost, however. As a "reward" for her hard work, she will probably end up getting a tax refund. Why? Because from her day job, Mary earned $32,500. Her employer (the law firm) took out taxes each payday at the rate of someone in the $32,500 tax bracket. However, Mary is now actually in a lower tax bracket since she had all those business expenses which she can subtract from her gross income to lower her taxable income. With her taxable income lowered, she pays less taxes. Read this paragraph again to make sure you understand the concept. You will see how this is actually reported and claimed on her 1040 form.

Line 32   All investment is at risk

Schedule C-Business Profit or Loss (Page 1; Loss Scenario)

SCHEDULE C
(Form 1040)

Department of the Treasury
Internal Revenue Service

Profit or Loss From Business
(Sole Proprietorship)

▶ Partnerships, joint ventures, etc., must file Form 1065 or 1065-B.
▶ Attach to Form 1040 or 1041. ▶ See Instructions for Schedule C (Form 1040).

OMB No. 1545-0074

Millennium
Attachment
Sequence No. **09**

Name of proprietor — **MARY P. ROBINSON**

Social security number (SSN) **123 45 6789**

A Principal business or profession, including product or service (see page C-1 of the instructions)
RETAIL SALE OF HATS

B Enter code from pages C-7, 8, & 9 ▶ **448150**

C Business name. If no separate business name, leave blank.
HEADSTRONG HATS

D Employer ID number (EIN), if any **13 1234567**

E Business address (including suite or room no.) ▶ **P.O. BOX 123**
City, town or post office, state, and ZIP code **CLEARVIEW CA 90210**

F Accounting method: (1) ☐ Cash (2) ☐ Accrual (3) ☐ Other (specify) ▶

G Did you "materially participate" in the operation of this business during 2002? If "No," see page C-3 for limit on losses . ☑ Yes ☐ No

H If you started or acquired this business during this year check here . . . . ▶ ☐

Part I   Income

1	Gross receipts or sales. **Caution.** If this income was reported to you on Form W-2 and the "Statutory employee" box on that form was checked, see page C-3 and check here . . . . . . ▶ ☐	1	6500
2	Returns and allowances	2	500
3	Subtract line 2 from line 1	3	6000
4	Cost of goods sold (from line 42 on page 2)	4	1300
5	**Gross profit.** Subtract line 4 from line 3	5	4700
6	Other income, including Federal and state gasoline or fuel tax credit or refund (see page C-3) . . .	6	
7	**Gross income.** Add lines 5 and 6 . . . . ▶	7	4700

Part II   Expenses. Enter expenses for business use of your home **only** on line 30.

8	Advertising	8	2000	19	Pension and profit-sharing plans	19	
9	Bad debts from sales or services (see page C-3) . .	9		20	Rent or lease (see page C-5):		
				a	Vehicles, machinery, and equipment	20a	
10	Car and truck expenses (see page C-3)	10	775	b	Other business property . .	20b	
11	Commissions and fees . .	11		21	Repairs and maintenance . .	21	
12	Depletion	12		22	Supplies (not included in Part III) .	22	500
13	Depreciation and section 179 expense deduction (not included in Part III) (see page C-4) . .	13		23	Taxes and licenses . . .	23	
14	Employee benefit programs (other than on line 19) . .	14		24	Travel, meals, and entertainment:		
15	Insurance (other than health) .	15		a	Travel	24a	700
16	Interest:			b	Meals and entertainment	100	
a	Mortgage (paid to banks, etc.) .	16a		c	Enter nondeductible amount included on line 24b (see page C-5) .	50	
b	Other	16b		d	Subtract line 24c from line 24b	24d	50
17	Legal and professional services	17	200	25	Utilities	25	1200
18	Office expense	18	400	26	Wages (less employment credits) .	26	
				27	Other expenses (from line 48 on page 2) .	27	2000

28	Total expenses before expenses for business use of home. Add lines 8 through 27 in columns . . . ▶	28	7825
29	Tentative profit (loss). Subtract line 28 from line 7	29	(3125)
30	Expenses for business use of your home. Attach **Form 8829**	30	
31	**Net profit or (loss).** Subtract line 30 from line 29.		
	• If a profit, enter on **Form 1040, line 12,** and **also** on **Schedule SE, line 2** (statutory employees, see page C-6). Estates and trusts, enter on Form 1041, line 3.	31	(3125)
	• If a loss, you **must** go to line 32.		
32	If you have a loss, check the box that describes your investment in this activity (see page C-6).		
	• If you checked 32a, enter the loss on **Form 1040, line 12,** and **also** on **Schedule SE, line 2** (statutory employees, see page C-6). Estates and trusts, enter on Form 1041, line 3.	32a ☑ All investment is at risk.	
	• If you checked 32b, you **must** attach **Form 6198.**	32b ☐ Some investment is not at risk.	

For Paperwork Reduction Act Notice, see Form 1040 instructions.   Cat. No. 11334P   Schedule C (Form 1040) Millennium Ed.

Part III — Cost of Goods Sold

Line 33   The value of the inventory is based on the actual cost to Mary.

Line 34   Mary used the cost method for determining the value of both opening and closing inventories

Line 35   Mary started with an initial inventory of 20 hats which cost her $200 to create.

Line 36   Since she creates her hats herself, Mary does not purchase her inventory

Line 37   Mary does the work herself, for now, so there is no cost of labor

Line 38   Mary spends $1,000 on the materials and supplies necessary to create the hats

Line 39   Shipping charges for supplies and other miscellaneous costs to produce the hats total $100

Line 40   Lines 35 through 39 total $1300

Line 41   By the end of the year, Mary has sold every single Swerve in the house! Her inventory at the end of the year is, therefore, valued at $0.

Line 42   Cost of goods sold is $1,300   ·

Part IV — Information on Your Vehicle

Mary completes this section with information on her car which she uses for business as well as personal matters.

Part V — Other Expenses

In this section Mary lists the specific expenses she summed and entered on line 27.

Promotion	$ 500 (mailing costs, photocopying, etc.)
Website Design	$ 500
Website host fees	$ 300 (12 months @ $25/month)
Hire models for show	$ 400
Miscellaneous	$ 300
Total	$ 2000

Schedule C-Business Profit and Loss (Page 2; Loss Scenario)

Schedule C (Form 1040) Millennium Version

Page **2**

Part III Cost of Goods Sold (see page C-6)

33 Method(s) used to value closing inventory: a ☑ Cost b ☐ Lower of cost or market c ☐ Other (attach explanation)

34 Was there any change in determining quantities, costs, or valuations between opening and closing inventory? If "Yes," attach explanation . . . . ☐ Yes ☑ No

35	Inventory at beginning of year. If different from last year's closing inventory, attach explanation . .	35	200
36	Purchases less cost of items withdrawn for personal use	36	
37	Cost of labor. Do not include any amounts paid to yourself	37	0
38	Materials and supplies	38	1000
39	Other costs	39	100
40	Add lines 35 through 39	40	1300
41	Inventory at end of year	41	0
42	Cost of goods sold. Subtract line 41 from line 40. Enter the result here and on page 1, line 4 . .	42	1300

Part IV Information on Your Vehicle. Complete this part **only** if you are claiming car or truck expenses on line 10 and are not required to file Form 4562 for this business. See the instructions for line 13 on page C-4 to find out if you must file.

43 When did you place your vehicle in service for business purposes? (month, day, year) ▶ . . . . . /. . . . . /. . . . .

44 Of the total number of miles you drove your vehicle during this year, enter the number of miles you used your vehicle for:

a Business . . . 2500 . . . . . . b Commuting . . . 7500 . . . . . c Other . . . .

45 Do you (or your spouse) have another vehicle available for personal use? . . . . ☑ Yes ☐ No

46 Was your vehicle available for personal use during off-duty hours? . . . . ☑ Yes ☐ No

47a Do you have evidence to support your deduction? . . . . ☑ Yes ☐ No

b If "Yes," is the evidence written? . . . . ☑ Yes ☐ No

Part V Other Expenses. List below business expenses not included on lines 8-26 or line 30.

PROMOTION	500
WEBSITE DESIGN	500
WEB HOSTING FEE	300
HIRE MODELS FOR SHOW	400
MISCELLANEOUS	300
48 Total other expenses. Enter here and on page 1, line 27 48	2000

Schedule C (Form 1040) Millennium Edition

Explanations
Form: **8829 - (BUSINESS USE OF HOME) Page 1 of 1**
Scenario: **LOSS**

Line 1   The area of her apartment that she uses as her office is about 420 square feet

Line 2   The total area of her apartment is approximately 1200 square feet (S.F.)

Lines 3, 7   Therefore, the percentage of space in her apartment that is used for business is 420 divided by 1200 = .35 or 35%

Line 8   The business loss ($3125) that she computed and entered on line 29 of her Schedule C is entered here.

Line 19   This amount, $350, is the electric portion of her utility bills for the year. It is an indirect expense because it would have to be paid whether or not Mary were running a company from her home. Therefore it is not an expense that's directly related to the business.

Line 20   This amount $7200, is the rent she paid for the year.
12 months x $600 = $7200

Line 21.   The total of these indirect expenses is $7550. Indirect expenses are expenses which benefit the entire home. Both her electric bill and her rent fall into this category.

Line 22,24   She is allowed to deduct only the percentage of these expenses that apply to the business. In this case 35% of $7550 = $2642 apply to the business.

Line 25,34   Her allowable operating expense, however, is $0. (see summary below)

Summary: The IRS allows you to deduct expenses for business use of your home ONLY up to the amount of your profit earned in your business. In other words, if, after subtracting operating expenses, your business earned, say $500 in profit, even if your home use expenses total $2000, you can only deduct a maximum of $500 for home expenses. However, one nice advantage is that you can carry over into next year the $1500 that you couldn't deduct this year. (That amount would be entered on line 41 of this form, and entered on line 23 of next year's form). In Mary's case, since she incurred a loss for her business for the year, (remember, a negative number is less than zero), she won't be allowed to deduct anything this year for the business use of her home. However, she
will carry over the $2642 into next year's tax return.

Form 8829-Expenses for Business Use of Home (Loss)

Form **8829**	**Expenses for Business Use of Your Home**	OMB No. 1545-1266
Department of the Treasury Internal Revenue Service	▶ File only with Schedule C (Form 1040). Use a separate Form 8829 for each home you used for business during the year. ▶ See separate instructions.	**Millennium** Attachment Sequence No. **66**

Name(s) of proprietor(s): **MARY P. ROBINSON**
Your social security number: **123 45 6789**

Part I — Part of Your Home Used for Business

1	Area used regularly and exclusively for business, regularly for day care, or for storage of inventory or product samples (see instructions)	1	**420 S.F.**
2	Total area of home	2	**1200 S.F.**
3	Divide line 1 by line 2. Enter the result as a percentage	3	**35 %**
	• For day-care facilities not used exclusively for business, also complete lines 4–6.		
	• All others, skip lines 4–6 and enter the amount from line 3 on line 7.		
4	Multiply days used for day care during year by hours used per day	4	hr.
5	Total hours available for use during the year (365 days × 24 hours) (see instructions)	5	8,760 hr.
6	Divide line 4 by line 5. Enter the result as a decimal amount	6	
7	Business percentage. For day-care facilities not used exclusively for business, multiply line 6 by line 3 (enter the result as a percentage). All others, enter the amount from line 3 ▶	7	**35 %**

Part II — Figure Your Allowable Deduction

		(a) Direct expenses	(b) Indirect expenses		
8	Enter the amount from Schedule C, line 29, plus any net gain or (loss) derived from the business use of your home and shown on Schedule D or Form 4797. If more than one place of business, see instructions			8	**(3125)**
	See instructions for columns (a) and (b) before completing lines 9–20.				
9	Casualty losses (see instructions)	9			
10	Deductible mortgage interest (see instructions)	10			
11	Real estate taxes (see instructions)	11			
12	Add lines 9, 10, and 11	12			
13	Multiply line 12, column (b) by line 7		13		
14	Add line 12, column (a) and line 13			14	
15	Subtract line 14 from line 8. If zero or less, enter -0-			15	
16	Excess mortgage interest (see instructions)	16			
17	Insurance	17			
18	Repairs and maintenance	18			
19	Utilities	19	**350**		
20	Other expenses (see instructions)	20	**1200**		
21	Add lines 16 through 20	21	**1550**		
22	Multiply line 21, column (b) by line 7		22 **2642**		
23	Carryover of operating expenses from last year's Form 8829, line 41		23		
24	Add line 21 in column (a), line 22, and line 23			24	**2642**
25	Allowable operating expenses. Enter the **smaller** of line 15 or line 24			25	
26	Limit on excess casualty losses and depreciation. Subtract line 25 from line 15			26	
27	Excess casualty losses (see instructions)		27		
28	Depreciation of your home from Part III below		28		
29	Carryover of excess casualty losses and depreciation from last year's Form 8829, line 42		29		
30	Add lines 27 through 29			30	
31	Allowable excess casualty losses and depreciation. Enter the **smaller** of line 26 or line 30			31	
32	Add lines 14, 25, and 31			32	
33	Casualty loss portion, if any, from lines 14 and 31. Carry amount to **Form 4684**, Section B			33	
34	Allowable expenses for business use of your home. Subtract line 33 from line 32. Enter here and on Schedule C, line 30. If your home was used for more than one business, see instructions ▶			34	**0**

Part III — Depreciation of Your Home

35	Enter the **smaller** of your home's adjusted basis or its fair market value (see instructions)	35	
36	Value of land included on line 35	36	
37	Basis of building. Subtract line 36 from line 35	37	
38	Business basis of building. Multiply line 37 by line 7	38	
39	Depreciation percentage (see instructions)	39	%
40	Depreciation allowable (see instructions). Multiply line 38 by line 39. Enter here and on line 28 above	40	

Part IV — Carryover of Unallowed Expenses to next year

41	Operating expenses. Subtract line 25 from line 24. If less than zero, enter -0-	41	**2642**
42	Excess casualty losses and depreciation. Subtract line 31 from line 30. If less than zero, enter -0-	42	

For Paperwork Reduction Act Notice, see page 4 of separate instructions.   Cat. No. 13232M   Form **8829** Millennium Version

Explanations
Form: **1040 - (US INDIVIDUAL INCOME TAX RETURN) Page 1 of 2**
Scenario: **LOSS**

As a sole proprietor, Mary completes a 1040 form just as she does every year. Form 1040 includes personal income and expenses as well as business income or loss.

Filing Status   Mary completes her address in the "Label" section, checks box 1 for her filing status (single), and lists herself in box 6a as her only exemption

Line 6a-d.   Mary is single, lives alone, and has no dependents. Therefore, she has only one exemption: herself.

Line 7.   On this line, Mary puts the $32,500 she earned as legal secretary.

Line 8a.   On this line, she puts the $250 in savings account interest she earned. (This was found on the end-of-year statement she received from her bank.)

Line 12.   On this line she puts the $3125 business loss which was computed and entered on line 31 of the Schedule C.

Line 22.   Mary's total income, therefore, is $29,625.
                    Remember, since line 12 is negative (a loss), it should be placed in parentheses ("($X,XXX)"") and subtracted from the other income listed. Therefore:
                    $32,500 + $250 - ($3125) = $29,625

Line 35.   With no other adjustments to income, Mary's Adjusted Gross Income, therefore, is $29,265

NOTE: Please read all the possible adjustments to income. Your situation may vary. You may, for example be paying interest on a student loan, alimony, or other allowable expense which would entitle you to further adjustments to your income.

Form 1040-US Individual Tax Return (Page 1; Loss Scenario)

1040 Department of the Treasury—Internal Revenue Service
U.S. Individual Passion Profit Income Tax Return

For the years 2000 and beyond!

OMB No. 1545-0074

Label (See instructions on page 21.)

Use the IRS label. Otherwise, please print or type.

Your first name and initial: *MARY P.* Last name: *ROBINSON*
Your social security number: *123 45 6789*

If a joint return, spouse's first name and initial / Last name
Spouse's social security number

Home address (number and street). If you have a P.O. box, see page 21. Apt. no.
401 PASSIONFRUIT LANE

City, town or post office, state, and ZIP code. If you have a foreign address, see page 21.
CLEARVIEW CA 90210

▲ **Important!** ▲ You must enter your SSN(s) above.

Presidential Election Campaign (See page 21.)
Note. Checking "Yes" will not change your tax or reduce your refund.
Do you, or your spouse if filing a joint return, want $3 to go to this fund? ► You ☐Yes ☐No Spouse ☐Yes ☐No

Filing Status
Check only one box.

1 ☑ Single
2 ☐ Married filing jointly (even if only one had income)
3 ☐ Married filing separately. Enter spouse's SSN above and full name here. ►
4 ☐ Head of household (with qualifying person). (See page 21.) If the qualifying person is a child but not your dependent, enter this child's name here. ►
5 ☐ Qualifying widow(er) with dependent child (year spouse died ►). (See page 21.)

Exemptions

If more than five dependents, see page 22.

6a ☑ Yourself. If your parent (or someone else) can claim you as a dependent on his or her tax return, **do not check box 6a** . . . .
b ☐ Spouse . . . .

No. of boxes checked on 6a and 6b: **1**

c Dependents:

(1) First name Last name	(2) Dependent's social security number	(3) Dependent's relationship to you	(4) ✓ if qualifying child for child tax credit (see page 22)
			☐
			☐
			☐
			☐
			☐

No. of children on 6c who:
• lived with you
• did not live with you due to divorce or separation (see page 22)
Dependents on 6c not entered above

d Total number of exemptions claimed . . . .

Add numbers on lines above ► **1**

Income

Attach Forms W-2 and W-2G here. Also attach Form(s) 1099-R if tax was withheld.

If you did not get a W-2, see page 23.

Enclose, but do not attach, any payment. Also, please use Form 1040-V.

7	Wages, salaries, tips, etc. Attach Form(s) W-2	7	*32300*
8a	Taxable interest. Attach Schedule B if required	8a	*250*
b	Tax-exempt interest. **Do not** include on line 8a . . .	8b	
9	Ordinary dividends. Attach Schedule B if required	9	
10	Taxable refunds, credits, or offsets of state and local income taxes (see page 24) . .	10	
11	Alimony received	11	
12	Business income or (loss). Attach Schedule C or C-EZ	12	*(3125)*
13	Capital gain or (loss). Attach Schedule D if required. If not required, check here ► ☐	13	
14	Other gains or (losses). Attach Form 4797	14	
15a	IRA distributions	15a	b Taxable amount (see page 25)	15b	
16a	Pensions and annuities	16a	b Taxable amount (see page 25)	16b	
17	Rental real estate, royalties, partnerships, S corporations, trusts, etc. Attach Schedule E	17	
18	Farm income or (loss). Attach Schedule F	18	
19	Unemployment compensation	19	
20a	Social security benefits	20a	b Taxable amount (see page 27)	20b	
21	Other income. List type and amount (see page 29)	21	
22	Add the amounts in the far right column for lines 7 through 21. This is your **total income** ►	22	*29625*

Adjusted Gross Income

23	Educator expenses (see page 29)	23	
24	IRA deduction (see page 29)	24	
25	Student loan interest deduction (see page 31) . . .	25	
26	Tuition and fees deduction (see page 32)	26	
27	Archer MSA deduction. Attach Form 8853	27	
28	Moving expenses. Attach Form 3903	28	
29	One-half of self-employment tax. Attach Schedule SE	29	
30	Self-employed health insurance deduction (see page 33)	30	
31	Self-employed SEP, SIMPLE, and qualified plans . .	31	
32	Penalty on early withdrawal of savings	32	
33a	Alimony paid b Recipient's SSN ►	33a	
34	Add lines 23 through 33a	34	*0*
35	Subtract line 34 from line 22. This is your **adjusted gross income** ►	35	*29625*

For Disclosure, Privacy Act, and Paperwork Reduction Act Notice, see page 76.   Cat. No. 11320B   Form **1040** Millennium Edition

Line 36.   This line is the same as line 35 ($29,625).

Line 38   By itemizing her deductions Mary calculated her deductions to
                   be $4,000. As you can see, however, she is better off using the
                   STANDARD IRS deduction of $4,700.

Line 37.   Line 36 [$29,625] minus line 38 [$4700] = $24,925. In other
                   words, she is now in the $24,925 tax bracket.

Line 40.   Her one (1) exemption, from line 6d, allows her to deduct an
                   additional 1 x $3,000 from her adjusted gross income.

Line 41   Her taxable income is now $24,925 - $3,000 = $21,925. In other
                   words, she is now in the $21,925 tax bracket. (Note: If Mary
                   had a dependent, the number on line 6e would have been "2"
                   and she would have been allowed to deduct 2 X $3,000, or
                   $6,000. This would have put her in an even lower tax bracket.

Line 44   Her tax due on $21,925, based on the tax tables, is $2,989.

Lines 45-53.   Mary has no other credits which she can claim. She enters "0"
                   on line 54. Note: If she had a dependent, she would be able to
                   claim additional deductions by completing form 2441.

Line 50.   Since Mary incurred a loss this year, she is not required to file
                   form SE and therefore owes no self-employment tax.

Line 61   So, even though Mary made $32,500 at her job at the law firm,
                   because of her business activities, she was able to put herself in
                   a lower tax bracket. So the amount of tax she has to pay the
                   government will be based on $21,925 instead of $32,500. That
                   amount, $2,989, is entered here.

Lines 62,69   As mentioned earlier, taxes already have been deducted from the pay
                   check from her day job. From her W-2 statement she finds that the law
                   firm withheld a total of $5114 since they assumed she was in the $32,500
                   tax bracket. She enters that amount on line 62 and on line 69.

Line 65.   As you can see, her day job withheld MORE than she is actually
                   required to pay. Therefore, Mary is entitled to a refund of $5,114
                   - $2989 = $2,125. This will definitely come in handy to be put
                   back into the business.

It won't always be like this, however. Someday Mary will be required to pay
more in taxes than she ever dreamed of (That's a good thing!). At that point, she will
need to look for ways, like bonds, and IRA's to shelter her income from Uncle Sam!

Form 1040-US Individual Tax Return (Page 2; Loss Scenario)

Form 1040 created exclusively for Passion Profit

Page 2

Tax and Credits	36	Amount from line 35 (adjusted gross income)	**36** 29635
	37a	Check if: ☐ **You** were 65 or older, ☐ **Blind**; ☐ **Spouse** was 65 or older, ☐ **Blind**. Add the number of boxes checked above and enter the total here . . . . . ▶ 37a	
Standard Deduction for—	b	If you are married filing separately and your spouse itemizes deductions, or you were a dual-status alien, see page 34 and check here . . . . . ▶ 37b ☐	
• People who checked any box on line 37a or 37b or who can be claimed as a dependent, see page 34.	38	**Itemized deductions** (from Schedule A) or your **standard deduction** (see left margin) . .	**38** 4700
	39	Subtract line 38 from line 36	**39** 24925
	40	If line 36 is $103,000 or less, multiply $3,000 by the total number of exemptions claimed on line 6d. If line 36 is over $103,000, see the worksheet on page 35	**40** 3000
• All others:	41	**Taxable income.** Subtract line 40 from line 39. If line 40 is more than line 39, enter -0- .	**41** 21925
Single, $4,700	42	**Tax** (see page 36). Check if any tax is from: a ☐ Form(s) 8814 b ☐ Form 4972 . .	**42** 2989
Head of household, $6,900	43	**Alternative minimum tax** (see page 37). Attach Form 6251	**43**
Married filing jointly or Qualifying widow(er), $7,850	44	Add lines 42 and 43 . . . . ▶	**44** 2989
	45	Foreign tax credit. Attach Form 1116 if required	45	
	46	Credit for child and dependent care expenses. Attach Form 2441	46	
Married filing separately, $3,925	47	Credit for the elderly or the disabled. Attach Schedule R . .	47	
	48	Education credits. Attach Form 8863	48	
	49	Retirement savings contributions credit. Attach Form 8880 .	49	
	50	Child tax credit (see page 39)	50	
	51	Adoption credit. Attach Form 8839	51	
	52	Credits from: a ☐ Form 8396 b ☐ Form 8859 . .	52	
	53	Other credits. Check applicable box(es): a ☐ Form 3800 b ☐ Form 8801 c ☐ Specify _____	53	
	54	Add lines 45 through 53. These are your **total credits**	**54** 0
	55	Subtract line 54 from line 44. If line 54 is more than line 44, enter -0- . . . ▶	**55** 2989
Other Taxes	56	Self-employment tax. Attach Schedule SE	**56** 0
	57	Social security and Medicare tax on tip income not reported to employer. Attach Form 4137	**57**
	58	Tax on qualified plans, including IRAs and other tax-favored accounts. Attach Form 5329 if required .	**58**
	59	Advance earned income credit payments from Form(s) W-2	**59**
	60	Household employment taxes. Attach Schedule H	**60**
	61	Add lines 55 through 60. This is your **total tax** . . . . ▶	**61** 2989
Payments	62	Federal income tax withheld from Forms W-2 and 1099 .	62	5114
	63	2002 estimated tax payments and amount applied from 2001 return	63	
If you have a qualifying child, attach Schedule EIC.	64	**Earned income credit (EIC)**	64	
	65	Excess social security and tier 1 RRTA tax withheld (see page 56)	65	
	66	Additional child tax credit. Attach Form 8812 . . .	66	
	67	Amount paid with request for extension to file (see page 56)	67	
	68	Other payments from: a ☐ Form 2439 b ☐ Form 4136 c ☐ Form 8885 . .	68	
	69	Add lines 62 through 68. These are your **total payments** . . . . . ▶	**69** 5114
Refund	70	If line 69 is more than line 61, subtract line 61 from line 69. This is the amount you **overpaid** ▶	**70** 2125
Direct deposit? See page 56 and fill in 71b, 71c, and 71d.	71a	Amount of line 70 you want **refunded to you** . . . . ▶	**71a** 2125
	▶ b	Routing number 02001 2 345 ▶ c Type: ☑ Checking ☐ Savings	
	▶ d	Account number 12345678	
	72	Amount of line 70 you want **applied to your next year's estimated tax** ▶ 72	
Amount You Owe	73	**Amount you owe.** Subtract line 68 from line 61. For details on how to pay, see page 57 ▶	**73**
	74	Estimated tax penalty (see page 57) 74	
Third Party Designee	Do you want to allow another person to discuss this return with the IRS (see page 58)? ☐ **Yes.** Complete the following. ☐ **No**		
	Designee's name ▶	Phone no. ▶ ( )	Personal identification number (PIN) ▶

Sign Here

Under penalties of perjury, I declare that I have examined this return and accompanying schedules and statements, and to the best of my knowledge and belief, they are true, correct, and complete. Declaration of preparer (other than taxpayer) is based on all information of which preparer has any knowledge.

Joint return? See page 21.
Keep a copy for your records.

Your signature	Date	Your occupation	Daytime phone number
Mary Raham		LEGAL SEC'Y	000/123-4567
Spouse's signature. If a joint return, **both** must sign.	Date	Spouse's occupation	

Paid Preparer's Use Only

Preparer's signature ▶	Date	Check if self-employed ☐	Preparer's SSN or PTIN
Firm's name (or yours if self-employed), address, and ZIP code ▶		EIN	
		Phone no. ( )	

Form **1040** Millennium Edition

TAX SCENARIO #2: PROFIT YEAR 2

Whew!

That's what happened to Mary in her first year. By year two, however, someone who cared about her sent her a copy of *Turn Your Passion Into Profit*. She put it to good use. She was so inspired, she quit her job!

Then, armed with the desire to succeed, having conquered her fears and opened herself up to divine guidance and inspiration, Mary had some winning ideas about marketing her passion. She read several of the books recommended in the appendix of *Turn Your Passion Into Profit*, changed a few words in her classified ad to appeal to her customers' personality types, and "overnighted" a sample of the hat to a fashion editor who loved it so much, she wrote an article about her in a prominent magazine.

She found a new supplier who was able to reduce her unit cost to $3.00, and Mary sold about 4,000 hats for about $14.00 each. Her ideas proved so successful, that at the end of her first year, she made more selling hats than she did as a legal secretary!

Here is Mary's return for her winning second year!

Explanations on form: SCHEDULE C - (PROFIT OR LOSS FROM BUSINESS)
Page 1 of 2   Scenario: PROFIT

Line	Explanation
	Mary enters her name and social security number as the proprietor
Line B	According to Principal Business and Professional Activity Code list included in the instructions for this form, her business falls under "Retail Trade", sub-category "Clothing and Clothing Accessories" code 448150 for Clothing Accessory Stores
Line C	The official name of the business is HeadStrong Hats.
Line D	Mary enters her employer ID number from Form SS-4.
Line F	Cash accounting method to value inventory
Line G	Mary does participate materially in the business. She checks "yes."
Line 1	Mary sold 4000 hats during at approx $14 each for a total of $57,000 in gross receipts.
Line 2	Twenty-eight people returned their hats, so her returns were $400
Line 3	Line 1 - Line 2 = $57,000 - $400 = $56,600
Line 4	After completing Part III, it's determined that it cost Mary $12,000 to make the hats that were sold.
Line 5	Her gross profit, therefore, is $56,6000 - $12,000 = $44,600
Line 6	She had no other business income, so she leaves this item blank.
Line 7	Mary's gross income for the year, therefore, was $44,600
Line 8	Mary spent $2,000 to advertise her hats in various fashion magazines
Line 10	Mary put 10,000 miles on her car for the year. She estimates that 25% of those miles were for business purposes. The IRS allows a deduction of 31 cents per mile traveled for business use. Therefore, car expense is: 10,0000 miles X .25 X .31 =$775
Line 17	Mary paid a lawyer and a business consultant to advise her on her business

Line 18   Office expenses for the year were $425. Included in this figure is the $25 she spent to overnight a sample of her hat to the magazine editor.

Line 22   Mary spent $500 on additional supplies.

Line 24   Mary attended a trade show during the year. She spent a total of $700 in plane fare, hotel fees and other travel-related expenses.

Line 25   Her utilities expenses include local and long distance telephone bills which total $1200 (Electric bills will be factored in on form 8829-Business Use of Home)

Line 27   Mary's "Other Expenses" total $2,675 (see itemization on pg 2)

Line 28   Her business expenses for the year, therefore, total $ 8,475

Line 29   Tentative profit is $44,600 - $8,475 = $36,125

Line 30   Expenses for business use of home (see form 8829) total $7,742

Line 31   Mary's net profit is $36,125 - $7,742 = $28,383

Schedule C-Business Profit and Loss (Page 1; Profit Scenario)

SCHEDULE C
(Form 1040)

Department of the Treasury
Internal Revenue Service

Profit or Loss From Business
(Sole Proprietorship)

▶ Partnerships, joint ventures, etc., must file Form 1065 or 1065-B.

▶ Attach to Form 1040 or 1041. ▶ See Instructions for Schedule C (Form 1040).

OMB No. 1545-0074

Millennium

Attachment
Sequence No. **09**

Name of proprietor **MARY P. ROBINSON**

Social security number (SSN) **123 45 6789**

A Principal business or profession, including product or service (see page C-1 of the instructions) **RETAIL SALE OF HATS**

B Enter code from pages C-7, 8, & 9 ▶ **448150**

C Business name. If no separate business name, leave blank. **HEADSTRONG HATS**

D Employer ID number (EIN), if any **13 1234567**

E Business address (including suite or room no.) ▶ **P.O. BOX 123**
City, town or post office, state, and ZIP code **CLEARVIEW CA 90210**

F Accounting method: (1) ☐ Cash (2) ☐ Accrual (3) ☐ Other (specify) ▶

G Did you "materially participate" in the operation of this business during 2002? If "No," see page C-3 for limit on losses. ☐ Yes ☐ No

H If you started or acquired this business during this year, check here ▶ ☐

Part I Income

1 Gross receipts or sales. Caution. If this income was reported to you on Form W-2 and the "Statutory employee" box on that form was checked, see page C-3 and check here ▶ ☐	1	57000
2 Returns and allowances	2	400
3 Subtract line 2 from line 1	3	56600
4 Cost of goods sold (from line 42 on page 2)	4	12,000
5 Gross profit. Subtract line 4 from line 3	5	44600
6 Other income, including Federal and state gasoline or fuel tax credit or refund (see page C-3)	6	
7 Gross income. Add lines 5 and 6 ▶	7	44600

Part II Expenses. Enter expenses for business use of your home only on line 30.

8 Advertising	8	2000	19 Pension and profit-sharing plans	19	
9 Bad debts from sales or services (see page C-3)	9		20 Rent or lease (see page C-5):		
			a Vehicles, machinery, and equipment	20a	
10 Car and truck expenses (see page C-3)	10	775	b Other business property	20b	
			21 Repairs and maintenance	21	
11 Commissions and fees	11		22 Supplies (not included in Part III)	22	500
12 Depletion	12		23 Taxes and licenses	23	
13 Depreciation and section 179 expense deduction (not included in Part III) (see page C-4)	13		24 Travel, meals, and entertainment:		
			a Travel	24a	700
14 Employee benefit programs (other than on line 19)	14		b Meals and entertainment		
15 Insurance (other than health)	15		c Enter nondeductible amount included on line 24b (see page C-5)		
16 Interest:			d Subtract line 24c from line 24b	24d	
a Mortgage (paid to banks, etc.)	16a		25 Utilities	25	1200
b Other	16b		26 Wages (less employment credits)	26	
17 Legal and professional services	17	200	27 Other expenses (from line 48 on page 2)	27	2675
18 Office expense	18	425			

28 Total expenses before expenses for business use of home. Add lines 8 through 27 in columns ▶	28	8475
29 Tentative profit (loss). Subtract line 28 from line 7	29	36125
30 Expenses for business use of your home. Attach Form 8829	30	7742
31 Net profit or (loss). Subtract line 30 from line 29.	31	28383

- If a profit, enter on Form 1040, line 12, and also on Schedule SE, line 2 (statutory employees, see page C-6). Estates and trusts, enter on Form 1041, line 3.
- If a loss, you must go to line 32.

32 If you have a loss, check the box that describes your investment in this activity (see page C-6).
- If you checked 32a, enter the loss on Form 1040, line 12, and also on Schedule SE, line 2 (statutory employees, see page C-6). Estates and trusts, enter on Form 1041, line 3.
- If you checked 32b, you must attach Form 6198.

32a ☑ All investment is at risk.
32b ☐ Some investment is not at risk.

For Paperwork Reduction Act Notice, see Form 1040 instructions.   Cat. No. 11334P   Schedule C (Form 1040)Millennium Ed.

Part III — Cost of Goods Sold

Line 33   The value of the inventory is based on the actual cost to Mary.

Line 34   Mary used the cost method for determining the value this year too

Line 35   Mary started with an initial inventory of 0 hats which cost her $0

Line 36   Mary's purchase of her new inventory of hats totals $12,000

Line 40   Lines 35 through 39 total $12,000

Line 41   By the end of the year, Mary has 0 hats left (for simplicity)

Line 42   Cost of goods sold is $12,000

Part IV — Information on Your Vehicle
                 Mary completes this section with information on her car which
                 she uses for business as well as personal matters.

Part V — Other Expenses
                 In this section Mary lists the specific expenses she summed and
                 entered on line 27.

Promotion	$ 500 (mailing costs, photocopying, etc.)
Website host fees	$100 (one fee for the year)
Graphic Design	$350
Hire models for show	$ 450
Photography	$ 1,000
Internet Access	$ 275
Total	$ 2675

Schedule C-Business Profit and Loss (Page 2; Profit Scenario)

Schedule C (Form 1040) Millennium Version   Page **2**

Part III   Cost of Goods Sold (see page C-6)

33	Method(s) used to value closing inventory: **a** ☑ Cost **b** ☐ Lower of cost or market **c** ☐ Other (attach explanation)		
34	Was there any change in determining quantities, costs, or valuations between opening and closing inventory? If "Yes," attach explanation . . . . ☐ Yes ☑ No		
35	Inventory at beginning of year. If different from last year's closing inventory, attach explanation . .	35	*O*
36	Purchases less cost of items withdrawn for personal use	36	*12,000*
37	Cost of labor. Do not include any amounts paid to yourself	37	
38	Materials and supplies	38	
39	Other costs	39	
40	Add lines 35 through 39	40	*12,000*
41	Inventory at end of year	41	*O*
42	Cost of goods sold. Subtract line 41 from line 40. Enter the result here and on page 1, line 4 . .	42	*12,000*

Part IV   Information on Your Vehicle. Complete this part **only** if you are claiming car or truck expenses on line 10 and are not required to file Form 4562 for this business. See the instructions for line 13 on page C-4 to find out if you must file.

43   When did you place your vehicle in service for business purposes? (month, day, year) ▶ . . . . / . . . . . . / . . . .

44   Of the total number of miles you drove your vehicle during this year, enter the number of miles you used your vehicle for:

a Business . . . . *12,000* . . . . **b** Commuting . . . . **c** Other *3,000*

45	Do you (or your spouse) have another vehicle available for personal use?	☑ Yes	☐ No
46	Was your vehicle available for personal use during off-duty hours?	☑ Yes	☐ No
47a	Do you have evidence to support your deduction?	☑ Yes	☐ No
b	If "Yes," is the evidence written?	☑ Yes	☐ No

Part V   Other Expenses. List below business expenses not included on lines 8-26 or line 30.

PROMOTION	500
WEB HOSTING	100
GRAPHIC DESIGN	350
HIRE MODELS	450
PHOTOGRAPHY	1,000
INTERNET ACCESS	275

48	Total other expenses. Enter here and on page 1, line 27	48	*2675*

Schedule C (Form 1040) Millennium Edition

Explanations for form: 8829 (Business Use Of Home)
Scenario: PROFIT

Line 1.	The expanded area of her apartment that she uses as her business is about 600 S.F. (square feet)
Line 2.	The total area of her apartment is still approximately 1200 S.F.
Lines 3, 7.	Therefore, the percentage of space in her apartment that is used for business is 600 divided by 1200 = .50 or 50%
Line 8.	The business profit [$36,125) that she computed and entered on line 29 of her Schedule C is entered here.
Line 17	She spent $1000 on property insurance for her inventory
Line 19	She spent $1000 on electric utilities
Line 20.	This amount, $7200, is the rent she paid for the year. 12 months x $600 = $7200
Line 21a	The total of her DIRECT expenses is $1,000. Direct expenses are expenses which are related directly to the business and do not benefit the home. Her property insurance falls into that category.
Line 21b.	The total of these indirect expenses is $8200. Indirect expenses are expenses which benefit the entire home. Both her electric bill and her rent fall into this category.
Line 22,24	She is allowed to deduct only the percentage of these expenses that apply to the business. In this case 50% of $8200 = $4100
Line 23	Mary also includes a carryover from the year before of $2642
Line 25,34.	$7742 is how much Mary may deduct as an expense of doing business at home $1,000 + $4,100 + $2,642 = $7742

Summary: The IRS allows you to deduct expenses for business use of your home ONLY up to the amount of your profit earned in your business. In other words, if, after subtracting operating expenses, your business earned, say $500 in profit, even if your home use expenses total $2000, you can only deduct a maximum of $500 for these expenses. In this case, Mary is able to claim all of her expenses for business use of her home. In the earlier scenario, she couldn't claim any more than the profit she actually made through the business, but had $2642 that she was allowed to carry over into this year's return.

Form 8829-Expenses for Business Use of Home (Profit Scenario)

Form **8829**	**Expenses for Business Use of Your Home**	OMB No. 1545-1266
	▶ File only with Schedule C (Form 1040). Use a separate Form 8829 for each home you used for business during the year.	**Millennium**
Department of the Treasury Internal Revenue Service	▶ See separate instructions.	Attachment Sequence No. **66**

Name(s) of proprietor(s) **MARY P. ROBINSON**   Your social security number **123 45 6789**

Part I   Part of Your Home Used for Business

1	Area used regularly and exclusively for business, regularly for day care, or for storage of inventory or product samples (see instructions)	**1**	600 S.F.
2	Total area of home	**2**	1200 S.F.
3	Divide line 1 by line 2. Enter the result as a percentage	**3**	50 %

- For day-care facilities not used exclusively for business, also complete lines 4–6.
- All others, skip lines 4–6 and enter the amount from line 3 on line 7.

4	Multiply days used for day care during year by hours used per day	**4**		hr.
5	Total hours available for use during the year (365 days × 24 hours) (see instructions)	**5**	8,760 hr.	
6	Divide line 4 by line 5. Enter the result as a decimal amount	**6**		
7	Business percentage. For day-care facilities not used exclusively for business, multiply line 6 by line 3 (enter the result as a percentage). All others, enter the amount from line 3 ▶	**7**	50 %	

Part II   Figure Your Allowable Deduction

		(a) Direct expenses	(b) Indirect expenses		
8	Enter the amount from Schedule C, line 29, **plus** any net gain or (loss) derived from the business use of your home and shown on Schedule D or Form 4797. If more than one place of business, see instructions			**8**	36125
	See instructions for columns (a) and (b) before completing lines 9–20.				
9	Casualty losses (see instructions)	**9**			
10	Deductible mortgage interest (see instructions)	**10**			
11	Real estate taxes (see instructions)	**11**			
12	Add lines 9, 10, and 11	**12**			
13	Multiply line 12, column (b) by line 7		**13**		
14	Add line 12, column (a) and line 13			**14**	
15	Subtract line 14 from line 8. If zero or less, enter -0-			**15**	36125
16	Excess mortgage interest (see instructions)	**16**			
17	Insurance	**17**	1000		
18	Repairs and maintenance	**18**			
19	Utilities	**19**		1000	
20	Other expenses (see instructions)	**20**		7200	
21	Add lines 16 through 20	**21**	1000	8200	
22	Multiply line 21, column (b) by line 7		**22**	4100	
23	Carryover of operating expenses from last year's Form 8829, line 41	**23**	2642		
24	Add line 21 in column (a), line 22, and line 23			**24**	7742
25	Allowable operating expenses. Enter the **smaller** of line 15 or line 24			**25**	7742
26	Limit on excess casualty losses and depreciation. Subtract line 25 from line 15			**26**	28383
27	Excess casualty losses (see instructions)	**27**			
28	Depreciation of your home from Part III below	**28**			
29	Carryover of excess casualty losses and depreciation from last year's Form 8829, line 42	**29**			
30	Add lines 27 through 29			**30**	0
31	Allowable excess casualty losses and depreciation. Enter the **smaller** of line 26 or line 30			**31**	0
32	Add lines 14, 25, and 31			**32**	7742
33	Casualty loss portion, if any, from lines 14 and 31. Carry amount to **Form 4684**, Section B			**33**	
34	Allowable expenses for business use of your home. Subtract line 33 from line 32. Enter here and on Schedule C, line 30. If your home was used for more than one business, see instructions ▶			**34**	7742

Part III   Depreciation of Your Home

35	Enter the **smaller** of your home's adjusted basis or its fair market value (see instructions)	**35**	
36	Value of land included on line 35	**36**	
37	Basis of building. Subtract line 36 from line 35	**37**	
38	Business basis of building. Multiply line 37 by line 7	**38**	
39	Depreciation percentage (see instructions)	**39**	%
40	Depreciation allowable (see instructions). Multiply line 38 by line 39. Enter here and on line 28 above	**40**	

Part IV   Carryover of Unallowed Expenses to next year

41	Operating expenses. Subtract line 25 from line 24. If less than zero, enter -0-	**41**	0
42	Excess casualty losses and depreciation. Subtract line 31 from line 30. If less than zero, enter -0-	**42**	

For Paperwork Reduction Act Notice, see page 4 of separate instructions.   Cat. No. 13232M   Form **8829** Millennium Version

Explanations
Form: **SCHEDULE SE - (SELF-EMPLOYMENT TAX)**
Scenario: **PROFIT**

On the next page is a completed copy of Schedule SE. The form is fairly straight-forward and arrives at figures through calculations based on numbers entered on form 1040.

Line 5.   Mary is required to pay $4010 in Self-Employment tax for the year

***

Schedule SE-Self Employment Tax (Profit Scenario)

SCHEDULE SE
(Form 1040)

Department of the Treasury
Internal Revenue Service

Self-Employment Tax

▶ **Attach to Form 1040.** ▶ **See Instructions for Schedule SE (Form 1040).**

OMB No. 1545-0074

Mi**llennium**

Attachment
Sequence No. **17**

Name of person with **self-employment** income (as shown on Form 1040)

MARY P ROBINSON

Social security number of person
with **self-employment** income ▶ **123 45 6789**

Who Must File Schedule SE

You must file Schedule SE if:

* You had net earnings from self-employment from **other than** church employee income (line 4 of Short Schedule SE or line 4c of Long Schedule SE) of $400 or more **or**

* You had church employee income of $108.28 or more. Income from services you performed as a minister or a member of a religious order **is not** church employee income. See page SE-1.

Note. Even if you had a loss or a small amount of income from self-employment, it may be to your benefit to file Schedule SE and use either "optional method" in Part II of Long Schedule SE. See page SE-3.

Exception. If your only self-employment income was from earnings as a minister, member of a religious order, or Christian Science practitioner and you filed Form 4361 and received IRS approval not to be taxed on those earnings, **do not** file Schedule SE. Instead, write "Exempt–Form 4361" on Form 1040, line 56.

May I Use Short Schedule SE or Must I Use Long Schedule SE?

Section A—Short Schedule SE. Caution. Read above to see if you can use Short Schedule SE.

1	Net farm profit or (loss) from Schedule F, line 36, and farm partnerships, Schedule K-1 (Form 1065), line 15a	1	
2	Net profit or (loss) from Schedule C, line 31; Schedule C-EZ, line 3; Schedule K-1 (Form 1065), line 15a (other than farming); and Schedule K-1 (Form 1065-B), box 9. Ministers and members of religious orders, see page SE-1 for amounts to report on this line. See page SE-2 for other income to report	2	28383
3	Combine lines 1 and 2	3	28383
4	**Net earnings from self-employment.** Multiply line 3 by 92.35% (.9235). If less than $400, do not file this schedule; you do not owe self-employment tax ▶	4	26211
5	Self-employment tax. If the amount on line 4 is:		
	• $84,900 or less, multiply line 4 by 15.3% (.153). Enter the result here and on **Form 1040, line 56.**	5	4010
	• More than $84,900, multiply line 4 by 2.9% (.029). Then, add $10,527.60 to the result. Enter the total here and on **Form 1040, line 56.**		
6	**Deduction for one-half of self-employment tax.** Multiply line 5 by 50% (.5). Enter the result here and on **Form 1040, line 29**	6	2005

For Paperwork Reduction Act Notice, see Form 1040 instructions   Cat. No. 11358Z   **Schedule SE (Form 1040) Millennium Version**

Explanations
Form: **1040 - (US INDIVIDUAL INCOME TAX RETURN)**
Scenario: **PROFIT**

Form 1040 includes both personal income & expenses as well as business income & loss.

Line 6a-d   Mary is single, lives alone, and has no dependents. Therefore, she has only one exemption: herself.

Line 8a   On this line, she puts the $100 in savings account interest she earned. (This was found on the end-of-year statement she received from her bank.)

Line 12   On this line she puts the $28,383 business profit which was computed and entered on line 31 of Schedule C.

Line 22   Mary's total income is $28,483 ($28,383 + $100)

Line 29,34   Because of the profit she made this year, Mary will have to pay Self Employment tax. This has been computed on form Schedule SE. She is allowed to take a deduction of half the amount of her tax [$2005]

Line 35   Her adjusted gross income is line 22 minus line 34: $28,483 - $2005 = $26,478.

Form 1040-US Individual Tax Return (Page 1; Profit Scenario)

Form 1040

Department of the Treasury—Internal Revenue Service

U.S. Individual Passion Profit Income Tax Return

For the years 2000 and beyond!

OMB No. 1545-0074

Label

(See instructions on page 21.)

Use the IRS label. Otherwise, please print or type.

Your first name and initial: **MARY P.**
If a joint return, spouse's first name and initial. Last name

Last name: **ROBINSON**

Your social security number: **123 45 6789**
Spouse's social security number

Home address (number and street). If you have a P.O. box, see page 21. **401 PASSIONFRUIT LN** Apt. no.

City, town or post office, state, and ZIP code. If you have a foreign address, see page 21. **CLEARVIEW CA 90210**

▲ **Important!** ▲
You must enter your SSN(s) above.

Presidential Election Campaign (See page 21.)

Note. Checking "Yes" will not change your tax or reduce your refund.

Do you, or your spouse if filing a joint return, want $3 to go to this fund? ▶

	You	Spouse
	☐ Yes ☐ No	☐ Yes ☐ No

Filing Status

Check only one box

1. ☑ Single
2. ☐ Married filing jointly (even if only one had income)
3. ☐ Married filing separately. Enter spouse's SSN above and full name here. ▶
4. ☐ Head of household (with qualifying person). (See page 21.) If the qualifying person is a child but not your dependent, enter this child's name here. ▶
5. ☐ Qualifying widow(er) with dependent child (year spouse died ▶). (See page 21.)

Exemptions

6a. ☑ Yourself. If your parent (or someone else) can claim you as a dependent on his or her tax return, do not check box 6a . . . .

b. ☐ Spouse . . . .

c. Dependents:

(1) First name Last name	(2) Dependent's social security number	(3) Dependent's relationship to you	(4) ✔ if qualifying child for child tax credit (see page 22)
			☐
			☐
			☐
			☐
			☐

If more than five dependents, see page 22.

No. of boxes checked on 6a and 6b: **1**

No. of children on 6c who:
• lived with you
• did not live with you due to divorce or separation (see page 22)

Dependents on 6c not entered above

Add numbers on lines above ▶ **1**

d. Total number of exemptions claimed . . . .

Income

Attach Forms W-2 and W-2G here. Also attach Form(s) 1099-R if tax was withheld.

If you did not get a W-2, see page 23.

Enclose, but do not attach, any payment. Also, please use Form 1040-V.

7	Wages, salaries, tips, etc. Attach Form(s) W-2	7	
8a	Taxable interest. Attach Schedule B if required	8a	*100*
b	Tax-exempt interest. Do not include on line 8a	8b	
9	Ordinary dividends. Attach Schedule B if required	9	
10	Taxable refunds, credits, or offsets of state and local income taxes (see page 24)	10	
11	Alimony received	11	
12	Business income or (loss). Attach Schedule C or C-EZ	12	*28 383*
13	Capital gain or (loss). Attach Schedule D if required. If not required, check here ▶ ☐	13	
14	Other gains or (losses). Attach Form 4797	14	
15a	IRA distributions 15a	b Taxable amount (see page 25)	15b	
16a	Pensions and annuities 16a	b Taxable amount (see page 25)	16b	
17	Rental real estate, royalties, partnerships, S corporations, trusts, etc. Attach Schedule E	17	
18	Farm income or (loss). Attach Schedule F	18	
19	Unemployment compensation	19	
20a	Social security benefits 20a	b Taxable amount (see page 27)	20b	
21	Other income. List type and amount (see page 29)	21	
22	Add the amounts in the far right column for lines 7 through 21. This is your total income ▶	22	*28 483*

Adjusted Gross Income

23	Educator expenses (see page 29)	23		
24	IRA deduction (see page 29)	24		
25	Student loan interest deduction (see page 31)	25		
26	Tuition and fees deduction (see page 32)	26		
27	Archer MSA deduction. Attach Form 8853	27		
28	Moving expenses. Attach Form 3903	28		
29	One-half of self-employment tax. Attach Schedule SE	29	*2005*	
30	Self-employed health insurance deduction (see page 33)	30		
31	Self-employed SEP, SIMPLE, and qualified plans	31		
32	Penalty on early withdrawal of savings	32		
33a	Alimony paid b Recipient's SSN ▶	33a		
34	Add lines 23 through 33a	34		*2005*
35	Subtract line 34 from line 22. This is your adjusted gross income ▶	35		*26 478*

For Disclosure, Privacy Act, and Paperwork Reduction Act Notice, see page 78.

Cat. No. 11320B

Form **1040** Millennium Edition

Line 34.   This line is the same as line 33: $58,779

Line 38.   By itemizing her deductions using Schedule A, Mary calculated her deductions to be $4,000. She is better off using the IRS standard deduction of $4,700.

Line 39.   Line 36 minus line 38 ($26,478 - $4,700) = $21,778. In other words, she is now in the $21,778 tax bracket.

Line 40.   Her one (1) exemption, from line 6d, allows her to deduct an additional 1 x $3,000 from her adjusted gross income. (Note: If Mary had a dependent, the number on line 6e would have been "2" and she would have been allowed to deduct 2 X $3,000, or $6,000)

Line 41.   Her taxable income is now $21,778 - $3,000 = $18,778 In other words, she is now in the $18,778 tax bracket.

Line 42,55   Because of her business activities, the amount of tax she has to pay the government will be based on $18,778 instead of $28,383. Her tax, therefore, based on the tax tables in the 1040 instruction booklet is $2,516

Line 56   Since Mary made a profit of more than $400 this year, she is required to file Schedule SE and pay self-employment tax. Her SE tax is $4010.

Line 61   The total tax she is required to pay, therefore, is $2,516 + $4010 = $6,526

Line 68.   Everything has its price. The price for success is that Mary will actually have to pay more in taxes. That's a good thing! Mary will need to look for ways, like bonds, IRA's and other perks of being a corporation to shelter her income from Uncle Sam's taxes!

***

Form 1040-US Individual Tax Return (Page 2; Profit Scenario)

Form 1040 created exclusively for Passion Profit

Page 2

Tax and Credits	36	Amount from line 35 (adjusted gross income)	36	*26478*
	37a	Check if: ☐ You were 65 or older, ☐ Blind; ☐ Spouse was 65 or older, ☐ Blind. Add the number of boxes checked above and enter the total here ▶ 37a		
Standard Deduction for—	b	If you are married filing separately and your spouse itemizes deductions, or you were a dual-status alien, see page 34 and check here ▶ 37b ☐		
• People who checked any box on line 37a or 37b or who can be claimed as a dependent, see page 34.	38	Itemized deductions (from Schedule A) or your standard deduction (see left margin)	38	*4700*
	39	Subtract line 38 from line 36	39	*21778*
	40	If line 36 is $103,000 or less, multiply $3,000 by the total number of exemptions claimed on line 6d. If line 36 is over $103,000, see the worksheet on page 35	40	*3000*
• All others: Single, $4,700	41	Taxable income. Subtract line 40 from line 39. If line 40 is more than line 39, enter -0-	41	*18778*
Head of household, $6,900	42	Tax (see page 36). Check if any tax is from: a ☐ Form(s) 8814 b ☐ Form 4972	42	*2516*
Married filing jointly or Qualifying widow(er), $7,850	43	Alternative minimum tax (see page 37). Attach Form 6251	43	
	44	Add lines 42 and 43 ▶	44	*2516*
Married filing separately, $3,925	45	Foreign tax credit. Attach Form 1116 if required	45	
	46	Credit for child and dependent care expenses. Attach Form 2441	46	
	47	Credit for the elderly or the disabled. Attach Schedule R	47	
	48	Education credits. Attach Form 8863	48	
	49	Retirement savings contributions credit. Attach Form 8880	49	
	50	Child tax credit (see page 39)	50	
	51	Adoption credit. Attach Form 8839	51	
	52	Credits from: a ☐ Form 8396 b ☐ Form 8859	52	
	53	Other credits. Check applicable box(es): a ☐ Form 3800 b ☐ Form 8801 c ☐ Specify _____	53	
	54	Add lines 45 through 53. These are your total credits	54	*0*
	55	Subtract line 54 from line 44. If line 54 is more than line 44, enter -0- ▶	55	*2516*
Other Taxes	56	Self-employment tax. Attach Schedule SE	56	*4010*
	57	Social security and Medicare tax on tip income not reported to employer. Attach Form 4137	57	
	58	Tax on qualified plans, including IRAs, and other tax-favored accounts. Attach Form 5329 if required	58	
	59	Advance earned income credit payments from Form(s) W-2	59	
	60	Household employment taxes. Attach Schedule H	60	
	61	Add lines 55 through 60. This is your total tax ▶	61	*6526*
Payments	62	Federal income tax withheld from Forms W-2 and 1099	62	
	63	2002 estimated tax payments and amount applied from 2001 return	63	
If you have a qualifying child, attach Schedule EIC.	64	Earned income credit (EIC)	64	
	65	Excess social security and tier 1 RRTA tax withheld (see page 56)	65	
	66	Additional child tax credit. Attach Form 8812	66	
	67	Amount paid with request for extension to file (see page 56)	67	
	68	Other payments from: a ☐ Form 2439 b ☐ Form 4136 c ☐ Form 8885	68	
	69	Add lines 62 through 68. These are your total payments ▶	69	*0*
Refund Direct deposit? See page 56 and fill in 71b, 71c, and 71d.	70	If line 69 is more than line 61, subtract line 61 from line 69. This is the amount you overpaid	70	
	71a	Amount of line 70 you want refunded to you	71a	
	▶ b	Routing number ▶ c Type: ☐ Checking ☐ Savings		
	▶ d	Account number		
	72	Amount of line 70 you want applied to your next year's estimated tax ▶	72	
Amount You Owe	73	Amount you owe. Subtract line 69 from line 61. For details on how to pay, see page 57 ▶	73	*6526*
	74	Estimated tax penalty (see page 57)	74	

Third Party Designee
Do you want to allow another person to discuss this return with the IRS (see page 58)? ☐ Yes. Complete the following. ☐ No

Designee's name ▶	Phone no. ▶ ( )	Personal identification number (PIN) ▶	

Sign Here
Under penalties of perjury, I declare that I have examined this return and accompanying schedules and statements, and to the best of my knowledge and belief, they are true, correct, and complete. Declaration of preparer (other than taxpayer) is based on all information of which preparer has any knowledge.

Joint return? See page 21
Keep a copy for your records.

Your signature *Mary Roth*	Date	Your occupation *PASSION SEEKER*	Daytime phone number *(000) 123-4567*
Spouse's signature. If a joint return, both must sign.	Date	Spouse's occupation	

Paid Preparer's Use Only

Preparer's signature ▶		Date	Check if self-employed ☐	Preparer's SSN or PTIN
Firm's name (or yours if self-employed), address, and ZIP code ▶			EIN	
			Phone no. ( )	

Form **1040** Millennium Edition

Ways to Reduce Your Taxable Income

Itemizing Your Deductions

If the total of your medical and dental expenses, state and local income taxes, gifts to charity, employee expenses, casualty or theft losses total more than the standard IRS deduction, then instead of the $4,300 you deducted on form 1040, you would have been able to deduct an amount greater than $4,300 and thus reduce your taxable income even further. Here are some of the expenses which could be itemized. Expenses for

• Children/Dependents
• Elderly
• Alimony
• Student Loans
• Moving
• Individual Retirement Accounts (IRAs)
• Medical Insurance

Hire the Kids

If you operate a sole proprietorship or husband-wife partnership, consider hiring your children if they're under the age of 18. You get a business deduction for money you may give the kids anyway. That deduction reduces both your income and self-employment tax. There are no Social Security or federal unemployment taxes, and each child can shelter up to $4,300 of wage income with his or her own standard deduction. So you get a tax break, and there's zero tax cost to your children with this perfectly legal method.

Buy New Equipment

Most business equipment must be depreciated over either five or seven years. This generally translates into a first-year deduction of only 20% of the cost of a five-year property and 14.29% of the cost of a seven-year property. However, there's a special break available to most sole proprietors (and most other small businesses as well). It's called the "section 179 deduction," and it permits an immediate write-off for up to $18,500 of equipment additions. Even last-minute additions qualify, as long as you started using the equipment before the end of the year.

Incorporate

It's almost a fact of life, and not just a quaint saying, that the rich get richer and the poor get poorer. One of the reasons for this has to do with access to information about how to shelter your income as a corporation. You owe it to yourself to investigate the tax loopholes that come with owning a corporation.

A Word About Getting Audited

Audit. The word strikes fear in the hearts of many. It shouldn't. Many taxpayers are called in for audits on a random basis every year. Others are called in because some deduction or claim in their return may have widened a few eyes. Whatever the reason, unless you are doing some intricate (or shady) manipulation of tax codes, you don't need a lawyer, you don't need an accountant, or financial advisor. All you need is PROOF. Even if you make what turns out to be a mistake on your taxes, if you can justify it and explain how you came up with it, you'll be on better ground. Most auditors understand that the tax laws can at times be a bit tricky to decipher. Generally, if you explain your reasons for your entries, AND show some sort of proof of the expenditure, you will be better off. It will be hard for an IRS tax-reviewer to believe that you took 20 reps out to dinner and spent $3000 during the year and you can't show a single receipt.

NOTE: If it is determined that you underpaid your taxes, you will simply have to pay the difference. You may be able to work out a payment plan, so don't despair. Make this your number one priority over the time period that you are given. You definitely DON'T want the government as one of your creditors.

Even though fewer than 2% of all tax returns filed are actually audited, there are a few things which increase your chances of being picked out of the crowd. Here are some of the items that tend to draw attention to you:

Filing Schedule C. If you own your own business, deal in large amounts of cash and file Schedule C, your chances of being audited rise sharply.

Taking a home-office deduction. The rules here are so complex and limiting that IRS agents figure they have a good chance of squeezing more revenue out of many taxpayers who claim a home office. The tax law enacted in 1997 will allow more consultants and other self-employed workers to qualify for the deduction, but not until 1999. And it won't remove many other ambiguities and limitations. So don't expect the IRS to ease up on its scrutiny.

Writing off large amounts of travel and entertainment expenses. Don't try to write off personal expenses as business. Your pool party that you threw last summer is not a business expense because all the invited guests were your customers.

Continuously filing a loss. You are allowed to claim a loss for 3 consecutive years before the IRS starts to question whether you're really in business, or just claiming deductions for an expensive hobby.

Taking large casualty-loss deductions. Very few people qualify for such deductions. Thus, says a former IRS official, those filers who take them tend to stand out and get asked questions, even if they are innocent.

Being careless or lying. Report all income. It's important to make sure whatever you write down matches exactly whatever is on an "information return" such as the W-2 form you receive from your employer.

Living better than you seem able to afford. If, for example, your minimum wage income is providing you the resources to have a Beverly Hills home/business address, you might raise the curiosity of IRS officials.

Geography. Being in the wrong place at the wrong time. Where you live plays an important role in your chances of being audited. Local IRS offices decide how many of their employees to commit to doing audits. So each office has a different rate of audits. Los Angeles tends to have the most audits, while Ohio has the least.

MAIN POINTS FOR CHAPTER 11
"Accounting and Taxes"

• Profit is not what you get, but what you get to keep. It is what's left over from a dollar of income after you've accounted for all your production costs and expenses.

• The Balance Sheet, Income Statement and Cash Flow Analysis are the tools you need to run your business effectively and to make sure you actually make a profit.

• As a business owner, your mission is simple: make money and reduce the amount of taxes you pay by claiming as many legal deductions as allowed by the IRS. The IRS provides incentives to encourage small business owners to stay in business. It's up to you to find out what these incentives are and use them to your advantage. A majority of the commerce transacted in the US is as a result of small business owners just like you who are turning their passions into profit.

• In the loss scenario described, Mary Robinson spent more on running her business than she made selling her Swerve hats. However, she was able to use that loss to lower her taxable income and thus receive a tax refund.

• In the profit scenario described, Mary Robinson made more turning her passion into profit than she did as a legal secretary. In the future, she will need to shelter her income by claiming more deductions.

• There are ways you can reduce your income.

• There are ways to increase your chances of being audited that you should avoid.

FOLLOW-UP FILE FOR CHAPTER 11
"Accounting and Taxes...."

INSPIRATION: Passion Seeker Profiles

"A Passion for the Environment"
The Wooden Duck was started in 1995 when Amy Ferber & Eric Gellerman began importing recycled Teak furniture from Indonesia. They explain:

"Over the years, we have gradually expanded our scope to include production in various countries throughout the world (India, Hungary, Slovakia and Poland), as well as offering local craftspeople working with reclaimed materials the space to show and sell their furniture.

In April of 1998 we opened a factory in San Francisco and began producing a line of furniture from recycled Douglas Fir. Today our 17,000 sq ft warehouse is filled to capacity with recycled wood furniture from around the world.

Our principal goal has always been to offer our customers high quality, simply styled furniture at the lowest prices possible while maintaining our commitment to the environment by using recycled materials whenever possible."

With sales of over 3 million, it seems environmentalism certainly pays too!

IDEAS: The Right Questions To Ask
• What specific IRS forms and publications apply to my particular situation?
• What specific ways of sheltering my money from taxes can I begin to implement now?
• What specific tax-related questions do I have for my SCORE adviser?

Chapter 12: Enough to Pay the Rent?
"Meeting expenses, quitting your job & beyond!"

Reviewing the Journey

Before we explore this exciting topic in this final chapter of *Turn Your Passion Into Profit,* let's recap what you've accomplished thus far. You've made the courageous decision to do something different and turn your passion into profit. You've identified the activity, talent or hobby you'll pursue and develop. You've identified the value that your passion can offer to the world. Using your unique talents and gifts, you've developed a product or service-- or the idea for one-- which offers that value to your chosen people. You've launched a passion-centered business through which you'll present your idea to the world. In addition, if you're already making initial sales and generating income, you've proven to yourself that there is indeed value in the thing you love to do. You should feel proud.

Now, however, comes the critical question: Can you make enough at your new passion-centered business to pay your rent? Will this venture simply provide income to supplement your current job, or does it have the potential to replace it and create the sort of freedom and the life-style you envisioned in chapter one? By now, you've no doubt surmised that the answer to these questions has more to do with your commitment, belief level, self-esteem and thoughts about money than anything else. Therefore, you already know the answer: "It can, if you want it to. You can if you think you can!"

While this is, in fact, true, beyond the mental and metaphysical aspects of creating enough income to survive and also thrive, there are practical considerations, strategies and techniques for growing your business. Let's explore some of them!

What Does it Mean to Grow YOUR Business?

Whatever your long-term aspirations, focusing on growing your business is an integral part of turning your passion into profit. In the world of business, there's no such thing as cruising at a steady pace. You're either rising or falling. So focusing on growth ensures that your business will be around tomorrow to help you accomplish your goals and create the life-style about which you've given yourself permission to dream.

However, growing a business means different things to different people. Some people want to make a bit more money. Others desire more free time. Others want the option to walk away from their jobs. Still others want to make enough money to provide jobs for others. For some, business growth means nothing less than making the move to millionaire, taking their company public and changing the world!

Therefore, here are some practical considerations for accomplishing the 4 ultimate passion profit growth milestones (i.e. the "holy grail" of the passion profit quest)

Making more Money
Matching your Income
Leaving Your Job & Creating Jobs for Others
Making the Move to Millionaire

1. Making More Money

Even if your sales are going well, it is wise to be proactive about growth. In business, if you're not moving forward, you're falling behind. To keep growing, perform frequent Opportunity Gap Analyses. An Opportunity Gap Analysis is simply the process of asking the questions that will help you move forward. Think about these questions:

• What other ways can I sell my product?
• What additional customers are there for my product?
• How can I modify my product to make it more attractive?
• What current non-customers are out there who could be using my product?
• What else do my current customers need?
• How else can I get my product to my customers?
• What new products could I develop?
• What existing products could I sell through my current distribution channel?

In addition, being aware of trends in your industry, in the country and in the world is important to growing your business. There are major changes in society that are redefining life and the way we do business in this new era. Here are the trends that will define the coming years and will affect how you stay in business and grow.

The homebound habit

As computer technology affects the traditional workplace and our life-style, there is a growing tendency to do more things from home. People are shopping, banking, and working from the comfort of their homes. Products and services that cater to this growing market of homebodies will be more and more in demand.

Fragmented customer loyalty

Globalization has created a new landscape. Because of the increased number of choices available to the average consumer, the wise business owner must focus on relationships before revenue. Emphasis has shifted from acquiring market share to acquiring mind-share (more and more of the customer's loyalty). Rather than selling one thing to more and more customers, seek to sell more things to the same customers over and over.

The aging of the baby boomers

The 97 Million people born between 1946 and 1964 are known as "baby boomers." As this mass of consumers moves from one stage of life to another, their needs define which services and products can be counted on to be profitable. The products and services the baby boomers will increasingly demand as they now move into their 50s, are: health-related products, investment advice, technology and entertainment.

Evolving customer expectations

What and how you sell your products and services must also respond to trends. As people get more technologically comfortable, and as familiarity with the Internet increases, your customers will expect to purchase online, interact via email and websites, or perhaps download information rather than order by mail. Your new customers, who may now be anywhere in the world, will expect to communicate with you in their native language, purchase in different currencies, and receive culturally sensitive customer service.

2. Matching Your Income

How realistic is it to expect to make enough money to survive, and even prosper from your passion? Using the same Break-even Analysis we learned earlier, let's look at an ideal scenario to determine what it would take to match your present income and consider leaving your job. Let's assume:

1. You are single, have a child and are debt-free
2. You currently earn $40,000 per year as an employee
3. Your product sells for $30 each, plus $4.00 shipping
4. It costs you $4.70 to produce your product
5. You sell your product by mail order and fill the orders yourself

Sale Price per item $34.00 ($30 + $4 shipping)

Variable Cost
Batch of 1000 units cost $4700 $4.70 each
Shipping $4.00 $4.00
inserts 3 @.05 $0.15
VARIABLE COST PER UNIT IS $8.85
SALE PRICE OF PRODUCT IS $34.00
VARIABLE COST RATIO IS 8.05/34.00=26.0% = .260

Yearly Fixed Costs

Rent/mortgage	$9600/year
Food	$3600/year
Utilities	$600/year
Auto insurance	$1596/year
Child Care	$960/year
Advertising	$1860/year
Telephone	$1200/year
Gas/Electric	$720/year
Box rental	$60/year
Miscellaneous	$1200/year

FIXED COSTS FOR YEAR $21,396

• Sales needed to break even = 21,396/ 1-.260 = $28,913

• Units to sell to make $28,913 / $34 = 850

• Units to sell to make $40,000 = 1176

In other words, at the point that you sell 850 units of your product, you will have just broken even. At that point, all your living expenses will be paid for and the rest will be profit. At 1176 units sold, your income will be just what it is on your day job. Is this a realistic expectation? To sell 850 units in a year, you would have to sell 71 units in a month. That's 18 per week. Is it doable? If you don't think so, you have two choices: 1. increase the price you charge for your product, or 2. reduce your expenses by finding a way to produce your product for less than $4.70 each, or cut back on other expenses.

3. Leaving Your Job

If one of your reasons for pursuing your passion is to free yourself from having to work for someone else, then you probably envision with excitement and a bit of fear the day you will walk away from your job. What thoughts might you find going through your mind when you're thinking seriously about leaving your day job to follow your passion? What doubts, fears and hopes might haunt you at that moment when it seems your dreams are just about to come true? Here's your opportunity to take a peek into one person's thoughts on that very topic. Mine.

In this next section, I offer a few personal thoughts in the form of excerpts from my private journal. They date back fully two years before I actually made the leap into being a full time entrepreneur. They sometimes read like a conversation between myself and two other characters: the me of my doubts and the me of my dreams. You may find that your thoughts are the same. Italicized items are actual private journal entries from 1993-1994. Some notes and some formatting have been added just so you can make sense of my sometimes erratic thoughts. Many people have said they like this section because they are able to see their own quirks and doubts and relate to what I went through. Here's hoping you can extract some benefit as well.

Walt's Private Journal -1993: Fears of Failure

I desperately want to be on my own. But I doubt my ability to make it happen. I think about what things would work to keep me at this job? Here's what I came up with
1. business failure - my business ventures failing would make it difficult
2. massive debt - if I just racked up so much debt that I had to stay
3. limited creative potential - if I simply had no other options to make money
4. attachment to the people here-
5. no resources
6. dependence on job income
7. my own negative thinking
8. a rethinking of my goals - if I decided that staying was in my best interest
9. hanging on to the fear of failure

That's about all I can come up with. So in order for that not to happen, what am I doing to eliminate these as possibilities?

1. Business failure—Though it is not possible to rule this out completely, I am taking steps to make my business more profitable. I am cutting costs at every corner. I've made necessary plans to cut down on my long distance bills, my bank fees, my shipping expenses and advertising.

2. Massive Debt— I am now working to reduce this. I might even cancel my trip to the DC Trade Show in order to put more money into debt elimination. I anticipate being at least at zero level by December 25 of this year. I continue to work diligently at reducing my debt.

3. Limited creative potential—I have revived the [New Idea], and intend to sell it to a major company. The Music Entrepreneurs calendar is a success!

4. Attachment to the People Here—I must remind myself that the people themselves are not the place. I can still have an attachment to them and not feel that I'm trapping myself here. I can always continue to interact with the people I like even after I leave

5. No resources—I am building up my savings and investments even now.

6. Dependence on job Income—Upon the suggestion of my cousin, Zoy, I have "quit" [my job] financially as of August. By this I mean that I will not touch the [job] income. I will use the next 6 months to live on my business income. In this way, my decisions will tend toward truly severing the attachment and dependency, as well as spending more wisely. I will also need to ensure a minimum income rather than leave it up to chance. It is an excellent precursor to my future departure decision. An added bonus of this idea is that I will accumulate 6 months of income in the process with which to increase my resources.
I am afraid to commit to a date because I fear that the date may come and I won't be ready or be able to.

Let's see.... How does one break free? I just spoke to [a close friend] in the elevator. She told me that her son is 3 years old! Wow! I felt the reality of the old saying that "time flies." I felt immediately that I am wasting time and not moving fast enough.

Somehow I feel that it won't last; that the years will stretch on and the prosperity will die and I won't be able to sustain the necessary income. And that I will need to return to working for someone else. The fear of that humiliation is what is holding me back!

The fear of needing to return to the [job] is what is keeping me tied here!

I need to envision endless prosperity. Need to remind myself that my prosperity is an endless gift from the Universe. The universe alone is responsible for my prosperity, not people or things!

[NOTE: This is me visualizing]

I monitored my income for 6 months and maintained a constant minimum income of $5000 plus per month. This was all the support I needed to make my final move. During that six month period, I didn't touch the [job] income, and was thus able to put all of it into mutual funds, CD's and tax free bonds. At the end of the six-month period, with 20,000 saved from [my job], and another 20,000 from a company called W, I took the most fulfilling move of my life by writing a resignation letter and submitting it to [my boss]. I gave them 2 weeks notice and then jumped out into the world! I spent the next two weeks mentioning my good fortune to a few key people. Soon word spread rapidly and people stopped by to give encouragement and support. On the last Friday, I felt both excited and a bit depressed as well.

[NOTE: This is me envisioning the day of freedom]

That first day of not going into [work]. I laughed. I laughed for joy for having made what I thought was such an awe-inspiring bold move. I laughed after realizing how great the power of the universe manifested in me really is. I laughed that I had thought it so difficult a thing to do. I laughed because I still had the friends I thought I would have to leave behind. I laughed because I realized that I would now meet even more people, and in more socially conducive settings than ever before. I laughed because I felt that my mind and soul were now really awakening into freedom!

I felt and continue to feel stable in my decision. It has afforded me an entirely different view of life and reality. I am 27 years old, and I have done it! I have done what few who took the path I took dare to do! I harnessed the power of the universe within my mind and created the opportunity to experience a different reality. I knew it was something I had to do, so I did it! I use the days to travel, drive my 325i convertible, meditate and meet people. I travel to Africa, Japan, China, Europe. I've resurrected my interest in photography and I enjoy it even more now.

[NOTE: This is me having a conversation with myself in which I discover what I'm actually afraid of.]

My chief aim in life right now is the attainment of the self confidence necessary for making the leap into full-time entrepreneurship!

In those moments when I give in to my fear, I think of losing the job, and then needing it (or the steady income "it" provides) in order to survive. Let's take a look at this.

Obviously, [my job] isn't the only organization that can provide a salary.

Yes, but what about the fact that the work is easy and the pay is substantial?

Well, my mail order business is easy as well. There is nothing "easier" than plac-ing ads, stuffing envelopes, and checking mailboxes. [By then I had already written my first book which was selling well through mail order] *And the compensation I receive for that is sometimes $700 a day!*

"Sometimes" $700 a day. But what about if it stops? What about if the prosperity now is but a peak? a fluke?

I can always and I have the potential to create new products. I already have two new ones which are on the drawing board, and sure to be successes. This I know! Again, [job] is not the only company that pays a salary. I already had a job offer from [another job]! And a job like that would put me in closer proximity to the business with which I am happiest.

If what I am saying is that I need the assurance that a steady income is out there should I need to avail myself of it, then I need either to get that assurance, or rid myself of the need. First I'll get the assurance. I will research for jobs in the entertainment field.

As I contemplate all of this, I realize what it is I couldn't possibly be fearing. [It's obvious that] I do not fear getting a job. For I have had job offers from within the industry. I have had job offers from the educational field—when I was looking to be a counselor.

Obviously I do not fear being unqualified. I have a Bachelor of Science from Columbia University.

It can't be that I fear that I may have a lack of ambition. I have more ambition than most considering what I have accomplished while still holding a full-time job.

Maybe I'm afraid of ending a relationship. I am in a "relationship" with my em-ployer. And maybe I have a fear of ending relationships. Even with [my ex fiance], I didn't actually end the relationship—I just offered no resistance to her leaving.

The bottom line also is that my very existence; my chief aim in life is the conquest of these fears and the creation of something of my own.

[END OF JOURNAL EXCERPT]

In an Instant!

As I shared with you in "Walt's Story" (see "Purpose" chapter), after all the mental gymnastics, the worrying and fretting, when the moment came for me to walk away, it was simply due to a mental shift that occurred in an instant at a workshop. Once that shift occurred, I took action--despite the doubts and the fears and those crazy voices in my head--within 48 hours!

No one can tell you if and when you should leave your job. It's a decision that only you can make. However, when you're weighing the consequences and battling your own fears, here are a few questions to ask yourself. *Do I see myself living my ideal day while still being here at this desk at this job? Is it possible for me to be a world-famous painter/writer/performer and still come here every day? Did any of my visions in the Discovery exercises involve me being here? What will I think about myself 20, 30, 40 years from now if I'm still right here? What am I afraid of?*

A Tip for "Quitters"

One of the questions I suggest in this chapter's Follow-up File is *"who do I know who has done this, and from whom I can ask advice?"* This is very important. In deciding whether to leave the security and mindset of the workday world, you should seek advice from people who have done it. Too often, we seek advice not from people who know, but simply people we know.

We take guidance not from people who've done it and know what to do,
but from people who failed and really don't have a clue.
For the best teacher is experience, best advice is "follow me."
Learn your lessons from others who are where you wish to be.

If you accept someone's views and opinions, you accept their life-style. Who would you listen to for advice on how to make money in real estate? Donald Trump, or your uncle who lives in a trailer park? Accept advice from people whose life-styles you wish to duplicate.

Support from others was the key to me having the courage to walk away from my job. In the chapter on "Purpose" I told the story of the leadership workshop that changed my whole outlook on life. The courage came not from the money I was making from my passion, because nothing had changed financially between the Friday before the workshop and the Monday following it. It didn't come from the two people at my job who knew of my plans, and who advised me to wait. It came from people who were on the same path I was, people with whom I could talk who would understand my frustrations and who wouldn't belittle my aspirations as baseless fantasies. It cam from people for whom a life lived with uncertainty but with passion was infinitely more desirable than one lived with security, but with frustration. It came from people I could meet with on a regular basis whenever I needed to remind myself of my potential.

It's important to learn that the people who do the things we want to do are no different than us. They have the same fears, the same doubts, the same crazy voice talking to them and urging them on, and the equally forceful voice knocking them down. My point is that even with these doubts and ramblings, I was able to make the leap.

And so shall it be for you as well. Those closest to you may never fully appreciate what you are determined to create for yourself. Their worlds may be limited by their past, their courage may be mitigated by their beliefs, and their faith in you may be colored by their expectations of themselves. Like me, you may feel that though all of us may be on the same journey, that you're sometimes too far out in front in your thinking to communicate with others traveling right beside you.

OK. So, When Do I Quit My Job?

I say all of that to say this: that for some of you out there, the act of quitting your job will have nothing to do with money at all. It won't matter how much you've saved, or even how much you're making in your passion business. I suggest to you that you'll quit your job when you're ready to succeed.

During a recent conference call, someone asked that very question, "So, Walt, when do I quit my job?"

To have some fun with the answer, I replied, "You quit your job when you want to be successful." Other answers include "You quit your job when you don't want to work there anymore!" Or "You quit your job when you want the alternative bad enough."

Most people would like to have a formula to determine when they can cheerfully and confidently wave goodbye to their boss! The truth is, the answer to the question has nothing to do with any facts or figures and everything to do with your identity. When you are an entrepreneur in the deepest concept of yourself, you'll know the answer to "When do I quit my job?" For you see,

Your question begs an answer
but assumes one lie is true
that somehow cause for what you'll do
exists outside of you

The critical decision
is not based on time or tide
whoever claims a formula
quite frankly, friend, they lied

You'll need to choose your view of you
despite what terms are met
and asking "when" might simply mean
you haven't chosen yet

> *For fish will do what fish will do*
> *and that's the reason why*
> *no pension, perk or paycheck*
> *ever gets a fish to fly!*

Identity decides
the why and when of what we do
Decide first who you are
and then you'll know what you should do

Don't complicate the matter, then
with all this extra "stuff"
But simply choose by asking
"Do I want it bad enough?"

Walt's Life Rhyme #209
When Do I Quit?

Hiring Employees

Never do yourself what you can hire someone else to do. Of course, the key word here is "can". If you can afford to, however, then hire wisely. For you can do more harm to your business by hiring the wrong person than you will by not hiring at all.

The best business advice suggests not hiring family when seeking to staff your business. Business partnerships often put stress on marriages, and can destroy friendships overnight. Issues of money, equity, and the negotiation of contracts can lead to the break up of otherwise healthy relationships.

People will often look first to the most trusted, rather than the most qualified people to run their businesses. Focus on competence rather than camaraderie. Many stories exist of performers who hire their relatives to run multimillion dollar enterprises which then end up bankrupt for the simple reason that loyalty is no substitute for business experience. Like many of us, they too make emotional decisions.

If the benefit you will receive from hiring someone will increase sales, reduce your burden so you can focus on setting the vision of the company, then you can't afford NOT to bring them on board.

4. The Move To Millionaire

passion-aire n. 1. a combination of the words "PASSion" and "millIONAIRE".
Used to denote a person who has used their passion to become a millionaire.

According to Verne Harnish, author of *Mastering the Rockefeller Habits* and CEO of Gazelles, Inc., an executive development firm for fast growth companies, "Only 4% of all companies ever make it past the million per year revenue mark. (And of those, only 10% ever get around the ten million mark or larger!) So what's the secret?

Growing your business into a million-dollar enterprise involves adopting all of the skills techniques mindsets and methods shared throughout this book, with particular emphasis on a special few keys. It's fueled by a desire to do more. It hinges on a willingness to invest in the personal growth that such a shift in realities requires. It is aided by the ability to take risks, have faith and trust others. It's the unique result of a combination of timing, opportunity, perseverance and a host of other internal and external conditions. Entire books have been written on this topic, so I won't create another.

In the years that I've been discovering, learning, teaching, researching, proving and sharing the Passion Profit philosophy and formula, I've come across a rare breed of Passion Seeker I call the *passionaire*. A passionaire is someone who has taken his or her passion and used it to become a millionaire. I've interviewed several of these unique individuals and uncovered the following secrets they wish to share with you to help you do the same. The question I posed was simply, *"What does it take to grow a million-dollar passion-centered business?"*

Money's never the issue. Learn to think more creatively.

Every business needs cash. However, if you think that the lack of money is preventing you from moving forward, then you're simply not thinking creatively enough. Value is what you need. "They paid me in furniture!" recalls Eric Gellerman, 35, co-founder of The Wooden Duck. When Eric and his partner Amy Ferber needed recycled wood to create the furniture to pursue his environmental passion, he negotiated with the partners from a previous furniture venture to pay him his share of ownership in furniture rather than money. He adds, "I was then able to mark that up and turn it into money." The Wooden Duck is now the largest retailer/manufacturer of furniture from recycled wood in northern California.

Bartering and factoring are two other ways to trade value for what you need.

Say, for example, that as a result of your promotional efforts, a large chain contacts you to order 10,000 units of your new product. With a purchase order in hand, you can approach a "factor", who will then give you up front cash (less a fee) for your invoice. There are always ways to make things happen even if your finances are tight. Contact your local Small business Administration for more leads. For creative ideas, brainstorm on the following two questions: 1. *What specific things would I do if I had the money I needed?* And then, 2. *What specific ways can I get them done anyway?*

Things change. Be flexible. Even though Gregg Levin's Perfect Curve Cap Curver was a stunning success, the industry soon changed. Baseball cap makers soon started making their cap visors with the curves already built in. This would have spelled doom for many young companies, but Levin had a flexible vision. He was constantly scanning the industry for new opportunities and also creating new products. In fact, it was his company's fourth product—a cap rack—that helped him make the move to millionaire, and that now accounts for a significant portion of annual sales.

If you see this entire undertaking as an ongoing journey, or a continuously unfolding story, in which the destination, vehicle of choice, plot and climax may be everchanging, then you'll have stumbled upon one secret to turning your passion into profit. Don't expect that the thing you initially decide to pursue will be the one that makes your dreams of freedom come true. You might stumble upon a different idea, a new market, a new passion next week that takes you a few steps further in your journey. You may, as I did, start a record label, but end up hitting a home run with a book about that label. You might start a restaurant that fares poorly, but which leads you to riches with a cookbook. Set your sights high, but don't be too attached to any particular outcome. Have the flexibility to go with the flow, experiment, try new directions and opportunities as they present themselves. It is that willingness to change course as required that will lead you to the ultimate fulfillment of your dreams.

Find a mentor

Almost without exception, this secret was the most often quoted by those I interviewed. While many Passion Seekers tend to be mavericks blazing a trial-and-error trail towards the goal of business success, the majority of the million-dollar-plus entrepreneurs interviewed all have one thing in common: a mentor they meet with regularly to help guide them. Your mentor need not be an expert in a particular field or even share your passion. However, he or she should know the business of business.

"We and our mentor meet for two hours twice a month to go over sales, books, taxes, real estate and even personal stuff too, to make sure we have balance in our lives," says environmental passion seeker Eric Gellerman. "He [our mentor] also provides a much-needed balance between my headstrong nature and my partner Amy's more cautious personality. We wouldn't be where we are today without his guidance."

To find a mentor, put the word out to your peers that you're in search of one. Study your niche to identify the "Bill Gates" of your industry and simply request his/her assistance. "You'd be surprise how many of the really successful will gladly give of their time to help you," as passionaire Tracee McAfee-Gates says, "just for karma points!"

You may feel isolated. Walk with giants.

The third secret all passion seekers agree upon is having a network of similar-minded individuals to associate with. I call such mentors and associates "giants."

Giants are people who by virtue of their stature, step wider, see more and reach farther, and encourage you to do the same. Having a network of giants can help quell that sense of isolation and loneliness that haunts many entrepreneurs, especially passion seekers. Join organizations, attend meetings, and sign up to online networks to surround yourself with others like you!

Learn to leverage other people's time, talents and cash (The Assembly Line)

In an assembly line, each person is responsible for adding one part, or turning one screw on the product, before it passes on a conveyor belt to the next person who has their unique job to do. Similarly, you can create an assembly line for your passion so that you can pass the responsibility of marketing, for example, to someone who enjoys or is better skilled at it.

Everyone has different skills, talents, knowledge and contacts. Each phase of your venture, from research, to creation, to marketing, to sales requires different skills. Identify the phase your venture might be entering, and what skills it requires. If you don't possess the necessary skills to take it through that phase, then find someone who does.

You're going against the grain. Make it easy for people to accept.

When any new idea is introduced, people's habits and perceptions often stand in the way of widespread acceptance. When presented with Levin's Cap Curver, (think shoe-tree for baseball caps), many people would say, "Why do I need that? I can just curve my cap visor with my hands!" To counter this objection, Levin gave away literally thousands of samples of the Cap Curver in order to get people to use it. "If the product is good, people will accept it and speak well about it," he adds. In Levin's case, it was, and they did!

Anything you can do—from giving away samples, to providing easy-to-assemble store displays, to rewarding people for spreading the word—will help overcome the inertia associated with every new idea. Seth Godin's book *Unleashing The Idea Virus* can give you a wealth of tools and ideas for creating a powerful word-of-mouth campaign!

Success may be a LONG, LONG journey. Commit now.

Don't do it for the money. Not because there's no money to be made, but because the journey getting there may require patience and commitment. If your experience mimics that of many passion seekers, you might find yourself foregoing your own salary while you grow your business. It helps, therefore, to believe in what you're selling and to be really committed.

Eric Gellerman remembers the exact moment in the growth of The Wooden Duck that he realized he was in it for the long haul. "There was one time when, in order to make payroll, I had to go to several different banks to take out cash advances on all my credit cards," he explains. "But, rather than it being a low moment in my life, I remember feeling great! I remember thinking that if I was willing to max out all 6 of my credit cards in order to pay people who worked for me, even though I hadn't paid myself for a few years, then I truly was in the right business, because it meant I wasn't going to give up. I remember thinking, 'Wow I must really love what I do!' "

You'll hear more "NOs" than most. Listen to your intuition.

It's challenging enough starting any business. Passion seekers, though, are often cursed with a unique vision that makes them even less understood than other entrepreneurs. Don't be surprised, therefore, if the world is slow to accept your vision of the future, and tells you "No". It's at those moments when your intuition, your unique insight into the way things will be that will carry you through. Trust the still small voice within.

There will be competition. Always go for the Wow!

"Your dreams come true much quicker," according to *The Art of Wow* "when you make the world go wow." In business, one sure way to do that is to find out what is being offered by your competitors, and do it better than the customer, client, or industry ever expected. Take a tip from Tracee McAfee-Gates, shopper extraordinaire.

"Sure, there are others making presentations of unique items to clients," she explains, "But we make *our* presentations virtual media events, and create an experience that appeals to all the senses!" No one expects it, and it puts some excitement in their otherwise hum-drum days!" McAfee-Gates is so good at "going for the wow" in her passion for shopping, in fact, that others have used her closely guarded ideas to launch competing businesses.

You'll need fuel. Find the feeling.

How do you keep going when the rent is overdue, and the creditors are calling, and the phones are about to be turned off? Ask Rebecca Litwin, 40, president of Down Etc., LLC, who turned a childhood passion for "pillows and life's finer fabrics" into a 3 million dollar business.

Rebecca suggests to "close your eyes and remember the first time that you wanted something really bad. Focus on the feeling of what it was like to receive something that you really wanted. If the memory of that pleasure is still alive within you, then you've found the fuel for turning your passion into profit! Never let it go!"

****

What To Do If You Run Out Of Steam

The single greatest contributing factor to failure among those who pursue their passions, is the failure to stick with their dreams until they're successful. Nine out of ten people will quit a project before it's completed. Success at anything in life, therefore, is like running a race with nine other competitors. If 9 out of 10 of those running the race will drop out, then the only thing that's required for you to win is simply to stay in the race.

It's often said that success is a journey, not a destination. Many people seem to forget this and drop out of the journey when it seems that they're "not getting anywhere." If you've always been paid weekly for your efforts, it's easy to develop a habit of expecting immediate gratification and rewards for your efforts. Turning your passion into profit often requires adopting a different mindset. If you expect the same structured compensation, you'll miss the big picture of what it is you're creating. Success is indeed a journey. If you don't stick around to experience the joy of the journey, you'll fail; because failure is nothing more than stopping and allowing the race to go on without you.

Selling The Business

This topic often causes anxiety for the new entrepreneur. Many entrepreneurs consider their business to be their "child." It's something that they conceived, gave birth to, nurtured and raised. They feel an emotional attachment that won't allow them to consider the thought of separation. If the business activity is truly a passion, then the thrill is in the day-to-day doing. The reality, however, just like our own parent-child relationship, is that sometimes for your business to grow, it needs to grow without you.

Of course, there's no law that says you have to sell your business. And if you find fulfillment in the activity that is your passion, then you really never have to stop doing it. It depends on your motivation for launching your business in the first place. If, however, your motivation was to create personal freedom for yourself, or a bright future for your children, then thinking about selling your business forces you to do several things.

First, it forces you to think about how your business can be run without you so that it can bring you the freedom and the financial rewards even if you are not actively involved in it. Many entrepreneurs have invested so much of who and what they are into it that it requires their constant presence, energy and spirit to keep it alive. They've truly become the "soul" proprietor of their business. They are what keeps the business alive. If they are not around, the business doesn't exist. They have all the expertise, all the knowledge, and the only keys to the front door. If this describes the sort of business you've created, then this is not freedom. You've simply traded in one form of confinement for another.

Thinking about selling your business encourages you to look at where the value lies in your business. Is it in the products, the process, the people, or primarily the person with the passion (i.e.you)? Once you determine that, you can grow your business by focusing on the things that can be increased in value, and/or shifting value to the things that should really matter. It can help you to systemize, delegate and operate so that you own your business without it owning you.

Finally, thinking about selling your business forces you to ask the all important question: "why would anyone want to buy my business?" As we learned earlier, people buy things to fulfill a need. What need could your business fulfill for someone else?

Perhaps the same need it fulfilled for you? Is your business fulfilling your need for freedom, financial independence, or whatever motivated you to start it in the first place? If not, then you have some work to do. How can you sell your business as the answer to someon else's dreams, if it hasn't made yours come true? The answer is you can't.

However, thinking in terms of selling your business is a good exercise that can help you sell *yourself* on your business, and may even show you if you have a franchise opportunity on your hands—an opportunity that can help others achieve what your passion has provided you.

The Final Word on Growth

Growing your passion-centered business to provide you with the financial freedom, independence and security you desire requires being proactive. It requires anticipating change, planning accordingly, and thinking differently from others. It also requires that you see your personal growth as being inextricably linked to the growth of your business. As you grow, so will your business. As you pass each new milestone, you'll reflect on how far you've come, and you'll be an example for others who are traveling the same path. As you continue your journey, there may be international distribution, multiple locations, increased sales and even public stock offerings. You are limited only by your ability to dream. The sky's the limit! You can do it!

A FINAL SECRET TO SUCCESS

So there you have it! My step-by-step guide for transforming any talent, hobby or idea into a profit-making passion-centered business.

In order to be successful at this undertaking, you'll need to develop certain traits and qualities. There's desire, commitment, perseverance, honesty, courage, a positive mental attitude, good health, high self-esteem, patience, understanding, and the ability to listen. You need to be resourceful, innovative, and a visionary. In addition, I must add what I've found to be the most important trait of all: you must be willing to grow.

Personal growth is the desire, the decision and the deed to make yourself better and better. It is the personal commitment to always know more, be more, do more, and have more. Yes, for you to be successful in business, you will need to grow. Physically, you will need to grow in your appreciation of your body, its health and well-being, for no success is worthwhile unless you are well enough to enjoy it. Mentally, you will need to develop your skills, to become better at selling, better at marketing and better at business. You will need to respond differently to challenges and come up with better solutions, for your thoughts must be in alignment with your goals.

Ultimately, however, any success that you seek will come as a result of who you become on a much deeper level. It will be decided on by the journey that your spirit takes in the act of becoming.

That's right. How successful you are in business will be determined by something that appears to have absolutely nothing to do with writing a business plan, filling out a balance sheet, creating brochures, or making sales, but it is ultimately the only secret you'll really ever need. It is also the secret to help you be successful in love, in relationships, and in every aspect of your life. In fact, your path to turning your passion into profit in a lasting, satisfying and fulfilling way is part of a lifelong personal growth lesson with financial compensation as a measure. The profit you achieve will be spiritual as well as financial. In other words, as you grow, your success will be reflected in your wealth.

Did you ever find yourself asking yourself "why am I here?" If you're like most people, and surely the majority of people who are destined to read this book, you have asked that question at some point. That question is what prompts many people to seek their passion so that they can find more meaning in their lives. Whether you realize it or not, that single question, which has plagued mankind since the beginning, is a spiritual question. The answer is that we are all here on this plane in order to remember who we are. And our physical manifestation is an opportunity for our spirits to experience different aspects of that. Only in the act of experiencing do we truly become who we are.

We attract circumstances into our lives from which we can learn valuable lessons. Every situation we'll ever encounter here presents us with an opportunity to grow and to become. From birth to death, from sickness to health, from the words and actions of others, to getting cut off on the highway all happen because we want them to. We attract them because on a spiritual level we understand that they are necessary for our growth. Your growth is the real reason you are here. At every moment, you have the choice of whether or not to use the lessons to move to the next level of awareness. However, if you choose not to, then just as in school, you'll be forced to repeat that stage of your development until you pass the test. Spirit is a patient taskmaster.

We are here to grow in our awareness and remembrance of our true nature. And since happiness and abundance is our true state of being, then whatever we do to become that fulfills our mission for being here.

Your passion is an expression of that true nature. It is a statement by you to the universe that not only is this who you want to be, but it is who you've always been. Turning your passion into profit is symbolic of the discovery that who you are, has value, both here and in ultimate reality. And it can be as valuable here as you determine it to be.

Your profit is just one measure of the value you allow yourself to accept for who you are. It is an act of expression and acceptance of your true worth. It is an act of love. As we learned in the discussion of fear and love: you can tell how much you love yourself by what you allow yourself to experience.

Ultimately, therefore, the challenge in turning your passion into profit is not a challenge of economics, or of business, but one of spirit. Embrace the circumstances that present themselves as you move in the direction of your dreams. They are a necessary part of the journey. Know, too, that the journey is nothing more than becoming more of who you are and who you were meant to be.

Begin the journey with my support and blessings!

MAIN POINTS FOR CHAPTER 12
"Enough to Pay the Rent?"

• Growing your business means taking it to new levels of profitability, adding new products, hiring employees, getting national distribution, even going public through an Initial Public Offering (IPO). You decide what level you are comfortable with.

• A Break-even analysis can quantify your goal and give you a specific number of sales or clients to aim for to be able to match and exceed your present income.

• One possible outcome of the success of turning your passion into profit is the decision to leave your day job to focus exclusively on your passion. For some it is a major step fraught with doubt and indecision. For others it is a simple act. In dealing with the "voices" of doubt you may encounter, seek the support of others who are where you wish to be.

• Passionaires--people who have used their passions to become millionaires--share their secrets of success. One of the most-often emphasized is their advice to find a mentor.

• An Opportunity Gap Analysis can help you identify areas of potential growth and expansion. Recognizing and capitalizing on trends will help you to stay on the cutting edge of business growth.

• Once you realize that you are limited only by your views about yourself, then you'll realize as well that the sky's the limit on your dreams!

***

FOLLOW-UP FILE FOR CHAPTER 12
"Enough To Pay the Rent?"

INSPIRATION: Passion Seeker Profiles

_____

"The Kite Flier's Passion"

Mark Reed's passion is kites "On my travels [around the world]," he explains. "I always brought kites and flew them in some wild places; it was always a thrill to draw a crowd and then introduce people to the sport (it's quite addictive once you get the hang of it). I was constantly asked if my kites were for sale, so it was a logical step to look into building them for profit. To make a long story short, in early '92 a couple of friends and I pooled our credit cards to buy a sewing machine, fax, and computer, rented a tiny house, and built a little kite factory in the basement. We had no clue what we were doing but we were passionate about the sport and convinced that more people would try it if the equipment was cooler and better designed...." Last year's sales were between 1 and 2 million!

_____

IDEAS: The Right Questions To Ask

• What skills/talents will I need in order to take my business to the next level?

• What specific people do I know who might have these skills/talents?

• What additional streams of income can I think of for my current product/service?

• Who do I know who has turned their passion into profit successfully, and from whom I can ask advice?

Appendix:

APPENDIX I: Passion To Profit Master Checklist

DO RIGHT AWAY

- Decide that you're "IN" (i.e. commit to the journey)
- Set short term (6 month) and long term (3-5 year) personal goals
- Set up an email account and Internet access.
- Start compiling email addresses in anticipation of business launch
- Contact Nightingale-Conant for latest personal growth catalog (800)323-3938
- Contact Copyright Office/Patent & Trademark Office for brochures/booklets
- Request an information kit from any mutual fund company
- Request membership information packages from every appropriate organization
- Request IRS forms and publications
- Locate and contact nearest SBA and SCORE offices
- Open personal savings/checking account (set up a recurring investment plan.)

DO TO DISCOVER YOUR PASSION

- Take Passion Personality Test
- Identify your purpose and role
- Complete the Discovery Exercises
- Complete Talent Gold Mine Exercise
- Put on a Passion Party to determine your passion
- Define your passion.
- Pose the Overnight Question; Listen for your passion idea
- Apply the Magic Questions
- Put on a Passion Party to determine your passion idea
- Determine your product or service
- Decide which passion idea you will follow first
- Put your passion idea and plan into words
- Determine your mission; Create a personal mission statement
- Set goals (Visualize, act out, live from the feeling of the wish fulfilled)
- Do something to make it real (i.e. create a prototype)
- Put on another Passion Party to come up with your strategy

DO TO BUILD A BUSINESS AROUND YOUR PASSION IDEA

• Learn the different types of income • Learn the different business models • Open yourself up to money-making ideas • Start something. Anything • Head in the direction of your dreams.
- Determine your Wow Factor (Unique Selling Point)
- Choose your company name; test it on friends, relatives and strangers
- Choose structure (Sole Proprietorship, Corporation, Partnership, LLC)
- Apply for EIN (form SS-4)

PHASE 3 – Establish your online identity
• Read *Webonomics* by Evan Schwartz for ideas and tips
• Visit www.passionprofit.com or registrar to see if your URL is available
• Reserve your Internet URL (your "dot com" business address)
• Download Netscape/Internet Explorer (IE) Browser, Microsoft Outlook or find some means that allows you to send out emails to your mailing list as "yourname@yourdomainname.com" as in walt@hiphopbiz.com. This adds a level of professionalism to your email correspondence.
• Set up hosting for the domain. (We do that, too! Visit www.passionprofit.com)
• Visit other sites to get a feel for what yours might look like
• Design your site. Remember to include
      - products/merchandise page
      - news and event announcements
      - links to other related sites
      - contact information
      - online media kit
      - include information on shipping charges
      - add po box or physical address for customers who wish to mail checks
      - add fax number for customers who wish to fax orders
      - add guarantee and privacy information
• Upload your site
• Create the following email accounts
      [yourname]@yourdomain.com
      orders@yourdomain.com
      info@yourdomain.com
      events@yourdomain.com
      news@yourdomain.com
      advertise@yourdomain.com
• Determine your business model (business to consumer, business to business, etc.)
• Determine your method of selling
• Obtain and complete a D/B/A or "Fictitious name" form, corporate kit, etc.
• Create Business Mission Statement
• Start Your Business Plan
• Contact SBA and SCORE for advice on all the above
• Research your market, industry, customers, business type, etc.
• Research other websites selling similar products
• See Thomas Register for suppliers and manufacturers
• Set the price for your product or service
• Request brochures/media kits from various organizations and associations
• Open business checking/savings account with company name
• Set up a simple accounting system to keep track of all expenses
• Obtain Post Office Box if necessary
      • (Optional) Set up a Portable 800 Number through any long distance carrier
      • (Optional) Establish a Dedicated fax/internet line

- • (Optional) Use a Call Answering service
- • (Optional) Retain an Order Fulfillment Company to actually ship the orders
- • (Optional) Set up UPS or other business shipping account
- • Lease space/equipment/vehicles if applicable
- • Buy supplies for office.
- • Design and print stationery, business cards, envelopes, etc.
- • Trademark logo if necessary; start patent process if applicable; copyright as required
- • Subscribe to trade magazines
- • Set up Merchant Account to be able to process your customers' credit cards
- • Get your terminal/printer for offline sales.
- • Set up an "internet gateway account" which allows for real-time credit card processing through your website; Processing Software :$99-$295

DO TO SELL WITH PASSION

- • Read *IdeaVirus* by Seth Godin;
- •Decide how you will distribute your product
- • Practice passionately selling your passion

- • Create your selling tools (brochures, fliers, etc.)
- • Write Press Release
- • Create Media Kit
- • Implement any and/or all of the Code Cracker Tips
- • Find magazines that cater to your audience
- • Advertise in trade magazines
- • Send out press releases to magazines, newspapers or use wire services
- • List your site with Google.com and other search engines
- • Find similar community sites to swap links with
- • Prepare for these daily tasks
  - -Check & respond to email
  - -Charge customer credit cards
  - -Prepare and fill orders
  - -Send out brochures
  - Update site as necessary
- • Prepare for these weekly tasks
  - -Communicate with your subscribers
- • Swap ads with other webmasters

DO TO KEEP MORE OF WHAT YOU MAKE

- • Read *The 9 Steps to Financial Freedom* by Suze Orman
- • Read *Rich Dad, Poor Dad* by Robert T. Kiyosaki

DO TO GROW YOUR BUSINESS

- Read *The E-Myth* Revisited by Michael Gerber
- Build Your Assembly Line Team of key people
- Do an Opportunity Gap Analysis
- Read The *E-myth* by Michael Gerber for tips on how to work on your business.
- Create an Operations Manual for your business

DO ALWAYS

- Commit to personal growth. It is the key to your success
- Learn to think differently
- Learn and practice the behaviors that coincide with your new beliefs.
- Conquer your fears daily
- Develop The Success Attitude
- Read books and listen to audio tapes to inform and inspire you.
- Read books on what you love
- Use the tools affirmations, self talk, meditation, treasure maps, tapes
- Develop the winner's mentality.
- Pay attention to media coverage of your interests
- Meet and model the people who are doing what you love to do
- Start a journal; keep track of your ideas and thoughts

APPENDIX II. MY CHOSEN PEOPLE

Your product or service can be targeted to:

accountants	actors	Africans	air traffic worker
animal trainers	announcers.	appraisers	architects
artists	aunts	authors	BabyBoomers
babysitters	bachelors	bankers	barbers
bartenders	beekeepers	bookworms	builders
bus drivers	businesses	carpenters	catholics
cattle ranchers	cheerleaders	children	Chinese
choir members	churches	clerks	clowns
comedians	construction	cooks	counselors
cousins	day traders	defendants	designers
disc jockeys	doctors	editors	elderly
electricians	engineers	entrepreneurs	Europeans
executives	farmers	fathers	fathers-in-law
firemen	flight attendants	foster parents	contestants
gardeners	Generation X	gigolos	golfers
grandfathers	grandmothers	grandparents	hairdressers
healthconscious	Hispanics	hotel owners	housewives
hunters	husbands	hypnotists	immigrants
interior designers	investors	journalists	judges
juries	lawyers	lawyers	leaders
librarians	lifeguards	lottery winners	magicians
maids	make-up artists	managers	media
midwives	milkmen	ministers	models
mothers	mothers-in-law	moviegoers	musicians
nieces	nephews	non-profits	nuns
nurses	optometrists	orphans	painters
parents	passengers	pharmacists	philanthropists
photographers	photographers	pilots	pilots
plaintiffs	plumbers	poets	police officers
politicians	postal workers	priests	prisoners
programmers	promoters	prostitutes	psychiatrists
psychics	public speakers	public speakers	publishers
rappers	sailors	scientists	secretaries
shoppers	singers	smokers	soldiers
sports figures	spies	storeowners	street performers
drug abusers	teachers	tellers	the affluent
the disabled	the famous	the homeless	the overweight
the poor	therapists	tourists	translators
travel agents	travel agents	travelers	uncles
union workers	vegetarians	veterans	volunteers
volunteers	waiters	web surfers	wives

APPENDIX III. TRIZ and INTERNET PROFITS

The Passion Profit Principles and TRIZ: a Study in Innovative Solution-Finding

History of Triz

    In 1942, a Russian scientist who believed innovation could be taught set about to prove his theory. The Theory of Solving Inventive Problems, TRIZ (its Russian acronym) was founded in 1946 by a Russian engineer and scientist, Genrich Altshuller. He analyzed over 400,000 patents from different fields of engineering. Altshuller studied those patents with the most effective solutions. His empirical studies revealed objective laws, or trends, in the evolution of technical systems. From these he formulated his main postulate: the evolution of engineering systems is not a random process, but obeys certain laws. From these laws Altshuller formulated his eight Patterns of Evolution of technical systems. These patterns can be utilized for conscious system development -- including solution-finding. Some of these laws briefly described:

The Law of Ideality. Systems evolve toward increasing Ideality. An Ideal system being a system that requires no energy to operate, costs nothing to produce and occupies no space. It performs function without form.

The Law of Transitioning to Microlevel using Energy Fields. Systems will become smaller, replacing mechanical systems with alternative energy fields performing the required function.

The Law of Dynamization. In the course of their evolution, systems develop from rigid structures into flexible ones.

    In its original manifestation, TRIZ was envisioned as "..an algorithmic approach for solving technical and technological challenges. By utilizing this methodology engineers, planners and executive managers will be able to:

    Visualize technical systems from new perspectives.

    Reveal all possible solution concepts.

    Seek IDEAL solutions.

    Develop superior products by overcoming system contradictions.

    Predict future product and technology evolution.

    Establish an ABSOLUTE competitive advantage.

    One premise of Altshuller's theory -- that inventiveness and creativity can be taught -- represents a fundamental shift in attitude towards technical creativity.
TRIZ is all you need to develop Innovative products.

TRIZ Comes of (Internet) Age

In 2003, 61 years after Altshuller made his discovery, a Jamaican engineer turned author and career coach, inspired by that same idea, created a philosophy and formula for teaching creative innovation to help people develop unique solutions to the challenge of turning one's passion into profit.

"As an engineer steeped in much of the engineering-influenced thought processes that undoubtedly influenced Altshuller, I've always believed in process as the basis of innovative solution-finding. So, when I read about Triz in 2003," explains Walt, "I saw similarities between our two approaches. I set about combining the two concepts, and patterned the "Code Cracker" in *Turn Your Passion Into Profit* along the same lines of the 44 Principles in the Triz Matrix."

"Coming up with ideas is a process. Creating a product is a process. Selling is a system of beliefs that can be quantified, so it becomes a process, too. It is that belief that forms the basis of the Cycle of Success Philosophy and Formula within my book *Turn Your Passion Into Profit.* The result is a set of marketing principles that can be applied to just about any business and industry.

"In the books I've published, I've used this belief system to help aspiring entrepreneurs achieve success in the pursuit of their passion. There are flow charts to decide how to distribute a product, checklists to master the steps to launch a product, charts of interchangeable ideas used to create new business ideas, tables to decide the appropriate target audience, and so on.

"Anything that you'll ever achieve can be seen as a series of steps in a greater journey. Every step you take changes your position along the path, and thus your view of the landscape. Take a step, assess the landscape in relation to your destination, make a choice, and take another step. Keep doing that until you get to the desired destination.

"As the guide on that journey, if I can anticipate the choices at each junction, predict the resulting landscape, provide people with the necessary information to make the next choice of direction, then they can take another step. There's one desired outcome in every journey. There's one optimal choice for every decision. With that as my premise, I can create a map that can take anyone from where they are to where they want to be.

On the following pages is a map of the principles as they might apply to the process of selling products on the Internet. It takes each principle of the TRIZ Matrix and offers a solution for increasing traffic, reducing shopping cart abandonment, and increasing sales on internet sites."

TRIZ Principle	Standard Application	Internet Adaptation
1. Segmentation	Divide complex tasks into sub-tasks; make an event easy to dis-assemble; increase the degree of fragmentation or segmentation	Single page websites with one item are more profitable. Incorporate other sales agents; affiliate program
2. Taking Out	Eliminate the extraneous compo-nents, properties related to an event	Remove distracting links not related to the desired action of "click here" to order
3. Local Quality	Change an event's structure from uniform to non-uniform; Make each person/system in an event fulfill a function related to it	Create different site for each product; Target personality types in ad copy
4. Asymmetry	Change the shape from symmet-rical to asymmetrical	Set up different sites to target different languages and cultures
5. Merging	Merge similar components, events or systems to perform parallel operations; Make opera-tions contiguous or parallel	Have site collect information with cookies
6. Universality	Make a person/system perform multiple functions; eliminate the need for other persons	Make site as interactive as possi-ble; serve as a place for visitors to interact with each other
7. Nested Doll	Place one event inside another	Capture email address at the same time visitor requests free report
8. Anti-weight	To compensate for the weight of an event, merge it with other events that provide lift	Align your website, company efforts with third parties that provide credibility (Amazon, Better Business Bureau, reputa-ble magazine)
9. Preliminary anti-action	If it will be necessary to do an action with both harmful and useful effects, this action should be replaced with anti-actions to control harmful effects	Add security assurances, testi-monials, along the path in shop-ping cart

TRIZ Principle	Standard Interpretation	Internet Adaptation
9. Preliminary anti-action	If it will be necessary to do an action with both harmful and useful effects, this action should be replaced with anti-actions to control harmful effects	Add security assurances, testimonials, along the path in shopping cart process.
10. Preliminary action	Perform, before it is needed, the required change of an event	Provide website directory for visitors to site
11. Beforehand cushioning	Prepare emergency means beforehand to compensate for low reliability of an event	Prepare necessary bandwidth to handle surge in visits
12. Equipotentiality	In a potential field, limit position changes	Design site and offer content that speaks to lowest common denominator
13. The Other Way Round	Invert the actions used to solve the problem	Have the customer sell or serve himself; Have the website visit the customer; do something different
14. Curvature	Instead of rectilinear persons, surfaces or forms use curvilinear ones	Take the shortest path to the customer by asking for the sale right away.
15. Dynamics	Divide an event into systems capable of movement relative to each other	Have links open in separate windows
16. Partial or excessive actions	If 100% of an event is hard to achieve using a given solution, use slightly less or slightly more of the same method	Make "buy" button a bit harder to find OR make it very large and easy to find
17. Another Dimension	Move an event into 2 or 3 dimensions; tilt or re-orient;	Incorporate rotating graphics
18. Mechanical vibration	Cause an event to rotate or oscillate; increase frequency	Change look of website periodically
19. Periodic Action	Instead of continuous action, use periodic or pulsating action; use pauses between actions to perform different action	Communicate with customers, affiliates on a periodic basis
20. Continuity of useful action	Carry on work continuously; make all persons of an event work at full load all the time.	Eliminate website downtime
21. Skipping	Conduct a process or certain stages at high speed	Act quickly; Respond to customer inquiries quickly; listen to intuition.
22. Lemons to Lemonade	Use harmful factors to achieve positive effects; eliminate one harmful action by combining with another	Use resolved customer complaints as testimonials for great customer service; change thinking about challenges
23. Feedback	Introduce feedback to improve a process	Set up on-site visitor suggestion box, surveys, polls

TRIZ Principle	Standard Interpretation	Internet Adaptation
24. Intermediary	Use an intermediary carrier article or process	Escrow accounts for payment; ie. Paypal;
25. Self service	Make an event serve itself by performing auxiliary helpful functions; use waste resources or energy	Automate fulfillment process so customers serve themselves; Download e-books automatically
26. Copying	Use simpler and inexpensive replicas or facsimiles	Use page layout and format that successful sites use; find free cgi scripts
27. Use cheap replacement events	Replace expensive evens with multiple inexpensive events	Use overseas design labor; use free templates available online
28. Substitution for mechanical means	Replace a mechanical means with sensory means	Use email or website FAQ to communicate with customers
29. Pneumatics and hydraulics	Use gas and liquid systems instead of solid systems	Look at website traffic as a fluid phenomenon
30. Flexible shells and thin films	Use flexible shells and thin films instead of 3-D structures	Allow customer interaction with different departments, tech support, cust svc, et. al
31. Porous materials	Make an event porous or add porous elements	Encourage visitors to contribute to development of site
32. Color changes	Change the color of an event or its external environment; change the transparency of an event	Increase diversity; Make navigation more intuitive and apparent
33. Homogeneity	Make events interacting with a given event of the same material	Provide bilingual customer service representatives
34. Discarding and recovering	Make portions of an event that have fulfilled their functions go away (disappear, dissolve, evaporate) or be transformed	Provide dialog box or survey box that minimizes once an action is taken
35. Parameter changes	Change an event's physical state (from gas to solid); change concentration; flexibility; temperature	Re-train visitors to interact in different ways with website
36. Phase transitions	Utilize the results of phase transitions (volume changes, heat loss	Win over dissatisfied customers;
37. Thermal expansions	Use thermal expansion or contraction of materials	Self-monitoring discussion groups
38. Strong oxidants	Replace common air with oxygen-rich air	Introduce customization of content or product
39. Inert atmosphere	Replace a normal environment with an inert on; add neutral additives to an vent	Be exceedingly patient and nice to customers; seed discussion postings or online events with other participants
40. Composite materials	Change from uniform to composite materials	Hire diversely talented individuals

APPENDIX IV. *Creating Compelling Copy*

The following exercise will help you to create the compelling copy for
1. the e-book of your unique expertise,
2. the press-release that announces your product/service/event to the media,
3. the copy on your web page,
4. the advertising copy for your direct mail pieces
5. the article based on your expertise that you send to magazines
6. the winning Investor Proposal
7. the Passion-Centered Business Plan

Goal: To get people to take a desired action in relation to your product or service
The Process:
-Choose a headline (get free online report "350 of the Best Headlines Ever Written")
-Decide on the desired action (click here; order now; call us; sign up, etc.)
-Determine your target audience (press; public; business owners)
-Determine the motivational benefits for each Personality type
-Incorporate the Code Cracker Analysis

-What's the desired action? (What do you want people to do as a result of reading this? eg. click here; order now; call us; sign up, etc.)

_____

What's your WORD? (What's your brand identity or the concept you own or wish to own in the customer's mind?)

_____

What's the Big Deal? (Why should we be interested? Human interest angle; This will be the lead/opening paragraph.)

_____
_____
_____

Press Basics:
Who? _____
What? _____
Where? _____
When? _____
Why? _____
How Much? _____

What's the benefit that people will receive if they take the desired action?
(Survival? Comfort? Kinship? Status? Self-fulfillment? See Value Tree)

_____

What's the pressing need, desire, challenge or want that is addressed?
(What's going on in the world right now that makes this important?)

_____

What makes you the expert? (List your credentials, experience)

_____
_____
_____

What's the main thing you've learned/ discovered that makes this necessary?
(a quote from you)

_____
_____

Who else supports your beliefs and findings?

_____
_____
_____

Who has used your product/service or attended your event, and what have they said about you/it?

_____
_____
_____

Who is your audience? What makes them valuable?

_____
_____
_____

What special incentive can you offer?

_____
_____

What are the 10 or 20 most important things to know, do, believe, or say about your topic or area of expertise? (This will become the free report, e-book, and bullets for the article you write)

1. _____
2. _____
3. _____
4. _____
5. _____
6. _____
7. _____
8. _____
9. _____
10. _____

Describe the exact sequence of steps people need to take to accomplish some goal that your expertise makes possible (This will become your e-book!)

1. _____
2. _____
3. _____
4. _____
5. _____
6. _____
7. _____
8. _____
9. _____
10. _____

Tell a moving story of triumph attached to this whole experience (Your own story or of someone you know)

_____
_____
_____

Outline the history of your expertise or the concept behind your expertise?
This will become a chapter in your book or an article.

_____
_____
_____

APPENDIX V. Reading, Research Resources "MILLIONAIRE UNIVERSITY"

Much of turning my own passion into profit was about individual steps, and sporadic epiphanies rather than any one grand leap. Millionaire University are the books that influenced my thoughts and direction. Each book was another light that added to the brightness. Each new idea was another step towards the prize. Each revelation lifted the curtain that veiled my desires, and kept them from sight.

The following resources--books as well as magazines, websites, etc.--are provided to help you on your passion to profit journey. I've organized them according to the chapters to which they are relevant.

Each book in the reading list holds valuable life lessons. Treat each one as a separate classroom, a distinct leg of your journey. Don't look for the easy way through. There's no way to take the express lane. There's no cheating allowed. No "Cliff Notes" available here. There are things you need to experience in order to get to the other side. As you read a particular book the right question to ask is: *"What specific things can I do to make what I've just read applicable to my own situation?"* Take notes when you read, and create an immediate task list from your notes. Any new concept that you encounter can act as "The Switch" for your own divine idea.

If you've read a particular book before, try reading it again from a different perspective. Imagine you're collecting information, inspiration and ideas to teach someone else how to turn their passion into profit. You teach best what you most need to learn. So become a teacher of the very thing you are in the process of doing.

CHAPTER 1. PERMISSION TO DREAM

Million Dollar Home-Based Businesses: Successful Entrepreneurs Who Have Built Substantial Enterprises from Their Homes by Sunny Baker, Kim Baker
ISBN 1558502467
This book is one of the most inspiring books I've read as it's packed with stories of others who were doing what I wanted to do.

Why Should White Guys Have All the Fun: How Reginald Lewis Created a Billion-Dollar Business Empire
ISBN 0471145602
Who wouldn't be inspired by Reginald's story? Since I couldn't meet with Mr. Lewis in person to learn how he thinks differently from the rest of us, this book served as my meeting with the great man himself.

Jerry Seinfeld, The Entire Domain by Kathleen Tracy
ISBN 1559724749
Ok, so maybe I do read a little for entertainment! However, this book is a biography. The real reason Seinfeld appeals to me lies in what he was able to accomplish in creating a brand. Very inspiring.

Playing for Keeps: Michael Jordan and the World He Made by David Halberstam
ISBN 0767904443
Can there be any greater example of a man who's followed his passion?

King of the World: Muhammad Ali and the Rise of an American Hero by David Remnick
ISBN 0375702296

The Muhammad Ali Reader by Gerald Lyn Early (Editor), Muhammad Ali
ISBN 0688166202
As long as there are new books written about Ali, I will continue to read them. I'm not alone in being profoundly inspired by the story of The Greatest!

Visioning: 10 Steps to Designing the Life of Your Dreams by Lucia Capacchione
ISBN: 1585420875

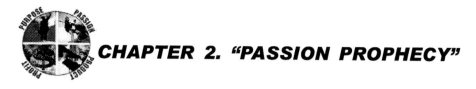

CHAPTER 2. "PASSION PROPHECY"

Rich Dad's Prophecy: Why the Biggest Stock Market Crash in History Is Still Coming... and How You Can Prepare Yourself and Profit from It! by Robert T Kiyosaki/Lechter (Author),
As recent events have proven, when it comes to retirement, relying solely on a 401K plan is a sure recipe for disaster. By the year 2012-10 years from now-the vast majority of Baby Boomers will be on the verge of retirement-and they'll be looking to cash in on their hefty 401K retirement packages. The situation, according to Kiyosaki and Lechter, is that all of these people who religiously pumped thousands of dollars over their working years into their 401Ks are going to be crushed if their mutual funds just haven't performed. To avert this financial crisis, Kiyosaki and Lechter provide a detailed financial plan to help forward-looking people prepare for the worst and start planning now.

CHAPTER 3. THINKING DIFFERENTLY

The Magic Carpet
Don't go looking for this one in the business section of your bookstore, it's the first children's book I owned (and still do), and was probably my first exposure to magical thinking.

The Cat In The Hat by Dr. Suess; ISBN 039480001X
Ok, so it may not be a practical guide on starting a business, but it probably helped me appreciate the joy and excitement that books could provide.

Flatland by Edwin A. Abbott; ISBN 048627263X
"Flatland is one of the very few novels about math and philosophy that can appeal to almost any layperson. Published in 1880, this short fantasy takes us to a completely flat world of two physical dimensions where all the inhabitants are geometric shapes, and who think the planar world of length and width that they know is all there is. One inhabitant discovers the existence of a third physical dimension, enabling him to

finally grasp the concept of a fourth dimension. Watching our Flatland narrator, we begin to get an idea of the limitations of our own assumptions about reality, and we start to learn how to think about the confusing problem of higher dimensions. The book is also quite a funny satire on society and class distinctions of Victorian England." — [review courtesy of Amazon.com]

I thank Joseph Latto, my high school geometry teacher, for introducing me to this book. I found myself using it just a week ago to explain to a friend the concept of reality as we know it, and how some people's ability to predict the future (i.e.psychics) can be explained as the ability to experience reality in what can only be described as another dimension.

Think And Grow Rich by Napoleon Hill; ISBN 0449214923
An all-time classic in personal growth.

Master Key To Riches by Napoleon Hill; ISBN 0449213501
My personal favorite of Hill's books.

How To Win Friends And Influence People by Dale Carnegie; ISBN 0671723650
I've always found the title to be a bit misleading. I guess it's a bit late to change it now. Everyone who is involved with other people, and that's all of us can learn a lot from the techniques in this book. This book showed me the secret to getting things done with other people's help.

The Power of Positive Thinking by Norman Vincent Peale; ISBN 0449214931
Another classic. Translated into fifteen languages with more than 7 million copies sold, *The Power of Positive Thinking* is unparalleled in its extraordinary capacity for restoring the faltering faith of millions.

As A Man Thinketh by James Allen;ISBN 0836278976
This must-read gem remains one my favorites.

The Game Of Life & How To Play It by Florence Scovel Shimm; (ISBN 0852073259
Shimm's books are easy but deep reading. This book reminded me of the basic laws of the universe I need to keep in mind as I play the game.

A Return To Love by Marianne Williamson; ISBN 0060927488
In my Top 5 of all time! If you run your life and your business with the basic premise in mind, you'll find things to be much easier and more fulfilling all around. Which reminds me, I need to read this one again!

Scientology-A New Slant On Life by L.Ron Hubbard; ISBN 1573180378
This book was recommended to me by the first millionaire I ever knew personally. I picked it up short time later as a supplement to the Scientology courses I took.

The Psychology of Achievement by Brian Tracy; ISBN 1555253539
My all time favorite success tape. A six-cassette audio which I recommend as the starting point for anyone whom I select to be part of my organization. I think the goal-setting exercise in this series was the most helpful.

Acres of Diamonds by Russell H. Conwell; ISBN 051509028X
A classic within self-help circles, Russell Conwell's story of the wealth in our own backyard is a powerful must-read.

Unlimited Power by Anthony Robbins

7 Habits of Highly Effective People by Stephen Covey; ISBN 0671708635
Mr. Covey helped me to structure the many roles I was playing in my life. Life was a confusing mish-mosh of tasks until I learned the secrets that helped me prioritize and tackle them appropriately. With over 5 million copies sold, in over 32 languages, it seems I'm not the only one who's been in need of what this book offers.

Creative Visualization by Shakti Gawain; ISBN 0553270443
Provides great exercises for honing my mind's-eye muscle.

It Works by R.H. Jarrett; ISBN 0875163238
Another little gem which taught me that "If you know what you want, you can get it." The famous little red book that makes your dreams come true. I realize that I can never have enough reminders of the power of the human mind to create a desired reality. This book is another of the servings of, as Brian Tracy calls it, "mental protein."

Celestine Prophecy: An Adventure by James Redfield; ISBN 0446671002

Three Magic Words by US Andersen; ISBN 0879801654
1996 Was a year of tremendous spiritual growth for me. My network marketing business was in full swing. This book is one of the major influences. Our team was on an almost fanatical binge of mental, spiritual and physical housecleaning, and this book was a major influence. I recommended this book to just about everyone who would listen. I drilled the concepts into my mind by memorizing, writing and rewriting the complete text. I won't tell you what the three magic words are, but they were my introduction to a liberating secret I have found reiterated in other milestone books I've since read. Once you learn the 3 magic words, and how to use them, you'll have the power to create anything you want in life. I've given lectures on success and have credited this book as being in the top 3 most influential works in my spiritual, mental as well as financial growth!

Master Cleanser by Stanley Burroughs; ISBN 0963926209
As a passionate vegan, not only am I concerned with what I put into my body, but I'm conscious that there are things I need to take out. The *Master Cleanser* provided a practical means of putting into practice some of Arnold Ehret's teachings.

Diet for a New America : How Your Food Choices Affect Your Health, Happiness and the Future of Life on Earth by John Robbins; ISBN 0915811812

Once destined to be heir to the Baskin Robbins Ice Cream empire, John Robbins, abdicated his soon-to-be throne when he learned of the industry's inhumane and unsanitary practices. He is now a famous advocate of animal rights and practices which benefit mankind as a whole, save the environment, and spare animals needless suffering. This book will open your eyes.

Ageless Body Timeless Mind by Deepak Chopra; ISBN 0517882124

Why Do Vegetarians Eat Like That? Everything You Wanted to Know (And Some Things You Didn't About Vegetarianism) by David Gabbe (out of print)

Perhaps the most straightforward book on being a vegetarian which answers many of the questions most people ask about the nutritional benefits, misconceptions, half-truths, about the life-style.

Arnold Ehret's Mucusless Diet and Healing System & Rational Fasting by Arnold Ehret; ISBN 0879040041

From Arnold, I learned that the foundational cause of all disease is congestion, constipation, and the accumulation of stuff in the body. I recommend this little book to everyone who comes to me for advice on eating better. This where I got the concept of flow as it relates to the body's health.

Body Ecology Diet by Donna Gates; ISBN 0963845829

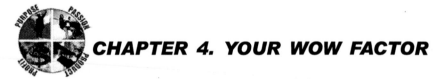 **CHAPTER 4. YOUR WOW FACTOR**

The Tao of Wow --The Art of Wow by Walt Goodridge; ISBN 096292024X
Discover your "wow factor." Become a "wow master." Impress and grow rich.

 **CHAPTER 5. PURPOSE**

Adventures of a Psychic : The Fascinating Inspiring True-Life Story of One of America's Most Successful Clairvoyants by Sylvia Browne; ISBN 1561706213
Spiritual Growth continues. Be willing to think differently. Even if you're not open to believing in psychic phenomenon, you might you just might find this an interesting station along the way in your journey.

The Other Side and Back: A Psychic's Guide to Our World and Beyond by Sylvia Browne (Contributor), Melvin L. Morse; ISBN 0525945040

Conversations With God : An Uncommon Dialogue (Book 1) by Neale Donald Walsch; ISBN 0399142789
Life-changing.

Seat of the Soul by Gary Zukav; ISBN 067169507X
By now, I've determined that my success in turning my passion into profit has been a result of my spiritual journey. Zukav's book provides more spiritual fortitude for the enlightened traveler.

The Road Less Traveled: A New Psychology of Love, Traditional Values and Spiritual Growth by M.Scott Peck; ISBN 0684847248
One of the first books through which prompted me to incorporate more spiritual growth in my journey. I probably wasn't as open to them then as I would be today. It's been a while since I took a look at it to see how the concepts sit with me since I've grown. [I also read *A World Waiting To Be Born*, and *People of the Lie : The Hope for Healing Human Evil* both by M.Scott Peck.]

Resurrection/Your Faith Is Your Fortune/Awakened Imagination/ Seed Time & Harvest and any book by Neville; ISBN 087516076X
Right after reading US Andersen's books, I was then introduced to Neville, from whom I learned practical techniques to create my desire reality. One of Neville's most enduring qualities is his ability to explain concepts simply. His instructions on how to "live from the feeling of the wish fulfilled" have helped me to stay focused on the real secret to creation.

 **CHAPTER 6. PASSION**

Turn Your Passion Into Profit: Information, Inspiration and Ideas to Help You Make Money Doing What You Love by Walt Goodridge; ISBN 0962920290

Yikes! He's listed his own book! That's right. And it's not just a shameless plug either. I learned a long time ago that there is only one writer, one painter, one artist, one creator in the universe, and we are all simply channels for this one source. As such, I learned as much writing this book as I hope you did reading it.

Your Secret Wealth by Jay Abraham; ISBN 9990804842

Even though at the time I was busy with at least 5 different streams of income, I was determined to keep searching for another breakthrough idea or business concept. Jay, who charges upwards of $4000 per hour for a consulting session, is himself a great inspiration for those of us seeking to truly realize the value of our time and talents.

The Artist's Way : A Spiritual Path to Higher Creativity by Julia Cameron; ISBN 0874776945

This book was recommended reading during a creativity workshop I took at Unity Church. The practice of writing my "morning pages" as a way of purging my mind at the beginning of each day and adding clarity to my thoughts is something I still do to this day as a result of what I learned from *The Artist's Way*. "With the basic principle that creative expression is the natural direction of life, Julia Cameron and Mark Bryan lead you through a comprehensive twelve-week program to recover your creativity from a variety of blocks, including limiting beliefs, fear, self-sabotage, jealousy, guilt, addictions, and other inhibiting forces, replacing them with artistic confidence and productivity." [online synopsis]

The Path by Laurie Beth Jones; ISBN 0786882417

If you need help creating your mission statement, this book can help you. Even though I had already created my mission statement ("I share what I know, so that others may grow") by the time I read The Path, it was a source of great research for the creation of the Passion Finder Chart in *Turn Your Passion Into Profit*.

 **CHAPTER 7. PRODUCT**

Why Didn't I Think of That? : Bizarre Origins of Ingenius Inventions We Couldn't Live Without by Allyn Freeman, Bob Golden; ISBN 0471165115

Another great idea generator. I always like to expand my mind to think differently. I also still dream of coming up with my own ingenious invention that I can sell to everyone in the world!

Infopreneurs : Turning Data into Dollars by H. Skip Weitzen; ISBN 0471528242

This is a great book! It finally gave a name to my passion! By this time, having taken the personality test and recognizing my affinity for compiling and sharing information, I got this book to explore the different ways of doing what it was I was good at.

How to License Your Million Dollar Idea : Everything You Need to Know to Make Money from Your New Product Idea by Harvey Reese; ISBN 0471580503

As a closet inventor, I'm always collecting information on getting my ideas out into the market. I also like to take ideas from one industry or business and use them to help me promote and market ideas from other industries.

The Complete Guide to Self-Publishing: Everything you need to know to write, publish, promote and sell your own book by Tom & Marilyn Ross; ISBN 0898796466

Yes, I'm reading this one again! It's been revised yet again, and is still the only book I recommend on self-publishing. This book was the beginning of me being able to create my freedom through writing.

AUDIOTAPES
• *Your Secret Wealth* by Jay Abraham (visit www.nightingale-conant.com)

MAGAZINES
• Entrepreneur Magazine; $16.97/year; (800)274-6229;
www.entrepreneurmag.com
• Business Start-Ups Magazine; $11.00/year; (800)274-6229;
www.entrepreneurmag.com

WEBSITES
• Visit www.howstuffworks.com for explanations of everyday products that may spark ideas of your own.
• Visit www.irs.gov. Get a copy of the instructions for Schedule C. It lists hundreds of business categories your venture can fall into.

 **CHAPTER 8: PROFIT**

Rich Dad, Poor Dad by Robert T. Kiyosaki/Sharon L Lechter; ISBN 0964385619
 After reading this book, I now recommend it highly along with Suze Orman's *9 Steps to Financial Freedom* as a two step process to getting to the other side of money. Suze Orman's book helped me to discover the childhood associations I've had with money which have kept it out of reach. Kiyosaki's book provided the knowledge that should be provided to all children to help them develop more fulfilling relationships with money.

The Trick To Money is Having Some by Stuart Wilde; ISBN 1561701688
 Attitude is everything.

9 Steps To Financial Freedom by Suze Orman; ISBN 0517707918
 A powerful book which helped me make the connection between my past associations with money and the accumulation of money in my present.

Spiritual Economics: The Principles and Process of True Prosperity by Eric Butterworth; ISBN 0871592118
 Like many people, I was raised with conflicting views and values with respect to money and spirituality. Somehow, many of us, while desirous of a prosperous life, push that very reality away from us because we believe that it is inherently wrong and evil to be wealthy. Eric Butterworth offers clarification that helped me see the connection between my beliefs about money and my resulting financial situation. I moved closer towards embracing prosperity as my birthright and a natural gift from the universe.

WEBSITES *(for money management, investing)*
- www.smartmoney.com (advice, information)
- www.armchairmillionaire.com (money management advice)
- www.morningstar.com (stock market reports)
- www.fidelity.com (mutual funds)
- www.americancentury.com (mutual funds)
- www.etrade.com (online trading)
- www.ameritrade.com (online trading)

 ## CHAPTER 9. STARTING YOUR BUSINESS

Multiple Streams of Income by Robert G. Allen

I listened to the audio version of this classic and was inspired beyond belief. In his explanation of the Money Tree concept which I touch on in this book, I realized I had found a recipe for creating the life-style I had always dreamed of. It came at a time during which I was hard at work building my network marketing business, and this book broadened my appreciation of how that venture fit into the bigger picture of wealth creation. It also reminded me that I needed to keep my other streams of income alive. I had made the mistake of seeing each stream of income as a replacement for the one before, as I searched for the best one. Now, I understand that the key is to create many streams each strong enough to support me should one falter. (6 cassette audio series)

Weaving the Web : The Original Design and Ultimate Destiny of the World Wide Web by Its Inventor by Tim Berners-Lee, Mark Fischetti; ISBN 0062515861

The E-Myth Revisited : Why Most Small Businesses Don't Work and What to Do About It by Michael E. Gerber; ISBN 0887307280

When it comes to my business, I'm quite possessive. So, it was a jolt to my system to learn the cold hard truth, according to Michael Gerber, that "the only reason to start ANY business is to sell it." It makes sense. If the reason you started it was to achieve freedom, then it defeats the purpose for you to be perpetually tied to it. I learned techniques and ways of thinking that will enable my business to function without me. Another milestone in my understanding of business.

Webonomics : Nine Essential Principles for Growing Your Business on the World Wide Web by Evan I. Schwartz; ISBN 0767901347

I read this book at the point where I was building the nichemarket.com website. This book was so powerful, that it took me twice as long to read it as it usually would. I would find myself so inspired with ideas that I had to take notes continuously and pause and brainstorm after every other sentence. Success on the Internet is truly a whole different ball game, and this book really gets into the nuts and bolts of how to prosper in this new frontier.

Doing Business Boldly: The Art of Taking Intelligent Risks by Daniel Kehrer ; ISBN 0671706160

As a civil engineer, I wasn't being trained to be a risk-taker. However, I knew that if were going to leave corporate America and follow my passion, that I would have to think differently. This book helped me to incorporate more risk-taking into how I did business.

Save Your Business a Bundle : 202 Ways to Cut Costs and Boost Profits Now-For Companies of Any Size by Daniel Kehrer (Out of Print); ISBN 0671788930
> I've been called *cheapskate* before in my life, but this took me to a new level.

MAGAZINES

- Entrepreneur Magazine; www.entrepreneurmag.com
- Business Start-Ups Magazine; www.entrepreneurmag.com

BOOKS/booklets (Business start-up, naming)

- *Form Your Own Limited Liability Company* by Attorney Anthony Mancuso
- *Legal Guide for Starting & Running a Small Business*, by Fred S. Steingold
- *Small Business Legal Guide* by Robert Friedman
- *Trademark—How to Name a Business or Product* by Kate McGrath and Stephen Elias with Attorney Sarah Shena
- *Naming for Power: Creating Successful Names For The Business World* by Naseem Javed
- *The Small Business Start-Up Guide* by Robert Sullivan
- *The Gold Book of Venture Capital Firms* by Kennedy Information; (800)531-1026; www.kennedyinfo.com
- *Roget's College Thesauru*s for coming up with names for your
- A good dictionary

ORGANIZATIONS

- Small Business Administration (SBA) call information for local chapter
- Small Business Administration Answer Desk; (800) 827-5722
- Service Corps of Retired Executives; ask local SBA for information
- Nat'l Assoc of Women Biz Owners; MD; (800)55-NAWBO
- National Federation of Independent Business; TN; (800) 634-2669
- Nat'l Business Incubation Assoc (NBIA); OH; (740) 593-4331 www.nbia.org
- Retail Council or similar retail member organization in your state.
- International Franchise Association; DC; (202) 628-8000
- US Department of Commerce; www.doc.gov
- Register of Copyrights Library Of Congress, DC; (202) 707-5959
- US Patent/Trademark Office; DC;(800)786-9199;(703)308-4357 www.uspto.gov
- Society of Am Inventors (SAI); (330) 253-2225 www.inventorshelp.com
- International Trademark Association; NY; (212) 768-9887
- Nat'l Assoc of Home-Based Businesses (NAHBB); (410)363-3698 www.ameribiz.com
- International Reciprocal Trade Association (IRTA); IL; (585)424-2940
- National Association of Trade Exchanges; OH; (440) 205-5378
- Manufacturers Agents National Association (MANA); CA; (949) 859-4040
- Nat'l Business Incubation Assoc; 20 East Circle Dr., Suite 190, Athens, OH 45701
- International Venture Capital Institute, P.O. Box 1333, Stamford, CT 06904;
- Internat'l Licensing Industry Merchandisers' Assoc; NY, (212)244-1944 licensing.org
- Insurance Information Institute; NY; (212) 669-9200; www.iii.org

MISCELLANEOUS
- The SBA Financing Kit; ask your local SBA chapter about it.
- www.Garage.com; CA; service@garage.com (contact by email preferred)
- Capital Network, TX; (512) 305-0831 www.thecapitalnetwork.com
- JumpStart Investments www.angelmoney.com
- Capital Connection; AZ; (602) 837-9590 www.capital-connection.com

SOFTWARE (Business Plans, naming your company)
- Business Resource Software, Inc.; (800)423-1228 Fax: (512)251-4401; www.brs-inc.com; info@brs-inc.com;
- The NameStormers, TX; (512)267-1814; www.namestormers.com

 **CHAPTER 10. SELLING WITH PASSION**

The 22 Immutable Laws of Branding by Al Ries
My new top 5 book!

Rene Gnam's Direct Mail Workshop by Rene Gnam, Bob Stone; ISBN 0137734336
This book, as well as *The Complete Guide to Self Publishing* were all I needed to set up a business to use writing to share my knowledge. I incorporated just about every tip I could into the sales materials for my first book and went on to sell $175,000 worth of product within the first several months. These books continue to sell today.

Mail Order Selling : How to Market Almost Anything by Mail by Irving Burstiner; (ISBN 0471097594
I remember reading somewhere that reading 2 or 3 books on any subject pretty much makes you an expert. Whenever I enter new business territory, I always get at least two books on the subject just to see if the information varies by much. Turns out the body of knowledge is pretty consistent. Both books were very instrumental in helping me set up my first business.

Rules For Revolutionaries by Guy Kawasaki, Michele Moreno; ISBN 0887309968
At the suggestion of a fellow entrepreneur, I flipped through this one at a local bookstore and got a wealth of creative marketing strategies which allow me to work smarter rather than harder at growing my business.

The End of Marketing As We Know It by Sergio Zyman;
Former chairman of Coca-Cola provides an excellent perspective on marketing.

BOOKS/Publications

- *Rules For Revolutionaries* by Guy Kawasaki
- *Guerilla Advertising* by Jay Conrad Levinson
- *Guerilla Selling: Unconventional Weapons and Tactics for Increasing..* by Bill Gallagher, Orvel Ray Wilson and Jay Conrad Levinson
- *How to Master the Art of Selling* by Tom Hopkins, J. Douglas Edwards
- *How To Sell Anything To Anybody* by Joe Girard
- Guides Concerning Use of Endorsements and Testimonials in Advertising (Federal Trade Commission 16CFR Part 255) ; DC; (202)326-2222; Free

MAGAZINES/Newsletters

- Selling Magazine; $39.95/year; (800)360-5344

ORGANIZATIONS

- SBA Publications PO Box 30 Denver CO 80201
- Sales & Marketing Executives-Int'; GA; (770) 661-8500; www.smei.org

MISCELLANEOUS

- Home Shopping Network; CA; www.hsn.com
- QVC; 484-701-8282; www.qvc.com
- Diversified Concepts helps you get your product to market on QVC or HSN; (303) 477-2100; email: DCMktng@aol.com

 # CHAPTER 11. ACCOUNTING AND TAXES

Loopholes of the Rich by Diane Kennedy
Part of the Rich Dad Series of books.

BOOKS (To learn more about business and taxes)

- *Kiplinger's Sure Ways to Cut Your Taxes* by Kevin McCormally

PUBLICATIONS

These are just a few of the more popular of the IRS' publications

- Pub 17   Your Federal Income Tax
- Pub 334   Tax Guide for Small Business
- Pub 463   Travel, Entertainment, Gift and Car Expenses
- Pub 503   Child And Dependent Care Expenses
- Pub 504   Divorced or Separated Individuals
- Pub 521   Moving Expenses
- Pub 530   Tax Information for First-Time Homeowners

- Pub 533   Self Employment Tax
- Pub 535   Business Expenses
- Pub 541   Partnerships
- Pub 542   Corporations
- Pub 583   Starting a Business and Keeping Records
- Pub 587   Business Use of Your Home
- Pub 946   How To Depreciate Property
- Pub 1853   Small Business Talk

SOFTWARE

- Quicken (Windows, Dos) by Intuit the bestselling finance program
- Microsoft Money (Windows) by Microsoft
- QuickBooks (Windows)
- Free downloadable programs are also available at www.shareware.com

CHAPTER 12.ENOUGH TO PAY THE RENT?

Mastering the Rockefeller Habits: What You Must Do to Increase the Value of Your Fast-Growth Firm by Verne Harnish

" During America's early oil-boom, tycoon John D. Rockefeller's disciplined approach to business replaced the helter-skelter methods of the original pioneering speculators. "These important disciplines need to be embraced by all companies that want to prosper in the upcoming decade," avers expert Harnish, founder of Gazelles, Inc. and creator of the Master of Business Dynamics program. His new book offers up the tools and habits Rockefeller implemented with such notable success.

ORGANIZATIONS

- Young Entrepreneurs Organization; www.yeo.org
- Landmark Education; www.landmarkeducation.com

APPENDIX VI. ONLINE RESOURCES

This section includes website information on many companies mentioned throughout *Turn Your Passion Into Profit*, as well as others which have very valuable information.

I. PERSONAL GROWTH

Self Growth Online

"The definitive guide to personal growth, self-improvement and self-help. Featuring resources for health, diet & nutrition, psychology, relationships, recovery and more! www.selfgrowth.com

Mars and Venus Institute

The Mars-Venus Institute teaches workshops around the world based on the writings of Dr. John Gray, author of *Men Are From Mars, Women Are From Venus* www.marsvenus.com

Anthony Robbins - Resources for Creating an Extraordinary Quality of Life

Your online, interactive chance to assess your life in several critical areas - physical health, emotional fitness, finances, time management, relationships, and drive www.tonyrobbins.com

Nightingale Conant Corporation

For audio tapes on Business, Health & Wellness, Mind Technology, Personal Development, Sales Skills, Spiritual Growth & Wealth Building, Nightingale Conant is the place to go.
www.nightingale-conant.com

The Keirsey Character Sorter

The website for the Keirsey Temperament Sorter and Keirsey Temperament Theory www.keirsey.com

A Visual Personality Test

Asks you to select the picture that most appeals to you in both form and color and then reveals a short personality summary.
www.ullazang.com/personality.html

II. MONEY AND INVESTING

The Armchair Millionaire

The Armchair Millionaire's goal is to help you build a million dollar portfolio using what they call The Five Steps to Financial Freedom. You'll also find the essential tools and information you'll need to get started on your own path to financial freedom. www.armchairmillionaire.com

Smart Money
The Wall Street Journal magazine of personal business. A wealth of information on stocks funds, investing, and much more.
www.smartmoney.com

III. TAXES

Internal Revenue Service
The IRS site features forms, publications, statistics, taxpayer assistance news and more.
www.IRS.gov

Tax Update Newsletter
This email will come to you periodically to keep you up-to-date on the latest tax law changes, court cases, audit results, and other developments that could affect your business. Sign up at www.mytaxman.net

IV. SMALL BUSINESS/HOME-BASED BUSINESS INFORMATION

a. Associations/Non-Profit Organizations/Government Resources

American Association of Home-Based Businesses-MD;
This nonprofit organization supports, promotes and encourages businesses in the home. www.aahbb.org

American Bar Association (ABA)-DC/IL
Features a "Lawyer Locator", news and information for lawyers as well as the public. www.abanet.org

American Management Association (AMA)-NY; (212) 586-8100
A nonprofit, membership-based educational organization that assists individuals and enterprises in the development of organizational effectiveness
www.amanet.org

Bureau of Labor Statistics (BLS)-DC; (202) 691-5200
An independent national statistical agency that collects, processes, analyzes, and disseminates essential statistical data to the American public, the U.S. Congress, other Federal agencies, State and local governments, business, and labor. The BLS also serves as a statistical resource to the Department of Labor.
www.bls.gov

Better Business Bureau (BBB)-VA; (703) 276-0100
"Helping consumers and businesses to maintain an ethical marketplace."
www.bbb.org

Educational Society for Resource Mgmt- (800) 444-2742 or (703) 354-8851
Provides educational programs to help your business bottom line (formerly known as American Production and Inventory Control Society)
www.apics.org

Home Business Institute (HBI)-NY;
National membership organization of small and home based businesses. The institute prides itself in bringing to its members vital information to help them anticipate opportunities and avoid pitfalls, as well as difficult to obtain services and benefits at substantial savings.
www.hbiweb.com

National Association for the Self-Employed (NASE)-DC/TX; (800) 232-6273
Advocacy group provides benefits, health, insurance, bankcard processing and more
www.nase.org

National Association of Home Based Businesses (NAHBB)
Provides support and development services to home managed businesses.
www.usahomebusiness.com

National Black Chamber of Commerce (NBCC)-DC;
A nonprofit, nonpartisan, and nonsectarian organization dedicated to the economic empowerment of African American communities
www.nationalbcc.org

Minority Business Development Agency (MBDA)-DC/PA/NY/GA/FL/IL/TX
The Minority Business Development Agency (MBDA) is part of the U.S. Department of Commerce, specifically created to encourage the creation, growth and expansion of minority-owned businesses in the United States.
www.mbda.gov

National Business Incubation Association (NBIA)-OH; (740) 593-4331
A clearinghouse of information on the Incubation industry.
www.nbia.org

National Foundation for Women Business Owners (NFWBO)-MD;
Its mission is to support the growth of women business owners and their enterprises by conducting research, sharing information and increasing knowledge.
www.nfwbo.org

National Minority Supplier Development Council (NMSDC)-NY; (212) 944-2430
Providing a direct link between corporate America and minority-owned businesses is the primary objective of the National Minority Supplier Development Council, one of the country's leading business membership organizations. Chartered in 1972 to provide increased procurement and business opportunities for minority businesses of all sizes.
www.trainingforum.com/ASN/NMSDC/

Online Women's Business Center (OWBC); Offices Nationwide

Whether you want to become your own boss or find information on how to run your business better, this SBA sponsored site has the information and resources you need.
http://www.onlinewbc.gov/

Small Business Administration (SBA); Offices Nationwide

Official site with information on government services, regulations and resources
www.sba.gov

Service Corps of Retired Executives (SCORE); Offices Nationwide

Dedicated to aiding in the formation, growth & success of small businesses nationwide.
www.score.org

US Patent &Trademark Office VA;(703) 308-9726 or (800) 972-6382

Their mission is to promote the progress of science and the useful arts by securing for limited times to inventors the exclusive right to their respective discoveries
www.uspto.gov

US Bureau of Census- MD;

Research information by industry; demographics; economic data; population and more.
www.census.gov

US Department of Commerce-DC/MD; Numerous offices

The Department of Commerce promotes job creation, economic growth, sustainable development and improved living standards for all Americans by working in partnership with business, universities, communities and workers
www.doc.gov

US Business Advisor

Business Development; How to get Financial Assistance; Taxes and how to pay them; The various Laws and Regulations governing business enterprises; International Trade; Workplace Issues; Buying and Selling a business, and more.
www.business.gov

Young Entrepreneurs Organization (YEO)-VA; (703) 519-6700

The YEO mission is to support, educate and encourage young entrepreneurs to succeed in building companies and themselves. Members must be under 40 and have sales of 1 Million or more
www.yeo.org

b. Commercial

About.com Small Business Information Page
(click on Home > Business/Careers > Business > Small Business Information >Guide Extra)
www.about.com

Biztalk Small Business Community
Small and home business daily entrepreneur magazine and guide. Chat with experts and get personal advice.
www.biztalk.com

Bplans.com
Download business plans. Submit yours for review and advice on marketing plans.
www.bplans.com

Briefme Online Magazine
I love this one! Very relevant. I recommend it highly. Tons of topics to choose from.
www.briefme.com

Business Week Frontier
www.businessweek.com/smallbiz/index.html

Chain Store Age
"The online resource for Retail executives"
www.chainstoreage.com

Entrepreneur Magazine
Entrepreneur Magazine's online small business publication with information to help you start, grow or manage your small business.
www.entrepreneurmag.com

HOMEBusiness Journal
Online magazine with featured articles, a business forum, contests and tips of the day.
www.homebizjour.com

INC.
Inc.com's mission, according to its website, is to "select the best business information, Web-based applications, products, and research available to the small biz market "
www.inc.com

Jayde Newsletter
www.Jayde.com

Money Making Mommies
Legitimate Work At Home Jobs With No Strings Attached
www.moneymakingmommy.com

National Federation of Independent Business (NFIB)-TN; (800) NFIB-NOW
NFIB was created to give small and independent business a voice in governmental
decision-making. Today, we remain true to our charter of advancing the concerns of
small-business owners among state and federal legislators and regulators.
www.nfibonline.com

Nolo Press Website
Publishing company of law-related books
www.nolo.com

Onvia
"Taking care of the business of running your small business"
www.onvia.com

Small Biz Findlaw
Step-by-step checklists, model business plans, forms, and other business documents,
selected Web sites, government documents and articles specifically chosen to help
you run your business.
http://smallbiz.findlaw.com

Small Business School 2000
www.sb2000.com

SmartOnline
Smart Online will walk entrepreneurs through research and planning tactics,
marketing ideas, and business-building skills.
www.smartonline.com

Society of American Inventors (SAI)-OH; 800-747-3109
For a fee, this company offers to take you from IDEA, to FEASIBILITY, to
PATENT and to MARKET!
www.inventorshelp.com

Successful Entrepreneur, Inc.
www.bizroadmap.com

Working Mother Magazine
www.workingmother.com

V. FINANCING YOUR BUSINESS & MONEY MATTERS

American Accounting Association (AAA)-FL; (941) 921-7747
The American Accounting Association promotes worldwide excellence in accounting education, research and practice
http://aaahq.org/index.cfm

America's Business Funding Directory (Online)
A free search engine for locating business capital.
www.businessfinance.com

The Technology Capital Network (TCN)-MA;
The Technology Capital Network (TCN) is a not-for-profit organization whose mission is to "Make money flow between investors and entrepreneurs".
www.tcnmit.org

Commercial Finance Association (CFA)-NY; (212) 594-3490
A trade group bringing together financers and entrepreneurs.
www.cfa.com

The Grant-Getting Page
A service of the University of Illinois at Chicago
www.uic.edu/depts/ovcr/ors/

Idea Cafe: The Small Business Channel
www.businessownersideacafe.com

Minority Business Development Agency (MBDA)
www.mbda.gov

Nat'l Assoc of Small Bus. Investment Companies (NASBIC)-DC; 202-628-5055
The association acts as the voice of the SBIC industry before Congress and the Administration. Its goal is to build and maintain a strong and profitable small business investment company industry.
www.nasbic.org

National Association of Trade Exchanges (NATE)-OH; (440) 205-5378
NATE is the premier organization for trade exchange owners from across the country and around the world. www.nate.org

National Venture Capital Association (NVCA)-VA; (703) 524-2549
The NVCA is the leading public policy advocate for the venture capital and private equity industries. NVCA works with all branches of government and the media to foster a better understanding of the importance of venture capital to the U.S. economy.
www.nvca.org

Service Corps of Retired Executives (SCORE) [see Section IV]
www.score.org

US Small Business Administration (SBA) [See section IV]
www.sba.gov

VI. ONLINE BUSINESS INFO/TRENDS/SUPPORT

E-Commerce Times
Latest news on online commerce
www.ecommercetimes.com

e-Marketer
transforming information into intelligence
www.emarketer.com

VII. SALES/MARKETING

American Marketing Assoc (AMA)-IL; (800)AMA-1150; (312) 542-9000
The American Marketing Association is an international professional society of individual members with an interest in the practice, study, and teaching of marketing.
www.ama.org

Association for Interactive Media (AIM)-DC
Just as your company relies on a trade association in your main line of business, AIM provides the protection and promotion essential to the health of your Internet projects. By supporting AIM you cover an exposed area of risk while ensuring that the Internet remains a healthy marketplace for your products and services. AIM promotes and protects your Internet business by: defending the industry in Washington; promoting consumer confidence; providing business-to-business networking opportunities
www.interactivehq.org

Direct Marketing Association (DMA)-NY; (212)768-7277
"The DMA delivers the tools and services that members need to succeed! Whether it is the latest industry knowledge and techniques, legislative representation or targeted marketing opportunities - we've got it covered!" Membership is a bit steep ($825) but, as the premier information source for target marketing, mailing lists, catalog marketing, etc. it may be well worth it if you passion relies heavily on mail marketing.
www.the-dma.org

Marketing Science Institute (MSI)-MA; (617) 491-2060
MSI is a unique, not-for-profit institute established as a bridge between business and academia. Its mission is to initiate, support and disseminate leading-edge studies by academic scholars that address research issues specified by member companies.
www.msi.org

Public Relations Society of America (PRSA)-NY; (212) 995-2230
Provides a forum for addressing issues affecting the profession, and the resources for promoting the highest professional standards. It offers unequalled opportunities for improvement of skills and advancement of knowledge, as well as for exchange of information and experiences with other public relations professionals.
www.prsa.org

VIII. GROWING YOUR BUSINESS

American Association of Franchisees and Dealers (AAFD)-CA; (800)733-9858
The AAFD provides a broad range of member services designed to help franchisees build market power, create legislative support of interest to franchisees, provide legal and financial support, and provide a wide range of general member benefits.
www.aafd.org

Franchise Associations
www.franchise.org and www.franchisee.org

American Society of Appraisers (ASA)-VA;703-478-2228
The American Society of Appraisers is an organization of appraisal professionals and others interested in the appraisal profession
www.appraisers.org

Association of Small Business Development Centers-Numerous offices
The mission of the Association of Small Business Development Centers is to represent the collective interest of its members by promoting, informing, supporting and continuously improving the SBDC network, which delivers nationwide educational assistance to strengthen small/medium business management, thereby contributing to the growth of local, state and national economies.
www.asbdc-us.org

Federal Trade Commission (FTC)-DC; (202)326-2222
The Commission seeks to ensure that the nation's markets function competitively, and are vigorous, efficient, and free of undue restrictions. The Commission also works to enhance the smooth operation of the marketplace by eliminating acts or practices that are unfair or deceptive.
www.ftc.gov

Franchise Finance Corporation of America (FFCA)-AZ; (480)585-4500
FFCA is the nation's leading financing source for the chain restaurant, convenience store/petroleum marketing and automotive service and parts industries. A one-stop capital source, FFCA provides mortgage and equipment loans, long-term real estate leases, construction and acquisition financing and other custom financing solutions to the nation's most successful multi-unit operators.
www.ffca.com

Institute of Business Appraisers (IBA)-FL; (954)584-1144
The IBA's mission is to increase awareness of business valuation as a specialized profession; ensure that the services of qualified and ethical business appraisers are available to anyone in need of them; expand the available body of knowledge regarding the theory and practice of business valuation; provide members with both technical and professional advancement opportunities; develop and provide essential industry information, programs and services for members
www.instbusapp.org

International Business Brokers Association (IBBA)-IL; (888)686-IBBA (4222)
IBBA is the largest international nonprofit association operating exclusively for the benefit of people and firms engaged in the various aspects of business brokerage, and mergers and acquisitions.
www.ibba.org

Service Corps of Retired Executives (SCORE)
www.score.org

IX. RESEARCH

All The Web
Sponsored by Dell, this site is attempting to be the largest search engine on the planet with over 1 Billion URLs
www.alltheweb.com

ASK.com
www.Ask.com

How Stuff Works
www.Howstuffworks.com

RefDesk
www.refdesk.com
"The single best source for facts on the net" Everything from dictionaries, law, quotes, thesaurus, addresses, maps, exchange rates, EVERYTHING!
(Also try www.resourcehelp.com and www.itools.com)

X. INSPIRATION AND IDEAS

The Entrepreneur's Mind
www.benlore.com/files/archive.html

The NameStormers
A name-development firm that offers software for creating winning names, slogans etc.
www.Namestormers.com

Marketing Tips
www.Marketingtips.com

Self Growth Online
www.selfgrowth.com

XI. PROMOTION & PUBLICITY SERVICES

Internet Wire
Press Release distribution service. If your product or service is more technology related, this is a good service to use.
www.marketwire.com

PRweb
Press Release distribution service
www.PRweb.com

Xpress Press
Press Release distribution service to major media.
www.Xpresspress.com

Marketing Research Association (MRA)
www.mra-net.org

TradeShow Network
Trade shows provide one of the best avenues for finding customers and clients when you are trying to get your new venture off the ground.
www.tsnn.com/~tsnn

Media Post
www.mediapost.com

XII. MISCELLANEOUS

Post Master Direct
Get opt-in list email addresses you can use to market your product or service
10 - 30 cents per name minimum order $1000
www.Postmasterdirect.com

Visual Search Engine
Type in "cats" and get back images of cats from all over the Internet. Good for
graphics to add to your site.
www.Ditto.com

U.S.P.S. Stamps
www.stamps.com

Web Demographics/Internet Information
www.learnthenet.com

For Reserving URLS
Network Solutions was the first, but now other sites have been allowed to offer Domain
Name Registration.
www.powerpipe.com $7.99/year

Weekly Keyword Statistics
Find out what keywords people are using to search the Internet. This is a great
tool to know what to offer to attract more visitors to your site and to keep up
with the latest fads and trends.
http://www.mall-net.com/se_report/

***

APPENDIX VII. The Secret Sessions
"Wow! I never knew that!"

.

The original Secret Sessions manuscript was a book of actual consulting sessions with clients who wished to turn their passion into profit. It was scheduled to be published in 1999. However, many of the original secret sessions have actually been incorporated within the text of *Turn Your Passion Into Profit*. Here are 3 more which are important enough to provide as a bonus:

Secret Session #1: Keyword Advertising,
Secret Session #2: The Amazon.com SECRET
Secret Session #3: Do You Have Some Advice for My Passion?

SECRET SESSION #2: Keyword Advertising
Have you ever used a search engine (Google, Yahoo, et al) and noticed the "endorsed listings" or ad boxes that appear? This is an example of keyword advertising. This relatively new form of advertising might be the best kept secret in driving traffic to websites. You now have some control over what links appear when web surfers type specific words in their never-ending quest for information or products related to what you're selling.

Let's say your passion is hot sauce and you have an award-winning recipe for the world's hottest sauce that you sell for $20. Let's imagine also that someone is searching online for "hot sauce". Through Google's AdWord program or through Overture.com's program, for example, a link to your site can appear when that web surfer types in "hot sauce", "hot sauce recipe", "hottest hot sauce" or any specific phrasing.

You bid on each of these key words or phrases. Your position on the search page is determined by how much you bid. So, if you indicate that you'll pay 25 cents for every click that your ad generates, but another hot sauce vendor bids 26 cents, then that company's ad would appear above yours. In certain categories where there's a lot of competition, you may have to place a high bid in order to appear in the top 5 or ten spots on the search results page. In other categories with little to no competition, you can find yourself at the top of the list for as little as 10 cents per click (the current minimum).

It's one of the greatest ways I've found and used successfully to jumpstart visits to a website!

SECRET SESSION #2: The "Amazon.com Secret"

Before it expanded into music and most recently into personal auctions, Amazon.com called itself "Earth's Biggest Bookstore." With annual revenues of close to 1 Billion dollars and daily traffic of a million visitors per week, Amazon.com is definitely a place where people are hanging out online. So, how can you take advantage of that fact to boost your business? Well, if you've ever visited Amazon.com, you know that in addition to offering books for sale, the company also provides a unique feature which allows customers, authors and publishers to write reviews of books they've read, written or published. This gives new visitors a chance to read the opinions of other customers before they purchase. And believe me, people do read these reviews. With no other means of judging the content of a book online, these reviews are a wealth of sales-generating information.

When I first launched my website to sell my products online, I knew that having my books listed with Amazon.com would be a good move as well. I registered them at Amazon and then added author and publisher information to boost sales.

I also became a member of the Amazon.com associates program which allows websites to earn commissions of the sales of books they recommend. So, to generate sales, I also referred other authors' books on my site. I had books on the music industry, business success, MLM (multilevel marketing), personal growth, health and other topics which are now "niches" on my nichemarket.com site. As many of these books are quite popular, it occurred to me that I could add my own reviews of these books I'd read to the Amazon.com site and benefit from the popularity of those books, and that's exactly what I did.

In fact, here's an actual review I posted for a book called 3 Magic Words, a book I consider quite powerful in the way of personal and spiritual growth.

Walt Goodridge (walt@passionprofit.com) from USA , August 23, 1998
HAVE ANYTHING YOU DESIRE
Once you learn the 3 magic words, and how to use them, you'll have the power to create anything you want in life. I've given lectures on success and have credited this book as being in the top 3 most influential works in my spiritual, mental as well as financial growth! I recommend this book to just about EVERYONE I meet, and in the "Millionaire University Booklist" on my website!

Amazon frowns on using the customer review feature of their site to advertise, so you have to be a little tactful in what you say. I simply made what I said intriguing enough to pique someone's interest without actually advertising. Anyone reading this review is naturally going to want to learn more about the "millionaire university booklist" I mention and also "my website." The key, obviously, when posting your review, is to check the option which allows your email address to be posted along with your comments.

Sure enough, I've gotten many emails from people who wanted to know more about the books I've reviewed. Those leads have resulted in sales of my books, exposure for my website, prospects for my MLM business and simple friendships!

SECRET SESSION #3: Do You Have Some Advice For My Passion?

No two passions are identical. Because everyone has a unique perspective, even two fiction writers are pursuing two entirely different visions, and thus different passions. The world will always need another writer, inventor and performer. There are, however, some general categories which your passion may fall under. Consequently, there are books, videos, websites and the accomplishments of other people which can offer guidance and inspiration to you.

Often during public appearances, I have only enough time to give quick suggestions to the many people I meet. Similarly, because of the number of people seeking ideas and inspiration within these pages, these short "Passion Readings" are intended to start you off in the right direction of thought and action. I always suggest starting with magazines, books and organizations devoted to your interest as a way to first familiarize yourself with the world that revolves around your passion.

Writing
Pick up a copy of *The Complete Guide to Self-Publishing* by Tom and Marilyn Ross.

Poetry
Pick up a copy of *The Poets Market: 1800 places to publish your poetry* by Writers Digest Books. *Read The Artist's Way* by Julie Cameron; Visit www.poetsniche.com and sign up to the group. Learn the different ways available to earn money.

Art
Pick up a copy of *Artist's Market* by Writers Digest Books; *Read The Artist's Way* by Julie Cameron.

Acting
Subscribe to BackStage Magazine. Pick up *How to Sell Yourself As an Actor* by K. Callan; *Acting As a Business : Strategies for Success* by Brian O'Neil; *Read The Artist's Way* by Julie Cameron *The Ross Report; NY/LA Actor's Handbook* ; Check out *www.thecastingnetwork.com,* an online resource with a database of more than 500 agents and 1000 casting directors nationwide; Pick up a copy of *A Challenge for the Actor*, and *Respect for Acting,* both by Uta Hagen.

Stand-up Comedy
Read Jerry Seinfeld's biography. Contact local comedy clubs for calendar of auditions and open-mike nights. Investigate continuing education seminars and organizations (which provide workshops on everything from comedy to cooking!

Inventing
From Patent to Profit by Bob Dematteis;
Marketing Your Invention by Thomas E. Mosley;
How to License Your Million Dollar Idea : Everything You Need to Know to Make Money from Your New Product Idea by Harvey Reese

Stand Alone, Inventor! Make $ With Your New Product Ideas! by Robert G. Merrick
Inventing Small Products : For Big Profits, Quickly by Stanley I. Mason
Entrepreneur Magazine: Bringing Your Product to Market; by Don Debelak

Photography

The Business of Studio Photography : How to Start and Run a Successful Photography Studio by Edward R. Lilley; *Make Money With Your Camera* by David Arndt

My children

Check out www. moneymakingmommy.com for work at home opportunities. Look into home schooling as an option for your children. Pick up the 10 Greatest Gifts I Give My Children and The Greatest Gifts Our Children Give To Us both by Steven Vannoy.
The Totally Awesome Business Book for Kids : With Twenty Super Businesses You Can Start Right Now! by Adriane G. Berg, Arthur Berg Bochner;
Kid Cash : Creative Money-Making Ideas (For Kids by Kids) by Joe Lamancusa
Better Than a Lemonade Stand : Small Business Ideas for Kids (Kid's Books by Kids); by Daryl Bernstein, Rob Husberg (Illustrator)
50 Money Making Ideas for Kids by Larry Burkett

Anything to do with animals
Ideas: Pet-sitting services; Pet grooming; veterinarian; pet calendars; pet image licensing; a pet museum;

Food
Ideas: Sell your recipes; Start a Restaurant of the Month club; Bottle and sell your concoctions.

Weddings
Ideas: Arrange weddings; matchmaking service; wedding-lovers club.

Traveling/Foreign Languages
Ideas: Arrange tours for others; compile books, calendars or videos with images of your travels.

Cars
Ideas: a women's self-help auto workshop; Classic-car lovers calendar;

Whatever your passion, start with a visit to Amazon.com, type in the subject and see what comes up.

***

Please help me update the next edition!--Walt

To: Walt Goodridge
       Passion Profit Company
       P.O. Box 618
       New York, NY 10008-0618
       USA

Ooops! I found a typo!
Check the word_____ on page _____ line _____

I think the following resources should be added or dropped:

_____
_____
_____
_____
_____
_____

The following information needs updating.

_____ on page number _____
_____ on page number _____
_____ on page number _____
_____ on page number _____
_____ on page number _____
_____ on page number _____

Name: (optional but desired)_____
Address: (hey you never know what surprises you might receive in appreciation for your keen eye for detail!)

Visit us online!

Order more copies for your friends!
View the newest life rhymes!
Order business plans!
Interact with other Passion Seekers!
Meet Pasion Profit success stories
Join Walt's Weekly Life Rhymes mailing list!
Download Free Reports
Register for workshops!
Stay informed of upcoming events!

All this and more is available online at
www.PassionProfit.com

For interviews, review copies and workshop information,
contact us at
The Passion Profit Company
P.O. Box 618
New York, NY 10008-0618
United States of America
tel: (800)323-5197
fax: (323)693-9425
email : info@passionprofit.com

Index

O

P

X

Y